Divide and Deal

Divide and Deal

The Politics of Distribution in Democracies

EDITED BY

*Ian Shapiro, Peter A. Swenson,
and Daniela Donno*

New York University Press

NEW YORK AND LONDON

NEW YORK UNIVERSITY PRESS
New York and London
www.nyupress.org

Library of Congress Cataloging-in-Publication Data
Divide and deal : the politics of distribution in democracies / edited by
Ian Shapiro, Peter A. Swenson, and Daniela Donno.
p. cm.
Includes index.
ISBN-13: 978-0-8147-4058-3 (cl : alk. paper)
ISBN-10: 0-8147-4058-8 (cl : alk. paper)
1. Distribution (Economic theory)—Political aspects. 2. Income
distribution—Political aspects. 3. Distributive justice.
4. Democracy—Economic aspects. I. Shapiro, Ian. II. Swenson, Peter.
III. Donno, Daniela.
HC79.I5D58 2008
339.2—dc22   2008000893

Contents

Introduction   1
Ian Shapiro, Peter A. Swenson, and Daniela Donno

PART I   Institutions

1   Welfare Regimes and Redistribution in the South   19
Jeremy Seekings

2   Distributional Conflicts in Mature Welfare States   43
Isabela Mares

3   The Politics of Tax Structure   72
Steffen Ganghof

4   AIDS, Inequality, and Access to Antiretroviral Treatment   99
Nicoli Nattrass

5   Distributive Politics and Formal Institutions in New
Democracies: The Effect of Electoral Rules on Budget
Voting in the Russian State Duma, 1994–2003   118
Jana Kunicová

PART II   Individuals

6   Religion and Social Insurance: Evidence from the
United States, 1970–2002   149
Kenneth Scheve and David Stasavage

7   Moral Values and Distributive Politics: An Equilibrium
Analysis of the 2004 U.S. Election   186
Woojin Lee and John Roemer

8   Giving the People What They Want? Age, Class, and
     Distribution in the United States   221
        Christopher Howard

PART III   Coalitions

9   Good Distribution, Bad Delivery, and Ugly Politics: The
     Traumatic Beginnings of Germany's Health Care System   245
        Peter A. Swenson

10   Democracy and Distributive Politics in India   280
        Pranab Bardhan

11   The Political Uses of Public Opinion: Lessons from the
      Estate Tax Repeal   298
        Mayling Birney, Ian Shapiro, and Michael J. Graetz

     About the Contributors   341
     Index   343

Introduction

Ian Shapiro, Peter A. Swenson, and Daniela Donno

Wealthy people used to find democracy frightening. The reason was simple: the poor, once enfranchised, should be expected to soak the rich. This fear bred elite resistance to expanding the franchise, particularly beyond the propertied classes. Nor did this fear, and the reasoning behind it, go unnoticed on the political left. The failure of the revolutions of 1830 and 1848 to radicalize Europe's working classes sobered Marx, leading him— in later years—to endorse the "parliamentary road to socialism." Fighting for democracy might not be such a bad idea. Perhaps the workers would do through the ballot box what they had not done at the barricades. And this expectation of democracy was not limited to the nineteenth century. Millions of marginalized citizens greeted the "third wave" of democracy that swept across the global South in the last decades of the twentieth century with jubilation and hope. Political equality, it was widely believed, would naturally enhance economic equality.

Much academic writing has also assumed that majority rule with a universal franchise would lead to economic redistribution—at least in countries where income and wealth are as unequally distributed as they are in modern capitalist systems. Meltzer and Richard (1981) formalized this intuition through the median voter theorem, which holds that economic policy will reflect the preferences of the voter located at the median point of the income distribution. Given an unequal starting point and self-interested voters, it seemed to stand to reason that downward redistribution would continue until the income of the median voter reached that of the mean. Although appealing for its parsimony and its intuitive predictions, the median voter theorem has proven strikingly unsuccessful at explaining reality. Deep inequalities persist, both in established democracies with institutionalized welfare states and in the younger democracies of the developing world. There seems to be no systematic relationship between expanding the franchise and downward redistribution. Indeed, majority rule democracy can coexist with regressive redistribution in capitalist systems. Nineteenth-century elites need not have feared democracy, and the left, it seems, put too much faith in it.

This reality has real consequences for millions of people across the globe who expect democracy to ameliorate injustice. In recent years, we have witnessed increasing public frustration at the inability of governments to provide for basic needs and stem the widening gulfs between rich and poor. Governments the world over also fail to insure against economic losses due to the punitive effects of labor markets on childbearing, childrearing, bodily injury, physical and mental illness, skill obsolescence, and the infirmity of old age. Americans need look no further than the scenes from New Orleans in the aftermath of Hurricane Katrina to understand the depth of the problem within our own borders. Poverty and exposure to further loss go hand in hand.

Of course, the kind of poverty exposed by Hurricane Katrina is a minority phenomenon, in both a numerical and an ethnic sense, so there is perhaps no profound political puzzle in its tenacity in the face of majority rule. However, even majorities regularly lose out in distributional politics. The continuing failure to pass universal health insurance legislation —when strong majorities at the electoral and elite levels agree on its necessity—is a puzzling political failure of democracy in the United States.

Conventional economic theory discerns *market failure* in the inefficient underprovision of private, voluntary health insurance; political analysis is needed to explain *political failure* in remedying the market failure. In this case, and therefore perhaps in many others, democratic politicians consistently underperform in acting on behalf of majorities. It is therefore all too apparent that our understanding of the forces that drive distributive politics is woefully inadequate. The mismatch between theory and reality suggests that the complex web of motivations, actors, issue areas, and institutions in the political world is simply not captured by the assumptions informing the median voter theorem and its progeny. Fresh thinking and empirical research are needed.

This volume explores how processes at the institutional, group, and individual levels contribute to the often surprising twists and turns of distributive politics. The chapters explore a variety of psychological and institutional factors, collective action problems, and policy-design challenges that influence distributive politics. The contributors present different perspectives on a crucial question: *redistribution of what?* Research on the distribution of income and wealth dominates the political economy literature, but perhaps equally important are the distribution of risk, health care, education, status, values, and life chances. This volume includes chapters on these understudied topics, with an eye to improving our understanding of distributive politics not only in the advanced capitalist democracies but also in the developing world. The contributors also offer new insights into old controversies, notably those concerning the origins and consequences of the welfare state and the role of religion in politics.

A second question addressed in this volume is *redistribution to whom?* As several of the contributors show, despite the predictions of the median voter theorem, redistribution is not always downward. A more appropriate way to think about distributive politics may be based on the ways in which groups form coalitions to bargain over the allocation of the available resources. Imagine a society of three voters whose job it is to determine the division of a dollar among themselves by majority rule. Because every possible division is potentially vulnerable to upset by a new majority coalition, the key questions concern why one coalition rather than another is formed and sustained, when it is, and why distributive coalitions fall apart when they do. A coalitional perspective directs attention to the real chances of unlikely groups benefiting from lateral or even regressive distribution, depending on the alliances that they can form and sustain.

This book is divided into three parts. The chapters comprising part 1 explore the effects of political institutions on a wide range of distributive outcomes including state spending, unemployment, and legislator behavior. The first two chapters explore the sociological and economic origins of the welfare state, as well as the effects of welfare state maturation in the advanced capitalist democracies. Chapters 3 through 5 examine a diverse set of formal institutions, from electoral rules to taxation systems, and assess their influence on distributive outcomes. Taken together, the chapters encompass a range of theoretical perspectives: from a rational choice conception of institutions as exogenous constraints that alter actors' incentives to a thick historical conception of institutions as networks of formal and informal rules with long-term, path-dependent effects.

In part 2 the authors turn from institutions to individuals, examining how preferences and beliefs shape voting behavior and policy outcomes.

These chapters provide compelling evidence for the importance of preferences that would be considered "unusual" from the standpoint of pure economic rationality. Chapters 6 and 7 explore the micromechanisms behind the way religious beliefs and moral values affect political behavior concerning distributive questions. Chapter 8 centers on the normative contours of distributive preferences, uncovering a disproportionate concern for the elderly vis-à-vis other needy groups in the United States.

Part 3 moves from individual- to group-level analysis, exploring how political groups of various stripes bargain and form coalitions in support of distributive arrangements. These chapters offer new insights into the divide-a-dollar logic of distributive politics, in which powerful coalitions, rather than the median voter, are the key locus of influence. They trace how durable coalitions can be forged based on common economic interest but also based on side payments or (mis)perceptions of common interest that may be strategically constructed by political entrepreneurs.

I. Institutions

The core set of policies associated with the modern welfare state—pensions, unemployment compensation, and health care—have a major impact on distribution and redistribution. Esping-Andersen's (1990) pathbreaking study of the three "worlds" of welfare capitalism traced how different modes of state intervention have solidified over time into what we now think of as different welfare systems or regimes. Chapter 1 provides a much-needed corrective for the lack of scholarly attention to welfare regimes in the developing world. In a sweeping historical survey of Latin America, Asia, and Africa, Jeremy Seekings traces the origins and distributional consequences of different welfare systems in the global South. Examining Esping-Andersen's three-part typology of welfare regimes in the advanced capitalist democracies—liberal, corporatist, and social democratic—Seekings finds them inadequate to explain the political and economic dynamics of welfare provision in the developing world. He highlights two key structural differences in developing economies that cause social policy to have different effects there than in the advanced industrial economies of the Organisation for Economic Co-operation and Development (OECD). First, large segments of the population in the global South work in informal sectors, rendering corporatist welfare systems that rely on employment-based policies highly inegalitarian. Countries where labor unions have historically been strong—most notably in Latin America— have adopted corporatist models to the severe detriment of those working in the informal sector. Second, the state has historically been weaker and economies more agrarian in developing countries, leading to a central role for kin and family in serving many of the functions traditionally associated with the welfare state—particularly health care and provision for the elderly.

Seekings puts forward a new threefold typology of welfare states in the global South: *workerist,* in which assistance is employment-based and centers on providing insurance against social risk; *pauperist,* based on means-tested downward redistribution; and *agrarian,* in which redistribution is achieved primarily through state-sponsored land reform, which in turn empowers families and kin to provide for their own welfare. He identifies four key factors that explain which of the three paths was taken. A large immigrant working class and an open, trade-based economy tend to spur the development of exclusionary, workerist systems. De-agrarianization tends to produce agrarian welfare regimes. And democratization through the expansion of suffrage generates electoral incentives for the adoption of redistributive, noncontributory (pauperist) systems that benefit the poor.

Whereas Seekings traced the differences between welfare states in the developed and developing worlds, Isabela Mares turns our attention in chapter 2 to some of the unintended consequences of welfare state maturation. She is particularly interested in explaining why in recent decades the tradeoff between taxation (which sustains the welfare state) and unemployment has become more acute. Whereas influential models in political economy hold that union wage moderation reduces unemployment, in reality the 1980s and 1990s saw increasing levels of unemployment in Western Europe in spite of centralized wage-bargaining institutions that imposed wage moderation. Mares draws insights from the literature on social policy and wage determination to develop a new model that better specifies the relationship between the tax burden, the composition of social spending, wage-bargaining institutions, and the resulting level of unemployment.

An innovative feature of Mares's account is the assumption—supported by evidence drawn from primary sources—that trade unions care about social policy in addition to wages, taxes, and transfer payments. This aspect of unions' utility, she argues, formed the basis for the durable political exchange between unions and governments that sustained the welfare state throughout the postwar period: unions provided wage moderation in exchange for the expansion of social policy. But as Mares shows, this political exchange has recently been undermined by a growth in governments' social policy commitments, resulting from both exogenous demographic change (aging populations) and endogenous expansion. Her model identifies two mechanisms by which these changes in social policy tend to increase equilibrium levels of unemployment. First, a growth in the number of labor market outsiders, namely pensioners and the unemployed, has reduced the willingness of unions to engage in wage moderation, since fewer of the benefits from state social provision accrue to union members. Second, the growth in the size of the tax burden limits the effectiveness of wage moderation in reducing unemployment, since a lower portion of employers' total wage bill is affected by the actual wage rate. Mares tests these propositions using data on wage bargaining and taxation in fourteen OECD countries. Mares's model highlights the sometimes acute tradeoffs that governments face in deciding the composition of social expenditures.

Chapter 3 focuses on a different institutional tradeoff. Shifting from consideration of state expenditures to state income, Steffen Ganghof illuminates the challenges that governments face in designing efficient tax systems that can sustain the robust level of public spending required to support advanced welfare states without driving out capital investment. Ganghof forwards a schema for classifying tax structures according to (a) the vertical distribution of the tax burden over different income levels (i.e., the degree to which the system is progressive or regressive) and (b) the horizontal distribution of relative tax burdens on different types, rather than levels, of income (i.e., financial versus wage income). Different arrangements exhibit different levels and types of *tax-structure efficiency,* which can be conceived in political terms (systems that are electorally sustainable), economic terms (arrangements that bring in higher tax yields), and administrative terms (systems with lower processing, auditing, and enforcement costs).

Drawing from the experiences of European countries, Ganghof explores the political and economic consequences of the tradeoff between vertical and horizontal tax efficiency. He builds from the work of Przeworski and Wallerstein (1988), which showed that increasing capital taxation tends to decrease the investment needed for economic growth. In addition, Ganghof argues, moderate capital taxation increases the economic and administrative efficiency of the tax structure, thereby making possible higher levels of public spending. But whereas horizontal efficiency requires limited taxation of capital, vertical efficiency (and equity) requires progressivity of wage taxation. The paradoxical result, however, is incentives for high-income tax payers to transform their highly taxed (wage) income into more lowly taxed (capital) income—increasing administrative costs and perhaps decreasing overall tax revenues. To make matters even more difficult for tax-structure design, international tax competition —commonly associated with the "race to the bottom"—places further restraints on governments' ability to tax capital. Ganghof provides cross-national evidence for the existence of these tradeoffs, controlling for total tax burden (as percentage of GDP) and degree of wage coordination.

Finding a sustainable balance between these countervailing forces is inherently difficult, Ganghof argues, and will depend on the political climate and institutions specific to each country. However, he does issue a qualified endorsement of the dual income tax system, implemented by Finland, Norway, and Sweden, which combines features of flat income taxes (for capital) with progressive expenditure and wage taxes. Whether these arrangements prove politically stable in the long run remains to be seen, but policy learning and incremental innovation continues.

In chapter 4, Nicoli Nattrass turns our attention to a different set of tradeoffs associated with an essential aspect of state expenditure in the developing world: public health. If inequality is conceived broadly as the distribution of life chances in a society, the AIDS epidemic and government policies for prevention and treatment carry enormous implications for inequality in developing countries. The statistics speak for themselves: according to Joint United Nations Programme on HIV/AIDS (UNAIDS) and World Health Organization (WHO) estimates, 37.5 million people were living with HIV/AIDS at the end of 2004; but just 12 percent of the people needing treatment were actually getting it. Ninety percent of those infected with HIV/AIDS live in countries at low and middle levels of development.

In a cross-national statistical analysis, Nattrass explores the economic and political correlates of AIDS infection and government-sponsored treatment—in the form of Highly Active Antiretroviral Therapy (HAART). HAART provision is a clear and compelling example of a government policy that can directly improve the life chances of large portions of a country's population. A complication, however, is that poverty is strongly implicated in HIV infection, meaning that governments with limited budgets may face a tradeoff between combating infection directly through HAART provision and combating it indirectly by promoting economic growth. Nattrass finds that economic factors—per capita income and health expenditures—have a strong positive effect on HAART provision. But regional effects remain: Latin American and Caribbean countries are significantly better at providing treatment than other regions, though, surprisingly, sub-Saharan Africa is also doing better than expected, after controlling for economic and political factors. Nattrass also finds that established democracies provide significantly higher levels of treatment, which suggests that popular pressure for HAART rollout is more effective in democracies or, alternatively, that international assistance is directed primarily toward democracies.

Moving from the focus on explaining the historical origins of institutions and tradeoffs associated with institutional design, Jana Kunicová in chapter 5 explores the behavioral effects of institutions. Students of electoral systems have long argued that single-member district (SMD) electoral rules create incentives for legislators to distribute resources and projects to their districts, creating an inefficient "pork-barrel" allocation of resources. By contrast, the larger constituency size of PR systems has been shown to reduce pressure for locally based spending, leading to more distributive spending that benefits the population as a whole, through pensions or a minimum wage, for example.

But due mainly to lack of data, we have little knowledge as to how these findings about the effects of electoral rules travel to new democracies in the developing world, where rules are in flux and political actors are still learning the game. Using roll-call data from three sessions of the Russian Duma in the 1990s—a mixed legislature where half the deputies were elected by SMD and half by PR—Kunicová examines the effects of electoral mandate on legislators' votes on redistributive issues. Because the institutional variation in electoral rules is located within one legislature, the research design controls for country-specific factors, such as legislative norms and context-specific distributive issues.

In keeping with findings from cross-national studies, Kunicová finds that legislators elected by SMD are significantly more likely than those elected by PR to break with their legislative faction on votes related to distributive spending to Russia's regions. Her results indicate that the relationship between electoral mandate and distributive politics does hold in new or developing democracies. The rules of the game may be new in Russia, but their effects are nonetheless robust.

II. Preferences

Having explored the institutional side of distributive politics, the contributors in part 2 ask how we can explain the surprisingly weak propensity of individuals to vote according to their economic self-interest—the "what's the matter with Kansas" problem (Frank 2004). The authors examine evidence from the United States to test for the effects of a set of factors long prominent in political science and sociology—religion, morality, and values—in newly rigorous ways.

In chapter 6, Kenneth Scheve and David Stasavage explore how religiosity affects preferences for state provision of social insurance. They draw from findings in psychology showing that religious beliefs serve to diminish the psychic costs of adverse life events, such as unemployment or injury, that affect the ability to work. Whereas previous work has explored how religious communities can serve as substitutes for the state in providing for the material well-being of their members following adverse life events, Scheve and Stasavage's focus on the psychic benefits of religion—i.e., reducing stress and loss of self-esteem—suggests an alternative mechanism by which religion affects political preferences, independent of differences in denomination or creed.

Scheve and Stasavage find cross-country evidence of a strong relationship between high religiosity and low social-insurance provision, in which the United States is the most pronounced example among the advanced industrial countries. They test their proposed relationship between religiosity and social insurance using data from the U.S. states, allowing them to hold constant possible unobserved factors at the country level that might drive patterns in social spending. At the individual level, they find a robust, negative correlation between religiosity and preferences for social insurance, even after controlling for socioeconomic status, for religious denomination, and for other possibly confounding beliefs about the role of effort versus luck in determining an individual's economic success. They then test for the effect of these beliefs on state-level unemployment and workers'-compensation provision, finding support for the link between religiosity and policy outcomes.

Scheve and Stasavage argue that the relationship between religiosity and economic-policy preferences is based on a substitution effect, whereby religious beliefs serve as a (partial) substitute for social insurance. Beginning with the same puzzle of the unexpectedly low rate of redistribution in the United States, Woojin Lee and John Roemer in chapter 7 argue that the relationship between morality and economic preferences is based on an ideological complementarity between religiosity and conservative economic causal beliefs. Lee and Roemer conduct a comprehensive formal and empirical analysis of the role of moral values in shaping both party platforms and voting behavior. Putting the puzzle in the context of the 2004 U.S. presidential election, they seek to explain why the Republican Party was able to win a majority of votes when their proposed economic policies were arguably geared toward the economic interest of a small minority of voters.

Lee and Roemer employ a party-unanimity Nash-equilibrium (PUNE) model with two issue dimensions to examine the effect on party policy platforms of adding a moral-values issue dimension to the standard economic issue dimension. They posit two mechanisms by which a moral-values dimension could confound the economic dimension: First, in what the authors term a "policy bundling" effect, high salience of moral values could lead some people to vote for a less-preferred economic-policy outcome. Or alternatively, moral values could be ideologically connected to the conservative economic belief that effort trumps luck, a phenomenon akin to Max Weber's Protestant work ethic, which Lee and Roemer term the "moral Puritan" effect. The authors show that (a) high salience of moral values and (b) a large number of voters who connect their conservative values to conservative economic preferences (the "moral Puritan" effect) both tend to diminish the level of redistribution proposed by the two parties in equilibrium. When moral values are highly salient to voters, the effect on economic policies (operationalized as size of the public sector) proposed by the two parties can be quite large. The Lee-Roemer model of the moral-values issue dimension also accounts for voting behavior that is manifestly surprising from a purely economic standpoint.

In chapter 8, Christopher Howard explores the preferences that underpin another puzzling aspect of distributive politics in the United States: the fact that public spending is heavily skewed toward the elderly and the affluent. Moreover, the increase in inequality in recent years has not prompted demands for redistribution away from these groups. A standard political explanation for this puzzling policy mix is one of small-group "capture" of government; policy is distorted as a result of the disproportionate political power of the elderly and wealthy, who exhibit higher political awareness, activism, and interest-group activity.

In Howard's revealing exploration of American public opinion, however, he shows that there is a robust intergenerational consensus for high spending on the elderly and, even more surprisingly, that there is little demand from the poor and middle class for state-sponsored redistribution. In 1996, fewer than half of Americans said that government should reduce income differentials between rich and poor—in stark contrast to European countries, where more than two-thirds support government-led redistribution. Even more surprisingly, less than 40 percent of the poor in America reported wanting government to redistribute income. Howard's findings raise important questions about public awareness and beliefs on the demand side of distributive politics and suggest that the elderly and wealthy do not have disproportionate "power" in the sense of enacting policy against the preferences of the rest of the country. Thus, Howard argues, the common assumption that things would look very different in the United States if the wealthy and elderly were not as politically powerful may not hold.

III. Coalitions

Individual preferences are one building block in understanding the role of demand in distributive politics, but we also must consider group preferences and power. As the contributors to part 3 show, distributive coalitions, forged by attending to considerations about power and commonalities of interest, serve as an analytical bridge between preferences and outcomes. Bringing the volume full circle, these chapters illustrate how coalitions are often responsible for institutional change.

In chapter 9, Peter A. Swenson examines the long-term institutional effects of coalitions. He traces how shifting coalitions among capital, labor, and medicine shaped the landscape of Germany's relatively egalitarian health care system. His innovative analysis introduces a new collective actor—organized medicine—to the standard capital-labor divide and highlights the presence of complex overlapping interests that facilitate, under conditions of economic crisis, major coalitional shifts and therefore transformation of institutions and policy regimes. Swenson also illuminates how maintaining egalitarian accomplishments in the political sphere is an ongoing process in which allocation of control over institutions is as much contested as allocation of material resources.

Swenson's explanation emphasizes the role of macroeconomic context, particularly periods of economic crisis, in opening up windows of opportunity for policy change. Entrenched coalitions crumble, and new ones emerge without a change of key actors' basic and relative distributional preferences. Thus, during the depression of the 1930s, the consequences of inefficiencies in the health care system and the tradeoff between quality and economy were exacerbated. Swenson locates the coalitional foundations of the unique system that emerged from an unexpected alliance between labor and organized medicine in 1931, a system that was reinstalled largely intact after World War II and endured relatively unchallenged until the 1990s.

Swenson's account hinges on the swing vote of organized labor, which sought a negotiated alliance that would best protect its interest in a centralized system that would provide for quality and equality in health care for all its members. A July 1930 presidential decree reorganizing the health care system, supported by capital and tentatively by labor, ended up disadvantaging workers, who lost sick pay and who had to pay a share of fees. Doctors would in principle share the sacrifices through a lowering of fees and flow of patients, but they did not suffer in relative terms. Because doctors were paid on a fee-for-service basis, they could avoid loss of income and circumvent the system simply by performing excess, unnecessary services. It soon became clear that the arrangement was economically dysfunctional and politically untenable, leading to a dramatic about-face by labor and a victory for doctors just one year later.

A 1931 presidential decree, resulting from the labor-medicine alliance, mandated collective bargaining between monopolistic physicians' associations and health insurance funds. Doctors retained a high degree of autonomy and income protection under the arrangement by assuming, at least in principle, the collective responsibility to monitor the practice of medicine to achieve cost control. Labor, in return, saw potential in the new system for the insurance funds they controlled to gain membership ground at the expense of health funds controlled by large employers.

Pranab Bardhan's account of distributive politics and democracy in India, in chapter 10, supports a decidedly more pessimistic view of the economic effects of coalitions. He paints a vivid picture of contemporary politics in India, characterized by a "bewildering crisscross" of interest groups connected for the most part by mutual suspicion. The frequency of national and regional elections creates an environment of constantly shifting political coalitions based on the narrow, short-term electoral calculations of politicians. Distributive politics is "short-run" and group based. Newly powerful regional parties tend to use elected office to redistribute to their own region.

The pernicious effects of these ethnic, regional, and class "logrolling" coalitions are far-reaching. Most importantly, they stymie the provision of much-needed public goods, namely comprehensive economic reform and investment—especially in infrastructure and irrigation—that would benefit the majority of the population. Culturally, the emphasis on group rights at the expense of individual rights has led to weak societal support for civil liberties such as freedom of expression and freedom from state interference. India's vast state apparatus is rife with corruption and is used largely as an instrument for the distribution of political favors. In sum, accountability and rule of law are eroding. Thus, in Bardhan's depiction, Indian politics adheres much more strongly to an Olsonian picture of interest-group capture than to a pluralist picture of benign cross-cutting cleavages. But it was not always so. Bardhan argues that the recent expansion of democracy to the lower rungs of the social hierarchy, though desirable in and of itself, has also led to the demise of intraparty democracy and coalition building that had previously sustained a more effective system of governance. The erosion of elite control has resulted in a concomitant erosion of administrative probity, the rule of law, and the insulation of economic decision-making.

In chapter 8, Howard provided evidence of surprisingly consensual distributive preferences in the United States despite economic realities that would predict deep cleavages. His implicit assumption is that preferences are exogenous to the political process. In chapter 11, Mayling Birney, Ian Shapiro, and Michael J. Graetz dispense with this assumption. They take malleable preferences as their starting point and show how unexpected distributive coalitions can be built through the strategic interpretation of public-opinion data. Their empirical puzzle is the repeal of the U.S. estate tax in 2001. Although the estate tax was highly progressive, affected less than 2 percent of the population, and had been on the books since 1916, repeal was nonetheless supported by a surprisingly diverse alliance of interest groups, cobbled together partly through the use of polling data that seemed to show support for full repeal. Birney, Shapiro, and Graetz trace how pro-repeal interest groups used this polling data as a political weapon to forge their coalition and ultimately to sway legislators' votes.

Birney, Shapiro, and Graetz propose a "running-room" model of public opinion in which interest groups and political entrepreneurs define the contours of latent opinion and then use their polling and focus group data to influence legislative votes. Contrary to prevailing theories of public opinion and policy, the running-room model emphasizes the indirect link between public opinion and policy, through legislators. Birney, Shapiro, and Graetz's findings imply, first, that public opinion is highly sensitive to framing and phraseology, particularly on low-salience issues like the estate tax. By using certain opinion-poll frames that emphasized procedural fairness and capitalized on public misperceptions about who is affected by the estate tax, pro-repeal entrepreneurs were able to convey the message that the public broadly favored repeal. Although opponents of repeal conducted polling that showed contrary results (i.e., that the public favored reform over repeal), they were slow and ineffective in broadcasting their message to legislators. Second—and echoing Howard—Birney, Shapiro, and Graetz argue that the deep cleavages over redistribution predicted by pure economic rationality should not be assumed. In this case, a surprisingly durable coalition was built among groups who were for the most part acting against their own economic interest; they persuaded legislators to vote for upward redistribution to the top 2 percent of the population. Birney, Shapiro, and Graetz are careful to emphasize that the general conclusion to be drawn from their analysis is not necessarily pessimistic for partisans of downward redistribution: distributive coalitions can be forged on both sides of every issue, and it is up to political entrepreneurs to seize the initiative.

The chapters comprising this volume engage a diverse set of questions and speak to several different literatures concerned with democracy and distributive politics. Yet they advance a single theme: the realm of distributive politics is occupied by a complex mix of actors, motivations, coalitions, and institutional contexts that belie the simplicity of the median voter theorem or the type of thinking about distributive politics that it encourages us to deploy. Institutions alter the incentives of political actors and influence policy outcomes that directly affect citizens' material well-being. Individual preferences concerning economic policy are complex and multidimensional. Psychological factors, including religious beliefs, cognitive biases, and misperceptions about self-interest influence citizens' demand for redistribution in significant ways.

And perhaps most importantly, a moral to be drawn from this volume is that politics matters. In seeking to explain the sometimes puzzling policy outcomes that shape the distribution of income, wealth, taxation, risk, status, and well-being in a society, we cannot ignore the role of shifting political coalitions and the often unexpected partnerships that they engender. A coalitional perspective directs our attention to the processes of competition, of bargaining, and of building and destroying the political alliances that serve as bridges between individuals and institutions. If, taken together, the chapters comprising this volume do not suggest that a grand theory of distributive politics will be in the offing any time soon, they do direct attention to fruitful research agendas and begin to explore them.

REFERENCES

Esping-Andersen, Gøsta. 1990. *The Three Worlds of Welfare Capitalism.* Princeton, NJ: Princeton University Press.

Frank, Thomas. 2004. *What's the Matter with Kansas? How Conservatives Won the Heart of America.* New York: Henry Holt.

Meltzer, Allan H., and Scott F. Richard. 1981. A Rational Theory of the Size of Government. *Journal of Political Economy* 89(5): 914–27.

Przeworski, Adam, and Michael Wallerstein. 1988. The Structural Dependence of the State on Capital. *American Political Science Review* 82(1): 11–29.

Part I

|||||||||||||||||||||||||||||||||||||||||||||||||||||||

Institutions

Chapter 1

||||||||||||||||||||||||||||||||||||||||||||||||||

Welfare Regimes and Redistribution in the South

Jeremy Seekings

The word "crisis" has been widely used in discussions of welfare states and regimes in the late twentieth century. "Almost all advanced industrial democracies cut entitlements in some programs in this period," summarize Huber and Stephens in their book *Development and Crisis of the Welfare State* (2001, 1). The crisis could be seen in the developing world also; a key World Bank study was entitled *Averting the Old-Age Crisis* (1994), and commentators widely charged that the World Bank was imposing cuts in the form of the Chilean "neoliberal" model on countries across the South. But it is now clear that in the North it is politically difficult to roll back substantially the public provision of welfare (Pierson 1994, 2001; Huber and Stephens 2001), while across much of the South pressures to expand welfare provision have grown. It is true that the Chilean/World Bank model of privatizing the contributory pension system was extended to other parts of Latin America and post-Communist Eastern Europe and central Asia. But, at the same time, welfare provision has been extended to the poor in other parts of the South, especially through social-assistance schemes (including "conditional cash transfers") or other moves in the direction of a guaranteed or "basic" income.

Is it possible to discern clear patterns in the ways in which states have responded at the end of the twentieth century and start of the twenty-first to the evolving social and political pressures of poverty, inequality, and risk? Why do some states adopt expansionary reforms while others retrench? Answers to these kinds of questions applied to the countries of the North typically employ a variant of Esping-Andersen's typology of different "worlds of welfare capitalism" (for the original typology, see Esping-Andersen 1990).

Esping-Andersen identified three distinct patterns of state intervention in the advanced capitalist countries of the North (including Australia and New Zealand). In each case, the state intervened through social and (to a lesser extent) labor market policies to reduce inequality (both between individuals and across the life-cycle), but the form of that intervention differed in the scale of public expenditure and the extent to which the state displaced the market and family in determining the incomes and welfare of its citizens. At the end of the twentieth century, these different clusters of states responded differently to fiscal, demographic, and political pressures (Esping-Andersen 1999, 2002). Path dependence was not rigid and immutable, but the conditions that produced distinctive welfare regimes and the effects of the different regimes themselves certainly influenced the ways in which they later evolved.

This chapter provides a preliminary, comparative, historical analysis of the development of "welfare" systems in the South, so as to inform an analysis of contemporary reforms and of the prospects for further reform. Societies, economies, and polities across much of the South are rather different from those of the North, however. Esping-Andersen's analysis needs to be revised if it is to illuminate experiences in the poorer parts of the world.

Esping-Andersen identifies different forms (or "worlds") of "welfare capitalism" in the advanced capitalist countries according to the ways in which the state affects distribution through a combination of social policies (including especially the public provision of welfare through social insurance or social assistance) and labor market policies. His 1990 study was organized around the concept of "welfare state regimes." Use of the term "regime" was intended to emphasize the relationships between social policies, employment, and the social structure in general (Esping-Andersen 1990, 2). In later work, he prefers the simpler term "welfare regime," which reduces the emphasis on the state: "A welfare regime can be defined as the combined, interdependent way in which welfare is produced and allocated between state, market and family" (Esping-Andersen 1999, 34–35). Esping-Andersen considers also labor market policies, primarily with respect to the maintenance of full employment. Full employment (during the Golden Age of postwar capitalism) meant that the public provision of welfare could be largely confined to the young (through schooling), the elderly (through old-age pensions), and the sick (through the public-health system). Unemployment was contained through Keynesian macroeconomic policies and public-sector employment policies (which increased the demand for labor) and through social and tax policies that affected labor supply. Such policies constituted different kinds of "labor market regime," each corresponding to a different kind of "welfare state regime" (Esping-Andersen 1990).

The three "worlds" of welfare capitalism are characterized by their welfare state and labor market regimes. Liberal welfare regimes entail modest financial provision to targeted (generally means-tested) individuals in a limited array of situations. Public provision is residual in that the state only fills gaps left by the market, but its targeting means that it is nonetheless redistributive. The modal liberal welfare regime is the United States. By contrast, the social democratic welfare regime is much more generous and universal and aspires to cover (i.e., socialize) all risks, with the result that it is much more redistributive and egalitarian. The state actively assumes roles—such as child care—played hitherto by the family, and seeks to minimize the role played by the market. Full employment in these social democratic regimes entails very high participation rates, not just low unemployment rates. The social democratic regimes are mostly in Scandinavia, with Sweden treated as the modal regime (although Goodin et al. 1999 use the Netherlands as the modal social democratic regime).

The conservative welfare regimes of continental Europe (Austria, France, Germany, and Italy) share some features with each of the other two kinds of welfare regime. Like the social democratic regimes, they are generous. But they are unequally generous, with differentiated benefits; support is "mutualist" rather than redistributive. The basis is insurance, not assistance. These regimes emphasize the roles played by families: public policies buttress rather than undermine familial roles. Women are discouraged from working, so that full employment entails a low participation rate. Each of these regimes has its origins in different political and ideological contexts: liberal regimes where liberal traditions were strong and where liberty was the fundamental value; social democratic regimes where politics revolved around class and where social equality was the fundamental value; and conservative regimes where strong corporatist or Catholic traditions were strong (and liberal and socialist traditions weak) and where the fundamental value was social cohesion (Goodin et al. 1999).

Table 1.1 shows the key characteristics of each of Esping-Andersen's regimes (based on Esping-Andersen 1999, 85). The degree of "decommodification" refers to the extent to which the state provides income to citizens as a right independently of the market value of their labor as a commodity. Esping-Andersen also refers to "defamilialization," that is, the extent to

TABLE 1.1
Esping-Andersen's Typology of Welfare Regimes

	Liberal	Social democratic	Conservative
Role of:			
family	marginal	marginal	central
market	central	marginal	marginal
state	marginal	central	subsidiary
Welfare state:			
dominant mode of solidarity	individual	universal	kinship; corporatism; statism
dominant locus of solidarity	market	state	family
degree of decommodification	minimal	maximum	high (for breadwinner)
degree of defamilialization	medium	high	low
Extent of redistribution	low	high	medium

which the state assumes roles played by close kin (such as care for children and the elderly).

The final row of table 1.1 reflects the extent of direct redistribution through taxes and transfers. Esping-Andersen himself is less concerned with this measure, but other scholars have paid it careful attention, using cross-national data from the Luxemburg Income Study. Korpi and Palme (1998) showed that there was a close relationship between the size of the budget for redistribution (i.e., the public-welfare budget) and the extent of income redistribution through transfers and direct taxation (measured through the reduction in the Gini coefficient). The social democratic welfare regimes tended to spend more and redistribute more than the conservative welfare regimes of continental Europe, which in turn tended to spend and redistribute more than the liberal welfare regimes (see also Huber and Stephens 2001, Milanovic 1999, Przeworski and Gandhi 1999, Bradley et al. 2003). The differences between the three kinds of welfare state regime are evident also in the analysis of longitudinal data by Goodin et al. (1999).

One of the grounds on which the "three worlds" typology has been criticized is its failure to address the role of family or kin in caring for poor people. Welfare regimes in southern Europe (Italy, Spain, and Portugal) and in Japan are said to be "familialistic." Esping-Andersen (1999) concedes that his earlier work neglected the roles of family but argues on empirical grounds that the welfare regimes of southern Europe do not provide markedly less support to families than other conservative regimes in continental Europe.

Another criticism, made by Castles, is that Esping-Andersen's typology underestimates the importance of labor market policies designed to influence wages (and thereby earnings). Castles shows that in Australia, the material well-being of the citizenry was secured primarily through the regulation of earnings through, especially, the wage-arbitration system (Castles 1985, 1996; Castles and Mitchell 1993). The result was, in Castles's phrase, a "wage earners' welfare state," that is, a welfare state that sought to ensure a certain standard of living for Australians as (male) wage-earners (and their dependents) rather than as citizens.

Welfare Regimes in the Global South

The "three worlds" typology was developed for, and continues to fit reasonably well, the advanced industrialized countries of Europe and North America. It fits less easily the later industrializing countries of southern Europe, Japan, Australia, and New Zealand (see Esping-Andersen 1999, chap. 5). It fits even less easily the countries of Latin America and East Asia that industrialized still later or the post-Communist countries of central and eastern Europe. In an edited collection including chapters on each of these three parts of the world, Esping-Andersen and his contributors avoided developing his typology (Esping-Andersen 1996). There was, indeed, no mention of welfare *regimes*. Instead, he discussed the *trajectories* that these cases are following. Most of the countries (including Chile) were identified as following a liberal, market-oriented strategy. Others (e.g., Brazil) were seen to have taken tentative steps toward universalism (along what he later called a "proto-social-democratic path"; ibid., 267). A third group (in East Asia) had followed the Japanese lead in combining great emphasis on both the family and employment-related welfare; public provision is residual, although the model relies on a de facto job guarantee.

A typology in which welfare capitalism is categorized into "regimes" in the countries of the North but into "trajectories" in those of the South is clearly incomplete. At what point in the twentieth century did the Northern countries complete their own transitions from what Esping-Andersen might call "pre-regimes" into recognizable regimes? What are the criteria defining whether and when a regime is fully (or simply sufficiently) formed? Unfortunately, there is little research on the historical experiences of "welfare capitalism" in Southern societies. The set of cases that has attracted the most research in this vein comprises the East Asian "tigers." Many of the scholars concerned have emphasized how these countries do not fit Esping-Andersen's "*Western* welfare capitalist typology" (Jones 1993) but are instead distinctively "Confucian" welfare regimes. Latin American welfare systems have attracted considerable attention, although not so much within Esping-Andersen's framework. In general, however, few Southern regimes appear to be redistributive. Studies of the incidence of taxation and public expenditure in the South reveal a picture of very limited—even zero—redistribution from rich to poor. Because public expenditure is often captured by nonpoor groups, Gini coefficients for the distribution of income are not reduced by anywhere near as much as in the industrialized democracies of the North. Even taking into account the benefits in-kind from social spending (especially public education and health), Gini coefficients are rarely reduced by more than 5 to 7 percentage points, which is very substantially less than in the North.

Pro-poor forms of capitalism in the South have generally not emphasized social or labor market policies as much as a broader set of developmental policies. These forms of capitalism might be described as "developmental" more than "welfare," and the states as "developmental states" rather than "welfare states." Development economists have conducted many cross-national studies that show that growth strategies had profound effects on who gets what in these societies. The pioneers in this research (e.g., Adelman and Morris 1973; Chenery et al. 1974; W. Lewis 1976) were followed by multivolume projects such as the International Labour Organisation's "Income Distribution and Employment Programme," Princeton's series "Political Economy of Income Distribution in Developing Countries," and the World Bank's series "Political Economy of Poverty, Equity and Growth." Whereas Esping-Andersen takes the market-generated distribution of income largely as given and concentrates instead on how welfare states redistribute that income, development economists emphasize the relationship between the state, growth, and "market" distribution.

Extending Esping-Andersen's analysis to South Africa or other Southern societies suggests that different worlds of welfare capitalism are characterized by packages of welfare, labor market, *and* "growth-path" policies. These may be functionally interlocking, as are (in general) welfare and labor market policies in the North. Elsewhere, in a case-study of South Africa, Nattrass and I use the concept of a "distributional regime," combining (often uneasily) welfare, labor market, and growth-path policies (Seekings and Nattrass 2005). In the South African case, diverse policies promoted a growth path that increased inequality, by rewarding people with skills in industry and services while reducing opportunities for unskilled laborers and smallholding peasants.

If we narrow our analysis to the provision of welfare specifically, it is clear that many welfare regimes in the South attach considerable importance to kin and the family and do not rely on either the market or the state. The relative youth and weakness of both the (modern) state and the market has meant that the family has historically played a major role in providing for the poor. The World Bank estimated in the early 1990s that only 30 percent of the world's elderly were covered by formal arrangements, and only 40 percent of the world's working population participated in any formal arrangements for their future old age (World Bank 1994). Moreover, many Southern countries stipulate in statute or constitution that the family must provide for its members. The 1987 constitution of the Philippines declares that "the family has a duty to care for its elderly members" (cited in Ofstedal et al. 2002, 66), and there are statutory obligations on children to support their parents in Singapore, India, and Botswana, among many other cases.

In other, more industrialized settings, welfare regimes entail a mix of market and state. In the case of the larger economies of Latin America, the state typically assumes a massive role, which includes heavy subsidization of social insurance out of general tax revenues as part of a broader distributional regime that favors organized workers (and some domestic employers) and discriminates against the rural and urban poor. The East Asian cases have historically entailed a larger emphasis on the market (supplementing the family); the Latin American cases are more inegalitarian in that they entail more state subsidization of the already privileged formal-sector employees. But this orthodox distinction blurs some basic similarities between the Latin American and East Asian models. In both settings, the rights or claims that people can make are dependent on their prior employment status. In other words, rights are dependent on prior commodification. This is the case regardless of whether the claims are exercised through social insurance or through state-regulated market systems of risk-pooling or saving. White and Goodman (1998, 14) described the East Asian cases as "similar to what Esping-Andersen (1990) calls 'Bismarckian' welfare systems": state-sponsored but occupationally fragmented schemes that reflect and reinforce differences in status and power. This is a description that readily fits most Latin American cases. In a few countries across the South, welfare regimes include also an element of decommodification for the poor, through the recognition of rights that are entirely independent of employment, that is, through social assistance rather than social insurance. Such provision is almost always means-tested, along the lines of the poor laws or of social-assistance programs in the "liberal" welfare regimes of the North. A typology of Southern welfare regimes needs to distinguish between those entailing claims based on employment and those entailing claims based on rights of citizenship. This is especially important in the South because the population in formal employment is generally relatively privileged, that is, has incomes close to or above the median income. A welfare system that ties benefits to formal employment is likely to exclude most of the poor.

There is, in the South, a third alternative to employment-based and rights-based welfare. In many settings, both before and after decolonization, Southern states have sought to promote income security through promoting broad access to land. Land-reform programs, and ensuing government support for small farmers, can provide poor families with the opportunity to produce for either their own consumption or for the market. Most states sought to regulate prices for agricultural produce (especially exports) and inputs including credit. Although such agrarian policies promoted involvement in product markets and regulated that involvement, it does not seem appropriate to consider them as entailing either commodification or decommodification in the same way as through labor markets and cash transfers.

Welfare regimes in the South incorporate one or more of these distinct *agrarian, workerist,* and *pauperist* approaches.[1] The agrarian approach is defined by the private provision of welfare, dependent on access to land and/or kin, that is itself dependent on a set of supportive state policies. The workerist approach is defined by forms of risk-pooling and/or saving (such as retirement pensions) that are dependent on formal employment. Workerist approaches come in either a market-based version (through either provident funds, as in Singapore, or employer-based schemes, as in much of East Asia until recently) or the more statist form of social insurance. Finally, the pauperist approach is defined by the recognition of the rights of some citizens to income security through, especially, noncontributory social assistance. Insofar as the welfare regime in any country entails predominantly one of these approaches, we might talk of an agrarian, workerist, or pauperist welfare regime. These three kinds of South-

TABLE 1.2
Typology of Southern Welfare Regimes

	Agrarian	Workerist	Pauperist
Focus	peasants	workers	paupers
Incentive	social stability	industrial peace	social stability (nondemocracy); electoral gain (democracy)
Objective	development	income smoothing	poverty reduction
Role of:			
family	central	marginal	marginal
employment	marginal	central	marginal
state	varied	varied	central
Welfare state:			
dominant mode of solidarity	kinship	individual or corporate (occupational)	universal
dominant locus of solidarity	family	market or state	state
degree of decommodification	varied	minimum	maximum
degree of defamilialization	low	varied	medium to high
Extent of redistribution	varied	low	medium to high

ern welfare regime can be considered in the same framework as Esping-Andersen's three Northern regimes (see table 1.2).

In practice, the welfare systems in most Southern countries combine elements of two if not all three of these approaches. In South Africa, for example, there is a large employment-based semisocial insurance system, including both risk-pooling and individual savings, providing for the employed elite; there is an impressive set of noncontributory social-assistance programs, including especially old-age pensions; and there have been some (very inadequate) attempts to revive smallholder production and an agrarian society. A case like this entails a mixed workerist-pauperist regime. Other cases are more clearly agrarian (for example, parts of Africa) or workerist (as in the major countries of Latin America, at least until recently). Over the past twenty years, however, more and more countries have been adopting the pauperist approach as a supplement to their existing approaches. It is important to reemphasize that all three of these approaches or regime types entail active state interventions of one sort or another. Agrarian welfare regimes cease to be "welfare" regimes in any meaningful sense if the state does not provide support with infrastructure, marketing, tax and tariff policy, and even land reform.

The Making of Southern Welfare Regimes

Looking at the broad sweep of welfare-regime making in the global South over the course of the twentieth century, there seem to be five factors which play especially important roles in the pace and direction of change.

1. Is there an *immigrant working class* (as in Australia, South Africa, Brazil, Argentina, and Chile)? If so, there is more likely to be a rapid move toward a workerist approach which provides nonuniversal benefits to corporate groups of workers through some mix of state and market; welfare-regime making might be due to direct pressures from below or proactive reforms from above; the importance of the *immigrant* working class is that it lacks links to a productive peasantry (and might also bring socialist or trade-unionist ideologies and traditions).

2. Is there an agrarian crisis, that is, *deagrarianization*? And if so, is this considered irreversible, or might it be thought possible to revive an agrarian society and economy?

3. Is the *economy open or closed*? An open economy precludes employers passing the costs of social insurance on to consumers and encourages state and employers to consider seriously social-assistance programs funded out of central government revenues; the prospect of passing the costs of social insurance on to consumers is a strong additional incentive to coalitions of employers and workers to demand tariff protection and policies pushing the economy down the path of import substitution.

4. What is the relative salience of universal rather than employment-based *norms of welfare provision*? Is the country more exposed to the influence of the International Labour Organisation (with its workerist emphasis) or the British liberal welfare tradition (with its pauperist emphasis)?

5. Is there *electoral competition* for votes of nonunionized poor? This requires a degree of democratization; competition for the votes of the nonunionized poor provides an important stimulus to the promise of noncontributory social assistance, because the nonunionized poor are unlikely to be able or willing to be covered by a contributory system.

These five factors combined in different ways in four key stages of welfare-regime making. First, in the early twentieth century, industrial and public-sector workers struggled for or were given insurance-based welfare. Unionized immigrants were especially prominent in this struggle for state-subsidized risk pooling. Outside of these specific occupations, poverty was the concern of kin; only in exceptional circumstances did the state accept the need for state-funded social assistance to "deserving" poor (often through discretionary poor relief). Here lay the origins of *workerist* or employment-based welfare regimes. Second, in the mid-twentieth century, concerns with agrarian crisis and ensuing urban poverty led to reform in one of two directions: the predominant response was the "developmental" one (with an uneasy combination of economic modernization and social traditionalism, such that poverty is more effectively addressed by kin or through the extension of risk pooling among wage earners), leading to the formation of *agrarian* welfare regimes; a less common response was the extension and institutionalization of social assistance, leading to nascent *pauperist* regimes. In the second half of the twentieth century there was a widespread broadening of workerist regimes, as insurance systems were extended to cover a broader (but still very incomplete and generally nonpoor) section of the population. Finally, at the end of the century, a combination of demographic change, massive deagrarianization, and (especially) democratization increased pressures for welfare reform and the extension of income security to the poor through noncontributory social assistance.

Immigrant Workers and the Politics of Industrialization in the Early Twentieth Century

In urban and industrial areas across much of what was later to become known as the South, as in what was to become known as the North, welfare systems were born and grew primarily through the establishment of contributory insurance schemes for particular groups of workers. The groups with most power and influence were the same in most settings: soldiers, civil servants, and workers in key sectors such as railways, ports, and utilities. In some cases, these groups of workers secured protection through direct action; in other cases, elites provided protection to preempt such action. Immigrant workers rarely wielded electoral power to match their industrial power. They typically mobilized, or were provided for, as workers rather than as citizens. Insurance schemes developed more in those settings where the workers were immigrants, sometimes drawing on socialist or other ideologies from their countries of origin, and always with weak or no links to the agrarian economy outside the towns and industrial areas. Typically, these occupational groups obtained favorable welfare provision at the same time as favorable economic policies (often parts of a strategy of industrialization through import substitution, or ISI).

Brazil is a classic example of this pattern (see Malloy 1979). Brazil's welfare system had emerged in the 1920s in response to the industrial (but not electoral) strength of sections of the working class, in formal employment in key sectors. Prior to 1923, public-sector workers secured some social insurance. In 1923, state-enforced, compulsory social insurance (covering retirement, sickness, and invalidity) was introduced for private-sector railway workers, later extended also to dock and maritime workers. The scheme was funded through contributions from employees, employers, and the state. Unlike in South Africa, there was no supplementary social assistance covering those who had not contributed to the social-insurance schemes. After 1930, under Vargas, an elaborate system of social insurance was extended to cover most of the urban, formal sector—that is, approximately two million workers by the late 1930s. A substantial number of working people was thus covered by a state-subsidized welfare system. Chile's welfare regime developed along similar lines: better-paid workers secured better welfare provision; poorly paid workers, inferior benefits; and workers outside the formal sector, none at all (Borzutzky 2002).

The result, as Borzutzky argues forcefully for the Chilean case, was structured inequality. Indeed, as Huber (1996, 143–44) notes for Latin America in general (citing earlier work by Mesa-Largo), "these schemes did more than reproduce the inequality in the labour market; they aggravated inequality by imposing some of the burden of financing on groups not covered, mainly through indirect taxes and through the passing on of employer contributions to prices in protected markets." Formal-sector workers and existing employers were protected by tariff barriers. Tariffs enabled employers to pass on to domestic consumers both higher wages and the cost of employer contributions to social security (Huber 1996, 146). In terms of both their political origins (reform from above) and their occupationally structured inequalities, these Latin American welfare regimes were similar to the conservative or corporatist regimes of continental Europe (ibid., 148). Unlike the European cases, however, these regimes excluded the poor. While corporatist, these regimes were therefore doubly inegalitarian.

Amid this picture of inegalitarian social insurance, there are several deviant cases, including South Africa. The South African case illustrates the unusual circumstances in which social assistance developed alongside social insurance. The core of the South African welfare system was corporatist, with a variety of contributory schemes covering most semiskilled or skilled workers in formal employment. Most workers covered were white or "coloured," in the racial terms used in South Africa, with "native" workers excluded. The impetus to this social insurance was, as in Latin America, a combination of the industrial and electoral power of these groups of workers. But, in 1928, the South African state introduced noncontributory old-age pensions for white and coloured people, and later extended this social assistance to include grants for the disabled and for single mothers. The motivation for this change had been made four years earlier, in an official memorandum reviewing the options for old-age pensions. The arguments for noncontributory schemes were "(a) the increasing stress of modern industrialism and the competitive system throwing, as it does, men out of employment at an ever earlier age; (b) the lowness of wages leaving no margin for making adequate provision for declining years." These were issues related to urban poverty, and the concern was for poverty among a racialized and privileged group. The premise was that the state had an obligation to ensure that white (and coloured) workers enjoyed a "civilized" standard of living, leaving "native" people to rely on their own, kin-based resources. In 1936 as many as fifty-six thousand elderly white and coloured men and women were receiving the noncontributory pensions.

Although the South African system shared with its Latin American counterparts the exclusion of the poor majority, it needed to include some groups who were unable to provide for themselves on a contributory basis, that is, poor white and coloured people. They needed to be included because of the prevailing racist and Afrikaner nationalist ideologies and because deagrarianization among these groups meant that they could not be provided for through agricultural production. Indeed, many of the "poor whites" were immigrants into towns from farms, former sharecroppers, and tenants squeezed off the land by the spreading commercialization of agriculture.

Depression, War, Welfare, and Development

The welfare systems of the 1920s and 1930s were to be overtaken by events, with the Second World War following close on the Great Depression. The late 1930s and early 1940s were a period not only of profound social and economic change but also of extraordinary intellectual ferment. In Cape Town, Nairobi, and Mexico City, just as in London, Paris, and Stockholm, politicians and administrators and intellectuals alike were infused with new confidence in the capacity of the state to promote the welfare of its citizens and subjects, against the backdrop of the risks revealed in the Great Depression and the promises made during war.

The most radical innovation was the idea that a minimum income was a right, alongside guaranteed health care and education. This idea had most traction in contexts where the poor were citizens, and not subjects. Even before the First World War, Britain had begun to build a welfare state on the foundations of the poor laws, providing minimum income to the elderly and—after the First World War—most unemployed also (Thane 1996; Gilbert 1970). In the face of the Great Depression, the small British colony of Barbados introduced means-tested, noncontributory old-age pensions, for its nonvoting poor. The neighboring colonies of Trinidad and Tobago and British Guiana followed suit soon after. The British colony of Mauritius also considered seriously similar pensions, but such pensions were only actually introduced after a long delay more than a decade later.

Reforms in the global North fueled debate in the South. A universal old-age pension was introduced in New Zealand in 1938, but it was the 1942 Beveridge Report in Britain that caught the imagination of peoples and elites across much of the world. At much the same time the International Labour Organisation (ILO) began to promote more vigorously the public provision of welfare through social insurance. The context of the Second World War was crucial in driving forward the welfarist agenda. Article 5 of the 1941 Atlantic Charter committed Allied governments to the objective of "securing for all, improved labour standards, economic advancement, and social security." Other "allied" governments of the world promised a future free of insecurity and poverty through postwar "reconstruction." Even in racially segregated South Africa, the wartime government declared that "there will be no forgotten men": the specters of "want, poverty and unemployment" would be "combated to the best of our ability"; "the restoration after the war of the *status quo ante* is neither possible nor desirable. . . . everything practicable must be done to ensure a better life for all sections of the population"; "the native population also, both rural and urban, [would] participate in the enhanced well-being which it is desired to secure for the community as a whole" (see Seekings 2005).

In the less industrialized parts of the British Empire (and the Colonial Office in London), the process of policy change accelerated rapidly. The "welfare" of colonial subjects began to be taken seriously, in light of evidence on malnutrition and poverty, unrest (as in the Caribbean and Mauritius in 1937–38), and the value of good wartime propaganda. The 1940 Colonial Development and Welfare Act made more funding available, as well as marking an important discursive shift in colonial policy (Lee and Petter 1982; Constantine 1984; J. Lewis 2000). In 1942, the influential Lord Hailey used his report *Native Administration and Political Development in British Tropical Africa* to endorse emphatically the colonial state's role as "an agency for the active promotion of social welfare," and the following year he wrote that "our modern appreciation of the need for supplementing private initiative by state action has been reinforced by the fuller recognition of the function of the state as an organisation for promoting the economic welfare or safeguarding the standards of living of the population. That is a doctrine which has now been projected from domestic into colonial policy."

This concern for "welfare" could be realized in very different ways, however. One way was the replication in the South of the British kind of social-assistance program. South Africa followed the lead of Barbados in extending old-age pensions to its poor, African or black majority, in 1944. As in Barbados, this was a reform from above, driven by progressive officials rather than through struggles from below (although the threat of "unrest" was one factor motivating reforms). The British Colonial Office was, however, hostile to such reforms, for a mixture of financial concerns (the cost was recurrent) and ideological ones (for example, such reforms would encourage laziness among uneducated people). Partly in response to rising interest in old-age pensions and similar programs, especially after the publication of the Beveridge Report, the Colonial Office developed a new doctrine of "development" which emphasized raising the productivity of colonial populations through targeted investments in agricultural production. From this doctrine was born the agrarian approach, and the agrarian welfare regime.

The agrarian approach was compelling only if officials believed that an agrarian society and economy could be revived (or established anew). In some cases it was clear that such a revival was not realistic. In the sugar economies of Barbados and Mauritius, most obviously, the poor could only be settled on adequate land and given the opportunity to become a self-supporting peasantry if estates were expropriated from the landowners. This was not a political option. In South Africa, also, state officials in African-settled rural areas (the "reserves") and the employers of migrant workers from those areas agreed that agricultural production was well below subsistence levels, even in good years. Kinship-based protection against poverty was seen as breaking down. Any attempts to "develop" the reserves would reduce the supply of migrant labor to industry. Under these conditions, mitigating poverty through modest and tax-financed social assistance was an attractive option to employers as well as the state.

In Kenya, in contrast, colonial officials embraced the agrarian approach. Welfare officers would rebuild family life among "detribalized," urban African people and promote "community development." These welfare officers later became "development" officers. Initially, colonial officials saw themselves as the defenders of the egalitarian values of a (mythical) precolonial "Merrie Africa"; later, they embraced economic change, encouraging African peasant production of cash crops and especially export crops (J. Lewis 2000). In contrast to their counterparts in South Africa and Barbados, officials in Kenya believed that an agrarian economy and society could be revived without major costs to powerful local elites.

South Africa, Barbados, and Mauritius might have gone down the third route, of the workerist approach. The poor in each of these three cases were temporarily unemployed or retired workers and their dependents. Compulsory, contributory social-insurance schemes might have provided against such poverty. Indeed, in many colonies, the state began to develop contributory schemes at this time, as part of its efforts to "stabilize" wage workers (Cooper 1996). South Africa and Mauritius investigated such schemes carefully and repeatedly. But such schemes had one huge disadvantage. Barbados and Mauritius were small, open economies, heavily dependent on the export of a commodity (sugar) whose price was set externally. South Africa's economy was based on the export of another commodity (gold), which had a fixed global price. Most wages were too low for workers to contribute to insurance or pension funds themselves, and employers were unwilling or unable to pay higher wages or contributions because doing so would squeeze profits. Where an economy could reasonably expect to grow behind tariff barriers, the costs of a contributory scheme could be passed on to domestic consumers. This was not the case in an open economy.

"Modernization" and the Broadening of Inegalitarian Corporatism

Postwar development strategies in many countries revolved around "modernizing" the economy through expanding the modern formal sector, especially through ISI. Contributory systems provided for formal-sector workers, so the growth of the formal sector meant that the coverage of social-insurance schemes expanded across a wider section of the population. At the same time, hitherto uncovered formal-sector workers sometimes exerted pressure on the state to include them, while politicians sought new groups of clients. By the mid-1960s, over 60 percent of the economically active population in Chile was covered by social security (Borzutzky 2002, 51), and the situation was similar in Argentina (Huber 1996, 143).

Broader coverage did not mean that systems became more pro-poor. Most poor people remained excluded. Moreover, changes in the contribution and benefit arrangements may have meant that the systems actually exacerbated inequality. Most of these social-insurance schemes were heavily subsidized by the state. In Chile, the state paid about one-third of all social-security receipts in the 1960s; the proportion was lower in Brazil and Argentina (although it rose rapidly in Argentina after 1980) (Huber 1996, 153). In addition, higher-paid occupations paid the lowest contributions, as a share of earnings, and secured the most special privileges in terms of benefits (Borzutzky 2002, 55–60). But all contributing workers benefited at the expense of the excluded or uninsured. A 1964 inquiry in Chile assessed that the uninsured paid 41 percent of the cost of social security through taxation and higher prices; a subsequent study in 1971 put the figure at 50 percent (ibid., 56–57).

During this time there were some attempts to extend coverage much more widely. The experience of Brazil is documented by Malloy (1979). Here, as elsewhere in Latin America, reformers sought to unify the disparate existing social-insurance schemes and also to extend coverage to unorganized and poorer sections of the population, either through social assistance or heavily state-subsidized social insurance. The difficulty was that a substantial number of working people were covered by a state-subsidized welfare system and had good reason to oppose the extension of the welfare system to other, poorer groups. Their patrons in the political system had special reason to oppose reforms that removed their discretionary sources of patronage. In Brazil, from the 1940s to the 1960s, reforms were repeatedly initiated by technocrats but thwarted by coalitions of politicians, union leaders, and privileged groups of workers. Only in the 1970s did the military government bring rural workers under a noncontributory scheme. Even then, formal-sector workers retained access to heavily subsidized and very generous welfare schemes, while low-paid rural workers were only eligible for the minimal flat-rate benefits.

This was the period also of emergence and growth of public welfare systems in East Asia. In contrast to Latin American systems, East (and Southeast) Asian systems generally have defined benefits (Ofstedal et al. 2002), making them less inegalitarian. But they shared with their Latin American counterparts the linkage of benefits to contributions while in formal employment, meaning that they did not reach the poor. Some of the Asian schemes were also state subsidized and hence doubly regressive.

Amid this flurry of construction of contributory systems, there were a few deviant cases where a pauperist approach was also adopted. In both Costa Rica and Hong Kong, limited social assistance was introduced in the 1970s. In Brazil, the military regime finally succeeded in extending noncontributory old-age pensions to rural workers. But, overall, this was not an encouraging period for pro-poor welfare reforms.

Demographics, Democracy, and Social Citizenship at the End of the Twentieth Century

Beginning in the 1980s, in countries across the South, pressures for reform of the welfare system came from a range of factors. Population growth and deagrarianization resulted in rapid increases in the number of poor people in towns or otherwise detached from the land. Globalization might have accentuated the vulnerability of many groups to poverty. Trade liberalization also eroded the ease with which employers could pass on the costs of their social-security contributions to the consumers. At the same time, fiscal pressures compelled states to reassess their subsidization of social-insurance schemes, especially in Latin America. Most important of all, democratization strengthened the nonunionized poor. Political parties began to use promises of pro-poor welfare reform as a platform to build electoral support. Elections politicized welfare provision. The collapse of ISI models of development and the shift to more open economies might, perversely, have made it easier to consider tax-funded welfare reforms rather than contribution-funded ones.

In Taiwan, only 40 percent of the population was covered by social-insurance schemes in 1993. Social assistance was a municipal responsibility and was therefore very limited. In 1993, when the opposition party promised a universal old-age pension, the ruling Kuomintang copied or matched the promise. In the face of electoral competition, means-tested old-age pensions were introduced in 1993. Universal health insurance was introduced in 1994; although contributory, the government pays the employer's contribution if there is no employer. In 1995, special pensions were introduced for small farmers. Many municipalities give additional grants to the elderly (see Ku 1997, 1998; Aspalter 2002; Ofstedal et al. 2002). In South Korea, also, electoral competition led to the introduction of universal welfare provision between the late 1980s and mid-1990s (Kwon 1998, 2002; Kim 2004). And in Hong Kong, partial democratization led to the extension of the existing, limited social assistance.

South Africa's transition to democracy occurred at a time when, as we have already seen, a major set of social-assistance programs was already in place. Democratization did lead, however, to further extensions in coverage and generosity. The first effect was on the level at which the old-age pension was paid once racial discrimination was eliminated. In 1993, the National Party government, on the eve of South Africa's first democratic elections, set parity at a generous level, apparently with electoral considerations in mind. Second, the post-1994 government presided over the extension of noncontributory pension payments in two areas: child-support grants, to children in low-income households, and disability grants, including to people living with AIDS. South Africa's neighbor, Botswana, also extended its noncontributory old-age pension system in the late 1990s.

In Brazil, as in South Africa, democratic competition and the increased currency of progressive social ideas following the transition to democracy in the 1980s resulted in major extensions in the coverage of the public welfare system. In the 1990s, a new noncontributory rural pension (the *Previdencia Rural*) was introduced and then extended, and new pro-poor schemes were introduced in urban areas (Barrientos 2003, 5–6). The

Cardoso governments (1994–2002) established or expanded several new federal welfare programs, including the *Bolsa Escola* program, which provided means-tested grants to poor families conditional on children attending school. By early 2002 the program reached nearly five million families, including over eight million children. In 2003, President Lula launched the *Bolsa Familia* program, to integrate several hitherto fragmented social-assistance programs, including *Bolsa Escola* (Lavinas 2004, 9).

The 1990s were an unprecedented period of expansion of welfare provision to the poor in many Southern settings. Some of the reasons why are becoming clear. First and foremost must be the new electoral power of the nonunionized poor. With democratization in Brazil, South Africa, Taiwan, Korea, Hong Kong, and elsewhere, political parties began to compete earnestly for the support of these poor voters. But the ballot box seems to work more effectively for the poor if there is a not well entrenched system of social insurance providing for workers in formal employment. Reform was easier in East Asia, where contributory schemes were very recent and the contributory pension scheme was still not paying pensions to elderly people, than in Latin America, where organized (and politically powerful) groups of workers had major vested interests in the status quo (which meant state subsidies of their welfare).

Prospects for Further Reform

There are grounds for optimism, even in surprising places. The World Bank "model" is notorious for replacing publicly managed social insurance with privately managed individual savings and co-insurance schemes. But the other public "pillar" in the World Bank model is publicly managed social assistance, albeit with means testing and minimum benefits. The implementation of this pillar would mark a major pro-poor reform in most Southern settings. In practice, recent Brazilian and South African reforms are not far from this model, with means-tested grants targeted on deserving categories of poor people (poor families with children, the disabled, the elderly).

Other grounds for optimism are clearer. In South Africa, the government-appointed Taylor Committee of Inquiry into a Comprehensive System of Social Security for South Africa recommended, in its 2002 report, the gradual introduction of a basic income grant, with benefits that are low but are paid to all South Africans regardless of means. In Brazil, in

January 2004, President Lula signed a law to introduce a basic income grant (renda basica), in stages. Although the South African government has opposed the introduction of a basic income grant, and in Brazil the passage of a law does not preclude a very drawn-out process of implementation, there appears to be some momentum behind radical reforms of public welfare.

But there are also grounds for pessimism. The factors that frustrated Brazilian reforms for so long are still present, and not only in Brazil. Writing about Costa Rica, Clark (2001, 9) contrasts the politics of "first-stage" reforms (such as trade liberalization and deregulation) with "second-stage" reforms (including reforms of social security). The winners from first-stage reforms often organize quickly and effectively, out-muscling the losers. But, with second-stage reforms, "the political fallout often outweighs potential gains. The losers are represented by large public sector unions and professional associations while the potential beneficiaries of state reform, that is taxpayers and clients dependent on public services, are typically poor, unorganised and dispersed. In this case, politicians and their reform teams might feel that there is little to gain by attempting second-stage reforms at all." In Costa Rica, teachers were a leading opponent of reform: their pensions were paid at 100 percent of their final salary, and they could retire at a low age if they so chose. Unfortunately for the poor, it seems to be difficult to create the fiscal space for pro-poor expenditure without reforming any existing contributory system.

Welfare reform is more likely in some settings than in others. Deagrarianization and democratization together result in powerful pressures for reform: competition for the votes of poor, landless citizens leads to promises of redistributive welfare. Employers are more likely to be sympathetic in an open economy. But reform is most likely in those settings where there are fewer obstacles, and that means settings where there is a weakly entrenched system of social insurance with all the vested interests that arise from it. Fundamental shifts in the welfare regime are difficult in contexts such as Brazil, where organized workers have vested interests in the status quo, leaving little fiscal space for more pro-poor reforms.

NOTES

1. In earlier versions of this chapter, I employed a different terminology, labeling the "workerist" approach/regime as "inegalitarian corporatist" and the "pauperist" approach/regime as "redistributive."

REFERENCES

Adelman, I., and C. Morris. 1973. *Economic Growth and Social Equity in Developing Countries*. Stanford, CA: Stanford University Press.

Aspalter, Anthony. 2002. *Democratisation and Welfare State Development in Taiwan*. Aldershot, UK: Ashgate.

Barrientos, Armando. 2003. What Is the Impact of Non-contributory Pensions on Poverty? Estimates from Brazil and South Africa. Unpublished paper.

Borzutzky, Silvia. 2002. *Vital Connections: Politics, Social Security and Inequality in Chile*. Notre Dame, IN: University of Notre Dame Press.

Bradley, D., E. Huber, S. Moller, F. Nielsen, and J. Stephens. 2003. Distribution and Redistribution in Post-Industrial Democracies. *World Politics* 55, no. 2: 193–228.

Castles, Francis. 1985. *The Working Class and Welfare: Reflections on the Political Development of the Welfare State in Australia and New Zealand, 1890–1980*. Sydney: Allen and Unwin.

———. 1996. Needs-Based Strategies of Social Protection in Australia and New Zealand. In G. Esping-Andersen (ed.), *Welfare States in Transition: National Adaptations in Global Economies*. London: Sage.

Castles, Francis, and Deborah Mitchell 1993. Worlds of Welfare and Families of Nations. In F. Castles (ed.), *Families of Nations*. Aldershot, UK: Dartmouth.

Chenery, H., M. Ahluwalia, C. Bell, J. Duloy, and R. Jolly. 1974. *Redistribution through Growth*. Oxford: Oxford University Press.

Clark, Mary. 2001. *Gradual Economic Reform in Latin America: The Costa Rican Experience*. Albany: State University of New York Press.

Constantine, Stephen. 1984. *The Making of British Colonial Development Policy, 1914–1940*. London: Frank Cass.

Cooper, Frederick. 1996. *Decolonisation and African Society*. Cambridge: Cambridge University Press.

Esping-Andersen, Gøsta. 1990. *The Three Worlds of Welfare Capitalism*. Princeton, NJ: Princeton University Press.

———. 1996. Positive-Sum Solutions in a World of Trade-Offs? In G. Esping-Andersen (ed.), *Welfare States in Transition: National Adaptations in Global Economies*. London: Sage.

———. 1999. *Social Foundations of Post-Industrial Economies*. Oxford: Oxford University Press.

———. 2002. *Why We Need a New Welfare State*. Oxford: Oxford University Press.

Gilbert, Bentley. 1970. *British Social Policy, 1914–1939*. London: B. T. Batsford.

Goodin, R., B. Headey, R. Muffels, and H. Dirven. 1999. *The Real Worlds of Welfare Capitalism*. Cambridge: Cambridge University Press.

Huber, Evelyne. 1996. Options for Social Policy in Latin America: Neoliberal versus Social Democratic Models. In G. Esping-Andersen (ed.), *Welfare States in Transition: National Adaptations in Global Economies*. London: Sage.

Huber, Evelyne, and John Stephens. 2001. *Development and Crisis of the Welfare State*. Chicago: University of Chicago Press.

Jones, Catherine. 1993. The Pacific Challenge: Confucian Welfare States. In Catherine Jones (ed.), *New Perspectives on the Welfare State in Europe*, 198–220. London: Routledge.

Kim, Jo-Seol. 2004. Formation and Development of the Welfare State in the Republic of Korea: Processes of Reform of the Public Assistance System. *Developing Economies* 42, no. 2 (June).

Korpi, W., and J. Palme. 1998. The Paradox of Redistribution and Strategies of Equality: Welfare State Institutions, Inequality and Poverty in the Western Countries. *American Sociological Review* 63, no. 5: 661–87.

Ku, Yeun-wen. 1997. *Welfare Capitalism in Taiwan: State, Economy and Social Policy*. London: Macmillan.

———. 1998. Can We Afford It? The Development of National Health Insurance in Taiwan. In Roger Goodman, Gordon White, and Huck-ju Kwon (eds.), *The East Asian Welfare Model: Welfare Orientalism and the State*, 119–38. London: Routledge.

Kwon, Huck-ju. 1998. The South Korean National Pension Programme: Fulfilling Its Promise? In Roger Goodman, Gordon White, and Huck-ju Kwon (eds.), *The East Asian Welfare Model: Welfare Orientalism and the State*, 106–18. London: Routledge.

———. 2002. The Korean Welfare State: Development and Reform Agenda. In Anthony Aspalter (ed.), *Discovering the Welfare State in East Asia*. New York: Praeger.

Lavinas, Lena. 2004. Exceptionality and Paradox in Brazil: From Minimum Income Programs to Basic Income. Paper presented at the BIEN conference, Barcelona, September.

Lee, J. M., and Martin Petter. 1982. *The Colonial Office, War and Development Policy*. London: Institute of Commonwealth Studies.

Lewis, Joanna. 2000. *Empire State-Building: War and Welfare in Kenya, 1925–52*. Oxford, UK: James Currey; Athens: Ohio University Press.

Lewis, W. A. 1976. Development and Distribution. In A. Cairncross and M. Puri (eds.), *Employment, Income Distribution and Development Strategy: Problems of the Developing Countries*. London: Macmillan.

Malloy, James. 1979. *The Politics of Social Security in Brazil*. Pittsburgh: University of Pittsburgh Press.

Milanovic, B. 1999. Do More Unequal Countries Redistribute More? Does the Median Voter Hypothesis Hold? Unpublished paper.

Ofstedal, Mary Beth, Angelique Chan, Napaporn Chayovan, et al. 2002. Policies and Programs in Place and Under Development. In Albert Hermalin (ed.), *The Well-Being of the Elderly in Asia*. Ann Arbor: University of Michigan Press.

Pierson, Paul. 1994. *Dismantling the Welfare State? Reagan, Thatcher, and the Politics of Retrenchment.* Cambridge: Cambridge University Press.

———, ed. 2001. *The New Politics of the Welfare State.* Oxford: Oxford University Press.

Przeworski, Adam, and J. Gandhi. 1999. Distribution and Redistribution of Income. Paper presented at the conference on Democracy and Redistribution, Yale University, November.

Seekings, Jeremy. 2005. "Visions and Hopes and Views about the Future": The Radical Moment of South African Welfare Reform. In Saul Dubow and Alan Jeeves (eds.), *Worlds of Possibility: South Africa in the 1940s.* Cape Town, South Africa: Double Storey.

Seekings, Jeremy, and Nicoli Nattrass. 2005. *Class, Race and Inequality in South Africa.* New Haven, CT: Yale University Press.

Thane, Pat. 1996. *Foundations of the Welfare State.* 2nd edition. Harlow, UK: Pearson Longman.

White, Gordon, and Roger Goodman. 1998. Welfare Orientalism and the Search for an East Asian Welfare Model. In Roger Goodman, Gordon White, and Huck-ju Kwon (eds.), *The East Asian Welfare Model: Welfare Orientalism and the State.* London: Routledge.

World Bank. 1994. *Averting the Old-Age Crisis: Policies to Protect the Old and Promote Growth.* Oxford: Oxford University Press.

Chapter 2

IIIIIIIIIIIIIIIIIIIIIIIIIIIIIIIIIIIIIIIIIIIIIIIIII

Distributional Conflicts in Mature Welfare States

Isabela Mares

The welfare state has a large, nearly ubiquitous presence in the economic activity of all advanced industrialized societies. The average level of government expenditures in OECD economies grew from 28 percent of GDP (in 1960) to 51 percent of GDP in 1997 (OECD 1999). This growth in the size of the public sector has been accompanied by a commensurate growth in the level of taxes necessary to finance existing social policy commitments. Using an average figure for OECD economies, the amount of taxes grew from 27.6 percent of GDP in 1960 to 39.4 percent of GDP in 1995 (OECD 1995). However, the consequences of this massive expansion of the size of the welfare state on the employment performance of most economies varied significantly over time. During the initial decades of the postwar period, the growth in the size of the welfare state came at relatively low costs in terms of employment. The high levels of employment achieved by many European economies during this period suggested to many observers that the goals of full employment and welfare state expansion could be compatible policy goals.

The trade-off between the redistributive intentions of the welfare state and the goal of full employment accentuated, however, during the most recent decades. Many governments have begun to share the policy diagnosis that the high levels of income and payroll taxes required to finance the welfare state are one of the general causes of the economic malaise experienced by European economies during recent decades. The diagnosis that high levels of nonwage labor costs are an obstacle to employment growth is now being accepted even by social democratic governments, traditional defenders of the welfare state. As Fritz Scharpf concludes in a recent study, "a considerable range of perfectly decent jobs, which in the absence of payroll taxes would be commercially viable are eliminated from the private labor market of continental welfare states" (Scharpf 1998: 142). A number of policy changes enacted during recent years respond to the concern that high nonwage labor costs are inimical to employment expansion and overall economic competitiveness. Consider the following examples. Both left- and right-wing governments in France have attempted to address the persistent levels of unemployment, by introducing more than forty policy measures that have lowered the social charges of employers and exempted a number of firms from social security contributions to various branches of the French welfare state (Conseil Supérieur de l'Emploi 1996; Bourguignon and Bureau 1999). During recent years, the Belgian and Dutch governments have enacted policies reducing payroll taxes of employers in both the manufacturing and service sectors. In Germany, the red-green coalition government has considered both a broad reform in the mode of financing of the social-insurance system (involving a partial shift to taxes that are not employment based, such as ecological taxes) as well as various *Kombilohn* proposals, that is, policy measures combining low earnings with fiscal transfers that compensate social-insurance contributions at low income levels (Wanger 1999).

What are the consequences of the growth in the size of social policy commitments on the employment performance of European political economies? Does it vary across countries—in other words, do salient cross-national differences, such as differences in labor market institutions—affect the sensitivity of employment to taxation? How does the growth of the tax burden affect the optimal wage choices made by unions? And what is the effect of unions' wage choices on the equilibrium level of employment, given that a high share of the total wage bill is now committed in the form of taxes?

To analyze these questions, this chapter explores the impact of the growth of the welfare state on the wage demands of trade unions and on the level of unemployment. In an effort to account for both cross-national and intertemporal variation in the employment performance of OECD economies, I integrate the literatures on wage determination and comparative systems of social protection. By explicitly modeling unions' concern for social policy, I show how the optimal strategy of trade unions is to deliver wage restraint in exchange for social policy expansion (given a particular mix of social policy transfers and services). This proposition echoes an insight of many corporatist studies that have invoked the importance of the social wage for unions' wage demands (Cameron 1984: 143–178; Esping-Andersen 1990: 105–143). Moreover, I show how the structure of labor market institutions—more specifically the level of centralization of the wage-bargaining authority—affects the magnitude of the employment effects resulting from the wage restraint of trade unions. Building on the theoretical propositions advanced by Calmfors and Driffill and further refined by other scholars of corporatism, I hypothesize that one should expect a parabolic relationship between the level of centralization of the wage-bargaining authority and the level of unemployment (Calmfors and Driffill 1988). Economies with institutions of wage bargaining centralized at the sectoral level are expected to exhibit the worst employment performance.

In contrast to existing explanations, the argument presented here can, simultaneously, account for the steady deterioration of the employment performance of European economies. I show how demographic and fiscal developments have strained this political exchange, contributing to the gradual rise in the level of unemployment. The chapter identifies two mechanisms by which the growth in the size of social policy commitments impinge on the wage strategies of trade unions and on the equilibrium level of employment. The first of these developments is the growth in the size of the tax burden. A higher part of the wage bill is now committed in the form of income or payroll taxes. As a result, the effectiveness of the wage policies pursued by unions is severely curtailed. Since wages represent an ever smaller fraction of the total wage bill faced by firms, even sustained moderation of wage demands can have only a small impact on the level of employment. The second consequence of the growth of the welfare state on the wage choices made by unions is through a change in the composition of social policy transfers. A number of economies have experienced sharp increases in the number of "labor market outsiders"— in the form of early retirees, long-term unemployed, or persons unable to enter the labor market. If the increase in social policy expenditures committed to labor market outsiders has lowered the net transfers and benefits received by union members, unions' willingness to pursue a policy of wage moderation is expected to decline. Thus, while welfare states have become more overburdened, both the *willingness* of unions to sustain high levels of wage moderation and the *effectiveness* of income policies in reducing the level of unemployment have declined. In other words, the maturation of the welfare state has undermined the political exchange between unions and governments premised on wage moderation in exchange for social policy expansion. Whereas welfare state expansion and the pursuit of full employment were compatible policy goals during the first decades of the postwar period, the presence of a high tax burden has increased the trade-off between these policy objectives.

The remaining part of this chapter is organized as follows. I begin by reviewing recent theoretical developments in the political economy of advanced industrialized economies. Existing studies have been relatively successful in accounting for the cross-national variation in the labor market performance of these economies. However, these studies have been unable to provide an explanation for the temporal deterioration of employment outcomes. I argue that this limitation of the literature can be attributed to the absence of a discussion of the institutional advantages *and* constraints imposed by the welfare state on wage-bargaining actors. In the following section, I propose a theoretical remedy to this problem. My analysis highlights the main consequences of the process of welfare state maturation on the strategies of unions and on the effectiveness of unions' wage policies in lowering unemployment. The remaining part of the chapter provides an empirical test of the main implications of the model, by using data from advanced industrialized democracies for the period 1960–1995.

The Existing Theory: Wage-Bargaining Actors and Central-Bank Independence

The study of the impact of institutions on economic outcomes—such as inflation, unemployment, or inequality—has been at the center of research in political economy. The critical variable identified by most studies to account for cross-national variation in employment outcomes has been the centralization of the wage-bargaining system. The insight developed by this literature has been that unions in economies with centralized institutions of wage bargaining are likely to exhibit greater levels of wage moderation than unions in economies with fragmented labor market institutions. In economies with encompassing labor market institutions, wage setters are more likely to internalize the consequences of their actions on both prices and employment (Cameron 1984; Bruno and Sachs 1985). As a result of this Olsonian logic, the level of employment in economies with centralized labor market institutions is likely to be higher than the level of employment in economies with decentralized labor markets.

An important qualification to these earlier arguments is the proposition that the impact of labor market institutions on labor market outcomes exhibits important nonlinearities (Calmfors and Driffill 1988). As Lars Calmfors and John Driffill—the most important proponents of this explanation—argue, the relationship between the centralization of the wage-bargaining system and the level of unemployment exhibits a "hump-shaped" relationship, with economies with intermediately centralized wage-bargaining institutions exhibiting inferior higher level of unemployment than either economies with highly centralized or decentralized labor markets. The justification for this argument is as follows. When labor markets are decentralized, individual companies compete in product markets which are characterized by a high elasticity of substitution among goods. In these environments, the trade-off between unemployment and wage increases faced by trade unions is extremely steep, as a wage settlement that exceeds the wage rate paid by a competitor within the same industry contributes to a steep employment decline of a firm. As a consequence, firm-level bargaining results in high levels of wage restraint and low levels of unemployment. An increase in intrasectoral centralization of wage bargaining is associated with a decline in the elasticity of substitution among the goods produced by the firms that are subject to unified wage demands of trade unions. This economic and institutional environment increases the incentives of trade unions for wage militancy, thus leading to higher levels of unemployment. However, a further increase in the level of centralization of wage bargaining—from industry-level to economy-level centralization—creates incentives for trade unions to "internalize" some of the consequences of militancy. Thus, Calmfors and Driffill predict wage moderation and higher levels of employment in economies with highly centralized institutions of wage bargaining compared to intermediately centralized wage-bargaining systems. Figure 2.1 presents the relationship between centralization of wage bargaining and unemployment that is hypothesized by the Calmfors and Driffill analysis.

The analysis of Calmfors and Driffill and earlier studies by Bruno and Sachs and by Cameron attempted to explain variation in employment outcomes across advanced industrialized economies by using one single, yet powerful, variable, the level of centralization of the wage-bargaining system. In retrospect, however, these explanations appear excessively parsimonious. Labor market institutions are embedded in and interact with a variety of other institutions. As a result, in choosing their optimal wage demands, wage-bargaining agents respond to a number of additional

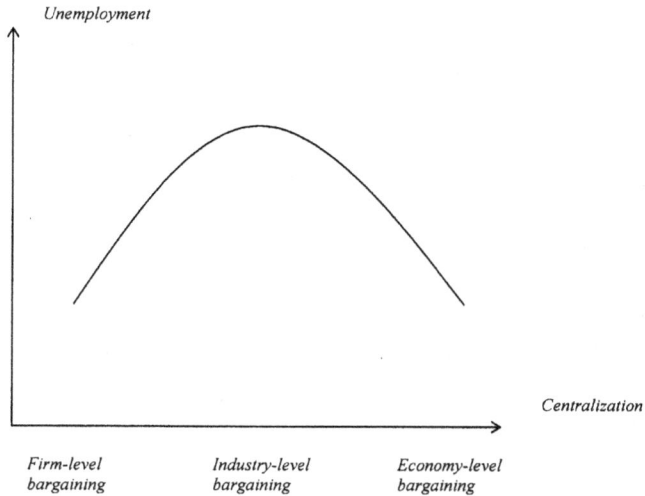

Fig. 2.1. Predictions of Calmfors and Driffill model about the relationship between centralization of wage bargaining and unemployment.

institutional constraints, in addition to those posed by labor market institutions. The policies pursued by actors such as governments or independent central banks also affect the mix of moderation and militancy pursued by trade unions. Thus, additional institutional and political variables can affect the functional form of the relationship between the centralization of the wage-bargaining system and the level of unemployment. As a result of these omissions, the predictions of this early literature can be highly inaccurate. Moreover, empirical results of regressions of measures of the centralization of the wage-bargaining system on the level of unemployment are likely to be severely biased.

During the past decade, a number of studies have taken up the theoretical challenge of understanding the interaction between wage-bargaining actors and other actors in the political economy (Hall and Franzese 1998; Iversen 1999; Soskice and Iversen 2000). Almost all of these studies have focused on monetary authorities as the key actor that is likely to influence the wage policies pursued by trade unions and, consequently, the equilibrium level of employment. David Soskice and Torben Iversen have provided one of the most influential analyses of the interaction between wage-bargaining agents and monetary authorities (Soskice and Iversen

2000). Soskice and Iversen build on the initial work examining the consequences of wage-bargaining systems but introduce an additional parameter modeling the degree of "accommodation" of a monetary policy. Monetary accommodation is defined as the overall responsiveness of the government to the increases in the aggregate price level. In the Soskice and Iversen framework, a central bank that is completely accommodating sets the real money supply equal to the price level, whereas in the case of a totally "nonaccommodating" monetary policy—the equivalent of independent central banks—the money supply is entirely independent of changes in the price level.

Using this set-up, Iversen and Soskice show that the impact of monetary policy on unemployment is conditional on the centralization of the wage-bargaining system. If the monetary policy regime is accommodating, their predictions for cross-national differences in the level of unemployment are in agreement with the analysis of Calmfors and Driffill. In this case, both models predict that the employment performance of economies characterized by intermediately centralized wage-bargaining systems is inferior to the performance of economies in which wage bargaining is either extremely centralized or extremely decentralized. The predictions differ, however, in the case of a nonaccommodating macroeconomic policy. Soskice and Iversen argue that a nonaccommodating monetary policy can in part deter some of the wage militancy of trade unions. As Iversen argues,

> if the monetary authority is non-accommodating, higher wages can no longer be externalized to the same extent and this will deter militant union behavior. The collective action problem facing unions in intermediately centralized systems—which can lead to excessive wage demands and unemployment—is thus "solved" (or at least dissipated) by an agent that is deliberately non-accommodating to union objectives. This crucial (and perhaps surprising) result is overlooked in all existing models of union behavior (such as Calmfors and Driffill's application of Olson's theory) because they fail to consider the conditioning effects of monetary policies on inter-union interactions. (Iversen 1998: 48–49)

Figure 2.2 summarizes the empirical predictions of this analysis.

The Soskice and Iversen model is extremely elegant and logically compelling. However, its main empirical implications are at odds with labor market developments in European economies. The central prediction

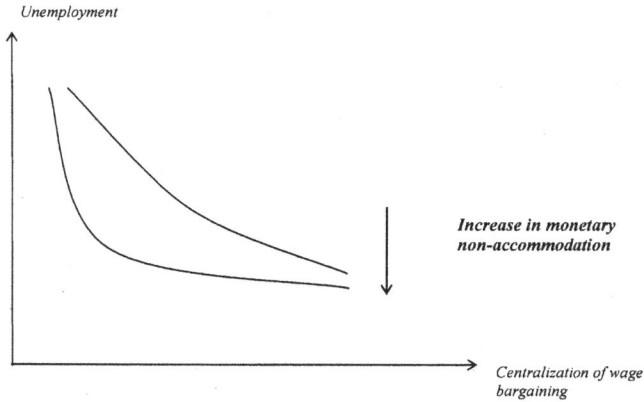

Fig. 2.2. Predictions of the Soskice and Iversen model.

of the model is that "an increase in monetary non-accommodation will have substantial benefits for long-term employment" (Soskice and Iversen 2000: 280). Given that most European economies have *de facto* shifted from an accommodating to a nonaccommodating monetary policy—either by increasing the independence of their central banks or by explicitly following the strict macroeconomic policies of the *Bundesbank*—the level of unemployment experienced by these economies should have declined between the 1970s and recent decades.

This divergence between the theoretical predictions of the Soskice and Iversen model and empirical outcomes can have several distinct causes. On the one hand, the theoretical mechanism postulated by this literature might be incorrect. In other words, an increase in the level of monetary nonaccommodation might not have the predicted "disciplining" effect on union behavior but instead might lead to greater union militancy. If, however, monetary policy has the effect on union behavior that is predicted by the Soskice and Iversen model, the rise in unemployment can be attributed to other variables that are missing from their analysis but that counteracted the effect of monetary nonaccommodation on union behavior. In other words, the excessive parsimony—shared by this "second-generation" corporatist literature with the earlier literature—is, again, a factor that prevents these studies from explaining both cross-national and temporal variation in employment outcomes.

In this chapter, I approach this problem by attempting to identify variables that are missing from the Soskice and Iversen framework but that counteract the effect of monetary policy on the strategies of unions. I argue that institutions and policies of the welfare state have effects on the wage strategies of trade unions that have not been studied systematically in previous studies. Under certain conditions—characterized by high transfers and services targeted to union members and a low level of taxes—social policies can act as a significant source of wage moderation. Under these conditions, the commitment to full employment and a large welfare state can be compatible policy goals. By contrast, a social policy regime characterized by high taxes and high levels of transfers going to labor market outsiders has different labor market implications. On the one hand, the high tax burden raises the labor costs faced by firms and lowers employment. On the other hand, both an increase in the level of transfers to labor market outsiders and an increase in the level of taxes lower unions' ability to deliver wage moderation. The net effect of these developments is a rise in the level of unemployment. The inability of previous studies to provide an explanation that accounts for cross-national and temporal differences in employment outcomes can be attributed to the absence of a discussion of social policy from existing models of wage bargaining.

A Theoretical Synthesis: Labor Market Institutions, Macroeconomic Policy, and the Welfare State

In related research, I have developed a formal model that extends the studies of Calmfors and Driffill and Iversen and Soskice (Mares 2005, 2006). The main goal of the analysis is to explore how differences in the level of social policy expenditures and in the composition of welfare state commitments affect the strategy of wage-bargaining agents and the equilibrium level of unemployment. I examine the consequences of social policies for unions' policies in a set-up that simultaneously pays attention to other institutional factors that affect the wage demands of the labor movement, namely the centralization of the wage-bargaining system and the level of central-bank independence.

Most wage-bargaining models assume a utilitarian objective function of the union (Farber 1986). Thus, for instance, Soskice and Iversen assume that unions maximize both employment and wages of their members (Soskice and Iversen 2000: 7). In the Calmfors and Driffill framework, unions seek to maximize wages and employment for their members as well as benefits for union members that are out of work (Calmfors and Driffill 1988). Iversen (1999) represents an interesting exception to these studies. In his framework, unions are concerned not only with the level of wages and employment of their members but also with the level of wage equality. In this framework, each union has an ideally sought relationship between the wage increases of high-earning and low-earning workers, and any discrepancy between the desired and realized wage equality enters unions' utility with a negative sign (Iversen 1999).

These analyses omit, however, considerations about social policy brought by unions to the wage-bargaining process. A vast qualitative and historical literature has emphasized unions' concern for the "social wage" (Katzenstein 1985; Cameron 1984; Esping-Andersen 1990), which includes concern for both benefits that are closely related to the employment relationship—such as paid vacations and maternity benefits—and also broader programs and policies of the welfare state, such as health benefits or old-age insurance. As publications of trade unions have repeatedly pointed out, the negotiation of these benefits should be, from the perspective of unions, of equal importance as the negotiation of salaries and wages (see for, example, Trades Union Congress 1958). Since wage negotiations unfold simultaneously with budget negotiations or other political deliberations surrounding the adoption of new programs, changes in the design of these policies or in their mode of financing can influence the demands formulated by labor unions during the wage-bargaining process.

To incorporate these considerations, one can assume that, in addition to wages and employment, unions' utility function incorporates an additional term which captures the gains from social policy received by union members. In order to make this different assumption about the behavior of wage-bargaining actors, we need to specify more carefully the nature of social policy benefits that are received by union members and contrast them to transfers and services going to other groups. Let us assume, for the sake of simplicity, that the total population can be divided into two broad groups, labor market insiders and outsiders. The former are union members that are currently working or are out of work. By contrast, labor market outsiders are a heterogeneous category that includes persons that enter the labor market only intermittently, the long-term unemployed, persons drawing on long-term disability benefits, and so on. The overall deterioration of the labor market has increased the size of these groups in many European economies.

Social policy expenditures are financed by a combination of taxes paid by unions and employers. The expenditures can be divided into three broad categories. First, we have social services—such as education and publicly provided child-care services—which are received by the entire population. A second category is social policy transfers that are received by working union members or by union members that are temporarily out of work, such as, for instance, unemployment or health-care benefits. A third category is the transfers going to labor market outsiders.

What are the implications of this assumption about the utility of unions for the equilibrium of wages and employment? This question can be studied by deriving the equilibrium wage demands in a model that assumes unions maximize the level of wages and employment of their members and comparing them to the equilibrium wage demands in a model which assumes that unions "care" about social policies in addition to wages. This analysis (presented elsewhere) yields the proposition that unions' concern for social policy acts as a source of moderation (Mares 2005). The equilibrium wage demands of unions that "care" about social policies are lower than the demands of unions that seek to maximize wages and employment only. An additional result is that this "wage-moderation" effect increases monotonically with the increase in the centralization of the wage-bargaining system, thus flattening the curve relating the centralization of the wage-bargaining system and unemployment (Mares 2005).

This model allows us to study systematically the impact of cross-national differences in the level and composition of social policies on the wage demands of unions and, thus, on the equilibrium level of unemployment. First, the aggregate size of the welfare state—more specifically the total level of taxation—affects the outcomes of the wage-bargaining process and, hence, the resulting level of employment. At the same time, the mix of social policy expenditures—among social services, programs benefiting labor insiders, and programs benefiting outsiders—also affects the equilibrium wage demands of unions. Welfare states with the *same* level of expenditures but with a different mix of transfers to insiders and outsiders affect the wage strategies of unions in different ways and thus lead to different levels of unemployment.

For the simplicity of presentation, let us examine the consequences of social policy for the wage strategies of unions in two distinct scenarios. The first case characterizes the early postwar period, in which the number of preexisting policies and, hence, the overall tax burden was small. By contrast, the second case is one of mature welfare states, characterized by a high density of policies and programs and by a high tax burden. Consider the nexus of wage and social policy during the early period of social policy development. In this case, the wage strategies of unions are influenced by the overall mix of services and transfers to labor market insiders and outsiders. If the share of social policy transfers received by labor market insiders is high, unions are more likely to forgo increases in wages and accept moderate wage settlements. This moderation on the wage front is the crucial variable that explains why, during the first decades of the postwar period, the expansion of the welfare state came at such low cost in terms of employment. However, the willingness of unions to accept low wage increases decreases as the share of transfers to labor market outsiders increases. Finally, the low level of taxes affects the resulting wage and employment outcomes in two ways. First, in this scenario, the overall labor costs of firms are low. This reinforces the effect of wage moderation, increasing the demand for labor. Secondly, in a context of low payroll and income taxes, unions and employers bargain over a large share of the total wage bill. As a result, the sensitivity of employment to changes in wages is high (Mares 2005). Wage settlements are likely to have a high impact on employment outcomes.

In agreement with the predictions of earlier studies, the resulting employment outcomes depend also on the level of centralization of the wage-bargaining system and on the macroeconomic policy orientation of the government. First, wage moderation is likely to be strongest in economies with the most centralized labor market institutions. Second, a more accommodating monetary policy increases unions' incentives for wage militancy, whereas monetary policies that are nonaccommodating are likely to lead to more moderate wage settlements. With few exceptions, most countries pursued accommodating monetary policies during the first decades of the postwar period. Thus, the social wage and monetary policy influence unions' wage behavior in opposite directions. The low level of unemployment achieved by most economies during the period until the first oil shock suggests that the dampening effect of social policy trumped the effect of an accommodating monetary policy.

Consider, by contrast, the case of a "mature" welfare state, characterized by a high tax burden. In economies in which the number of labor market outsiders is low, both services and transfers continue to be channeled towards union members, contributing to moderate wage settlements. An increase in the number of labor market outsiders will lower the share of social policy benefits received by union members and will erode some of

Equilibrium employment

Equil. level of unemployment as a function of centralization of wage bargaining system if (a) number of labor market outsiders is small, (b) monetary non-accommodation is low, (c) level of taxes is low

Equil. level of unemployment as a function of centralization of wage bargaining system if (a) number of labor market outsiders is large, (b) monetary non-accommodation is high, (c) level of taxes is high

Centralization of the wage bargaining system
Decentralized   Intermediately centralized   Highly centralized

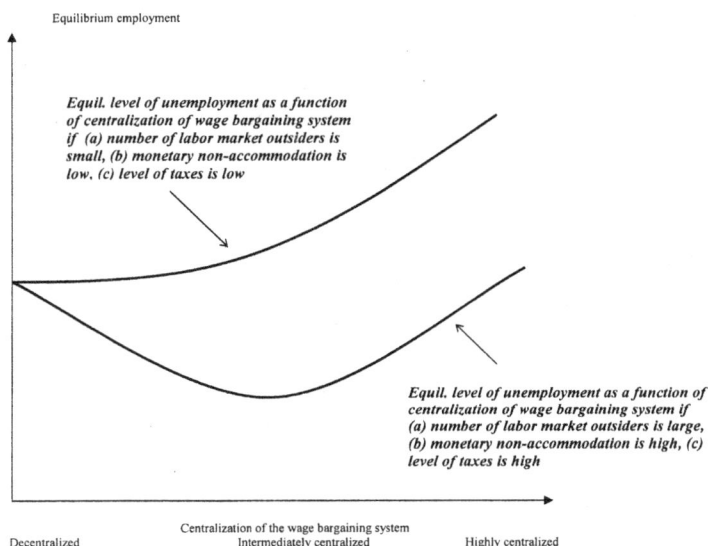

Fig. 2.3. Predicted level of employment as a function of (a) centralization of the wage-bargaining system, (b) degree of accommodation of monetary regime, and (c) number of labor-market outsiders.

the incentives toward wage moderation. In mature welfare states, the high tax burden also affects the outcome of the bargaining process. Given that a high share of the total wage bill is already committed in the form of taxes, unions' wage policy—either moderate (if the number of outsiders is small) or militant (if the number of outsiders is large)—has a much smaller impact on the level of employment. The sensitivity of employment to changes in wages is much lower in mature welfare states. An additional consequence of the rise in the tax burden is the reduction in firms' demand for labor, which results in lower levels of employment.

As in the earlier case, the net effect for unemployment depends on the centralization of the wage-bargaining system and monetary policy. As discussed earlier, the effect of the social wage on the level of unemployment increases monotonically with the degree of centralization of the wage-bargaining system, flattening the "hump" of the function linking labor market centralization and unemployment. In the case of a high number of labor market outsiders, we expect to see the opposite effect and a more pronounced hump-shaped relationship. An accommodating monetary policy further increases unions' incentives for militancy, whereas a nonaccommodating monetary policy leads to a higher moderation of unions.

I started this section by noting that the theoretical model of Soskice and Iversen is unable to account for the temporal variation in employment outcomes in advanced industrialized economies. Two questions remain unanswered. Why was the level of unemployment low during the first decades of the postwar period, given that monetary policies were generally accommodating? Why did the transition to monetary nonaccommodation not result in superior employment outcomes? The suggestion advanced in this chapter is that this empirical conundrum can be resolved if we add a series of parameters modeling cross-national differences across welfare states to existing wage-bargaining models. In the early postwar period, the effects of the social wage contributed to higher levels of wage moderation which counteracted the incentives toward greater militancy of an accommodating monetary policy. The effects of monetary policy and social policy on the optimal wage choices of unions worked in opposite directions. The overall deterioration of the employment performance of most economies suggests, again, that the effect of social policy was stronger than the effect of monetary policy.

A Cross-National Analysis

The preceding analysis yields both macro-level implications about the equilibrium level of unemployment as well as micro-level implications about the behavior of unions, given changes in the character of social policy. A test of the micro-level implications is presented elsewhere (Mares 2006). In the remaining part of the chapter, I will briefly test the macro-level hypotheses, using time-series data for fourteen OECD economies, covering the period between 1960 and 1995. The number of cases in my analysis has been limited by data availability on the incidence of tax rates. For the list of countries used in the cross-sectional analysis and the values on their explanatory variables, see the appendix.

The goal of this section is to examine three empirical implications of the analysis presented in the preceding sections. First, I test the prediction of a "hump-shaped" relationship between labor market institutions and the level of unemployment. As hypothesized, economies with intermediately centralized wage-bargaining systems will have an employment performance that is inferior to the performance of economies with highly centralized or highly decentralized labor market institutions. Second, an increase in the level of monetary nonaccommodation is expected to lower the level of unemployment. Finally, I test the implications concerning the impact of the growth and maturation of the welfare state on the level of unemployment. An increase in the level of expenditures devoted to labor market outsiders and an increase in the level of taxes is expected to shift the Calmfors-Driffill curve upward and to contribute to an increase in the level of unemployment.

To test the first proposition we can, fortunately, rely on an extensive empirical literature measuring cross-national differences in the structure of labor market institutions. Recent research has generated increasingly sophisticated measures that capture cross-national differences in the level of centralization of wage-bargaining authority, the concentration of union membership, and the level of union density. Although the available indices show a relatively high level of correlation, they still reflect differences in expert judgment among the various individuals or teams responsible for the coding effort (Golden 1993: 444). Rather than developing a new measure for the centralization of the wage-bargaining system, I have opted for a strategy that averages eight of the most widely used measures that are available. These are the measures developed by Schmitter (1981), Cameron (1984), Calmfors and Driffill (1988), Iversen (1999), Hall and Franzese (1998), Traxler and Kittel (2000), Golden, Lange, and Wallerstein (1998), and the OECD (1997: 71). This strategy has a number of advantages. First, it incorporates the expertise that has been accumulated in the literature during the past twenty years. The index used here combines some of the earliest measures of labor market institutions (developed by Schmitter and Cameron over two decades ago) with measures developed during recent years. Second, as Miriam Golden has pointed out, existing differences in measurement reflect differences in expert judgment among the various individuals or teams responsible for the coding effort (Golden 1993: 444). By averaging these measures, one can remove some of the measurement bias of individual scores. The centralization of the wage-bargaining index has been constructed as follows. First, I average the time-varying indices, such as Iversen and Golden-Lange-Wallerstein. For each of the individual indices, I order economies from economies with the most centralized labor market institutions (which take low values on the centralization score) to economies with the most centralized labor market institutions (which take high values on the centralization score). Then, I average these indices. Table 2.1 presents a rank-ordering of individual countries according to their degree of centralization of labor market institutions and the average of the eight different indices that are used in the analysis.

I begin by displaying some simple cross-tabulations, which describe some of the patterns in the data. Table 2.2 presents data on the employment performance of economies featuring different levels of coordination of the wage-bargaining system. The countries with decentralized labor markets have an average centralization score higher than 10 and include Canada, the United Kingdom, the United States, France, and Switzerland. Countries with a centralization score lower than 2.5 (Austria, Sweden, and Norway) are ranked as highly centralized. The remaining six cases (Belgium, Denmark, Finland, Germany, Italy, and the Netherlands) are classified as intermediately centralized. The figures in table 2.2 provide initial support for one of the hypotheses of the model. The employment performance of economies with intermediately centralized institutions of wage bargaining is inferior to the performance of economies with either extremely centralized or extremely decentralized labor market institutions. Although the level of unemployment has risen in all economies, economies with intermediately centralized institutions of wage bargaining have

TABLE 2.1
Centralization of Wage Bargaining

	Schmitter (1981)	Cameron (1984)	Calmfors-Driffill (1988)	Iversen (1999)	Hall and Franzese (1998)	OECD (1994, 1997)	Taxler and Kittel (2000)	Golen, Lange, Wallerstein (1998)	Average
Austria	1	3	1	5	1	1	6	8	3.25
Belgium	7	4	8	8	8	7	11	7	7.5
Canada	11	12	13	13	12	14	14	13	12.75
Denmark	4	6	4	3	4	5	5	2	4.125
Finland	4	5	5	4	4	6	2	6	4.5
France	12	14	9	12	10	10	10	9	10.75
Germany	8	8	6	7	4	3	8	10	6.75
Italy	15	11	11	10	10	9	4	5	9.25
Norway	2	2	2	1	1	2	1	1	1.5
Netherlands	6	7	7	6	8	10	8	4	7.00
Sweden	4	1	3	2	1	4	3	3	2.625
Switzerland	9	10	12	10	4	10	6	10	8.75
UK	13	9	10	11	12	8	12	12	10.875
USA	11	13	14	14	12	14	14	14	13.25

Sources: Schmitter 1981: 284; Cameron 1984: 165; Calmfors and Driffill 1988: 52–53; Iversen 1999: 56; Hall and Franzese 1998: 530; Traxler and Kittel 2000; 1164–1167; OECD 1997: 71; Golden, Lange, and Wallerstein 1998.

TABLE 2.2
Average Levels of Unemployment in OECD Economies under Different
Wage-Bargaining Arrangements and Social-Policy Arrangements

| | LEVEL OF UNEMPLOYMENT | | |
| | *Centralization of wage-bargaining system* | | |
Period	Decentralized	Intermediately centralized	Highly centralized
1960–1975	3.04	3.135	1.49
1976–1995	6.986	8.4616	3.166

Highly centralized countries: Austria, Norway, Sweden (centralization score < 4.0); intermediately centralized countries: Belgium, Denmark, Finland, Germany, Italy, Netherlands; decentralized countries: United Kingdom, United States, France, and Switzerland (centralization
score > 10).

experienced the strongest deterioration of their economic performance. Average levels of unemployment rose by 1.67 percent in economies with highly centralized labor markets, by around 4 percent in economies with firm-level wage bargaining, and by 5.33 percent in economies with intermediately centralized institutions of wage bargaining.

Next, I test the implications of the model based on pooled cross-sectional time-series analysis. Following a recent approach to this type of analysis, I use ordinary least-squares (OLS) regression with a lagged dependent variable and panel-corrected standard errors to take account of potential problems of heteroskedasticity in the data (Beck and Katz 1995). Omitting all controls, the simplest regression model is

$$U_{i,t} = a_i + b_1 U_{i,t-1} + b_2 CWB_i + b_3 CWB_i^2 + b_4 TRANSFERS.TO.OUTSIDERS_{i,t-1}$$
$$+ b_5 MONETNONACC_i + TIMETREND + b_5 \varepsilon_{i,t}$$

where $U_{i,t}$ is the unemployment rate for country i at period t, CWB_i is the index measuring the level of centralization of the wage-bargaining system, $TRANSFERS.TO.OUTSIDERS_{i,t-1}$ is a measure of social policy transfers to outsiders (lagged by one period), $MONETNONACC_i$ is a measure of the monetary nonaccommodation, and $\varepsilon_{i,t}$ is an error term. The predictions about the impact of the structure of wage-bargaining systems on the level of unemployment imply that the signs of the coefficients b_2 and b_3 should be + and –, respectively. All specifications also include a time trend (*TIME-TREND*) that attempts to capture the effect of variables that are not directly observable but that are correlated with time and might affect the dependent variable. In a second set of models, I estimate both the impact of the growth in the level of taxes and of the growth in the level of expenditures devoted to labor market outsiders on the level of unemployment.

The variable *MONETNONACC* operationalizes the degree of monetary nonaccommodation of the government (parameter β of the model). I have relied on Iversen's measure of the degree of conservatism of a monetary-policy regime (Iversen 1999: 57–60). The appendix presents the values of Iversen's hard-currency index for the countries in the sample. The empirical results are virtually unchanged if one uses the measure of central-bank independence developed by Robert Franzese, which is an average of frequently used indices (Franzese 2002).

The model developed in this chapter predicts that both the growth in the level of taxes and an increase in the social policy transfers going to labor market outsiders adversely affect the employment performance of OECD economies. A few considerations about the operationalization of the variable denoting social policy expenditures going to labor market outsiders are necessary at this point. To meet the definition of labor market outsiders proposed by this model, two separate criteria have to be met. First, these labor market groups have to receive some benefits, such as unemployment benefits, long-term disability benefits, and so on. The second criterion ascribing groups to the "outsider" category is intrinsic to unions' choices. If unions are unwilling to forgo wage increases in exchange for increases in the social policy transfers received by a group, then that group can be classified as labor market outsiders. By contrast, if unions respond to an increase in the social policy benefits received by a group by moderating their wage demands, that group cannot be classified as outsiders. In this case, an increase in expenditures devoted to the group is not expected to lead to an increase in unemployment.

To establish the "boundaries" of this group, I began by separating "demographic outsiders" and "labor market outsiders." Let "demographic outsiders" be defined as persons aged over sixty-five. By contrast, "labor market outsiders" are persons who fulfill the age requirement for participation in the labor market (i.e., persons who are aged between eighteen and sixty-five) but who are not in the labor force. I computed the ratio of demographic outsiders and labor market outsiders to the working-age population, based on data reported in OECD statistics (various years). To estimate the expenditures devoted to demographic and labor market outsiders, respectively, I multiplied the resulting number by the level of expenditures on pensions (for demographic outsiders) and unemployment benefits (for labor market outsiders). Next, I ran a number of preliminary statistical analyses to determine which variable has a significant effect on the level of unemployment. The results of these preliminary analyses

TABLE 2.3
Who Are Outsiders? Demographic versus Labor-Market Outsiders

Variables	Predicted sign	Regression Estimates and Standard Errors	
		Model 1	Model 2
CONSTANT		−3.13	−2.21
		2.13	2.77
$UNEM_{i,t-1}$		0.90***	0.75***
		0.12	0.15
CWB_i		0.41**	0.45**
	+	0.17	0.22
CWB_i^2		−0.02**	−0.02**
	−	0.11	0.01
$MONETNONACC_i$		−1.67**	−2.38**
	−	0.74	1.11
$TRANSFERS.TO.DEMOGRAPHIC.OUTSIDERS_{i,t-1}$		0.22	
	+	0.72	
$TRANSFERS.TO.LABOR.MARKET.OUTSIDERS_{i,t-1}$			0.86***
			0.27
TIMETREND		0.37	0.33
		0.28	0.34
N		73	73
$Adj.R^2$		0.89	0.83

Period dummies included but not reported.

(reported in table 2.3) suggest that only expenditures on labor market outsiders have a positive impact on the level of unemployment that is statistically significant. By contrast, transfers going to demographic outsiders do not have a statistically significant effect on unemployment. These findings suggest that unions approach labor market and demographic outsiders in different ways. Whereas unions are willing to respond to an increase in benefits to demographic outsiders by exercising a policy of wage moderation, they are unwilling to exercise the same restraint in the case of an increase in expenditures to labor market outsiders. Several qualitative studies—analyzing the linkages between pension reforms and unions' wage strategies—have reported results that are in agreement with this finding (Baccaro 1999; Lynch and Anderson 2004).

In the extended models (reported in tables 2.4 and 2.5), the variable *TRANSFERS.TO.OUTSIDERS* measures expenditures to labor market outsiders. To avoid potential endogeneity problems, I have lagged the variable by one period in all empirical estimations. Descriptive statistics (and country summaries) are presented in the appendix. As discussed earlier, one expects a positive relationship between this variable and the level of unemployment.

The second pathway by which the growth in the level of social policy commitments affects the level of unemployment is through a growth in the tax burden. As pointed out by a recent survey of empirical estimates of tax rates in OECD economies, the calculation of tax ratios poses immense methodological challenges, due to the complexity of tax codes (Volkerink and de Haan 2000; Volkerink, Sturm, and de Haan 2001; Eurostat 1997; European Commission 1997; OECD 2000a, 2000b). The most widely used measures for marginal effective tax rates have been developed by Mendoza, Razin, and Tesar (1994) and serve as the basis of tax measures used by the European Commission and the OECD. The tax measure used in this chapter is the effective average labor tax rate developed by Mendoza, Razin, and Tesar. The time series used in the empirical analysis updates Mendoza et al.'s measure and has been developed (and generously provided) by Tom Cusack. To avoid potential endogeneity problems, I have lagged the tax measures by one period ($TAXRATE_{i,t-1}$).

I have added a number of political and economic control variables to the analysis. The first variable, LEFTCAB, is a measure of the number of cabinet seats held by left-wing parties as a percentage of all cabinet portfolios. This variable has been developed by Huber, Ragin, and Stephens (1997) using data compiled in Browne and Dreijmanis (1982) and Keesings's World News Archive (www.keesings.com). A vast body of research has shown that left-wing parties demonstrate a higher level of concern for unemployment than conservative parties, and the theoretical and empirical results are robust even under assumptions of rational expectations (Hibbs 1977, 1992; Alesina 1989). Thus, I expect a negative relationship between this variable and the equilibrium level of unemployment. The second political control variable, COGRAVITY, is a measure of the "center of gravity of the government." This variable is computed by multiplying the share of seats of parties in government with an expert ranking of their ideological position. The ideological scale positioning various parties along a left-right dimension has been constructed by Francis Castles and Peter Mair based on "expert judgments" of these parties (Castles and Mair 1984: 83–88). The scale ranks from 5 (parties on the extreme right) to 1 (parties on the extreme left). As the summary presentation of the data reported in table 2.4 shows, this variable takes the lowest average value for Sweden (2.3) and Austria (2.4) and the highest values for the United States.

The additional economic variables examine the impact of various aspects of economic globalization on the aggregate level of unemployment.

First, I control for the impact of the trade exposure of an economy. The variable OPENNESS is computed as the sum of exports and imports as a percentage of GDP (using data reported in the IMF International Financial Statistics). The second variable—CAPFLOWS—measures the exposure of an economy to capital movements. It is calculated as the percentage of cross-border capital flows of GDP. One expects that both measures will be positively associated with unemployment.

In table 2.4, I present the results of a number of regressions that study the impact of the growth of expenditures devoted to labor market outsiders on the level of unemployment. Model 1 is a baseline model that includes the measure of the centralization of the wage-bargaining system and the stringency of the monetary regime, in addition to the variable measuring transfers to labor market outsiders. The results confirm the key hypotheses advanced in this chapter. First, in agreement with the

TABLE 2.4

OLS Estimates of Impact of Expenditures on Labor-Market Outsiders on the Level of Unemployment: Pooled Cross-Sectional Time Series 1960–1995 with Panel-Corrected Standard Errors

Variables	Predicted sign	Regression Estimates and Standard Errors				
		Model 1	Model 2	Model 3	Model 4	Model 5
CONSTANT		−2.21	−1.95	−2.73	−2.72	−2.11
		2.77	2.93	2.56	2.72	2.85
$UNEM_{i,t-1}$		0.75***	0.74***	0.73***	0.79***	0.74***
		0.15	0.16	0.15	0.15	0.15
CWB_i	+	0.45**	0.45**	0.45**	0.44*	0.47**
		0.22	0.22	0.22	0.23	0.23
CWB_i^2	−	−0.02**	−0.02**	−0.02**	−0.02*	−0.02**
		0.01	0.01	0.01	0.01	0.01
$MONETNONACC_i$	−	−2.38**	−2.45**	−2.65**	−2.16*	−2.56*
		1.11	1.09	1.19	1.10	1.39
$TRANSFERS.TO.OUTSIDERS_{i,t-1}$	+	0.86***	0.86***	0.91***	0.52*	0.96**
		0.27	0.26	0.31	0.31	0.41
$LEFTCAB_{i,t}$			−0.00			
			0.00			
$COGRAVITY_{i,t}$				0.28		
				0.49		
$OPEN_{i,t}$	−				0.08*	
					0.00	
$CAPFLOWS_{i,t}$						−0.00
						0.00
TIMETREND		0.33	0.33	0.32	0.30	0.33
		0.34	0.34	0.34	0.33	0.35
N		73	73	73	73	73
$Adj.R^2$		0.83	0.83	0.83	0.83	0.83

Note: *** $p < 0.01$; ** $p < 0.05$; * $p < 0.1$ Period effects are included but not reported.

Calmfors and Driffill hypothesis, we find an inversely U-shaped relationship between the centralization of the wage-bargaining system and the level of unemployment. Second, an increase in the level of central-bank independence leads to a reduction in the level of unemployment. Finally, an increase in the level of expenditures to labor market outsiders contributes to a rise in unemployment. The results remain robust to the introduction of additional controls. In model 2, I examine the impact of left-wing participation in government on the level of employment. Although the sign of the coefficient is in the predicted direction, surprisingly the effect of left-wing partisanship is not statistically significant. The level of the ideological polarization of the government also has no effect on the level of unemployment. In models 4 and 5, I introduce successively two additional economic controls, measuring the exposure of the economy to trade and capital flows. An increase in the level of trade openness is associated with higher levels of unemployment, and the variable has a statistically significant impact. By contrast, the exposure of the economy to capital movements does not affect the overall employment level.

Table 2.5 displays the results of a number of models that examine the effect exerted by the growth of expenditures devoted to labor market outsiders and the impact of an increase in the level of taxes on the level of unemployment. The results of the baseline model reported in the first column of table 2.5 support the hypothesis suggesting that the deterioration of the employment performance of European economies in recent years can be attributed both to an increase in the tax burden and to a change in the composition of social policy expenditures and an increase in the transfers to labor market outsiders. In contrast, an increase in the level of central-bank independence has a positive impact on the equilibrium level of unemployment. As in the models reported in table 2.4, we also find evidence that the impact of wage-bargaining institutions on employment outcomes is U-shaped, whereby economies with intermediately centralized wage-bargaining systems have the worst employment performance. The results of the initial model are robust to the introduction of additional control variables. Surprisingly, none of the political control variables (the measure of left participation in the cabinet and of the ideological composition) has a significant impact. Models 4 and 5 control for the impact of changes in the level of capital and trade flows but find no statistical effect of these variables.

In tables 2.6 and 2.7, I report the estimated impact of increases in the level of social policy commitments to labor market outsiders and of in-

TABLE 2.5

OLS Estimates of Impact of Taxes and Expenditures on Labor-Market Outsiders on the Level of Unemployment: Pooled Cross-Sectional Time Series 1960–1995 with Panel-Corrected Standard Errors

Variables	Predicted sign	Regression Estimates and Standard Errors				
		Model 1	Model 2	Model 3	Model 4	Model 5
CONSTANT		−3.55	−3.38	−3.97	−3.67	−2.84
		2.68	2.73	2.72	2.92	2.92
$UNEM_{i,t-1}$		0.71***	0.70***	0.70***	0.72***	0.66***
		0.17	0.17	0.16	0.19	0.17
CWB_i		0.45**	0.44**	0.44**	0.44**	0.50**
	+	0.19	0.19	0.19	0.20	0.20
CWB_i^2		−0.02**	−0.02**	−0.02***	−0.02*	−0.02**
	−	0.00	0.00	0.00	0.01	0.01
$MONETNONACC_i$		−2.77**	−2.84**	−2.94**	−2.72*	−3.59**
	−	1.27	1.22	1.27	1.39	1.67
$TRANSFERS.TO.OUTSIDERS_{i,t-1}$		1.32**	1.30**	1.32**	1.24*	1.90***
	+	0.53	0.52	0.52	0.75	0.64
$TAXES_{i,t-1}$		0.03**	0.03**	0.03**	0.03*	0.02*
	+	0.01	0.01	0.01	0.01	0.01
$LEFTCAB_{i,t}$		−0.00				
		0.00				
$COGRAVITY_{i,t}$				0.20		
				0.46		
$OPEN_{i,t}$	−				0.00	
					0.00	
$CAPFLOWS_{i,t}$						−0.01
						0.00
TIMETREND		0.35	0.35	0.34	0.35	0.40
		0.30	0.30	0.31	0.30	0.31
N		71	71	71	71	71
Adj.R^2		0.85	0.85	0.85	0.85	0.85

Note: *** $p < 0.01$; ** $p < 0.05$; * $p < 0.1$ Period effects are included but not reported.

creases in the labor tax rate on the equilibrium level of unemployment, for economies with different levels of the centralization of the wage-bargaining system. Both variables measuring the level of transfers to labor market outsiders and the tax variable have a lognormal distribution. I report the results of the simulation for the mean value as well as the highest and lowest values in the sample, respectively. Holding all other variables at their mean level, an increase in the level of expenditures to labor market outsiders contributes to an increase in the equilibrium level of unemployment by about 3 percentage points. Simulations of model 1 from table 2.4 (reported in table 2.7) suggest that an increase in the average tax rate and the expenditures to labor market outsiders lead to an increase in the equilibrium level of unemployment by 3.5 percentage points.

TABLE 2.6
Simulation Results of Model 1, Table 2.4

Labor-Market Outsiders	Centralization of Wage Bargaining		
Expenditures on Unemployment-Insurance Benefits	1.5 (Norway)	7.34 (~Netherl)	13.25 (USA)
Low (0.10)	4.10	5.16	5.26
Mean (0.47)	4.50	5.57	5.66
High (2.77)	6.49	7.56	7.65

TABLE 2.7
Simulation Results of Model 1, Table 2.5

	Centralization of Wage Bargaining		
Welfare Effort and Tax Rate	1.5 (Norway)	7.34 (~Netherl)	13.25 (USA)
Low transfers to outsiders Low taxes	3.22	4.46	4.89
Mean transfers to outsiders Mean taxes	4.30	5.54	5.90
High transfers to outsiders High taxes	7.80	9.04	9.47

These empirical results support the propositions advanced in this chapter. Consistent with the findings of earlier approaches, labor market institutions explain cross-national differences in the employment performance of OECD economies. The new variables added to existing models—measuring the growth in the level of social policy commitments to labor market outsiders and the growth in the level of taxes—help account for the deterioration of the employment performance of these economies over time and for the upward shift in the Calmfors-Driffill curve. The combination of labor market institutions, macroeconomic policies, and welfare state transfers to labor market outsiders can explain the cross-national and intertemporal variation in the employment performance of OECD economies.

Conclusion

During the past two decades, the literature examining cross-national differences in the structure of labor market institutions has generated important insights for the understanding of variation in economic performance across advanced industrialized democracies. By formalizing the Olsonian logic of collective action, these studies have specified the incentives for wage moderation of large wage-bargaining actors and have provided an explanation for the superior employment performance of economies with centralized institutions of wage bargaining during the first decades of the postwar period. In recent years a number of studies have added institutional complexity to earlier models, by specifying the strategic interaction between wage-bargaining actors and monetary authorities. However, although this literature has been especially successful in explaining cross-national differences in economic performance *until the first oil shock*, it is less successful in accounting for the deterioration of the employment performance of European economies during recent decades. The most significant limitation of this literature is its inability to specify the factors that have *undermined* the effectiveness of the policy of wage moderation in economies with corporatist institutions of wage bargaining and that account for the rise in unemployment in European economies during recent decades.

To explain both cross-sectional and intertemporal variation in the employment performance of OECD economies, this chapter has explored the consequences of the "maturation" of the welfare state on the equilibrium level of employment. The crucial insight of the chapter is that the *wage demands of trade unions are affected by the structure of welfare state commitments.* I show that the rational strategy of trade unions is to deliver wage restraint in exchange for the expansion of social policy commitments *if* a sizable part of these transfers affect union members and *if* the magnitude of the net benefits derived by unions from the provision of social policy transfers and services exceeds labor's share of the tax burden necessary to finance these commitments. This argument, stressing the importance of social policy as a source of wage moderation, formalizes a number of existing observations formulated by students of the welfare state. However, I show that this political exchange premised on wage moderation is less effective in combating unemployment in an environment characterized by high levels of taxes and sizable social policy commitments devoted to labor market outsiders. In other words, the maturation of the welfare state *undermines* the effectiveness of the political exchange which was at the basis of welfare state expansion during the first decades of the postwar period.

This chapter identifies two directions of social policy reform that could attenuate the negative impact of the welfare state on the employment performance of European economies. First, future reforms need to reduce the size of labor market outsiders. Policies that aim to improve the employment performance of occupational groups situated at the demographic extremes of the labor market—by stopping the trend toward early retirement or by improving the skill mix of younger workers and, thus, reducing youth unemployment—could, simultaneously, lower the fiscal burden of declining labor-force participation rates. Second, the chapter points to the importance of reforms of the mode of financing of social insurance. Potentially, these reforms could increase the effectiveness of the policy of wage moderation in improving employment.

Appendix

Country Averages

Country	UNEM	CWB	MONET-NONACC	TAX RATE	TRANSFERS. TO.OUTSIDERS	LEFT-CAB	COGRAVITY	OPEN	CAPFLOWS
Austria	2.4	3.25	0.52	38.14	0.38	67.9	2.4	65.9	13.60
Belgium	7.4	7.5	0.47	40.10	1.26	30.6	2.9	108.1	46.21
Canada	7.6	12.75	0.35	23.40	0.75		3.4	48.4	11.68
Denmark	6.1	4.125	0.42	33.55	0.53	52.3	2.9	63.2	18.76
Finland	5.0	4.5	0.38	28.80	0.13	37.4	2.7	52.5	14.29
France	5.4	10.75	0.39	39.36	0.65	27.5	3.5	37.3	11.47
Germany	4.4	6.75	0.60	36.95	0.50	34.2	3.2	51.5	10.79
Italy	7.9	9.25	0.29	34.50	0.34	14.2	2.8	38.2	13.77
Norway	2.4	1.5	0.40	38.55	0.06	66.3	2.5	81.9	18.66
Netherl	5.3	7	0.54	47.10	1.91	17.9	3.0	98.2	21.98
Sweden	2.4	2.625	0.29	47.65	0.10	72.5	2.3	55.8	19.60
Switzerl	0.7	8.75	0.67	29.10	0.07	29.3	3.4	66.6	15.96
UK	6.4	10.875	0.15	25.70	0.21	30.1	3.4	48.9	22.94
USA	6.1	13.25	0.47	27.20	0.38		3.6	15.9	5.03
Mean	4.77	7.34	0.44	33.22	0.47	32.11	3.06	57.04	16.87
St.Dev.	3.48	3.63	0.147	9.12	0.54	33.96	0.643	26.43	17.33

ACKNOWLEDGMENTS

This chapter draws on research presented in *Taxation, Wage Bargaining and Unemployment* (Cambridge University Press, 2006), and I gratefully acknowledge the permission of Cambridge University Press to publish this material. I have accumulated many debts to colleagues that have provided comments on draft versions of the manuscript. In particular, I would like to acknowledge suggestions from Pepper Culpepper, Keith Darden, Jim Fearon, Karl-Orfeo Fioretos, Miriam

Golden, Peter Gourevitch, Peter Hall, David Laitin, Margaret Levi, Kathleen Thelen, and Gunnar Trumbull.

REFERENCES

Alesina, A. 1989. "Politics and Business Cycles in Industrial Democracies." *Economic Policy* 8: 55–98.

Baccaro, L. 1999. "The Organizational Consequences of Democracy: Labor Unions and Economic Reforms in Contemporary Italy." Ph.D. dissertation, Sloan School of Management, MIT.

Beck, N., and J. Katz. 1995. "What to Do (and Not to Do) with Time-Series Cross-Section Data." *American Political Science Review* 89 (3): 634–647.

Bourguignon F., and D. Bureau, eds. 1999. *L'architecture des prélèvements en France: Etat des lieux et voies de réforme*. Paris: La Documentation Française.

Browne, E., and J. Dreijmanis. 1982. *Government Coalitions in Western Democracies*. New York: Longman.

Bruno, M., and J. Sachs. 1985. *Economics of Worldwide Stagflation*. Cambridge, MA: Harvard University Press.

Calmfors, L., and J. Driffill. 1988. "Coordination of Wage Bargaining." *Economic Policy* 6 (1): 14–61.

Cameron, D. 1984. "Social Democracy, Corporatism and the Representation of Economic Interests in Advanced Capitalist Societies." In *Order and Conflict in Contemporary Capitalism*, ed. John Goldthorpe, 143–178. New York: Oxford University Press.

Castles, F., and P. Mair. 1984. "Left-Right Political Scales: Some 'Expert' Judgements." *European Journal of Political Research* 12 (1): 83–88.

Conseil Supérieur de l'Emploi. 1996. *L'allègement des charges sociales sur les bas salaires*. Paris: La Documentation Française.

Esping-Andersen, G. 1990. *Three Worlds of Welfare Capitalism*. Princeton, NJ: Princeton University Press.

European Commission. 1997. "Effective Taxation and Tax Convergence in the EU and the OECD." Memo 5/1997. Brussels: Directorate General II of the European Commission.

Eurostat (Statistical Office of the European Communities). 1997. *Structures of the Taxation Systems in the European Union, 1970–1995*. Luxemburg: Eurostat.

Farber, H. 1986. "The Analysis of Union Behavior." In *Handbook of Labor Economics*, vol. 2, ed. O. Aschenfelter and R. Layard, 1039–1089. Amsterdam: North Holland.

Franzese, R. 2002. *Macroeconomic Policies of Developed Democracies*. New York: Cambridge University Press.

Golden, M. 1993. "The Dynamics of Trade Unionism and National Economic Performance." *American Political Science Review* 87 (2): 439–454.

Golden, M., P. Lange, and M. Wallerstein. 1998. "Union Centralization among Advanced Industrial Societies: An Empirical Study." Dataset available at http://www.shelley.polisci.ucla.edu/data.

Hall, P., and Franzese, R. 1998. "Mixed Signals: Central Bank Independence, Coordinated Wage Bargaining and European Monetary Union." *International Organization* 52 (3): 505–535.

Hibbs, D. 1977. "Political Parties and Macroeconomic Policy." *American Political Science Review* 71 (4): 1467–1487.

Hibbs, D. 1992. "Partisan Theory after Fifteen Years." *European Journal of Political Economy* 8 (2): 361–373.

Huber, E., C. Ragin, and J. Stephens. 1997. "Comparative Welfare States Dataset." Available at http://www.lisproject.org/publications/welfaredata/welfareaccess.htm, updated April 2004.

Iversen, T. 1998. "Wage Bargaining, Hard Money and Economic Performance: Theory and Evidence for Organized Market Economies." *British Journal of Political Science* 28: 31–61.

Iversen, T. 1999. *Contested Economic Institutions.* New York: Cambridge University Press.

Katzenstein, P. 1985. *Small States in World Markets.* Ithaca, NY: Cornell University Press.

Lynch, J., and Anderson, K. 2004. "Internal Institutions and the Policy Preferences of Organized Labor: The Effects of Workforce Aging on Unions' Support for Pension Reform." Unpublished manuscript.

Mares, I. 2005. "Wage Bargaining in the Presence of Services and Transfers." *World Politics* 57 (1): 99–142.

Mares, I. 2006. *Taxation, Wage Bargaining and Unemployment.* New York: Cambridge University Press.

Mendoza, E., A. Razin, and L. Tesar. 1994. "Effective Tax Rates in Macroeconomics: Cross-Country Estimates of Tax Rates on Factor Incomes and Consumption." *Journal of Monetary Economics* 34: 297–323.

OECD. 1995. *Statistical Compendium: Revenue Statistics.* Paris: OECD.

OECD. 1997. *Employment Outlook.* Paris: OECD.

OECD. 1999. *Taxing Wages.* Paris: OECD.

OECD. 2000a. *Effective Average Tax Rates on Capital, Labour and Consumption Goods: Cross-Country Estimates.* Paris: OECD.

OECD. 2000b. *Tax Burdens: Alternative Measures.* Paris: OECD.

Scharpf, F. 1998. *Governing in Europe: How Effective? How Democratic?* Oxford: Oxford University Press.

Schmitter, P. 1981. "Interest Intermediation and Regime Governability in Contemporary Western Europe and North America." In *Organizing Interests in Western Europe: Pluralism, Corporatism and the Transformation of Politics*, ed. Suzanne Berger, 287–327. New York: Cambridge University Press.

Soskice, D., and T. Iversen. 2000. "The Non-neutrality of Money with Large Price or Wage Setters." *Quarterly Journal of Economics* 115 (1): 1–20.

Trades Union Congress. 1958. *Report of Proceedings at the Annual Trades Union Congress*. London: Trades Union Congress.

Traxler, F., and B. Kittel. 2000. "The Bargaining System and Performance: A Comparison of 18 OECD Countries." *Comparative Political Studies* 33 (9): 1154–1190.

Volkerink, B., and J. de Haan. 2000. *Tax Ratios: A Critical Survey*. Paris: OECD.

Volkerink, B., J. Sturm, and J. de Haan. 2001. "Tax Ratios in Macroeconomics: Do Taxes Really Matter?" Working Paper 7/2001. Madrid: European Economy Group.

Wanger, G. 1999. "Soziale Sicherung im Spannungsfeld von Demokratie und Arbeitsmarkt." In *Herausforderungen an die Wirtschaftspolitik an der Schwelle zum 21. Jahrhundert*, ed. I. Nübler and H. Trabold, 77–91. Berlin: Sigma.

Chapter 3

IIIIIIIIIIIIIIIIIIIIIIIIIIIIIIIIIIIIIIIIIIIIIIIIIIIIIIIII

The Politics of Tax Structure

Steffen Ganghof

Governments that wish to redistribute through budgetary policy do so mostly on the spending side and not on the taxing side of the budget. The taxing side is nevertheless important, partly because less-efficient tax structure seems to be associated with lower taxation and spending levels. Hence, political struggles over spending levels may partly be fought as struggles over tax structure (e.g., Przeworski 1999: 43). A recent example of this logic is the *Wall Street Journal* editorial (20 Nov. 2002) that complained about the low income tax burden of a U.S. taxpayer earning twelve thousand dollars a year. These "lucky duckies" benefit so much from the progressive income tax structure that they pay little in income tax: "It ain't peanuts, but not enough to get his or her blood boiling with tax rage." If much less progressive income taxation could somehow be entrenched, so the argument goes, this would increase voters' overall resistance to taxation and thus reduce tax levels.

In this example tax-structure "efficiency" refers to the electoral costs of taxation (cf. Hettich and Winer 1999), but the general logic extends to economic and administrative costs. In continental European welfare states, for instance, which suffer from a high tax burden on low-skilled labor, progressive taxation of wages may be a matter of economic efficiency (Scharpf 2001). Similarly, the *vertical* distribution of the tax burden is only one dimension of tax equity and efficiency. The other dimension, the *horizontal*, has to do with the relative tax burdens on different types rather than levels of income. Along this dimension it is widely believed that moderate tax burdens on (certain types of) capital are efficient, both in general and within the income tax system (e.g., De Long and Summers 1991; Przeworski and Wallerstein 1988; Lindert 2004). For example, the "social democratic" welfare states of Finland, Norway, and Sweden operate so-called dual income taxes (DITs), which discriminate against wages in very systematic and visible ways: whereas capital income is taxed at a uniform low and proportional rate of 25–30 percent (or even lower), wages are taxed progressively up to top rates of almost 60 percent. Many observers find this system difficult to square with those countries' traditional redistributive ambitions. The former Conservative prime minister of Norway, Kaare Willoch (1995: 179), for instance, laments that whereas "social democrats once felt that financial income should be taxed more severely than income from work, they have now changed their minds"; and he is puzzled that the new tax policy goes together with continuing "demands for a large public sector." But these two observations may be causally linked rather than contradictory. For if moderate capital taxation increases the overall (i.e., electoral, economic, and administrative) efficiency of tax *structure*, it also tends to increase the *level* of public spending.

In this chapter I explore the politics of tax structure in comparative perspective, drawing on both quantitative and historical evidence. My focus is mainly on advanced EU and OECD countries and on the potential *tradeoffs between vertical and horizontal tax-structure efficiency*. These tradeoffs seem most salient in income tax policy: if horizontal efficiency does indeed require moderate and proportional taxation of (some) capital income, whereas vertical efficiency (and equity) considerations require progressive taxation of wages, the resulting tax rate differentials will give high-income taxpayers great incentives to transform highly taxed income into lowly taxed income. Trying to avoid this circumstance is difficult and costly in administrative terms, which in turn tends to decrease political support for tax-rate differentiation. Finding a balance between horizontal and vertical tax-structure efficiency is thus inherently difficult. I will explore the tradeoffs involved and show that this exploration can inform and connect a number of separate literatures on the political economy of taxation. Moreover, I will analyze how corporate tax competition has exacerbated domestic tradeoffs and how political institutions figure in the domestic politics of income tax structure.

In the next section, I clarify some basic concepts. Then I treat differentiated income taxation as an implication of the more general need to moderate the tax burden on capital income. Next I highlight basic tradeoffs in income taxation and interpret the tax reforms of the 1980s and 1990s as efforts to find systematic and efficient forms of differentiated income taxation. I then show how tax competition has exacerbated the economic and administrative problems of differentiated income taxation. Finally, I explore the politics of differentiated income taxation and the role of political institutions.

Definitions

In the political-science literature the terms "income tax" and "consumption tax" are typically understood in an *institutional* sense, following the usage in, say, the OECD Revenue Statistics: an income tax is a direct tax on corporations and individuals, whereas consumption taxes are indirect taxes (e.g., value-added taxes). Yet there is also an *analytical* meaning of these terms, which is unrelated to the method of implementation. A consumption or expenditure tax in this analytical sense can be implemented as a direct and progressive tax on corporations and individuals.[1]

So what is the analytical difference between income and expenditure taxes? Answering this question requires an analytical distinction between two types of what we typically call "capital income" (Slemrod and Bakija 2004: 203–4). The *normal return* to capital is the return to deferring consumption, the (risk-free) return to wealth. If I buy a machine, I want this investment to generate at least the return I would have received from buying government bonds. The normal return is the return that can be earned on a marginal investment in capital, which is competed down to a fairly low level. *Above-normal returns* go beyond that level. They include various things, for example, returns to innovation, returns to establishing a monopoly in some market, or returns to entrepreneurial skill. Bill Gates's income from his share of profits from Microsoft would typically be labeled "capital income," but it consists mostly of above-normal returns.

Based on this distinction, we can characterize, roughly, three analytical types of taxes: a *wage tax* taxes neither normal nor above-normal returns, an *expenditure tax* exempts the former but taxes the latter, and an *income tax* taxes both. All three, of course, also tax wages.[2] These distinctions are important because economic theory suggests that—at least in closed economies—above-normal returns can be taxed without distorting investment decisions, whereas taxation of normal returns discourages saving and investment (e.g., Przeworski and Wallerstein 1988). Many theorists also believe that there is an equity rationale for taxing normal returns at a concessionary rate or not at all. Since the normal return is a reward for the saver's willingness to postpone consumption, taxing it (highly) would result in overtaxation of individuals with relatively high savings propensities. In contrast, above-normal returns often represent windfall gains which ought to bear a high tax rate. Proponents of direct expenditure taxes (i.e., exemption of normal returns) also emphasize that they can achieve exactly the same overall degree of progressivity as income taxes.[3]

Efficient Tax Structure and Differentiated Income Taxation

There is widespread agreement that tax structures and tax levels are interrelated; more-efficient tax structures are associated with higher tax levels (Hettich and Winer 1999). "Structure" is here meant to include both the mix between different types of taxes and the internal structure of particular taxes. "Efficiency" is understood broadly, referring to the economic, political (electoral), and administrative costs of taxation. Some authors highlight the causal arrow from levels to structures. The argument is that, at least in democracies, a high taxation level enforces an efficient tax structure (Lindert 2004). Others highlight the opposite causal arrow: changes in tax efficiency entail changes in taxation and spending levels (Becker and Mulligan 2003; Kato 2003).

There is less agreement about what makes for efficient tax structure. For instance, some see flat tax rates as crucial to tax-structure efficiency (e.g., Becker and Mulligan 2003), while others make efficiency-based arguments in favor of (directly) progressive taxation (e.g., Frank 1999; Layard 2005; Røed and Strøm 2002). If there is an exception to these kinds of disagreements, it probably concerns the normal return to capital: since the economic, political, and administrative costs of taxing capital income seem to increase quickly, large welfare states may be predicated on moderate capital-income taxation. Many political scientists, following Przeworski and Wallerstein (1982, 1988), have adopted this perspective. They argue that left-wing governments generally keep the tax burden on (normal) capital income low in order to reconcile efficiency on the taxation side of the budget with equity on the spending side (e.g., Garrett and Lange 1991). In economics, Lindert (2004) has advanced a similar argument as one explanation for the relatively good economic performance of large-tax/welfare states. Although these arguments focus on the *average* effective tax burden on capital, a focus on *marginal* rates leads to parallel

TABLE 3.1
Selected Tax Data for EU and OECD Countries

Country	Taxes as percentage of GDP, 1995–2002	Average effective tax rates, 1995–2000/2002				Top income tax rate, 2004		Threshold top personal rate, 2003 Percentage of average production-worker wage	Income tax per percentage of GDP 1995–2002	
		Capital (total)	Capital income	Labor	Consumption	Corporate	Personal		Corporate	Personal
EU-15										
Belgium	46	27	17	44	22	34	54	95	3	14
Denmark	50	31	20	41	33	30	62	93	3	26
Germany	41	24	19	40	18	39	47	163	1	10
Greece	36	17	12	37	18	35	40	197	3	5
Spain	35	25	17	29	16	35	45	265	3	7
France	45	36	19	43	18	35	58	209	3	7
Ireland	32	27	20	29	26	13	42	208	3	9
Italy	43	28	20	41	18	37	46	317	3	11
Luxemburg	41	29	21	29	23	30	39	107	8	8
Netherlands	41	27	19	34	23	35	52	156	4	7
Austria	44	25	21	40	22	34	50	208	2	10
Portugal	35	28	18	33	20	28	40	602	3	6
Finland	47	31	26	44	29	29	53	191	4	14
Sweden	52	29	20	49	29	28	56	173	3	17
United Kingdom	36	31	22	25	22	30	40	150	3	10
Other										
USA	29	28	n.a.	24	6	39	39	932	2	12
Japan	27	26	n.a.	24	7	42	50	429	4	6
Canada	36	37	n.a.	30	14	36	44	261	4	13
Australia	30	32	n.a.	22	12	30	47	123	5	12
Norway	43	25	n.a.	36	27	28	55	284	6	11
Switzerland	30	28	n.a.	32	10	24	41	n.a.	3	10
New Zealand	35	n.a.	n.a.	24	18	33	39	154	4	15

Notes: n.a. = not available. All values are rounded to nearest percentage point. The OECD averages are for shorter periods (end year 2000 or 2001).
Sources: Revenue and average tax rate data for EU-15 comes from Eurostat (2005), for other countries from OECD (2004b). Statutory tax-rate data is assembled from various sources, specified in Ganghof (2006b). Thresholds are my own computations based on OECD (2004b).

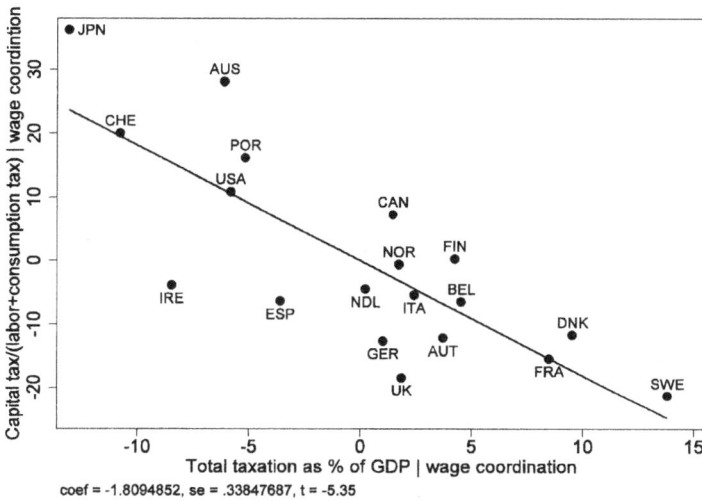

Fig. 3.1. The impact of total tax levels on the relative importance of capital taxation, unweighted averages for the period 1995–2002. *Sources*: See text and table 3.1.

results: taxing (normal) capital income with graduated and high marginal tax rates seems inherently problematic (Slemrod 1990).

These arguments imply that the ratio of capital taxes to labor and consumption taxes decreases systematically with the total tax burden. To show that this is the case in advanced OECD countries, I combine data from the Eurostat (2005) and Carey and Rabesona (2002) for the period from 1995 to 2002 (table 3.1).[4] Figure 3.1 shows the correlation between the total tax burden (revenue as percentage of GDP) and the capital / (labor + consumption) ratio after controlling for the degree of wage coordination. This control is included because it has been argued that in countries with corporatist decision-making, the efficiency costs of labor income taxes are reduced so that labor is taxed more heavily (Summers, Gruber, and Vergara 1993; cf. Cusack and Beramendi 2006).[5] As expected, the ratio of capital taxes to labor and consumption taxes clearly decreases with total taxation.

Now, how do we get from the assumption that tax efficiency requires a moderate overall level of capital taxation to the observation of differentiated forms of income taxation? Some political scientists seem to think that we do not get there at all, because they understand tax *structure* efficiency solely in terms of tax *mixes*. Their argument, as I understand it, is this: since "progressive" property and income taxes fall heavily on capital, whereas "regressive" consumption and social-security taxes do not, a high share of the latter in a country's tax mix is conducive to building and maintaining large-tax/welfare states (Wilensky 2002: 392; Kato 2003: 199).[6] I think this argument is flawed precisely because it ignores the variability of the internal structure of the income tax. Low income taxation is only one of two ways to keep the capital-income burden moderate; the other way is differentiated income taxation, which systematically discriminates against wages *within* the income tax system.

Consider the comparison between France and Denmark (all values are unweighted averages for the period 1995–2002; see table 3.1): France seems to have a very "regressive" tax mix (Kato 2003: 94–110), with a corporate and personal income tax burden of only 9.8 percent of GDP. In contrast, Denmark has a huge income tax burden of 28.8 percent of GDP. Based on the argument from tax mixes, the large size of Denmark's tax/welfare state is a major puzzle (Kato 2003: 197). Yet Denmark's outlier status disappears once we focus on the underlying tax burdens on capital and labor (Ganghof 2006a, 2007). Despite its low income tax burden, France has an average tax rate on capital (income and stocks) of 35.5 percent, the *highest* in the EU, whereas Denmark has one of only 30.5 percent. The reason for this is Denmark's highly differentiated income tax: employed labor is taxed at an average effective rate of 41 percent, with a top marginal rate that exceeds 60 percent and sets in *below* the earnings level of an average production worker (table 3.1). In contrast, many important types of capital income are taxed at marginal rates of 30 percent or lower, which contributes to an average effective tax burden on capital *income* of only 20.1 percent (France: 18.8 percent).

Hence, the difference between Denmark and France does not lie in the level of capital taxation but rather in the progressivity of wage taxation. In France the dominant form of direct wage taxation is payroll taxes; in Denmark it is income taxes. Payroll taxes, if regarded as taxes, are typically regressive because they do not have basic tax allowances, which reduce the relative tax burden on low-income earners, but do have ceilings on contributions, which reduce the relative tax burden on high-income earners. Therefore, countries with "small" income taxes such as France or Austria have also adopted differentiated income taxes that apply fairly high marginal tax rates to wages while treating sensitive types of capital income under separate and much lower rates. In these countries, the income tax partly fulfills a kind of *progressivity adjustment function* for wage taxation at large. Since a large share of labor taxation takes the form of payroll taxes and consumption taxes, income taxes with graduated rates and a large basic allowance can provide a progressive counterweight.

This argument can also help to explain the fact, highlighted in Ganghof (2006b), that the *total* tax burden (as percentage of GDP) is a much better predictor of top personal income tax rates than the *income* tax burden (as percentage of GDP). The logic is as follows: the difference between high-tax and low-tax countries is mainly accounted for by direct or indirect taxes on labor incomes (cf. figure 3.1), and a high labor-tax burden implies higher top personal income tax rates on labor incomes—either directly (if the share of income taxes in total taxes is large) or indirectly (if income taxes are relatively small but more progressive).

Tradeoffs and Trends

In this section, I use the assumption of fairly tight constraints on the taxation of (normal) capital income to offer a stylized interpretation of the postwar development of income taxes in advanced OECD countries. I argue that policy change can be understood as the result of efforts to move toward more-efficient ways of tax-rate differentiation. This interpretation will allow us to better understand the nature of existing income tax regimes, such as the Nordic dual income taxes, as well as the effects of tax competition (to be discussed in the next section). Because my interpretation differs somewhat from the "standard" view in political science, I summarize this view first.

Political-science explanations of income tax reforms in the 1980s and 1990s highlight the importance of ideational changes. Swank and Steinmo (2002: 645) speak of a "paradigm shift"; Kato (2003: 14), of a "reversal of the ideal of progressive income taxation." These accounts focus mainly on the *structure* of capital income taxation. Privileges for business investment are interpreted as efforts of "micro-management" of the supply side (Steinmo 2003) and tax privileges for personal savings (pensions, owner-occupied housing) as "hidden" welfare provision (Howard 1997; Ervik 2000). Policymakers, so the argument goes, learned these manipulations of the structure of capital taxation to be inefficient, so that the tax reforms of the 1980s and 1990s leveled the playing field and made income taxation more "market-conforming" (Swank 1998; Garrett 1998a, 1998b).

Although there is much truth to this view, it underestimates the extent to which tax privileges for capital income were aimed at reducing the *level* of capital-income taxation as well as the fundamental administrative problems of taxing many types of capital income. As a result, it also underestimates the extent to which the very same basic tradeoffs continue to structure the politics of taxation. To elaborate on these points, I start by reviewing, in a stylized way, what I consider to be the basic tradeoff faced by policymakers.[7]

As explained earlier, there are two ideal-type "income" taxes: truly uniform *income* taxes, which tax all types of incomes jointly and equally, and direct *expenditure* taxes, which exempt the normal return on capital. Under the assumption that taxing all normal returns on capital is very costly, politically acceptable versions of both ideal-types are likely to have very different tax-rate schedules. If policymakers followed the income tax ideal closely, tax rates would have to be moderate. Marginal income tax rates would be leveled down to the lowest common denominator—defined by what is acceptable for the most "sensitive" (i.e., costly to tax) types of capital income. In fact, given the inherent administrative problems of taxing certain types of capital income with graduated rates, a truly uniform income tax would most likely have a flat tax rate, with or without a sizable basic tax allowance (Slemrod 1990, 1997). In contrast, if policymakers followed the expenditure-tax model, a progressive rate structure would perhaps imply lower economic efficiency costs because normal returns are exempt. In addition, more-progressive taxation of above-normal returns and wages would be necessary to make up for this exemption in equity and revenue terms. Given real-world constraints on capital-income taxation, therefore, policymakers who want to implement a "market-conforming" income tax that does not intervene into the structure of savings and investment face the basic choice between a *flat income tax* and a *progressive expenditure tax*.

This choice is a difficult one because both ideal-types maximize certain dimensions or notions of tax efficiency and equity at the expense of others (Ganghof 2006b). It is not surprising, therefore, that policymakers in OECD countries eschewed a clear decision and instead tried to combine elements of both types of taxes. The problem was that the resulting "hybrids" or "compromises" (Aaron, Galper, and Pechman 1988) were ad hoc and proved to be very inefficient. One example of this problem is a type of direct expenditure tax at the business level, the so-called cash-flow tax, which allows investment outlays of businesses to be deducted immediately, thereby exempting the normal return on capital. However, if this "expensing" of investment outlays—or, less extremely, greatly accelerated depreciation of assets—is combined with the income tax feature of interest deductibility, as was done in the past by some OECD countries, the tax rate on the normal return to debt-financed investment becomes *negative*. This leads to significant distortions in the structure of investments.

Something similar happened with respect to owner-occupied housing, especially in the Nordic countries: if mortgage-interest payments are deductible, a feature of a pure income tax, but the resulting implicit rent earned by owner-occupiers is taxed lowly or not at all, an expenditure-tax feature, such housing investment is greatly subsidized (Sørensen 1998). This unsystematic combination of features of income and expenditure taxes compromised the efficiency, equity, and revenue goals of income taxes. For instance, it was estimated that in 1986 Danish taxation of personal (household) capital income resulted in a revenue *loss* of 1.6 percent of GDP, which was roughly balanced by the revenue from corporate taxation (Ganghof 2007). Denmark's huge income tax was thus largely a tax on wages and transfers.[8]

Although the tax reforms of the 1980s and 1990s responded, in part, to these kinds of pathologies, the underlying dilemma certainly did not disappear: if policymakers were unwilling to implement pure income or expenditure taxes, they had to look for a more systematic and practicable hybrid approach. I argue that this is what most advanced OECD countries did. One of the best results of this search is the dual income tax (DIT) model implemented in Finland, Norway, and Sweden, as well as, temporarily, in Denmark and Italy.[9] I start by briefly characterizing this model (Sørensen 1998; Cnossen 2000), as this will facilitate the subsequent discussion of the effects of corporate tax competition.

The DIT model combines features of flat income taxes and progressive expenditure taxes in straightforward ways (Ganghof 2006b: chaps. 3–4). Capital income is generally taxed at a moderate uniform proportional tax rate between 25 and 30 percent, while wages are taxed with graduated rates up to top rates of around 60 percent. The above-normal returns of businesses (as approximated by tax administrations) are, in part, taxed together with wages—as they would be under an expenditure tax. The reason is this: in order to split business income into its capital and labor components, tax administrations typically impute a "normal return" on the invested capital and tax all residual income as wages.

In the Nordic countries, these splitting regimes are only applied to un-incorporated businesses and small corporations in which (some of) the owners are active as managers. However, the Italian version of the DIT, introduced in 1998, applied the splitting regime to *all* businesses (but only to the *increase* in their net equity after the base year) (Bordignon, Giannini, and Panteghini 2001). Firms' normal returns were taxed at 19 percent; their residual profits, either at the corporate rate of 37 percent or at personal-income tax rates of up to 46 percent.[10] After a transition period, therefore, an ideal DIT of the Italian type would be a systematic compromise between a flat income tax and a progressive expenditure tax: the government would not manipulate the structure of savings and investments, but by varying the tax rate on normal returns it could approximate any position on the notional continuum between a pure income tax and pure expenditure tax. The latter is approximated if the (top) tax rate on normal returns is reduced to zero; the former, if this rate is aligned with the top rate on labor and above-normal returns.

As this discussion shows, policy learning in OECD countries can be described as a historical trial-and-error search for feasible compromises between two *ideal types* rather than a shift between incommensurable *paradigms*. The alternative interpretation is fruitful in that it highlights oft-neglected observations and questions: If policymakers and experts have found more-efficient ways of differentiating the tax burden, why has there been such a strong downward trend in marginal tax rates on wages and above-normal returns (cf. Wallerstein and Przeworski 1995)? Why has the Italian dual income tax recently been abolished rather than exported to other countries? The next section deals with these types of questions.

The "Spill-Over Problem" and the Role of Tax Competition

My basic argument in this section is that one of the main purposes of the corporation tax is to function as a "safeguard" for the personal income tax, and this function is best fulfilled if the corporation tax rate is not below the top rate on wages, or at least not too far below. However, corporate tax competition is strongest with respect to statutory tax rates and the rates on above-normal returns. As a result, tax competition tends to spill over into personal income taxation, increasing the costs of high marginal tax rates on less-mobile capital income and wages. Tax competition has thus contributed to the downward trend in personal income tax rates.

Political scientists have generally been skeptical about tax-competition explanations of corporate tax-rate cuts, on both empirical and theoretical grounds. The empirical objection is that corporate tax revenue (as percentage of GDP) has not fallen in most OECD countries (e.g., Garrett 1998a, 1998b). The theoretical objection is that if countries compete on the tax rates on normal returns to capital, income taxation in open economies is not fundamentally different than in closed ones. Expenditure taxes can still reconcile equity and efficiency goals (Wallerstein and Przeworski 1995). Yet both arguments, though correct, provide no challenge to the tax-competition explanation proposed here. First, corporate tax revenue as percentage of GDP tells us little about competitive dynamics, since it is influenced by several factors other than statutory corporate-tax provisions (share of profits in GDP, relative size of the corporate sector). Second, there is evidence that countries have competed mainly over statutory tax rates and effective rates on above-normal profits (i.e., inframarginal investments).[11] The first type of competition is mainly driven by the profit-shifting behavior of multinational firms (Hines 1999; Haufler and Schjelderup 2000); the second, by competition for highly profitable investments of such firms (Bond 2000; Devereux, Griffith, and Klemm 2002). Since very profitable investments, by definition, generate a high share of above-normal returns, tax allowances are less important. Revenue-neutral reforms that cut both statutory tax rates and allowances therefore shift the tax burden from more-profitable to less-profitable businesses. Such reforms imply higher taxation of normal returns of domestic firms, but in small open economies this negative effect may be mitigated by the lower statutory rates on inward investment (Bond 2000: 173).

There is robust evidence that the strong downward trend in corporate tax rates since the mid-1980s has been driven to a large extent by tax competition (for an overview, see Griffith and Klemm 2004). The simplest way to see this is to look at the relationship between tax rates and country size. Economic theory predicts that small countries will have lower tax rates in equilibrium because their own capital stock/tax base is small relative to potential inflows (Bucovetsky 1991). The data pattern displayed in figure 3.2 is in line with this prediction. The downward trend in corporate tax rates in advanced OECD countries is associated with an increasing correlation between tax rates and country size (fig. 3.2). Hence, although the absolute convergence of corporate tax rates as measured by the standard deviation has been moderate, the obvious pattern of

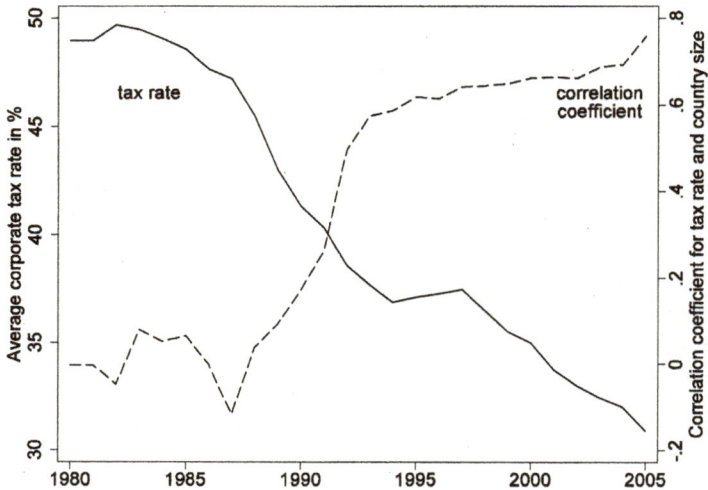

Fig. 3.2. Corporate tax rates and their correlation with country size in twenty-one advanced OECD countries, 1980–2005. The sample includes the cases included in table 3.1 except Luxembourg. The average is unweighted. Correlation coefficient = Pearson's *r*.
Sources: Population: World Bank (2003), corporate tax rates: Ganghof (2006b).

conditional convergence (Sala-i-Martin 1996) is consistent with the theory of asymmetric tax competition.[12]

Qualitative evidence supports this conclusion. In many countries, policymakers clearly would have maintained generous investment incentives for businesses (e.g., accelerated depreciation rules) had it not been for competitive pressures on statutory corporate tax rates. Examples include Australia, Canada, Denmark, and Germany (Ganghof 2006b). In addition, there is evidence that tax competition has created a bias *against* pure expenditure taxes, as these would require higher statutory corporate rates in order to achieve some given revenue level. In the United Kingdom this was one main argument against expenditure taxes (Isaac 1997: 313). Croatia did operate a pure direct expenditure between 1994 and 2001 but eventually decided to abandon this system and lower the corporate rate from 35 to 20 percent (Keen and King 2003).

Now, why can falling corporate tax rates create problems for income taxation as a whole? Consider first why there are corporation taxes at all.

After all, every tax falls eventually on individuals. One main reason is that the corporation tax functions as a safeguard for the personal income tax (Mintz 1995). If retained profits of incorporated businesses went untaxed, much personal income taxes could be avoided. For the same reason, tax designers and international institutions strongly recommend that "personal and corporate income taxes have the same top marginal rate" (Stotsky 1995: 282) or "not differ materially" (Tanzi and Zee 2000: 310). If the corporate tax rate is much below the top personal rate, high-income taxpayers have a large incentive to shift their income into the corporate sector (cf. Gordon and Slemrod 2000; Fuest and Weichenrieder 2002; Wallerstein and Przeworski 1995: 428).

These recommendations do not distinguish between income and expenditure taxes, because a taxation of above-normal returns is sufficient to complement the taxation of wages. A pure wage tax, by contrast, which also exempts above-normal returns, does create significant problems for tax administrations: "Under a wage tax, relabeling your labor compensation as capital income would be an easy avenue to escape taxation altogether. The difficulty of distinguishing what is labor income and what is capital income is an important reason that a pure wage tax would end up being highly inequitable and costly to enforce" (Slemrod and Bakija 2004: 204). This explanation implies that enforcement costs also tend to be high when the marginal tax rates on both normal and above-normal returns are well below the marginal rates on wages.

Hence, by putting pressure on the taxation of above-normal returns at the corporate level, tax competition makes it more difficult for the corporation tax to fulfill its safeguarding function for personal income taxation. Tax competition raises the costs of imposing high marginal tax rates on wages and on the above-normal returns of unincorporated businesses. The tax-reform experiments in Croatia and Italy exemplify this problem. When Croatia introduced a progressive expenditure tax in 1994, the Ministry of Finance proposed a corporate rate of 35 percent to align it with the top rate on personal income. Tax competition motivated the parliamentary majority to set it at 25 percent, but, as expected, the gap between the two top rates led to significant tax-avoidance problems (Rose and Wiswesser 1998: 272). The corporate rate was raised to 35 percent, but given tax competition it was only a question of time until it had to fall again. When it did (to 20 percent in 2001), the expenditure-tax approach was abolished altogether (Keen and King 2003). The Italian experience is similar. The Italian-style dual income tax had itself been a concession to tax competition: the tax rate on normal profits was set at 19 percent rather than zero—as under a pure expenditure tax—so that the tax rate on above-normal returns could be lower, given some revenue target (Bordignon, Giannini, and Panteghini 2001). As in Croatia, however, the preferential taxation of normal profits has recently been abolished in return for a slightly lower corporate tax rate.

It is not surprising, therefore, that Nordic-style dual income taxes do not tax above-normal returns more highly at the corporate level. The consequence, though, is that high-income earners, especially the owners of unincorporated businesses and small corporations, have greater incentives to transform wages into capital income (Hagen and Sørensen 1998). The resulting tax avoidance increases the administrative and political costs of differentiated income taxation and thus creates additional pressure to reduce marginal rates on personal income.

I do not intend to exaggerate the problem. There surely are ways to deal with a large tax-rate gap between corporate and personal income taxation. Perhaps the most systematic way is to retain the basic logic of the Italian-style dual income tax but shift the taxation of above-normal returns from the level of the corporation to the level of the shareholder (Sørensen, 2005). The idea is to include into the tax base of the progressive income tax the difference between the realized income from shares (dividends and realized capital gains) and the normal return. Norway recently introduced a variant of such a system (Ganghof 2006b: chap. 6). The problem, though, is that taxing shareholder's above-normal returns leads to great administrative complexity. In Norway a centralized, computerized register of all Norwegian personal shareholders was created to keep track of the adequately adjusted values of shares and of the utilization of tax allowances for normal profits. Moreover, the Norwegian model nevertheless required further cuts in the top marginal tax rates.

Hence, although there are ways to make a large tax-rate gap between corporate and personal taxation work, they are costly. As a result, the decks seem to be stacked in favor of flatter income taxes. We can already see this empirically. In eastern European transition economies flat income taxes rather than progressive expenditure taxes are spreading. Such taxes were adopted in Estonia (1994: 26 percent, to be reduced to 20 percent in 2007), Latvia (1995: 25 percent), Russia (2001: 13 percent), Serbia (2003: 14 percent), Ukraine (2004: 13 percent), Slovakia (2004: 19 percent), Romania (2005: 16 percent), and Georgia (2005: 12 percent) and are likely to be adopted in more countries such as Poland.[13] Although flat income taxes

TABLE 3.2

The Impact of Corporate Tax Rates on Top Personal Income Tax Rates in EU (Actual and Prospective) and OECD Member Countries, 2004

Independent variables	Dependent variable	Top personal income tax rate, 2004
Corporate tax rate	.35 (.13)	.30 (.11)
Total tax revenue as percentage of GDP	.58 (.17)	.59 (.15)
GDP per capita (in US$10,000)	2.61 (.85)	3.66 (.82)
Constant	5.06 (6.12)	4.80 (5.43)
Excluded outliers	None	Luxembourg
Adj. R-squared	.62	.71
N	38	37

Notes: OLS estimation, standard errors in parentheses. All taxation data are for general government. The tax-rate data are for 2004; the other data are for the latest available year.
Sources: Tax revenue is taken from Eurostat (2005) for EU members, from OECD (2004b) for the remaining OECD countries, and from IMF country reports for the rest. GDP per capita is taken from World Bank (2003).

are now also much more seriously discussed in advanced OECD countries such as Germany and Italy, the higher overall tax burdens on labor have mitigated against a radical flattening of income tax schedules (see the earlier section on efficient tax structure). Nevertheless, there is evidence that corporate tax cuts have contributed to cuts in the marginal income tax rates of individuals. Elsewhere I present case-study evidence for a number of countries, including Australia, Denmark, Germany, and New Zealand (Ganghof 2006b; Ganghof and Eccleston 2004). Here, I perform a simple cross-sectional regression analysis.

If low corporate tax rates increase the costs of maintaining high personal rates, we can expect a systematic positive association between corporate and top personal tax rates (cf. Slemrod 2004). I test this hypothesis with a simple OLS regression for the year 2004. The sample ($N = 38$) is the union of all OECD members and all actual and prospective EU members (i.e., including Bulgaria, Romania, and Turkey).[14] Tax rates are for general government and are taken from a variety of sources (Ganghof 2006b: appendix). I include two important control variables (cf. Slemrod 2004). Total taxation as percentage of GDP serves as a proxy of countries' overall average effective tax rate on wages. This average tax burden influences personal income tax rates either directly, if high total taxes go together with high income taxes, or indirectly, if income taxes are low but serve as a progressive counterweight to the extensive reliance on payroll taxes and indirect consumption taxes. The variable also accounts for the possibility that low overall taxation may be a common cause of low corporate and personal tax rates. The second control variable is GDP per capita.

The simple model performs surprisingly well. It accounts for around 60 percent of the variation in top income tax rates—70 percent if Luxembourg is dropped as an outlier—and suggests that higher (lower) corporate tax rates are systematically associated with higher (lower) top personal tax rates. Hence, if we treat corporate tax rates as the exogenous variable—a reasonable assumption given strong tax competition—the results suggest that lower corporate tax rates do indeed tend to pull down personal rates on high wages and above-normal capital income.

The point of this preliminary analysis is not to enter into the grand debates about the domestic effects of globalization but to highlight two important observations. First, the politics of income tax structure does have an international dimension. EU member states that want to maintain high marginal income tax rates on wages and above-normal returns would probably benefit greatly from a minimum EU corporate tax rate (Ganghof and Genschel, 2008). Second, tax-policy instruments like progressive expenditure taxes look more attractive "on paper" (Przeworski 1999: 43) than in real-world open economies. This fact contributes to limiting the differences between the policy preferences of left and right parties at the domestic level. I now turn to the politics at this level.

The Domestic Politics of Differentiated Income Taxation

It follows from the foregoing discussion that domestic political struggles about tax policy are to a large extent struggles about the *progressivity of wage taxation* in the tax system at large. In this section I focus on these struggles and argue that straightforward left-right differences exist but that they are often not very large. By extension, the importance of veto institutions is generally also reduced. But there are exceptions. I focus on Germany, where different powerful veto points and tax competition *interacted* in ways that forced a Social Democratic–led government to pursue regressive tax reforms.

Left parties are more likely than right parties to prefer more-progressive income taxation of wages, even if this implies a large tax-rate gap between corporate and personal taxation and thus significant administrative costs. This preference is, in part, based on efficiency considerations: progressive income taxes generally fall less heavily on low-wage earners than do payroll taxes and indirect consumption taxes, which may mitigate the employment problems of the low skilled (Scharpf 2000; e.g., Kemmerling 2005). Hence, progressive and differentiated income taxation is one main way to target tax reductions to the low skilled rather than cut wage taxes across the board, which is costly in revenue terms. Right parties, in contrast, are more likely to choose lower and flatter income taxes. As a result, it is possible to explain many features of income tax reforms in terms of the interaction of institutional power and partisan preferences. Elsewhere I provide systematic quantitative and qualitative evidence for this claim (Ganghof 2006b). Here, I only give examples, focusing on changes in top personal income tax rates.

In countries like France, Greece, New Zealand, and the United States, the alternation of right and left governments has been systematically associated with the fall and rise of top personal income tax rates. In countries like Norway and Sweden, veto players—or merely influential players —*outside* the government have also played an important role. Swedish Social Democrats implemented deeper cuts in the top personal tax rate when they needed the parliamentary support of the Liberals in the late 1980s/ early 1990s but later increased the top rate again to 57 percent with the support of the left parties in parliament. Similarly, the Norwegian Labor Party used its power as an opposition party vis-à-vis a small centrist minority government to increase the top personal rate to 55 percent in 2000.

As already noted, though, the differences between the policy preferences of left-leaning and right-leaning governments are typically not very large. In Finland, for instance, the economic constraints of the 1990s were so tight that policy preferences of left and right parties converged strongly. Marginal tax rates on capital had to be low, and tax relief for wages was desirable, but the combination of budget deficits, population aging, and unemployment required that the effective tax burden on capital *increase* significantly and that tax relief for wages be targeted to low wages— through lower income tax rates at the bottom and an earned-income tax credit. Similarly, center-right coalitions in Austria and the Netherlands accepted high marginal tax rates on wages in order to maintain a significant degree of wage-tax progressivity (compare table 3.1). In all these cases there is little evidence that the relevant right-wing actors deliberately pursued "inefficient" tax policies in order to reduce the level of taxation.

A case where the specific *interaction* of economic, partisan, and institutional factors did have a rather drastic effect on legislative outcomes, however, is Germany. When a left-leaning coalition of Social Democrats and Greens took office in 1998, Germany's total tax level was not particularly high (around 42 percent of GDP), but its tax structure was rather inefficient. The statutory corporate tax rate, like other marginal rates on capital, was extremely high by international standards (around 57 percent including local taxes; compare figure 3.2), and there was broad partisan consensus that it had to fall quickly and drastically. On the other hand, the top personal rate was only slightly above the EU average (57 percent, as compared to 53 percent), and the average effective tax burden on capital was rather low (table 3.1). This was partly due to the country's strong reliance on regressive payroll taxes (18 percent of GDP), which also financed expenditures unrelated to social insurance and which caused a heavy tax burden on lower wages. Finally, there was an urgent need to put public finances in order.

One should have expected a Social Democratic–led government to deal with this situation by following a strategy similar to that of governments in Scandinavia or the Netherlands: First, implement some kind of differentiated or dual income tax, which greatly reduces marginal tax rates on capital while maintaining or even increasing the revenue raised from capital and higher wages. Second, reduce the tax burden on low wages, for example, by introducing a sizable basic allowance into the system of payroll taxes (cf. Scharpf 2001). The last thing one would expect is large *general* cuts in the marginal tax rate on very high incomes—capital and labor incomes—and a large reduction of an already moderate income tax burden. Yet this is precisely what happened. The government cut income tax rates across the board and tried hard to limit the tax-rate gap between corporate and personal taxation. Hence, the top personal tax rate fell to 44 percent in 2005, which is low by international comparison, and the corporate rate fell to 39 percent, which is still high by international comparison. The government puts the overall net tax reduction achieved by its tax reforms between 1998 and 2005 at almost €60 billion. This amounts to around 3 percent of GDP and is roughly equal to Germany's structural budget deficits (in 2002).

A critical contributing cause of this puzzling outcome is Germany's combination of strong bicameralism and a far-reaching constitutionalization of tax policy (Ganghof 2006b). The initial tax-reform strategy of Social Democrats was indeed quite similar to the one I sketched earlier, but the government had to deal with two very powerful veto players. The first was the upper house (*Bundesrat*), in which the government lost its majority soon after getting into office. This gave veto power to an opposition that firmly rejected the idea of differentiated income taxes. That the oppositional Christian Democrats adopted this stance may seem surprising, given its own welfare state legacy as well as the pragmatic policies of Christian and Conservative parties in other countries. It is explained to a large extent by the existence of a second powerful veto player: the Federal Constitutional Court. Under the intellectual leadership of former judge and tax expert Paul Kirchhof, the Court deliberately removed central aspects of tax policy from the realm of democratic politics.[15] With respect to income taxation, it was widely and plausibly believed that the Court would not accept any significant gap between the corporate tax rate and the top rate on personal income. In fact, after Kirchhof left the Court in 1999, he immediately became Germany's leading proponent of a 25 percent flat tax and explicitly claimed that different tax burdens on labor and capital are, in principle, unconstitutional.[16] The implicit veto threat of the Constitutional Court was also substantiated by the Federal Fiscal Court in April 1999. It considered one type of differentiated income tax to be unconstitutional, on which the Red-Green government had based its initial tax-reform step: to cut the corporate rate without discriminating against unincorporated businesses, these businesses got a cut in the top personal tax rate as well; the top rate for other personal income, most notably wages, remained unchanged. After the Fiscal Court's decision, this simple model of differentiated income taxation was dead, and in the end the government could only achieve bicameral agreement on a significant reduction of the corporate tax rate by cutting income taxes across the board (for more detail, see Ganghof 2006b: chap. 7).

In sum, the puzzling outcome of German tax reforms is explained by the complex interaction of economic, partisan, and institutional factors. Strong tax competition rendered the legal status quo so unattractive that Social Democrats could not simply veto any policy change, as they had done during their time in opposition. At the same time, their preferred reform strategy—differentiated, revenue-neutral tax-rate cuts—was unacceptable to the relevant veto players. The result was not only neoliberalism *by surprise* (Stokes 2001) but also neoliberalism *by default*.

Conclusions

Large welfare states seem to require moderate capital taxation. Moderation can be achieved in two ways: shifting the tax burden onto payroll taxes and indirect consumption taxes (*low income taxation*) or privileging capital income within the income tax (*differentiated income taxation*). One elegant variant of the second option is a direct expenditure tax that fully exempts the normal return on capital, while taxing above-normal profits together with wages.

Compared with low income taxation, differentiated income taxation tends to lead to more-progressive taxation of wages, which may have both equity and efficiency advantages. However, large tax-rate differentials between different types of incomes are associated with economic, administrative, and political costs. High-income taxpayers can find ways to transform highly taxed incomes into lowly taxed incomes, and, partly as a result, voters may resent visible forms of differentiated income taxation. Low capital-income taxation can thus spill over into wage taxation and pull down marginal tax rates at the upper end of the wage scale. Tax competition exacerbates this problem by putting pressure on corporate tax rates on above-normal profits. It thus undermines governments' ability to use the corporation tax as a safeguard for the progressive personal income tax.

At the national level, political conflicts are to a large extent about the overall progressivity of wage taxation. Left parties prefer more-progressive taxation, even if this increases administrative complexity and implies visible discrimination against wages within the income tax. Left-right differences, however, are often not large, as governments face similar constraints. There is little evidence that right-wing governments or veto players deliberately opt for inefficient tax structures in order to create downward pressure on the overall tax level. As the German case shows, however, particular interactions of economic, partisan, and institutional factors may lock countries into rather inefficient tax structures, at least temporarily.

NOTES

I would like to thank the participants at the Yale conference on Distributive Politics, April 29–30, 2005, especially Kathleen McNamara and the late Michael Wallerstein, as well as Andreas Broscheid and Armin Schäfer, for helpful comments and discussions. All remaining errors are mine.

    1. I use the terms "expenditure tax" and "consumption tax" interchangeably.

    2. For the purpose of this chapter I ignore compensation for inflation and

returns to risk-taking, which need not be taxed under either income or consumption taxes.

3. For critical discussions of these and other arguments, see Murphy and Nagel (2002) and Avi-Yonah (2004).

4. Most data on average effective tax burdens on capital, labor, and consumption available for larger sets of countries, including that of Carey and Rabesona (2002), do not adequately reflect many forms of tax relief for capital income, which can lead to highly misleading data patterns. The Eurostat data seem more reliable because Eurostat has access to national sources on the breakdown of personal income tax revenue into its capital and labor components. These data are only available for the fifteen original EU member states and the period 1995–2002. Since the Eurostat estimates are at least roughly comparable to those of Carey and Rabesona, however, I combine the Eurostat data with the OECD data (for the period 1995–2000).

5. Wage-coordination scores (for the period 1995–2000) are taken from OECD (2004a: 151). The estimated equation (OLS) is this: $CapitalTax/(Labor + ConsumptionTax) = 135.42 - 6.87 WageCoordination - 1.81 TotalTaxation$. Adj. R-squared = .77.

6. Here and throughout, I assume that payroll taxes and indirect consumption taxes are largely shifted backward onto wages. Note also that the arguments of Wilensky and Kato are partly based on the *visibility* of income and property taxes. I will not comment on this mechanism here.

7. For a more detailed analysis of tradeoffs and the resulting conceptions of policy change, see Ganghof (2006b: chaps. 3–4).

8. Similar estimates for the United States are provided by Gordon and Slemrod (1988) and Gordon, Kalambokidis, and Slemrod (2004).

9. The DIT model has influenced tax reforms in many countries, even though only a few countries have so far implemented this model consistently (Ganghof 2005). The model is now also advanced as the most adequate model of pragmatic tax reform for developing countries (Bird and Zolt 2005).

10. The underlying model of expenditure taxation is of a "prepaid" kind. Rather than exempting savings but taxing returns (postpaid or cash-flow expenditure tax), savings are taxed, but normal returns are exempt. On the resulting alternative to cash-flow taxes, see Boadway and Bruce (1984) and IFS Capital Taxes Group (1991).

11. Some studies also find evidence for competition over effective tax rates on normal profits (i.e., "effective marginal tax rates"). See especially Devereux, Lockwood, and Redoano (2004).

12. Ganghof (2006b) uses regression analysis to investigate the relationship between country size and tax rates. Ganghof (2005) shows that the relationship between tax rates and country size also holds for a much larger sample of countries.

13. Note that in some of these countries, the corporate tax rate is higher than the flat tax rate on personal income.

14. Extending the sample is difficult because standard data sources such as World Bank (2003) only report tax-rate and revenue data for *central* government (cf. Slemrod 2004).

15. In the English summary to a recent article, Kirchhof (2003: 50) states, "The democratic hope that the parliamentary process—the decision-making of the representatives of all taxpayers—will guarantee a moderate and consistent tax law, has not been fulfilled. For this reason, the fundamental rights of taxpayers in Germany are increasingly becoming the primary measure of legislation."

16. In the autumn of 2005 Kirchhof joined the election campaign of the Christian Democrats as Shadow Finance Minister. His flat-tax proposal thus became one of the crucial campaign topics and, according to many observers, contributed significantly to the fact that the political right did not win a majority.

REFERENCES

Aaron, Henry J., Harvey Galper, and Joseph A. Pechman, eds. 1988. *Uneasy Compromise: Problems of a Hybrid Income-Consumption Tax*. Washington, DC: Brookings Institution Press.

Avi-Yonah, Reuven S. 2004. Risk, Rents, and Regressivity: Why the United States Need Both an Income Tax and a VAT. *Tax Notes International* 37 (2): 177–195.

Becker, Gary S., and Casey B. Mulligan. 2003. Deadweight Costs and the Size of Government. *Journal of Law and Economics* 46 (2): 293–340.

Bird, Richard, and Eric M. Zolt. 2005. Redistribution via Taxation: The Limited Role of the Personal Income Tax in Developing Countries. *UCLA Law Review* 52: 1627–1695.

Boadway, Robin, and Neil Bruce. 1984. A General Proposition on the Design of a Neutral Business Tax. *Journal of Public Economics* 24 (1): 231–239.

Bond, Stephen R. 2000. Levelling Up or Levelling Down? Some Reflections on the ACE and CBIT Proposals, and the Future of the Corporate Tax Base. In *Taxing Capital Income in the European Union*, edited by S. Cnossen. Oxford: Oxford University Press.

Bordignon, Massimo, Silvia Giannini, and Paolo Panteghini. 2001. Reforming Business Taxation: Lessons from Italy? *International Tax and Public Finance* 8 (2): 191–210.

Bucovetsky, Sam. 1991. Asymmetric Tax Competition. *Journal of Urban Economics* 30 (2): 167–181.

Carey, David, and Josette Rabesona. 2002. Tax Ratios on Labour and Capital Income and on Consumption. *OECD Economic Studies* 35 (2): 129–174.

Cnossen, Sijbren. 2000. Taxing Capital Income in the Nordic Countries: A Model for the European Union? In *Taxing Capital Income in the European Union*, edited by S. Cnossen. Oxford: Oxford University Press.

Cusack, Thomas R., and Pablo Beramendi. 2006. Taxing Work: Some Political and Economic Aspects of Labour Income Taxation. *European Journal of Political Research* 45: 43–73.

De Long, J. Bradford, and Lawrence H. Summers. 1991. Equipment Investment and Economic Growth. *Quarterly Journal of Economics* 106 (2): 445–502.

Devereux, Michael P., Rachel Griffith, and Alexander Klemm. 2002. Corporate Income Tax Reforms and International Tax Competition. *Economic Policy* 17 (35): 451–495.

Devereux, Michael P., Ben Lockwood, and Michela Redoano. 2004. Do Countries Compete over Corporate Tax Rates? Unpublished manuscript, University of Warwick.

Ervik, Rune. 2000. The Hidden Welfare State in Comparative Perspective: Tax Expenditures and Social Policy in Eight Countries. Ph.D. dissertation, University of Bergen, Department of Comparative Politics.

Eurostat. 2005. *Structures of the Taxation System in the European Union, Data 1995–2003.* Luxembourg: Eurostat.

Frank, Robert H. 1999. *Luxury Fever.* New York: Free Press.

Fuest, Clemens, and Alfons Weichenrieder. 2002. Tax Competition and Profit Shifting: On the Relationship between Personal and Corporate Tax Rates. *Ifo-Studien* 48 (4): 611–632.

Ganghof, Steffen. 2005. Globalisation, Tax Reform Ideals and Social Policy Financing. *Global Social Policy* 5 (1): 77–95.

———. 2006a. Tax Mixes and the Size of the Welfare State: Causal Mechanisms and Policy Implications. *Journal of European Social Policy* 16 (4): 360–373.

———. 2006b. *The Politics of Income Taxation: A Comparative Analysis.* Colchester, UK: ECPR Press.

———. 2007. The Political Economy of High Income Taxation: Capital Taxation, Path Dependence and Political Institutions in Denmark. *Comparative Political Studies* 40 (9): 1059–1084.

Ganghof, Steffen, and Richard Eccleston. 2004. Globalisation and the Dilemmas of Income Taxation in Australia. *Australian Journal of Political Science* 39 (3): 519–534.

Ganghof, Steffen, and Philipp Genschel. 2008. Taxation and Democracy in the EU. *Journal of European Public Policy* 15 (1): 58–77.

Garrett, Geoffrey. 1998a. *Partisan Politics in the Global Economy.* Cambridge: Cambridge University Press.

———. 1998b. Shrinking States? Globalization and National Autonomy in the OECD. *Oxford Development Studies* 26 (1): 71–97.

Garrett, Geoffrey, and Peter Lange. 1991. Political Responses to Interdependence: What's Left for the Left? *International Organization* 45 (4): 539–564.

Gordon, Roger H., and Joel Slemrod. 1988. Do We Collect Any Revenue from Taxing Capital Income? *Tax Policy and the Economy* 2: 89–130.

———. 2000. Are "Real" Responses to Taxes Simply Income Shifting between Corporate and Personal Tax Bases? In *Does Atlas Shrug? The Economics Consequences of Taxing the Rich*, edited by J. B. Slemrod. New York: Russell Sage/ Harvard University Press.

Gordon, Roger, Laura Kalambokidis, and Joel Slemrod. 2004. Do We Now Collect Any Revenue from Taxing Capital Income? *Journal of Public Economics* 88 (5): 981–1009.

Griffith, Rachel, and Alexander Klemm. 2004. What Has Been the Tax Competition Experience of the Last 20 Years? WP 04/05. London: Institute for Fiscal Studies.

Hagen, Kare Peter, and Peter Birch Sørensen. 1998. Taxation of Income from Small Businesses: Taxation Principles and Tax Reforms in the Nordic Countries. In *Tax Policy in the Nordic Countries*, edited by P. B. Sørensen. Basingstoke, UK: Macmillan.

Haufler, Andreas, and Guttorm Schjelderup. 2000. Corporate Tax Systems and Cross Country Profit Shifting. *Oxford Economic Letters* 52 (2): 306–325.

Hettich, Walter, and Stanley L. Winer. 1999. *Democratic Choice and Taxation: A Theoretical and Empirical Analysis*. Cambridge: Cambridge University Press.

Hines, James R., Jr. 1999. Lessons form Behavioral Responses to International Taxation. *National Tax Journal* 52 (2): 305–322.

Howard, Christopher. 1997. *The Hidden Welfare State: Tax Expenditures and Social Policy in the United States*. Princeton, NJ: Princeton University Press.

IFS Capital Taxes Group. 1991. *Equity for Companies: A Corporation Tax for the 1990s*. IFS Commentary no. 26. London: Institute for Fiscal Studies.

Isaac, John. 1997. A Comment on the Viability of the Allowance for Corporate Equity. *Fiscal Studies* 18 (3): 303–318.

Kato, Junko. 2003. *Regressive Taxation and the Welfare State: Path Dependence and Policy Diffusion*. Cambridge: Cambridge University Press.

Keen, Michael, and John King. 2003. The Croatian Profit Tax: An ACE in Practice. In *Integriertes Steuer- und Sozialsystem*, edited by M. Rose. Heidelberg: Manfred Rose.

Kemmerling, Achim. 2005. Tax Mixes, Welfare States and Employment: Tracking Diverging Vulnerabilities. *Journal of European Public Policy* 12 (1): 1–22.

Kirchhof, Paul. 2003. Der Grundrechtsschutz des Steuerpflichtigen. Zur Rechtsprechung des Bundesverfassungsgericht im vergangenen Jahrzehnt. *Archiv des öffentlichen Rechts* 128: 1–51.

Layard, Richard. 2005. *Happiness: Lessons from a New Science*. New York: Penguin.

Lindert, Peter H. 2004. *Growing Public: Social Spending and Economic Growth since the Eighteenth Century, vol. 1: The Story*. Cambridge: Cambridge University Press.

Mintz, Jack M. 1995. Corporation Tax: A Survey. *Fiscal Studies* 16 (4): 23–68.

Murphy, Liam, and Thomas Nagel. 2002. *The Myth of Ownership: Taxes and Justice*. Oxford: Oxford University Press.

OECD. 2004a. *Employment Outlook*. Paris: OECD.

———. 2004b. *Statistical Compendium* (CD-ROM). Paris: OECD.

———. 2004c. *Taxing Wages 2003–2004: Special Feature: Broadening the Definition of the Average Worker*. Paris: OECD.

Przeworski, Adam. 1999. Minimalist Conception of Democracy: A Defense. In *Democracy's Value*, edited by I. Shapiro and C. Hacker-Cordón. Cambridge: Cambridge University Press.

Przeworski, Adam, and Michael Wallerstein. 1982. Democratic Capitalism at the Crossroads. *Democracy* 2 (July): 52–86.

———. 1988. The Structural Dependence of the State on Capital. *American Political Science Review* 82 (1): 11–29.

Røed, Knut, and Steinar Strøm. 2002. Progressive Taxes and the Labour Market: Is the Trade-Off between Equality and Efficiency Inevitable? *Journal of Economic Surveys* 16 (1): 77–110.

Rose, Manfred, and Rolf Wiswesser. 1998. Tax Reform in Transition Economies: Experiences from the Croatian Tax Reform Process of the 1990s. In *Public Finance in a Changing World*, edited by P. B. Sørensen. Basingstoke, UK: Macmillan.

Sala-i-Martin, Xavier. 1996. The Classical Approach to Convergence Analysis. *Economic Journal* 106 (2): 1019–1036.

Scharpf, Fritz W. 2000. The Viability of Advanced Welfare States in the International Economy: Vulnerabilities and Options. *Journal of European Public Policy* 7 (2): 190–228.

———. 2001. Employment and the Welfare State: A Continental Dilemma. In *Comparing Welfare Capitalism: Social Policy and Political Economy in Europe, Japan and in the USA*, edited by B. Ebbinghaus and P. Manow. London: Routledge.

Slemrod, Joel. 1990. Optimal Taxation and Optimal Tax Systems. *Journal of Economic Perspectives* 4 (1): 157–178.

———. 1997. Deconstructing the Income Tax. *American Economic Review* 87 (2): 151–155.

———. 2004. Are Corporate Tax Rates, or Countries, Converging? *Journal of Public Economics* 88 (6): 1169–1186.

Slemrod, Joel, and Jon Bakija. 2004. *Taxing Ourselves: A Citizen's Guide to the Great Debate over Tax Reform*, 3rd ed. Cambridge, MA: MIT Press.

Sørensen, Peter B. 1998. Recent Innovations in Nordic Tax Policy: From the

Global Income Tax to the Dual Income Tax. In *Tax Policy in the Nordic Countries*, edited by P. B. Sørensen. London: Macmillan.

Sørensen, Peter B. 2005. Neutral Taxation of Shareholder Income. *International Tax and Public Finance* 12 (6): 777–801.

Steinmo, Sven. 2003. The Evolution of Policy Ideas: Tax Policy in the 20th Century. *British Journal of Politics and International Relations* 5 (2): 206–236.

Stokes, Susan C. 2001. *Mandates and Democracy: Neoliberalism by Surprise in Latin America*. Cambridge: Cambridge University Press.

Stotsky, Janet. 1995. Summary of IMF Policy Advice. In *Tax Policy Handbook*, edited by P. Shome. Washington, DC: International Monetary Fund.

Summers, Lawrence, Jonathan Gruber, and Rodrigo Vergara. 1993. Taxation and the Structure of Labor Markets: The Case of Corporatism. *Quarterly Journal of Economics* 108 (2): 385–411.

Swank, Duane. 1998. Funding the Welfare State: Globalization and the Taxation of Business in Advanced Market Economies. *Political Studies* 46 (4): 671–692.

Swank, Duane, and Sven Steinmo. 2002. The New Political Economy of Taxation in Advanced Capitalist Democracies. *American Journal of Political Science* 46 (3): 642–655.

Tanzi, Vito, and Howell Zee. 2000. Tax Policy for Emerging Markets: Developing Countries. *National Tax Journal* 53 (2): 299–322.

Wallerstein, Michael, and Adam Przeworski. 1995. Capital Taxation with Open Borders. *Review of International Political Economy* 2 (3): 425–445.

Wilensky, Harold. 2002. *Rich Democracies: Political Economy, Public Policy, and Performance*. Berkeley: University of California Press.

Willoch, Kaare. 1995. What Can Other Countries Learn from the Scandinavian Experience? II. *Nordic Journal of Political Economy* 22: 177–182.

World Bank. 2003. *World Development Indicators* (CD-ROM). Washington, DC: World Bank.

Chapter 4

||||||||||||||||||||||||||||||||||||||||||||||||||

AIDS, Inequality, and Access to Antiretroviral Treatment

Nicoli Nattrass

According to the median voter theorem, democracy should facilitate a more equal distribution of resources. This chapter explores whether this is the case with regard to the provision of highly active antiretroviral therapy (HAART) to people sick with the Acquired Immunodeficiency Syndrome (AIDS). It starts off by demonstrating that HIV (Human Immunodeficiency Virus) prevalence is itself in part a product of unequal income distribution and then goes on to show how HIV is affecting the distribution of life chances by underpinning sharp declines in life expectancy. Access to HAART is thus an important aspect of distributive justice, especially in countries with high HIV prevalence. The chapter then goes on to investigate, by means of a quantitative analysis, possible determinants of HAART coverage among seventy-five AIDS-affected developing and transitional counties. Whether a country is a democracy is a significant determinant of HAART coverage, but only when per capita income is not controlled for in the regression. As soon as per capita income is included, the overall explanatory power of the model increases, and the significance of being a democracy falls away. This, of course, relates to the well-known association between democracy and level of development —the implication being that it is per capita income rather than democracy that is the key driver of HAART coverage. Another important factor in the early phase of the HAART rollout was HIV prevalence (which was to be expected given that high-prevalence countries face greater challenges delivering HAART to large numbers of AIDS-sick people). However, by 2006 (presumably because foreign assistance for HAART was focused specifically on high-prevalence countries) HIV prevalence had lost statistical significance as a determinant. This demonstrates the powerful and important impact that global initiatives to provide universal HAART coverage have had on HIV-affected countries.

HIV Prevalence, Per Capita Income, and Inequality

AIDS is overwhelmingly a problem of developing countries, especially in Africa: of the forty million people estimated to be living with HIV, 62 percent are in Sub-Saharan Africa, 20 percent are in South and Southeast Asia, and 5 percent are in Latin America and the Caribbean. Southern Africa, where over one in five adults are HIV-positive, is at the epicenter of the global epidemic (figure 4.1). With the possible exception of India, more HIV-positive people live in South Africa than in any country on earth.

The striking predominance of AIDS in Africa has inspired some analysts to focus on poverty and underdevelopment as key drivers of HIV transmission. Stillwaggon (2002, 2006) argues that malnutrition and parasitic infections have rendered Africans especially vulnerable to AIDS, and Oster (2005) highlights the predominance of untreated sexually transmitted infections, itself an outcome of an underdeveloped health sector. But although there is some evidence of a link between poverty and AIDS-related health outcomes (e.g., Booysen 2002), there is no clear relationship

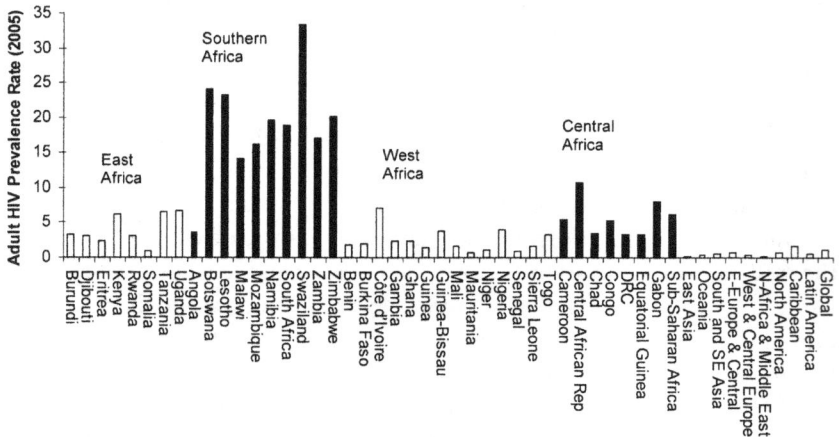

Fig. 4.1. Global HIV prevalence (data from UNAIDS 2006).

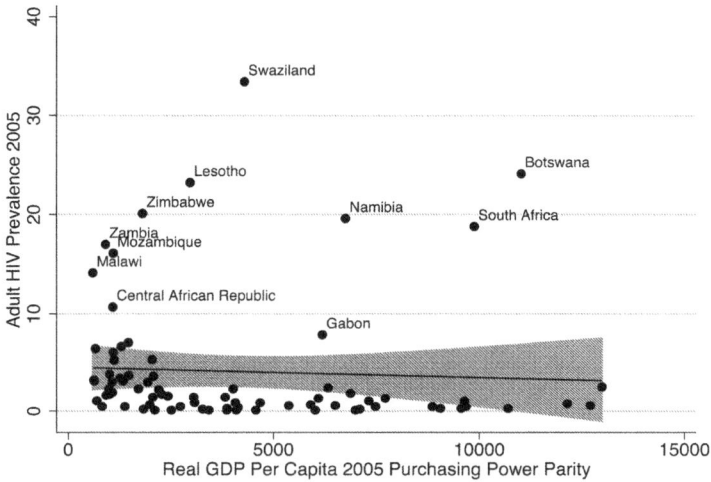

Fig. 4.2. HIV prevalence and GDP per capita.

between a country's level of development (proxied by per capita income) and HIV prevalence (see figure 4.2 and table 4.1).

Zanakis, Alvarez, and Li (2007) argue that the "spoilers" of the anticipated relationship between economic development and HIV prevalence are the "healthier of the wealthiest" and the "wealthier of the sickest." However, as is clear from figure 4.2, there is a strong regional dimension to the story, with the middle-income countries of Southern Africa (notably Namibia, Botswana, and South Africa) exercising strong "outlier" effects on the simple regression line. These same countries also exercise a disproportionate effect on the estimated relationship between HIV prevalence and income inequality (figure 4.3). There is thus something specific about the African AIDS epidemic—especially in Southern Africa—which needs to be taken into account when conducting cross-country analysis.

In his comprehensive history of the African AIDS epidemic, Iliffe argues that "Africa has the worst epidemic because it had the first epidemic established in the general population before anyone knew the disease existed" (2006, 2). His explicitly historical approach demonstrates the absurdity of comparing epidemics in different parts of the world—such as the oft-cited comparison between South Africa, notorious for tardy and inadequate AIDS policies, and Thailand, which had HIV prevalence levels

TABLE 4.1
Per Capita GNP, Inequality, and Adult HIV Prevalence

Dependent variable: Log of Adult HIV Prevalence (2005)	1.1	1.2
Constant		
Coefficient	−0.701	1.142
(standard error)	(1.856)	(1.990)
P > |t|	0.707	0.568
Log of per capita GDP in 2005		
Coefficient	−0.148	−0.128
(standard error)	(0.216)	(0.221)
P > |t|	0.497	0.566
Latest available Gini coefficient	*	
Coefficient	0.027	
(standard error)	(0.015)	
P > |t|	0.072	
Share of income going to the bottom 20 percent		**
Coefficient		−0.142
(standard error)		(0.066)
P > |t|		0.034
Southern Africa	***	***
Coefficient	3.175	3.173
(standard error)	(0.432)	(0.404)
P > |t|	0.000	0.000
Rest of Sub-Saharan Africa	***	***
Coefficient	1.572	1.574
(standard error)	(0.402)	(0.411)
P > |t|	0.000	0.000
Adjusted R-squared	0.6424	0.6481
Number of observations	63	65

* Significant at the 10% level, ** significant at the 5% level, *** significant at the 1% level

similar to South Africa's in 1990 but was able to act quickly to stop this sex-worker-driven epidemic in its tracks. Iliffe points out that, unlike Thailand, South Africa

> bordered a massive continental epidemic, . . . had no identifiable core group, but a great diversity of cross-border contacts that can scarcely now be traced. Of course, better political leadership could have reduced the impact of HIV, but trying to prevent the extensive infection of South Africa would have been like sweeping back the ocean with a broom. Thanks to its uniquely long, asymptomatic incubation period, HIV-1 could probably never have been prevented from reaching epidemic proportions once

established in a general heterosexual population. This happened not in South Africa but ten years earlier and 2,500 kilometers away in Kinshasa. (2006, 43)

Table 4.1 explores the relationship between HIV prevalence, level of development, and inequality in the presence of regional controls for Southern Africa[1] and for the rest of Sub-Saharan Africa. Note that HIV prevalence and per capita income are now expressed as logs (to reduce the effect of outliers and to provide a more normal distribution of the variable). The regressions reported in table 4.1 show that after controlling for overall inequality (measured by the Gini coefficient) or relative poverty (proxied as the share of income going to the bottom quintile) and for being an African country, there is no significant relationship between HIV prevalence and per capita income. Inequality and relative poverty were, however, significant. Regression model 1.2 predicts that for every 1 percentage point increase in the share of income going to the bottom quintile, HIV prevalence falls by 14 percent and that simply being a Southern African country increases HIV prevalence massively and significantly (HIV prevalence is twenty-four times higher for Southern African countries).[2]

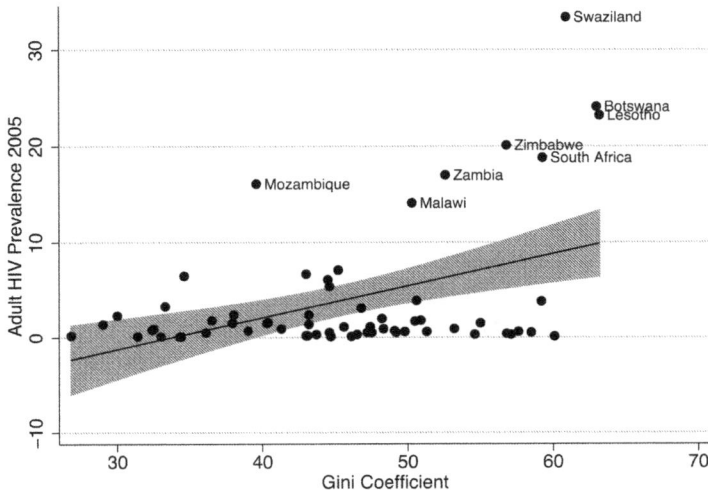

Fig. 4.3. HIV prevalence and inequality.

Although these regression models "explain" about 64 percent of the variation in HIV prevalence, the estimation must, of course, be treated with caution. For example, with regard to inequality, the causal direction is far from clear: just as inequality is likely to create conditions conducive to the spread of AIDS, it is also possible that high rates of HIV prevalence may well undermine economic growth, reduce economic security, and possibly result in greater inequality (see, e.g., United Nations 2004; Freire 2003; Barnett and Whiteside 2002).

How HAART Can Help Improve Life Expectancy

If inequality is conceptualized fairly broadly to include the distribution of "life chances," then it is clear that AIDS has had a significantly negative effect through its impact on life expectancy. As can be seen in figure 4.4, life expectancy has been declining sharply in AIDS-affected countries, particularly those in Southern Africa. For those countries where HIV prevalence is in excess of 5 percent, life expectancy in 2002 is now lower than it was in the 1960s. No wonder, then, that De Waal describes the AIDS pandemic as "development processes run in reverse" (2003, 11).

Government policy toward AIDS—both prevention interventions and the provision of HAART—can, of course, have a large positive impact on life expectancy. Not only does HAART enable HIV-infected adults to live longer, more productive lives, but it also helps increase average life expectancy by helping to prevent new HIV infections. This may seem counterintuitive given that HAART helps people with HIV live longer, thus potentially giving them more opportunities to spread the virus to others. However, it is now generally accepted in the academic literature that HAART is a form of prevention. There are three components to this argument: that people on HAART have reduced viral load and hence are less infectious (e.g., Porco et al. 2004; Cohen and Hosseinipour 2005; Montaner et al. 2006; Graham et al. 2007), that a HAART rollout encourages more people to participate in voluntary counseling and testing (VCT) programs and hence will expose more people to HIV-prevention messaging (e.g., VCTESG 2000; World Health Organization 2005b), and that mathematical modeling has shown that although HIV-positive people on HAART live longer and therefore have more time to infect others, the net impact, at least in the short to medium term, is probably to reduce the number of HIV infections (see, e.g., Blower, Gershengorn, and Grant

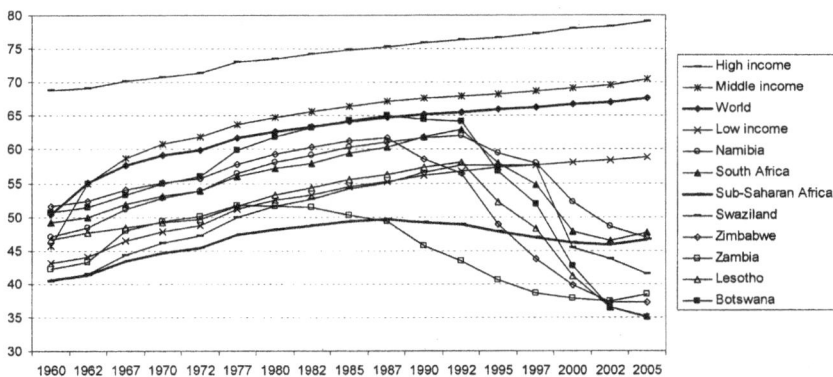

Fig. 4.4. Life expectancy at birth for AIDS-affected countries (population-weighted average for regional variables).

2000; McCormick et al. 2007). Demographic modeling by the Actuarial Society of South Africa of the impact of rolling out HAART predicts precisely this outcome for a HAART rollout in South Africa (see Johnson and Dorrington 2002; Nattrass 2004, 2007).

It is also now widely accepted that more people are likely to participate in VCT if there is hope of treatment (see, e.g., Harvard Consensus Statement 2001; De Cock, Mbori-Ngacha, and Marum 2002). This has proved to be the case in Haiti (Farmer et al. 2001) and in Khayelitsha, Cape Town (Coetzee and Boulle 2003). In other words, implementing a HAART program is likely to have further benefits through creating a social environment less conducive to the spread of HIV than would be the case in the absence of treatment possibilities. The provision of HAART by government thus can have a profound impact on the level and distribution of life chances. It should, in other words, be part of an intellectual agenda concerned with understanding the link between policy and distribution.

Government is generally understood to affect the distribution of life chances by influencing income distribution directly through taxes and transfers (to provide a minimum income floor) and by influencing the distribution of opportunities through the provision of subsidized services (especially education and health) for people too poor to make use of private services in these areas. In the case of epidemics (such as AIDS), there are clear public-health issues as well as concerns about the well-being of individuals. One would thus expect good governments (whether democratic or otherwise) to devote additional resources to such diseases. Low- and middle-income countries face further problems, however, because a disease like HIV is probably in part a function of poverty and because poverty undermines the resources needed to address the disease (either through prevention or treatment or both).

Given the limits on fiscal policy posed by globalization, developing countries are forced to confront the problem of allocating scarce resources between supporting economic growth and poverty alleviation and underpinning HIV prevention and treatment interventions (Nattrass 2004). The solution to this problem is not obvious, as equally well-meaning governments could opt for different policy strategies in this regard. Thus, a low level of government health expenditure could reflect either a lack of commitment to combating AIDS or the prioritization of combating poverty directly (and, to the extent that AIDS is a disease of poverty, to combating the epidemic indirectly). Governments may also believe that HAART is too expensive, even though evidence from South Africa indicates that providing treatment pays for itself by restoring AIDS-sick people to health and thereby taking pressure off the public-health system (see, e.g., Nattrass and Geffen 2005; Badri et al. 2006). The low level of expenditure may also reflect a situation in which the government genuinely believes that restrictive policy and, say, putting additional money into education rather than HAART is the best long-term strategy for fighting AIDS. However, as such governments are likely to face pressure from adults already infected with HIV, it is unlikely that such a strategy will be politically costless. For example, the South African government was forced to change its policies on HAART because of massive resistance from civil society spearheaded by the Treatment Action Campaign (Nattrass 2007). Certainly in democratic countries with high rates of HIV infection (such as South Africa), one might well expect that popular pressure for a HAART rollout would override such narrow economic approaches.

It is, however, important to note that the nation-state is not the only arena in which the struggle for antiretroviral treatment is played out. International pressure on national governments (for example, the international criticism of South African AIDS policy during the early years of the Mbeki presidency [Nattrass 2007]) and bilateral and multilateral foreign aid to AIDS-affected countries have also played major roles in shaping access to HAART internationally. Since 2003, there has been a sharp increase in international support for increasing HAART coverage in the developing world—most notably through the Global Fund to Fight AIDS,

TB, and Malaria and through the World Health Organization's "three by five" initiative to have three million people on treatment by 2005 (Piot 2006; Schwartlander, Grubb, and Perriens 2006; Feachem and Sabot 2006). Although the target was not met, this unique global effort resulted in the number of people on HAART in developing countries rising from 240,000 in 2001 to over two million by the end of 2006. However, despite this effort, only 28 percent of people in developing and transitional countries who needed HAART were actually getting it (see table 4.2). Unless coverage increases sharply, millions of people will continue to die untreated.

Even so, HAART coverage is profoundly shaped by national-level factors. As can be seen from figure 4.5, there is a wide discrepancy in country-level HAART coverage, and HAART coverage seems to be related positively with per capita income. Table 4.2 shows that substantial differences exist also on a regional level, with HAART coverage being substantially higher in Latin America and the Caribbean than is the case elsewhere. The question posed by such data is why are some countries more successful at ensuring that those who need HAART have access to it? What is the balance among economic, regional, demographic, and institutional factors? Does being a democracy matter after taking into account all these factors?

TABLE 4.2
Trends in the Global Rollout of HAART

	Total on HAART				HAART Coverage		
	Dec. 2003	June 2006	Dec. 2006	Average annual growth, Dec. 2003–6	Dec. 2004	June 2006	Dec. 2006
Sub-Saharan Africa	100,000	810,000	1,340,000	138%	8%	23%	28%
Latin America and the Caribbean	210,000	315,000	355,000	19%	65%	75%	72%
East, South, and Southeast Asia	70,000	180,000	280,000	18%	8%	16%	19%
Europe and Central Asia	15,000	21,000	35,000	12%	10%	13%	15%
North Africa and Middle East	1,000	4,000	5,000	71%	7%	5%	6%
Total	400,000	1,220,000	2,015,000	71%	12%	24%	28%

Sources: World Health Organization (2005b, 2006, 2007).

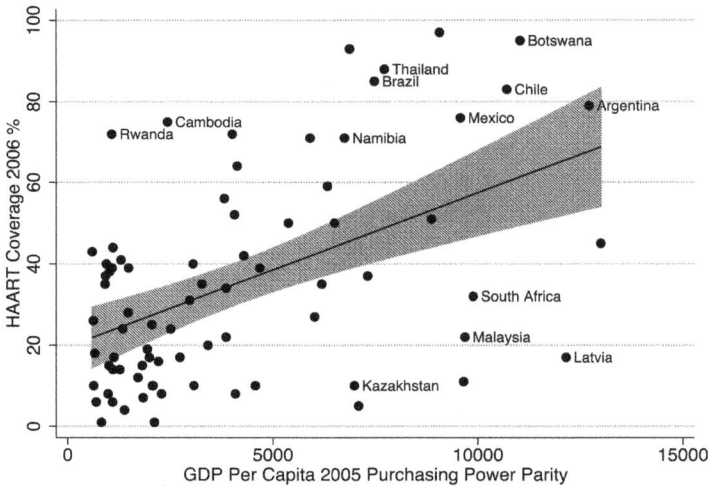

Fig. 4.5. HAART coverage (December 2004) and GNP per capita (2002).

What Determines HAART Coverage?

HAART coverage measures the proportion of people needing HAART who are actually receiving it. One would thus expect this measure to be driven by demographic factors (most obviously HIV prevalence, which determines the numbers of people needing HAART) and economic/institutional factors affecting the provision of HAART. HAART coverage is thus likely to be affected mainly by economic, political, and regional (rather than demographic) factors. As shown in figure 4.5, the level of HAART coverage in developing and transitional countries varies positively with per capita income. The relationship is clearly affected by strong positive outliers (especially from Latin America and the Caribbean) and negative outliers (such as Russia and South Africa).

HAART has been widely available in the advanced capitalist countries since the mid-1990s, but the very high initial price of HAART limited its early use in most developing countries (the notable exception being Brazil, which opted to challenge existing patent rights by producing and importing generic medication). Although some countries were more proactive than others in seeking foreign assistance to provide HAART and negotiating discounts with pharmaceutical companies prior to the widespread price declines (e.g., Botswana), it is nevertheless to be expected that for the same amount of effort, a developing country with a relatively low level of HIV prevalence would have been able to achieve a much higher HAART coverage than a country starting a HAART initiative with a relatively high HIV prevalence. This correlation, however, is likely to have changed over time, as HAART prices fell and as international efforts to provide HAART in developing countries helped overcome the economic obstacles faced by poor countries with a high HIV prevalence (Montaner et al. 2006). The regressions reported in table 4.4 show that this change did occur: whereas the level of HIV prevalence is a significant (negative) determinant of HAART coverage when using June 2004 data, its significance had disappeared by December 2004, and it remained insignificant into 2006 (see also Nattrass 2006).

Table 4.3 reports the results of four regression models of (the log of) HAART coverage: one for June 2004, another for December 2004, and two different regression models for December 2006. They include two economic explanatory variables (per capita income and per capita expenditure on health), two regional dummy variables (Sub-Saharan Africa and Latin America and the Caribbean), a political variable (whether the country is an established democracy or not), and two demographic variables: the differential between urban and rural HIV prevalence and the log of the adult HIV prevalence rate. As one would expect, both economic variables exercise a significant and positive impact on HAART coverage. The 2004 model predicts that controlling for the other explanatory variables, a 10 percent increase in per capita income results in an 8.5 percent increase in HAART coverage, and that a 1 percentage-point increase in the share of per capita health expenditure results in an 11.9 percent increase in HAART coverage. However, by 2006, the salience of these economic determinants had dropped to 3.2 percent and 8.7, respectively.

Also, as one would expect given the HAART-coverage data reported in table 4.2, being a Latin American country significantly increases HAART coverage (even after controlling for other factors, the regression analysis indicates that HAART coverage is three times higher in Latin America and the Caribbean than anywhere else). More surprising, perhaps, is the fact that the coefficient on the Sub-Saharan African dummy was significant and positive in 2004 (but not by the end of 2006). This implies that although HAART coverage was low in Sub-Saharan Africa at the end of 2004, it was nevertheless higher than predicted given international norms. However, by the end of 2006, other countries had caught up, and being an

TABLE 4.3
Determinants of HAART Coverage 2004 and 2006

Dependent variable: Log of HAART coverage	2004		2006 (December)	
	4.1 (June)	4.2 (Dec.)	4.3	4.4
Log of per capita income	***	***	**	
Coefficient	0.666	0.853	0.316	
(standard error)	(0.173)	(0.160)	(0.134)	
P > |t|	0.000	0.000	0.022	
Share of per capita income spent on health	*	**	*	*
Coefficient	0.114	0.119	0.087	0.092
(standard error)	(0.058)	(0.053)	(0.046)	(0.047)
P > |t|	0.054	0.030	0.061	0.054
Latin America and the Caribbean	***	***	***	***
Coefficient	1.138	0.995	1.089	1.056
(standard error)	(0.058)	(0.335)	(0.277)	(0.285)
P > |t|	0.003	0.004	0.000	0.000
Sub-Saharan Africa	**	**		
Coefficient	0.820	0.988	0.545	0.139
(standard error)	(0.456)	(0.422)	(0.354)	(0.319)
P > |t|	0.077	0.022	0.128	0.664
Log of Adult HIV Prevalence	**			*
Coefficient	−0.278	−0.135	0.124	0.173
(standard error)	(0.110)	(0.102)	(0.088)	(0.088)
P > |t|	0.014	0.190	0.164	0.054
Differential between urban and rural HIV prevalence		***	**	**
Coefficient	0.066	0.114	0.084	0.075
(standard error)	(0.045)	(0.042)	(0.035)	(0.036)
P > |t|	0.147	0.008	0.018	0.037
Established democracy				**
Coefficient	0.339	0.436	0.326	0.486
(standard error)	(0.306)	(0.283)	(0.239)	(0.237)
P > |t|	0.271	0.127	0.177	0.044
Constant	***	***		***
Coefficient	−4.662	−5.967	−5.985	2.035
(standard error)	(1.462)	(1.352)	(1.163)	(0.327)
P > |t|	0.002	0.000	0.608	0.000
Adjusted R-squared	0.5348	0.5770	0.4989	0.4654
Number of observations	75	75	75	75

* Significant at the 10% level, ** significant at the 5% level, *** significant at the 1% level

African country no longer conferred any benefits in terms of better-than-expected HAART coverage.

One of the reasons for the high HAART coverage in Latin America and the Caribbean may have to do with the nature of the AIDS epidemic in that region. Whereas poverty has played a role in Africa's heterosexual AIDS pandemic, injecting drug use and gay sex was much more strongly implicated (at least in the initial stages of the epidemic) in Latin America (Berkman et al. 2005). Thus, in the case of Brazil, people living with AIDS were more likely to be urban, middle class, and educated and thus in a better position to fight for greater access to HAART than was the case in Africa. In an attempt to capture this possible impact of an urban-led HIV/AIDS epidemic, the differential between urban and rural HIV prevalence was included as an explanatory variable. The coefficient on this variable turned out to be statistically significant, but the size effect is small (controlling for the other variables, a 1 percentage-point increase in the urban-rural HIV-prevalence differential results in about a 0.1 percent increase in HAART coverage).

Table 4.3 also includes a dummy variable taking a value of one if the country is an established democracy and zero if it is not. But although the sign on the coefficient was positive, and adding the variable increased the explanatory power of the model, the democracy variable was not a significant determinant of HAART coverage. Only in regression 4.4 (which dropped per capita income as an explanatory variable) was democracy a significant determinant of HAART coverage. In other words, the benefit of being a democracy is related more to the well-known positive relationship between democracy and level of development than to the impact of democratic forms of governance on government prioritization of HAART coverage.

The analysis so far has demonstrated the importance of regional and epidemiological factors and the level of per capita income for HAART coverage. But although the level of per capita income gives an indication of the resources available, it says nothing per se about the distribution of resources within the country. Could it perhaps be the case, even after controlling for per capita income, that within-country inequality has an effect on HAART coverage? Earlier research on 2004 data (see Nattrass 2004) showed that inequality was not a significant determinant of HAART coverage and that adding the Gini coefficient reduces the explanatory power of the model (in part because of the lower number of observations). This remained true for 2006 data.

This insignificance of inequality in affecting access to HAART may seem surprising. However, the relationship between inequality and HAART coverage is likely to vary depending on country-level circumstances. A negative relationship between inequality and HAART coverage may be expected in highly unequal societies where HIV affects the poor disproportionately and where elite-dominated governments may be less motivated to divert resources toward HAART. Such countries might also have limited health facilities in poor parts of the country (thus limiting access even further). However, HAART coverage is probably positively associated with inequality in those countries where inequality is driven primarily by the gap between the incomes of the rich and the rest of society and where the rich have access to private health insurance. Similarly, it is possible that in some unequal societies there are a significant number of HIV infections among the more politically powerful urban constituencies—and if these are not sufficiently covered by the private sector, then there will be pressure on government to ensure greater access to HAART. Ultimately, to test the relationship between within-country inequality and HAART coverage, we would need more disaggregated data—especially on the split between public and private provision of HAART and on the social profile of HIV infections. Such data is, as yet, unavailable.

Using regression 4.3, figure 4.6 plots the regression residuals, that is, the actual percentage of people on HAART minus the predicted percentage on HAART for each country. Residuals provide a picture of the degree of unexplained variation in the model (a model which predicts the actual distribution of people on HAART perfectly would have all residuals equal to zero) and provides us with a measure of how the various countries perform relative to what one would predict given our best available regression model. Countries such as South Africa, the Dominican Republic, Tanzania, Zimbabwe, India, Nigeria, and Russia—all of which have been criticized by international observers for poor leadership on AIDS (WHO 2005b, 15; ITPC 2005; and an editorial in the *Lancet* 365 [7 May 2005]: 1597)—had lower HAART coverage than predicted by international norms. By contrast, countries such as Brazil, Botswana, Uganda, Cambodia, Malawi, Thailand, Burundi, Zambia, and Ethiopia—all of which have been singled out for their relatively strong levels of political commitment on AIDS (see, e.g., Barnett and Whiteside 2002; WHO 2005b)—performed better than predicted. These data suggest that the political will to provide HAART can indeed make a great difference.

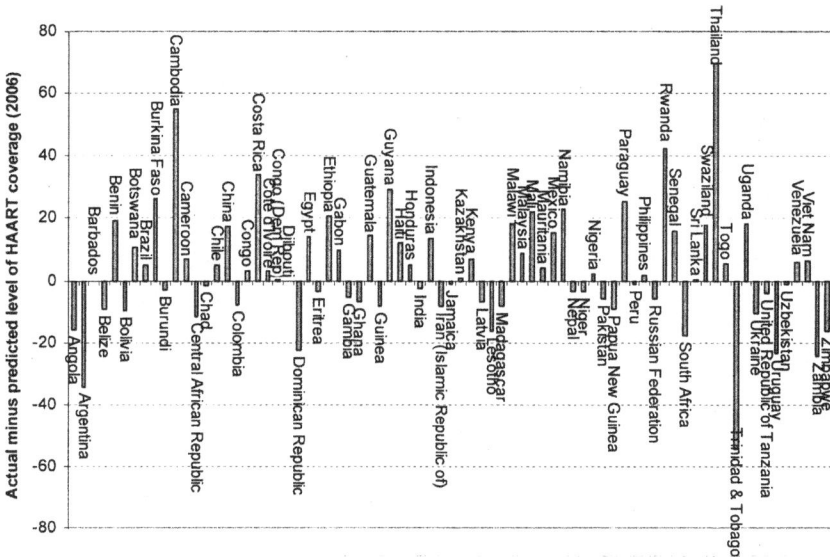

Fig. 4.6. Actual minus predicted HAART coverage (2006), regression 4.3.

Regression residuals, of course, capture all unexplained variation in the model—not simply the impact of "political will." An alternative strategy would be to try and use a measure of political will in the regression as an explanatory variable. For example, UNAIDS's political-support component of the "AIDS program effort index" is one such measure (see discussion in Bor [2007]). When included as an explanatory variable in the regression model, this measure indicates that political support is positively correlated with HAART coverage (and the coefficient is significant at the 5 percent level). Unfortunately, the index is not satisfactory for the purposes of this analysis as it does not cover all countries (including it as an explanatory variable reduces the number of data points from 75 to 46) and because it is, at heart, a qualitative measure which depends to a great extent on who allocates country scores. South Africa, for example, scores very highly on this measure—almost certainly because the data-collection protocol recommends that the qualitative scores be sourced from individuals such as the director or deputy director of the national AIDS Council or Commission and because access to HAART does not feature specifically as an issue. Using the regression residual as an indicator of political will to rollout HAART was deemed a better strategy.

Conclusion

This chapter has argued that health is an important aspect of distribution, illustrating the point with reference to the HIV epidemic, which has severely affected life expectancy in high-prevalence countries. Access to HAART has the potential to change the distribution of life chances significantly for the better. For this reason, one might expect that democracies would achieve higher levels of HAART coverage than other countries. However, exploratory cross-country regression on HAART coverage indicates that democracy is only a significant determinant if per capita income is not included in the regression. This suggests that level of development is a more important driver of HAART coverage than democracy per se.

The chapter also touches on the importance of international initiatives to assist in the provision of greater HAART coverage in developing countries. Such initiatives have enabled poorer countries, especially those with major epidemics, to overcome their initial relative disadvantage in rolling out HAART. This unique international effort has the potential to alter significantly the negative impact of HIV on the global distribution of life chances. Whether it is sustainable, however, is an open question.

NOTES

1. This includes the Southern African countries of Angola, Botswana, Lesotho, Mozambique, Namibia, Swaziland, South Africa, Zambia, and Zimbabwe.
2. The antilog of the coefficient on the Southern African dummy is 23.9.

REFERENCES

Badri, M., G. Maartens, S. Mandalia, L. Bekker, J. Penrod, R. Platt, R. Wood, and E. Beck. 2006. "Cost-Effectiveness of Highly Active Antiretroviral Therapy in South Africa." *PLOS Medicine* 3(1): 1–9.

Barnett, Tony, and Alan Whiteside. 2002. *AIDS in the 21st Century: Disease and Globalization.* New York: Palgrave Macmillan.

Berkman, A., J. Garcia, M. Muñoz-Laboy, V. Palva, and R. Parker. 2005. "A Critical Analysis of the Brazilian Response to HIV/AIDS." *American Journal of Public Health* 95(7): 1162–1172.

Blower, S., H. Gershengorn, and R. Grant. 2000. "A Tale of Two Futures: HIV and Antiretroviral Therapy in San Francisco." *Science* 287(5453): 650–654.

Booysen, F. 2002. "Poverty and Health in Southern Africa: Evidence from the Demographic and Health Survey." *South African Journal of Economics* 70(2): 391–413.

Bor, J. 2007. "The Political Economy of AIDS Leadership in Developing Countries: An Exploratory Analysis." *Social Science and Medicine* 64: 1585–1599.

Coetzee, D., and A. Boulle. 2003. "Adherence: Balancing Ethics and Equity, Selection Criteria and the Role of DOT." Paper presented at the seminar "Scaling Up the Use of Antiretrovirals in the Public Health Sector: What Are the Challenges?" University of the Witwatersrand, School of Public Health and Perinatal HIV Research Unit, August 1.

Cohen, M., and M. Hosseinipour. 2005. "HIV Treatment Meets Prevention: Antiretroviral Therapy as Prophylaxis." In K. Mayer and H. Pizer (eds.), *The AIDS Pandemic: Impact on Science and Society*, 137–161. London: Elsevier.

De Cock, K., D. Mbori-Ngacha, and E. Marum. 2002. "Shadow on the Continent: Public Health and HIV/AIDS in Africa in the 21st Century." *Lancet* 360 (July): 67–72.

De Waal, A. 2003. "How Will HIV/AIDS Transform African Governance?" *African Affairs* 102: 1–3.

Farmer, P., F. Leandre, J. Mukherjee, M. Sidonise Claude, P. Nevil, M. Smith-Fawzi, S. Koenig, A. Castro, M. Becerra, J. Sachs, M. Attaran, J. Yong Kim. 2001. "Community-Based Approaches to HIV Treatment in Resource-Poor Settings." *Lancet* 358 (August): 404–409.

Feachem, R., and O. Sabot. 2006. "An Examination of the Global Fund at 5 Years." *Lancet* 368 (August 5): 537–540.

Freire, Sandra. 2003. "HIV/AIDS Affected Households: Status and Temporal Impacts." In Jean-Paul Moatti, Benjamin Coriat, Yves Souteyrand, Tony Barnett, Jerome Dumoulin and Yves-Antoine Flori (eds.), *Economics of AIDS and Access to HIV/AIDS Care in Developing Countries: Issues and Challenges*, 365–381. Paris: ANRS, Collection Sciences Sociales et Sida.

Graham, S., S. Holte, N. Peshu, B. Richardson, D. Panteleef, W. Jaoko, J. Ndinya-Achola, J. Mandaliva, J. Overbaugh, and R. McClelland. 2007. "Initiation of Antiretroviral Therapy Leads to a Rapid Decline in Cervical and Vaginal Shedding of HIV-1." *AIDS* 21: 501–507.

Harvard Consensus Statement. 2001. "Consensus Statement on Antiretroviral Treatment for AIDS in Poor Countries." Individual Members of Harvard University, Harvard University.

Iliffe, John. 2006. *The African AIDS Epidemic: A History*. Oxford, UK: James Currey.

International Treatment Preparedness Coalition (ITPC). 2005. "Missing the Target: A Report on HIV/AIDS Treatment Access from the Frontlines." Available online at http://www.aidstreatmentaccess.org/itpcfinal.pdf.

Johnson, L., and R. Dorrington. 2002. "The Demographic and Epidemiological Impact of HIV/AIDS Treatment and Prevention Programmes: An Evaluation Based on the ASSA2000 Model." Paper presented at the 2002 Demographic Association of Southern Africa Conference, Cape Town.

McCormick, A., R. Walensky, M. Lipsitch, E. Losina, H. Hsu, M. Weinstein, A. Paltiel, K. Freedberg, and G. Seage. 2007. "The Effect of Antiretroviral Therapy on Secondary Transmission of HIV among Men Who Have Sex with Men." *Clinical Infectious Diseases* 44: 1115–1122.

Montaner, J., R. Hogg, E. Wood, T. Kerr, M. Tyndall, A. Levey, and R. Harrigan. 2006. "The Case for Expanding Access to Highly Active Antiretroviral Therapy to Curb the Growth of the HIV Epidemic." *Lancet* 368 (August 5): 531–536.

Nattrass, N. 2004. *The Moral Economy of AIDS in South Africa*. Cambridge: Cambridge University Press.

Nattrass, N. 2006. "Trading Off Income and Health: AIDS and the Disability Grant in South Africa." *Journal of Social Policy* 35(1): 3–19.

Nattrass, N. 2007. "Modeling the Relationship between Antiretroviral Treatment and HIV Prevention: Limitations of the Spectrum AIDS Impact Model in a Changing Policy Environment." *African Journal of AIDS Research* 6(2): 129–137.

Nattrass, N., and N. Geffen. 2005. "The Impact of Reduced Drug Prices on the Cost-Effectiveness of HAART in South Africa." Centre for Social Science Research, University of Cape Town. Available online at www.cssr.uct.ac.za.

Oster, E. 2005. "Sexually Transmitted Infections: Sexual Behaviour and the AIDS Epidemic." *Quarterly Journal of Economics* (May): 467–515.

Piot, P. 2006. "AIDS: From Crisis Management to Sustained Strategic Response." *Lancet* 368 (August 5): 526–530.

Porco, T., J. Martin, K. Page-Shafer, A. Cheng, E. Charlebois, R. Grant, and D. Osmond. 2004. "Decline in HIV Infectivity Following the Introduction of Highly Active Antiretroviral Therapy." *AIDS* 18: 81–88.

Schwartlander, B., I. Grubb, and J. Perriens. 2006. "The 10-Year Struggle to Provide Antiretroviral Treatment to People with HIV in the Developing World." *Lancet* 368 (August 5): 541–546.

Stillwaggon, E. 2002. "HIV/AIDS in Africa: Fertile Terrain." *Journal of Development Studies* 38(6): 1–22.

Stillwaggon, E. 2006. *AIDS and the Ecology of Poverty*. Oxford: Oxford University Press.

UNAIDS. 2006. "AIDS Epidemic Update, December 2006." Available online at http://data.unaids.org/pub/EpiReport/2006/2006_EpiUpdate_en.pdf.

United Nations Department of Economic and Social Affairs. 2004. *The Impact of AIDS*. New York: United Nations.

VCTESG (Voluntary HIV-1 Counselling and Testing Efficacy Study Group). 2000. "Efficacy of Voluntary HIV-1 Counselling and Testing in Individuals and Couples in Kenya, Tanzania and Trinidad: A Randomised Trial." *Lancet* 356: 103–112.

World Health Organization. 2005a. "'3 by 5' Progress Report, December 2004." Geneva: World Health Organization and UNAIDS. Available online at http://www.who.int/3by5/ProgressReportfinal.pdf.

World Health Organization. 2005b. "Progress on Global Access to HIV Anti-retroviral Therapy: An Update on '3 by 5.'" Geneva: World Health Organization. Available online at http://www.who.int/hiv/pub/progressreports/3by5%20Progress%20Report_E_light.pdf.

World Health Organization. 2006. "Progress in Scaling Up Access to HIV Treatment in Low- and Middle-Income Countries." Fact sheet, June. Available online at http://www.who.int/hiv/toronto2006/FS_Treatment_en.pdf.

World Health Organization. 2007. "Towards Universal Access: Scaling Up Priority HIV/AIDS Interventions in the Health Sector." Progress report, April. Available online at http://www.who.int/hiv/mediacentre/univeral_access_progress_report_en.pdf.

Zanakis, S., C. Alvarez, and V. Li. 2007. "Socio-Economic Determinants of HIV/AIDS Pandemic and Nations Efficiencies." *European Journal of Operational Research* 176: 1811–1838.

Chapter 5

IIIIIIIIIIIIIIIIIIIIIIIIIIIIIIIIIIIIIIIIIIIIIIIIIIIIIIIII

Distributive Politics and Formal Institutions in New Democracies

The Effect of Electoral Rules on Budget Voting in the Russian State Duma, 1994–2003

Jana Kunicová

Distributive Politics in Postcommunist Countries

Transition from authoritarianism to democracy in Eastern Europe and the former Soviet Union has brought about massive changes in distributive politics of the region. Most of the literature on the subject emphasizes the "dual" nature of this transition: the shift from a single-party authoritarian system to multiparty competitive democracy was accompanied by the move from centrally planned economy with state-owned means of production to market economy with private ownership. In this context, political scientists and economists alike have concentrated their attention on the massive redistribution of resources associated with privatization (Hellman 1998; Kaufmann and Siegelbaum 1999), price liberalization (Hellman, Jones, and Kaufmann 2000), and dismantling of the social safety net (Cook 2002).

That the aftermath of the economic reforms has brought dramatic increases in inequality and the concentration of wealth is well documented (Hellman 1998; Milanovic 1999). In addition, the duality of economic and political transition implied that these processes took place during the period of political flux. New democratic institutions—electoral rules, executive-legislative relations, federal structures—were being designed, adopted, and implemented. Both politicians and voters were learning to operate within these institutions. Winners and losers from the economic reform were attempting to learn and use the channels of representation to their advantage (Kaminski 1999; Moser 2001; Luong 2002; Filippov, Ordeshook, and Shvetsova 2004).

Importantly, once the process of economic transformation is completed, political institutions continue to channel distributive politics. In the aftermath of the dual transition, the "tectonic shifts" of privatization, price liberalization, and other profound redistributive reforms are replaced by mundane distributive pressures of democratic politics. Redistribution is now channeled through the allocation of the national budget. It may take place through redistribution from the young to the old (in the form of new national pension systems), from employed to unemployed (as state-provided unemployment insurance), or from healthy to ill (as nationally provided health care), or it can be regionally based, from the rich regions to the poor ones, from warm to cold ones, and so on. In established democracies, the distributive outcomes are expected to be influenced by the types of political institutions that govern democratic process. The main question that this chapter addresses is whether formal institutions, once established, have the same expected effects in new democracies. Do institutions begin affecting the behavior of political actors as soon as they are adopted, or is there a period of institutional "learning"? Is the direction of these effects the same as in developed democracies?

Anecdotal evidence from the Russian State Duma, the lower house of the Russian parliament, suggests that the members of parliament in Russia respond to distributive pressures channeled through electoral institutions. Students of the American Congress would recognize much of the pork-barrel politics that occurs there. Consider this impassioned plea for appropriating an additional twenty-six billion rubles (about $1 billion) in agricultural subsidies by the leader of the agrarian faction in the Russian State Duma in the course of debate on the 2001 budget:

> Dear friends, I will not try to wring a tear out of you, but I appeal to everyone, especially those who in their biography proudly write that they were born in the countryside, to vote for this amendment. You have a historically unique opportunity with your vote to stretch a hand out and give it to your ailing mother. Your mother today is called the countryside. We all say that we have only one natural mother. Our second mother is the countryside. (*Gosudarstvennaia Duma: Stenogramma zasedanii* [*The State Duma: Stenogram of Sessions*], Biulleten' No. 53 (501), October 20, 2000, pp. 46–47)

Despite his urging, and despite the near-unanimous support of the communist and agrarian factions, his amendment was defeated.

In the course of the same debate, a deputy from Saratov oblast proposed an amendment to the budget law increasing state spending on water-control projects. Arguing that dams and reservoirs all over the country were in a critical state of disrepair and urgently needed emergency repairs, he added, "This especially concerns the Volga falls." Students of legislative politics would hardly be surprised to learn that he was elected from a single-member district through which runs the Volga River.

However, the Russian electoral system provides that exactly half of the Duma deputies are elected in single-member districts, while the other half are elected on party lists. Consider the following incident on the Duma floor involving a party-list deputy. In the course of debate over the law on budget classification, a member of the Unity faction (which strongly supported President Putin and the government) from Tuva, K. A. Bicheldei, sponsored an amendment that would have added a separate line item in the budget for spending on nationality relations. Arguing that the time had come for Russia to pursue "an aggressive policy of harmonizing nationality relations," he declared that funding of this item would permit the establishment of a new "center for the Russian language" and other activity designed to promote harmony among Russia's nationalities. The amendment was defeated, receiving only 207 affirmative votes (the threshold for passage is 226 yea votes). The communists and agrarians, and many members of two pro-government factions, strongly supported his amendment. But his own faction, Unity, opposed it. Bicheldei had been elected on the Unity Party list but had a long background in Tuva politics, including four years as chairman of its legislature. He also chaired an interfactional group in the Duma called "The Friendship of Peoples—the Unity of Russia." Thus, despite being elected on the national list, he continued to advocate for his home region, over the opposition of his faction.

Likewise, consider the comment made by the head of one of the pro-government factions about the political costs that his members faced when they supported the government on fiscal policy. The communists, he complained, are able to appeal to the voters with budget-busting spending proposals, and the pro-government deputies have to take the heat for opposing them. Putin keeps his reputation intact, while the electoral onus of supporting the government falls most heavily on single-member district deputies, "who lack the protection of a party list" (*Segodnia*, April 12,

2001). Thus, even within the same factions, single-member-district and list deputies face different sets of electoral pressures.

This study attempts to provide more systematic evidence about the effect of electoral institutions on legislative behavior with regard to budget voting. Although the Russian case might be too specific to afford broad generalization, it is interesting in its own right. This study takes advantage of the availability of a body of roll-call voting data for the Russian State Duma (established following the adoption of a new postcommunist national constitution in 1993) across three convocations, in order to examine the effect of electoral mandate type on voting on distributive issues. We first discuss a theoretical framework of different electoral institutions providing different electoral incentives to politicians, and review the existing empirical research relevant to this question. The chapter then proceeds to describe the Russian State Duma as an environment in which we can test the link between electoral rules, legislative behavior, and distributive legislation. This is followed by a section on our empirical design, which attempts to take into account the institutional, behavioral, and historical features of the Duma. Finally, we discuss empirical results and conclude.

1. Electoral Rules and Distributive Politics: The Expected Effects

We proceed from the basic premise that legislators are office motivated and that their legislative behavior will reflect their wish to be reelected. Then, the relevant constituencies or other actors with whom the legislators will curry favor differ according to the rules governing the electoral process. These rules, in turn, are determined by the electoral formula. For simplicity, consider two basic formulae: single-member districts (SMD) and party-list proportional representation (PR). The electoral pressures in SMDs might dictate that the legislators please their constituencies by effectively channeling public funds to them. We might expect that these pressures would be very different in the PR systems, where electoral fortunes depend on the place on the list that the legislator can secure in the next election. These are assigned by party leaders, so toeing the party line on distributive legislation might be the best way to a high rank on the list.

What do we know empirically about these relationships? In the context of the most extensively studied SMD legislature in the world, the U.S. Congress, the analysis of particularistic legislation and its link to legislative behavior has a long and venerable tradition. Some of the seminal contributions in this field (Ferejohn 1974; Wilson 1986) focus on a particular type of spending that can be easily targeted geographically and for which the costs are shared by the entire nation—such as rivers and harbors legislation or the Corps of Engineers projects. The purpose of these studies is usually to determine the characteristics of the legislators who are most successful in securing such projects for their districts. Ferejohn finds that legislative power matters, so members of some committees receive more projects than nonmembers. Wilson, on the other hand, shows that there is support in the data for the theory of distributive universalism, in which coalitions tend to expand until all legislators eventually receive their share of the pie (cf. Weingast 1994). However, the results of both studies are consistent with the hypothesis that in an SMD-elected legislature, such as the U.S. Congress, geographically targeted projects will be an important tool for the office-motivated legislators. This tendency, in turn, has important implications for maintaining sound fiscal policy: by distributing locally concentrated, electorally helpful pork-barrel spending widely, and diffusing costs, legislators may wreck budget discipline. In some models, the collective dilemma that locally oriented legislators face in restraining their individually beneficial but collectively harmful tendency to overspend on pork creates an incentive to delegate strong veto or decree powers to presidents (Shugart 1998; Shugart and Haggard 2001).

The logical corollary question to that of the effect of SMD systems on distributive policy is this: how important, in terms of electoral success, is "bringing home the bacon" for SMD-elected legislators? Several more recent studies of the U.S. Congress have tried to establish the empirical link between the distributive spending and electoral success (Stein and Bickers 1994; Levitt and Snyder 1997). As Stein and Bickers note, the difficulty in documenting this link is akin to that between campaign spending and success at the polls: the candidates in the closest electoral contests tend to spend the most, and also have the most incentives to engage in pork-barreling. Their main finding is that the candidates who won by the tightest margins will most likely dole out pork for their districts. Levitt and Snyder build on this result and advocate the use of instruments that are unrelated to electoral vulnerability of the legislator in the district but that correlate with federal funding. Using such instruments, they show that raising targeted spending will lead to more votes for an incumbent, whereas transfer spending does not seem to affect electoral outcomes.

In sum, the studies of the U.S. Congress lend some support to our theoretical premise that SMD legislators are likely to rely on geographically targeted spending as one of the tools of securing their reelection. In addition, Levitt and Snyder's study directly contrasts a measure of "pork" with nongeographic redistributive spending, such as transfers. As we would expect, these do not matter electorally to SMD-elected legislators. However, our theoretical premise would imply that if the legislators are elected by PR, precisely this type of spending should receive relatively more attention. In large (often national) PR districts, party leaders will attempt to position their party clearly on a left-right redistributive spectrum. Hence, in order to please a party leader and secure a high rank on the party list, individual legislators should place more value on issues such as transfers that allow them to show loyalty to the party line, while "pork" should become less important as there are no ready-made geographic constituencies to please.

Milesi-Ferretti, Perotti, and Rostagno (2002) take up this point in a cross-country setting. They start from a premise that all spending is redistributive and distinguish between two kinds of spending: transfers aimed at voters of specific socioeconomic profiles and purchases of goods and services, typically targeted geographically. In order to test the prediction that the former will be more prevalent in PR and the latter in SMD, they use data from forty countries (both OECD and Latin American) over time. Their results corroborate their hypothesis but are significantly more robust for OECD countries than for the Latin American ones, which may be due to more noise in the data from developing countries.

However, the problems with studying the link between electoral rules and distributive politics in a cross-country setting might be deeper than what the authors are willing to admit, and the problems concern both the dependent and main causal variables. First, the legislators' behavior is fully absent from the analysis, thus making the analysis "reduced-form" and missing the vital link. Next, although the authors make an effort to acknowledge that not all PR systems are the same and develop an elaborate index of "PR-ness," it still misses important features of some institutions that can only be analyzed in a one-country setup. A good example is Brazil, which is classified as PR; so according to the theory, we ought to see more transfer than pork-barrel spending there. However, Brazil is an open-list PR federal system, in which the nomination of the candidates to the list is governed by state parties as opposed to national parties. So here we in fact have ready-made geographic constituencies, and, as both

Ames (1995) and Samuels (2002) document, Brazilian politics is generally state centered. The legislature behaves more like an SMD-elected one, as it tends to focus on state constituencies rather than on national issues. Both Ames and Samuels use budget amendment process in the legislature as a way to get at geographically targeted spending approved in the Brazilian Congress. Ames finds support for a hypothesis that deputies in fact gain electoral benefits by proposing budget amendments for their geographic constituencies. Samuels, on the other hand, argues that the link is indirect: "pork" pleases the businesses in a particular geographic region within the state, which then fund politicians' campaigns, and that brings in the votes. Overall, these studies of Brazilian politics illustrate how important it is to pay close attention to the details of the electoral rules as well as the actual legislative behavior.

As suggested earlier, these tasks can be very difficult to accomplish in a cross-country analysis. For this reason, if the research question is to study the effect of different electoral systems on the differences in the legislative behavior regarding distributive spending, countries with mixed electoral systems allow us to confine the analysis to a single country. In such systems, we have one legislative body that consists of legislators elected by two electoral rules. Such an environment allows us to hold constant the cultural, historical, and social factors that might influence distributive spending. Even more important, the meaning of "distributive" legislation is much easier to define within one country, as opposed to trying to classify all of spending as either "transfers" or "pork" across countries.

The German Bundestag is an example of such a legislature, where (normally) half of the seats are allocated in single-member districts and the other half based on the party lists with a 5 percent electoral threshold.[1] Lancaster and Patterson (1990) and Stratmann and Baur (2002) took advantage of this setting in an attempt to determine the effect of the different electoral pressures on SMD versus PR deputies on the distributive politics in the Bundestag. Lancaster and Patterson ran an attitudinal survey of the legislators and found that a higher proportion of legislators from single-member districts believed that provision of projects is important for their reelection than the proportion of the legislators from multimember districts. Also, more legislators from single-member districts believed that they can affect spending for their districts.

In a more recent study, Stratmann and Baur take a different approach to a similar question. The authors examine committee assignments in the Bundestag, as the incentives to be on particular committees differ depending on the electoral rule. PR legislators should have more incentives to participate in the issues that give them national visibility and further the cause of their party, whereas plurality representatives would be more likely to choose committees that allow them to cater to their geographic constituencies. The authors create a typology of the committees of the Bundestag that renders three categories—district, party, and neutral—depending on the type of issues with which the committees concern themselves. Consistent with the authors' hypothesis, distribution of legislators into the committees is dependent on the electoral mandate, with more PR representatives in the "party committees" and a higher proportion of SMD deputies in the "district committees."

These studies of the German Bundestag provide an important starting point for the analysis of the effect of electoral rules on distributive policies in the context of a mixed electoral system, and their results are consistent with our general hypothesis. However, the survey data are necessarily subjective, as Lancaster and Patterson readily acknowledge. In the case of Stratmann and Baur's data, the coding of the committees might also be endogenous to the authors' purpose. Ideally, we would like to study the actual legislative behavior of the members of a mixed legislature, such as roll-call votes on distributive issues, and see if this behavior varies systematically by the legislators' electoral mandate (PR or SMD). The dataset on the roll-call votes in the Russian State Duma provides just this opportunity.

The existing work on the Russian mixed electoral system and its effect on the behavior of the legislators has reached contradictory conclusions. There is no study concentrating specifically on distributive voting, but there are several that consider such aspects of legislative behavior such as party cohesion. Haspel, Remington, and Smith (1998) find no effect of the PR-SMD divide on party cohesion in the Duma in 1994–95. Thames (2001), however, finds a voting divide along mandate lines across all policy areas and in budgetary policy between 1994 and 1998. Smith and Remington (2001) show that the impact of electoral mandate varied systematically with the nature of the issues on which deputies voted. On some issues, particularly those most concerned with the rights and roles of factions themselves in the new legislative body, the effects of electoral mandate type were significant. On others, they were overwhelmed by the effects of policy preference and faction membership. We should expect, therefore, that the effect of electoral-mandate background on deputy behavior in floor voting will vary to the degree that the effects of a given piece of legislation concern a deputy's relationship with voters, party leaders, and influential organized interests.

Distributive legislation varies in the way in which material benefits are distributed. As the literature on American distributive voting reviewed earlier signifies, the SMD/separation-of-powers arrangement of American legislative policymaking introduces a systematic institutional bias toward legislation that "parcelizes" benefits in particular congressional districts and states. However, it has been argued (e.g., Rogowski 1987) that PR systems affect the organization of distributive legislation; larger constituencies may reduce pressure for narrowly based interests to collect rents or distribute local pork. The effect of a mixed electoral system such as the one that elects the Russian State Duma on the character of distributive policymaking should also be expected to be mixed, as a result, with pressure for both locally morselized benefits and more aggregate, sectoral benefits (such as higher pensions or minimum wages or lower profits taxes). The following section is devoted to the description of the Russian State Duma as an environment for exploring the effect of electoral rules on distributive policymaking, both as a system containing two different electoral institutions and as a mixed system with its own specific effects.

2. Russian State Duma: An Environment to Study the Effects of Electoral Rules on Distributive Voting

For all Duma elections from 1993 through 2003 (i.e., 1993, 1995, 1999, and 2003), Russian voters cast two votes: one for a party and another for a representative in a single-member district.[2] The result is a 450-member Duma, in which 225 legislators are elected in SMDs and the remaining 225 deputies come proportionally from those parties that cleared the 5 percent electoral threshold. We can think about Russian voters' two votes as if they were coming from two separate elections, one governed by PR and another by plurality rule, since the results of these two elections are not linked. This feature makes the environment particularly suitable for testing for the relationship between electoral rules, legislative behavior, and distributive politics.

Our dataset contains electronically recorded roll-call votes in three consecutive Dumas: the first (1994–1995), second (1996–1999), and third (2000–2003).[3] The dataset also includes some deputy characteristics: aside from the name and mandate (PR or SMD), we have deputy's age, gender, previous occupation, regional affiliation, party affiliation, faction membership at certain points in time, and other parameters for some years. As for the characteristics of the individual votes, we have the title of the vote, date, time, and outcome.

Although the coding of distributive legislation in one country allows a researcher to be more consistent than trying to define the classes of redistributive bills or spending across countries, it is still a daunting task. The main task here is to isolate the criteria that make legislation "particularistic" or "geographically distributive." Our first rough cut is to consider the votes on the federal budget, as the budget will inevitably contain redistribution of public funds to the regions, and spending decisions embodied in the budget reflect inherently distributive choices. Future research will examine a smaller subset of federal budget votes, namely the second and third readings of the federal budget bills, as these contain the amendments after the floor discussion and represent bills that are most likely products of legislative logrolling and are hence most likely particularistic (cf. Ames 1995 and Samuels 2002, who use the budgetary amendment process as a proxy for pork in Brazil). Finally, an even more intensive coding exercise would involve searching full texts of the bills passed in the third Duma (2000–2003) and isolating those bills that expressly mention the names of regions, cities, administrative entities, rivers, dams, and so on.[4] These bills are most likely to target public funds geographically. Keying them to the votes in the Duma will allow us to analyze the legislative behavior of the deputies with regard to the regionally particularistic legislation depending on deputies' characteristics, most notably whether they were elected on party lists or in the single-member districts.

However, the Russian State Duma has several institutional features that complicate our analysis. The following is a list of some of the most important challenges.

Electoral Parties versus Legislative Factions

Suppose we want to observe the mapping from electoral pressures into legislative behavior. If these electoral pressures come from the power of the party leaders above the rank of the deputy on the party list, then in terms of the legislative behavior we should observe office-motivated PR legislators toeing the party line on most issues. However, this prediction assumes that the legislator's *electoral party* is the same as his or her *legislative party*, which is not always the case in the Duma because of the peculiar system of legislative factions that developed in post-Soviet Russian politics.

Legislative factions in the Duma are of two kinds: those based on successful electoral parties (i.e., parties that cleared the 5 percent threshold) and those that are start-up groups (technically called "deputy groups") consisting of thirty-five registered members.[5] Elected deputies are free to affiliate with any faction. Those elected on party lists normally enter the Duma faction based on their party's list. Deputies elected in single-member districts may join either one of the party lists or a start-up group. Thus, the factions based on electoral parties typically comprise both list and SMD members, whereas start-up groups are composed overwhelmingly of SMD deputies plus a few strays from parties.[6] SMD deputies may consider themselves independents, but even independents generally face strong incentives to join an existing or start-up faction, because faction membership provides important benefits, such as administrative assistance or a better chance of obtaining a leadership position on a committee. These incentives mean that many factions based on electoral parties have substantial numbers of SMD deputies, some of whom may have been elected with relatively little assistance from the party. However, a PR-elected deputy who is dissatisfied with his or her electoral party may leave that party's legislative faction and either remain independent, form a new faction with thirty-four other legislators, or join an existing faction. Such movement is relatively common.

The details of legislative factions in the Duma are important, both in their effect on the operation of the Duma and in the relationship of the Duma with the executive branch. The fact that Duma factions are typically composed of two kinds of deputies shapes the internal dynamics of factions, since internal cohesion requires the use of different kinds of bargaining and disciplining mechanisms for the different categories of deputies. In addition, the dual system affects the relationship between the Duma and the executive, because the executive must take into account the different incentives that different kinds of members of factions face (Remington, forthcoming). Although the survival of the government is not directly dependent on maintaining a voting majority in the Duma, the president and government must bargain with factions and individual members for support on key legislative items unless they have overwhelming control over the Duma—which was not the case until the most recent Duma. As a result, both the internal operations of the Duma and its factions as well as the external relations of the Duma with the executive and other institutions in the political environment are affected by the mixed electoral system.[7]

Table 5.1a shows the partisan structure of each of the three Dumas in three different ways. The first column reports the results of the PR portions of the Russian parliamentary elections in 1993, 1995, and 1999. The

TABLE 5.1A

Electoral Results (PR) and Factional Composition of the Russian State Duma, 1994–2003

Electoral results (PR)		Initial faction membership of PR deputies		Initial faction composition of the entire Duma	
Party	Percentage	Faction	Percentage	Faction	Percentage
First Duma (1994–1995)					
LDPR	22.92	LDPR	24.68	LDPR	13.55
RC	15.51	RC	17.02	RC	16.77
KPRF	12.40	KPRF	13.62	KPRF	9.68
WR	8.13	WR	8.94	WR	4.95
AGR	7.99	AGR	8.94	AGR	11.83
YABLOKO	7.86	YABLOKO	8.51	YABLOKO	5.81
PRES	6.73	PRES	7.66	PRES	6.45
DPR	5.52	DPR	5.96	DPR	3.23
		NRP	0.00	NRP	14.19
		INDEPENDENT	0.43	INDEPENDENT	9.03
		Missing data	4.26	*Missing data*	4.52
Second Duma (1996–1999)					
KPRF	22.30	KPRF	30.70	KPRF	31.84
LDPR	11.18	LDPR	9.21	LDPR	10.90
NDR	10.10	NDR	13.16	NDR	13.89
YABLOKO	6.89	YABLOKO	8.77	YABLOKO	9.83
		AGR	9.65	AGR	7.48
		PPOWER	8.77	PPOWER	7.91
		RREGIONS	6.14	RREGIONS	8.76
		DVR	0.44	DVR	1.50
		INDEPENDENT	0.00	INDEPENDENT	4.06
		Missing data	9.21	*Missing data*	3.85
Third Duma (2000–2003)					
KPRF	24.29	KPRF	21.55	KPRF	18.58
UNITY	23.32	UNITY	28.02	UNITY	16.91
OVR	13.33	OVR	12.93	OVR	9.39
SPS	8.52	SPS	10.34	SPS	6.68
LDPR	5.98	LDPR	6.90	LDPR	3.55
YABLOKO	5.93	YABLOKO	7.33	YABLOKO	4.38
		RREGIONS	2.16	RREGIONS	7.93
		NARDEP	0.43	NARDEP	12.11
		APG	8.62	APG	8.56
		INDEPENDENT	1.72	INDEPENDENT	3.76
		Missing data	0.00	*Missing data*	8.14

TABLE 5.1B
Parties and Factions in the Russian State Duma, 1994–2003:
Acronyms and Leaders

Acronym	Faction/party	Leader
AGR	Agrarian Party	Rybkin
APG	APG	
DPR	Democratic Party of Russia	Travkin
DVR	DVR Group	
INDEPENDENT	Independent/No faction membership	
KPRF	Communist Party of the Russian Federation	Zyuganov
LDPR	Liberal Democratic Party of Russia	Zhirinovskiy
NARDEP	People's Deputy	
NDR	Our Home is Russia	Ryzhkov
NRP	New Regional Policy	
OVR	Fatherland–All Russia	Volodin
PPOWER	People's Power	
PRES	Party of the Russian Unity and Concord	Shakhray
RC	Russia's Choice	Gaidar
RREGIONS	Russia's Regions	
SPS	Union of Right Forces	Nemtsov
UNITY	Unity-Bear	Pekhtin
WR	Women of Russia	L'akhova
YABLOKO	Yabloko	Yavlinskiy

second column shows how PR deputies sorted themselves into factions at the beginning of each Duma's term. The third column lists the initial faction composition of the entire Duma. Looking at the middle column of the table, we can see that in each of the three Dumas there were some PR deputies who did not join their electoral party: in the first Duma, there was at least one independent PR deputy, and in the second and third Dumas, several PR deputies joined the newly formed People's Power, Russia's Regions, and Agrarian factions. Interestingly, this faction membership was recorded at the beginning of each convocation, which means that the "dissatisfaction" with the party on whose list these deputies secured legislative seats arose even before the legislative process began. Comparing the PR electoral results and the faction composition of the entire legislature after both SMD and PR deputies sorted themselves into factions (first and third columns), we can see that the partisan balance of power shifts from electoral to legislative parties. For example, although LDPR received the plurality of votes in the 1993 PR elections, it came third in legislative strength (13.55 percent of seats), behind Russia's Choice (16.77 percent) and a newly formed faction, New Regional Policy (14.19 percent). In developing the design of our empirical analysis in the next section, we will discuss the exact proportions of PR and SMD deputies in each faction.

The purpose of the descriptive statistics in table 5.1a is to emphasize that linking electoral motives to legislative behavior in the Russian Duma is complicated by the fact that electoral parties do not map perfectly into the legislative parties.

However, Table 5.1a is painting only a static picture. To make matters even more complicated, extensive *faction switching* occurs during each convocation. As an example, take the third Duma, in which between 12 and 17 percent of all deputies switched factions at some point.[8]

Table 5.2a breaks switching down by faction. For each deputy, a dummy variable "switch" was created. "Switch" takes value 1 if the deputy has switched factions at any point in 2000–2003 and value 0 otherwise, treating missing observations conservatively (see note 8). Table 5.2a reports frequency of "switch" values against the initial faction membership in January 2000. This way, switch = 1 records the "outflow" from each faction. We can see that all independents joined some other faction eventually, which is unsurprising given the institutional incentives. The faction with the highest proportion of members leaving (20 percent) was SPS, which was an electoral party; interestingly, the most loyal faction members (0 percent leaving) were in Russia's Regions, which did not run as a party and was created by mostly SMD deputies. As is clear from table 5.2b,

TABLE 5.2A
Faction Switching in the Third Duma, 2000–2003

Faction (January 2000)	Nonswitchers (N)	Switchers (N)	Total N
APG	38	2	40
CPRF	80	5	85
INDEPENDENT	0	13	13
LDPR	12	3	15
NAR DEP	48	6	54
OVR	40	3	43
RUS REG	37	0	37
SPS	24	6	30
UNITY	69	7	76
YABLOKO	17	3	20
Total N	365	48	413

TABLE 5.2B
Faction Switchers by Mandate in the Third Duma, 2000–2003

Faction switcher?	SMD	PR	Total N
No	164	201	365
Yes	27	21	48
Total N	191	222	413

faction switching occurred among both PR and SMD deputies, although it was slightly more common for SMD legislators. What is surprising is that the difference in frequency of switching by mandate is so small; our general theoretical framework would lead us to expect the PR deputies to be significantly more loyal to their electoral parties in their legislative faction incarnations because loyalty is important for being included in the party list in the next electoral cycle. On the other hand, SMD deputies should be free to switch factions at will whenever such a move might be electorally rewarded by their local constituencies. Russia's weak party system might be one of the reasons why the difference is not as stark as we would expect, which we will take into account when we design our empirical strategy for examining the effect of the mandate on distributive voting.

Electoral Hedging and Regional-Partisan Alliances

Besides joining legislative factions that are often based on electoral parties, SMD deputies might have additional party ties that go back to the electoral process. Although the results of the SMD and PR elections into the Duma are not linked, the Russian mixed electoral system has a peculiar feature: it allows politicians to run *both* on a party list and in a single-member district in any election. A significant number of deputies take advantage of this provision; in the 1999 elections, 97 (23.4 percent) of 415 deputies on whom we have such data did indeed hedge their electoral chances by running in both contests.[9] Out of these 97 deputies, the majority (62) won Duma seats in single-member districts, while the rest secured their seats on party lists. This electoral hedging, of course, poses the question of whether deputies also hedge in their legislative behavior: for example, being elected on a party list does not discipline a legislator who knows that he or she may run in a single-member district in the next election. On the other hand, cultivating two different potential constituencies is costly, which may outweigh the benefits of hedging.

But electoral hedging is not the only source of party ties of SMD deputies. Another is electoral nomination, which in the case of SMD deputies may be by voters, by the politician him- or herself, or by an electoral party. As table 5.3 shows, close to half of the elected SMD deputies were nominated by voters or by self-nomination, and the other half were nominated by parliamentary electoral parties. Nomination by a party saves the candidate from gathering signatures on nominating petitions and putting down a deposit, but in an environment in which party endorsements

TABLE 5.3
Nominations of SMD Deputies in the Third Duma
(1999 Elections)

Nominated by	N	Percentage
Voters	99	48
Self-nomination	3	1
Nonparliamentary parties	9	4
KPRF	41	20
UNITY	9	4
NDR	6	3
OVR	31	15
SPS	5	2
YABLOKO	3	1

usually carry little useful political capital and may associate a candidate with the party's negative reputation, many candidates prefer to remain independent of party affiliations or to minimize their ties to parties, and voters often prefer independents to party-related candidates (Rose and Munro 2002, 103–109). Thus, for many winning SMD deputies, party ties at the point of the election are relatively weak. Deputies' choices regarding faction affiliation are therefore based on considerations about how best to maximize policy influence while minimizing the loss of independence.[10]

Still, many SMD deputies, despite their local constituencies, might not be free of partisan allegiances in their electoral motivations. On the other hand, PR deputies might not be free of regional biases either. Besides natural links to their birthplaces and regions of residence, there is also often a particular territorial region to which a PR deputy has ties. These ties are often formalized in the structure of the electoral lists. The PR portion of the ballot uses an all-federal electoral district to calculate the share of the 225 PR seats that a given faction is entitled to fill. The election law requires, however, that parties create regional sublists and that the central list have no more than twelve names. This requirement is intended to encourage the recruitment of prominent regional politicians to the party lists. Thus, many elected PR deputies have specific territorial ties, and factions encourage those members to maintain those connections by periodic travel to their "home" region for consultation and fence mending. It is conceivable, then, that a PR deputy has an incentive to bring geographically targeted projects to his or her "own" region. On the other hand, this incentive should only be present when voting for such a project does not go against the wishes of the party leaders, who ultimately control deputies' place on the list.

Behavioral Norms and Learning-by-Legislating in a
New Democracy

In addition to the complications arising from institutional features of the Duma and peculiarities of the electoral process, we should also pay attention to the consequences of Russia being a "new democracy," which implies the fluidity of both formal and informal rules of the game. The formal rules have only recently been written and are regularly questioned, challenged, and amended. Informal rules also take time to develop and to be espoused by the legislators. For example, factions may coordinate on some level a factional discipline in voting, but this coordination takes time to achieve. Yet some informal rules specific to the Duma have developed and have taken root quickly and firmly. One of such norms is that instead of opposing a certain piece of legislation, deputies many times simply do not register to vote. Thus, in many cases "not voting" stands for a "nay" vote.[11]

However, as in any new democracy, it takes time for politicians and voters alike to learn about the consequences of the formal institutions within which they operate. As has been argued elsewhere (e.g., Kaminski 2002), often not even the designers of electoral laws fully understand their consequences, and it takes a few periods of "trial and error" for the participants in the new democratic process to grasp the payoffs of their alternative actions.

The institutional learning is made more difficult by the fact that many rules evolve during transition. For example, in the period analyzed here, Russia has seen strengthening of the presidency and weakening of the Duma, which may have changed the utility functions of the legislators considerably. All of these factors may weaken the empirical relationship between the mandate type and voting on distributive issues. We attempt to take some of these factors into account when we design our empirical strategy for isolating these effects in the next section.

3. Research Design

In the previous section we established that the imperfect correspondence between electoral parties and legislative factions compromises the premises of our theoretical framework. In order to maintain the link between electoral pressures and legislative behavior in our analysis, we will only

TABLE 5.4
Factions Admissible for Analysis: Number of
SMD and PR Members

Faction	SMD	PR	Total
First Duma (1994–1995)			
RC	33	39	72
KPRF	14	32	46
AGR	33	21	54
PRES	16	18	34
YABLOKO	8	19	27
Second Duma (1996–1999)			
KPRF	54	95	149
NDR	20	45	65
YABLOKO	15	31	46
Third Duma (2000–2003)			
KPRF	39	50	89
UNITY	16	65	81
OVR	15	30	45
SPS	8	24	32
YABLOKO	4	17	21

consider those factions that ran as "electoral parties" and have passed the 5 percent threshold to secure seats in the Duma. Within these factions, we would like to compare the legislative behavior of PR deputies to their SMD counterparts. However, this is only possible if there are enough of both PR and SMD members in a faction to make such comparison meaningful. Table 5.4 lists such factions for all three Dumas. Note that the use of Yabloko in the first Duma and Yabloko and SPS in the third Duma is doubtful, as the numbers of SMD deputies are rather low. Unfortunately, by restricting our analysis only to "balanced" factions, we select away those deputies who joined SMD-dominated factions, such as New Regional Policy in the first Duma or Russia's Regions in the second and third Dumas. However, our goal is to determine whether the voting on distributive issues differs between SMD and PR deputies. Such comparison in the Duma only makes sense if the factional effects are held constant.[12]

Furthermore, to address the problems that faction switching creates, we will only consider "loyal" faction members, that is, those who did not switch in or out of the faction during a convocation. Again, by doing so we are eliminating the least partisan (and hence potentially more particularistic) deputies; however, we gain the possibility of within-faction comparisons of PR and SMD deputies that avoids indexing factions by time. Also note that the resulting "loyal factions" may not exhibit the same patterns of factional discipline as observed in the "full factions" containing the switchers as well.

With this sample of deputies, a panel dataset with deputy-vote observations for each of the three Dumas was constructed. As discussed earlier, our first cut for regionally distributive projects are federal budget votes, which in the future will be replaced with a more precise coding based on the analysis of the text of the adopted laws.[13] For comparison purposes, we can extend the sample of roll-call votes to include a subset of expressly nondistributive legislation, such as that concerning symbolic issues (flag, hymn, emblem), the federal judiciary, treaty ratifications, and the regulation of religion.

To examine whether SMD deputies behave differently from their factional PR counterparts when voting on the regionally distributive issues, the dependent variable *dissent* was created. This dichotomous variable takes value 1 if the deputy's vote on a given issue differs from his faction leader's vote and takes value 0 otherwise.[14] To account for the behavioral norm in the Duma that in many cases renders "nonvoting" as a "nay," we have two different versions of *dissent*. The benchmark version treats "not voting" essentially as a missing observation, and another version codes "not voting" the same as "nay." Regardless of the measure of *dissent*, we would expect that PR deputies will dissent less than SMD members of the same factions on regionally distributive legislation, since their regional ties are presumably electorally less important than their incentives

TABLE 5.5
Frequency Analysis of Dissent by Faction and Mandate, 2000–2003

Election type	Faction	Frequency	Number of loyal members	Average dissent
SMD	KPRF	2,318	36	64.39
PR	KPRF	2,962	48	61.71
SMD	UNITY	402	15	26.80
PR	UNITY	1,552	59	26.31
SMD	YABLOKO	91	3	30.33
PR	YABLOKO	608	15	40.53
SMD	SPS	146	5	29.20
PR	SPS	640	21	30.48
SMD	OVR	548	14	39.14
PR	OVR	913	28	32.61

DISSENT IN THE THIRD DUMA, 2000-2003

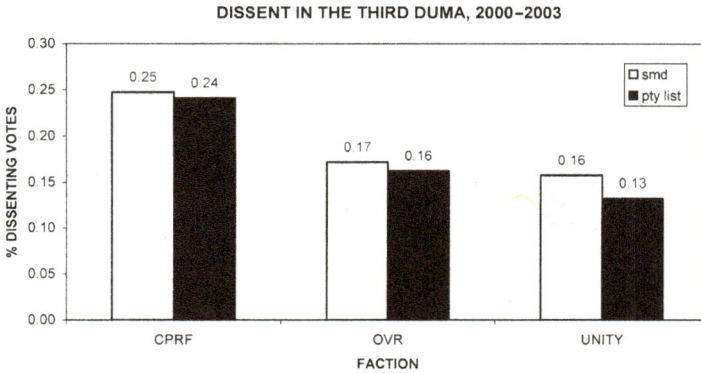

Fig. 5.1. Frequency analysis of dissent by faction and mandate, 2000–2003.

to demonstrate faction loyalty to their faction leaders. On the other hand, the SMD deputies will be more likely to stray from the faction leader's position on these regionally distributive projects, as their electoral incentives to cultivate a regional vote base should sometimes trump their partisan ties.

As an exercise to illustrate the shape of the data, we can perform a simple frequency analysis of *dissent* by mandate and faction. For simplicity, let us look only at the third Duma (2000–2003), where balanced factions based on electoral parties include KPRF, OVR, and UNITY—and perhaps, marginally, YABLOKO and SPS. We can then look at the *dissent* of loyal faction members on budget votes and "contract" our dependent variable by electoral mandate and faction, which gives us the number of times PR and SMD members of these factions disagree with their faction leaders. We weigh this frequency by the number of loyal PR and SMD deputies in each faction, respectively. The results are displayed in table 5.5 and figure 5.1.

When examining the three balanced factions (KPRF, UNITY, and OVR), the results are as expected: SMD deputies within each of the three factions are on average more likely to stray from the party leaders on budget legislation. However, note that the factions seem to coordinate on a level of faction discipline: KPRF appears to be much less disciplined than any other faction, while UNITY is most disciplined. Still, note that these are not full legislative factions; instead, we are dealing only with the subset of loyal faction members, so this may or may not correspond to how the discipline in these factions is commonly perceived by commentators and researchers. In addition, we are only looking at a subset of issues that are redistributive. The results for Yabloko and SPS go in the opposite direction (PR deputies are more likely to dissent), but given the scarcity of SMD members in both of these factions, this is hardly surprising.

The simple frequency analysis presented here is instructive as a first glance at the data and a hint that the relationship we are looking for might be present, but it certainly is much too crude. Our econometric method of choice is a probit model that estimates the probability of dissent as a function of the electoral mandate (SMD/PR) and faction, (eventually) controlling for some deputy and bill characteristics.

$$\Pr(\text{dissent}_{d,v}) = f(\text{mandate}_d, \text{faction}_d, \text{controls}_d, \text{controls}_v)$$

This model will be applied to each of the three Dumas on which we have data. Of course, many assumptions underlie this specification. The most restrictive one is that it treats all votes as equally important. Still, it can be argued that we have already selected a class of votes (budget) that are in principle comparable. In addition, with our benchmark version of *dissent*, we are only considering those votes for which the deputies were present. It might not be such a stretch to assume that those votes for which most deputies showed up are similarly important.

The theoretical framework discussed in the previous sections, as well as our observations about the institutional and behavioral features of the Duma, lead to the following hypotheses:

H1: Controlling for faction and for bill and deputy characteristics, SMD mandate should increase the probability of dissent of a deputy with his or her faction leader on distributive issues. Conversely, PR mandate should decrease this probability.

H2: Due to institutional learning, this effect should be more pronounced over time.

4. Results

In the regression of *dissent* on simple dummies for mandate and faction membership, the left-out (benchmark) category for the mandate type is

TABLE 5.6
*The Effect of Mandate and Faction Membership on Dissent over
Three Duma Convocations*

	1st Duma (1994–1995) Change in prob. (S.E. in parentheses)	2nd Duma (1996–1999) Change in prob. (S.E. in parentheses)	3rd Duma (2000–2003) Change in prob. (S.E. in parentheses)
Party list (PR)	−0.17% (0.006)	−1.99% (.003)***	−1.57% (.003)***
RC	21.97% (.008)***		
AGR	22.60% (.008)***		
PRES	21.27% (.011)***		
NDR		1.37% (.003)***	
YABLOKO		−6.07% (.003)***	
UNITY			−8.31% (.003)***
OVR			−1.14% (.006)*
Observations	29,054	130,457	57,251
|Pseudo R-sq.|	0.029	0.032	0.021

Notes: In our Probit models, we report changes in probability (%) of dissent given a change in each of the discrete variables (electoral mandate or faction dummy) from 0 to 1. Omitted categories are as follows: SMD (electoral mandate); CPRF (factions). Statistical significance reported at conventional levels: *** significant at 1% level; ** significant at 5% level; * significant at 10% level (statistically significant results in bold).

SMD and for faction *CPRF* in all three Duma regressions. Thus, if H1 holds, one would expect a negative significant sign on the PR dummy, as the probability of dissent on distributive issues should be lower for PR deputies than for SMDs. If H2 holds, we would expect this result to be stronger in the second and third Dumas. There are no strong priors about the signs or significance of the faction-membership dummies. However, figure 5.1 suggested that CPRF was relatively undisciplined in comparison to the other two factions that we consider in the third Duma, at least as far as budget votes and loyal faction members were concerned. If this is a true and robust pattern, then the signs of the coefficients on factional dummies should be negative and significant.

The results allow us to make the following observations. The first model specification yields a coefficient on the PR dummy that is statistically insignificant and has a wrong sign in the first Duma but is very significant and negative in the second and third Dumas. This suggests that controlling for factional membership, electoral type has had measurable influence on the probability of dissent in the two later Dumas. However, the absence of this relationship in the first Duma is consistent with H2, which is based on institutional learning.[15]

All of these specifications were repeated with our alternative measure of dissent that treats "not voting" as voting "nay." The results are mostly unchanged, if slightly weaker for the second Duma. In addition, in a companion paper (Kunicová and Remington 2005), we show that these effects are robust to inclusion of many controls, including ideology, incumbency, membership in the budget committee, and closeness of the vote.

Finally, we have attempted to compare distributive and nondistributive votes for the first Duma. (These will be replicated for later Dumas as soon as the data allow.) Interestingly, we find that there is actually *less* dissent on those issues that we code as "regionally distributive" (federal budget and other budget legislation) as compared to nondistributive issues. This is exactly the opposite of what we would expect, but we can offer several possible explanations of this finding. First, all our previous findings were either negative or counterintuitive for the first Duma, which might suggest that institutional learning, adaptation, and "trial and error" were in process during that time. In addition, as table 5.7 documents, the size and level of detail of budget legislation rose steadily over the decade, which may suggest that early on, budgets might have been vague and generalized and only have comprised broad categories of spending.

TABLE 5.7
Federal Budget Laws 1992–2002: Complexity and Detail

Budget year	Date signed	Number of articles	Number of pages
1992	7/17/1992	18	8
1993	5/14/1993	27	19
1994	7/1/1994	39	28
1995	3/31/1995	62	67
1996	12/31/1995	71	33
1997	2/26/1997	99	119
1998	3/26/1998	120	115
1999	2/22/1999	141	59
2000	12/31/1999	163	243
2001	12/27/2000	139	340
2002	12/30/2001	147	423

Notes: Number of pages refers to pages in official publication of law in Sobranie zakonodatel'stva Rossiiskoi Federatsii. Budgets for 1992 and 1993 are from Vedomosti S'yezda Narodnykh deputatov RSFSR i Verkhovnogo Soveta RSFSR.

It may also be the case that factions devoted more effort to ensuring a cohesive factional position regarding budget legislation than they did on other types of issues. Perhaps by presenting a united front in dealing with the government as the budget was being worked out, faction members developed their own intrafaction logrolls but exerted less effort to do so on other bills.

4. Conclusion

The foregoing examination of the effect of electoral rules on distributive voting provides evidence broadly consistent with expectations. Particularly in the second and third Dumas, SMD deputies were more likely to break with faction discipline on budget issues than were their list-based comrades, and this effect grew stronger after the first Duma. Future research will extend this analysis further by examining a set of bills with specifically localized impacts and by linking deputies from the relevant regions to such bills. The results for voting on issues that can be characterized as nondistributive in the first Duma also suggest that deputies were still engaged in a process of behavioral adaptation to their new environment.

On balance, the evidence presented here suggests that after some initial period (in Russia's case, the first Duma convocation), electoral rules affect distributive voting in new democracies in the same direction as we would expect in established democratic systems. The magnitude of the effect isolated in this study is rather small, which may be an artifact of institutional and societal features specific to Russia (cf. Kunicová and Remington, forthcoming). However, the consistent direction of this effect, as well as its robustness to various specifications in the second and third Dumas, are both remarkable and constitute a strong result in and of themselves.

Finally, the bifurcated nature of legislative factions with divisions along the mandate lines clearly influences their own internal operations and levels of voting cohesion, which in turn affects their ability to forge cross-factional coalitions and their bargaining influence with the executive. It is not too much to say that it is precisely the localizing pressures on deputy behavior arising from SMD representation that persuaded President Putin to eliminate SMD seats altogether from the Duma in the future.

The coexistence of two electoral mandate types in a single legislature will nonetheless continue to be an important feature of many other legislative bodies in the contemporary world.

NOTES

This chapter builds on Jana Kunicová and Thomas F. Remington, "Mandates, Parties, and Dissent: The Effect of Electoral Rules on Parliamentary Party Cohesion in the Russian State Duma, 1994–2003," *Party Politics* (forthcoming). The author is grateful to two anonymous referees for useful comments and to Sarah Hill for excellent research assistance.

1. Because Germany allows the "topping up" of a party's seat share based on its list vote, and does not penalize parties for seats won in SMDs, the actual number of mandates in the Bundestag can vary. At present there are 601 deputies.

2. Recently enacted electoral reforms, proposed by President Putin, eliminate the SMD seats entirely in favor of an all-PR system. All 450 seats will be filled based on the vote for party lists competing in the all-Russian federal electoral district. The electoral threshold will be raised to 7 percent. The new system is to take effect in the 2007 election.

3. The dataset was created on the basis of a proprietary product produced by the Moscow-based firm INDEM. The "first" Duma is, of course, the first modern Duma; however, it shares the name with the pre-1917 legislative body in tsarist Russia.

4. Slinko, Yakovlev, and Zhuravskaya (2005) assemble a similar dataset of regional legislation. They code regional laws as "captured" by industrial interests if they mention an enterprise by name.

5. As of 2004, the minimum number of deputies required for a registered deputy group was raised to fifty-five. This is one reason that there are no non-party-based deputy factions in the current Duma.

6. Sometimes the Communist Party of the Russian Federation (CPRF) faction has assisted the formation of friendly groups by assigning some of their members to join them. Deputies who have been seconded in this way may be presumed to maintain some relationship with their original party while members of the other faction.

7. It is not fanciful to speculate that it was the relatively high bargaining costs incurred by the government and president in dealing with two different types of members that led Putin to push through the electoral law reform eliminating SMD members.

8. We do not know the exact number of faction switchers because of the missing data. Faction membership is recorded at several points between 2000 and

2003. A conservative estimate of 12 percent is obtained by deleting all missing observations. However, it is likely that all the deputies for whom faction membership is unavailable after September 2000 were in fact faction switchers. If we make such a liberal assumption, we calculate that 17 percent of all deputies switched factions.

9. Data coded from official handbooks of the Duma: *Fond razvitiia parlamentarizma v Rossiia* 1994, 1996; Zapeklyi and Kozlov 2001).

10. Characteristic of the kind of calculations that elected SMD deputies make is the fact that one hundred independents chose to join the pro-Putin "party of power" faction in the Duma, United Russia. In all, some 80 percent of SMD deputies joined this faction, suggesting the power of the bandwagon effect.

11. For a discussion of the effect of nonvoting on analysis of roll-calls in the Duma, see Smith and Remington (2001), 163–165.

12. In the future, we hope to use more fine-grained measures of regionally distributive laws and analyze the legislative behavior of SMD-based factions with respect to these laws.

13. We have partially completed the coding of the regionally distributive laws based on whether the names of cities, regions, rivers, or administrative units appear in the text. The resulting subset of legislation includes a large number of federal budget laws, which gives us confidence in selecting budget legislation as our first rough measure of "pork."

14. There are four possible values that roll-call votes take: "yea," "nay," "abstain," and "not voting." If a deputy's vote value coincides with that of his faction leader, $dissent_{deputy, vote} = 0$; if they differ, $dissent_{deputy, vote} = 1$.

15. We obtain very similar results by running simple bivariate probits (not reported), regressing dissent within each faction in the three Dumas on electoral type of the deputy. In the first Duma, the coefficient on PR changes signs and lacks statistical significance. However, in the second and third Dumas, the PR coefficients are negative and significant. This gives us further confidence in the validity of our hypotheses. We also ran all of these specifications with a measure of dissent that treats "not voting" as voting "nay." The results are mostly unchanged, if slightly weaker for the second Duma.

REFERENCES

Ames, Barry (1995). "Electoral Rules, Constituency Pressures, and Pork Barrel: Bases of Voting in the Brazilian Congress." *Journal of Politics* 57(2): 324–343.

Cook, Sarah (2002). "From Rice Bowl to Safety Net: Insecurity and Social Protection during China's Transition." *Development Policy Review* 20 (5): 615–635.

Filippov, Mikhail, Peter C. Ordeshook, and Olga V. Shvetsova (2004). *Designing*

Federalism: A Theory of Self-Sustainable Institutions. Cambridge: Cambridge University Press.

Ferejohn, John (1974). *Pork Barrel Politics: Rivers and Harbors Legislation, 1947–1968.* Stanford, CA: Stanford University Press.

Fond razvitiia parlamentarizma v Rossii (1994). *Federal'noe Sobranie: Sovet Federatsii. Gosudarstvennaia Duma. Spravochnik.* Moscow.

Fond razvitiia parlamentarizma v Rossii (1996). *Federal'noe Sobranie: Sovet Federatsii. Gosudarstvennaia Duma. Spravochnik.* Moscow.

Haspel, Moshe, Thomas F. Remington, and Steven S. Smith (1998). "Electoral Institutions and Party Cohesion in the Russian Duma." *Journal of Politics* 60 (2): 417–439.

Hellman, Joel S. (1998). "Winners Take All: The Politics of Partial Reform in Postcommunist Transitions." *World Politics* 50 (2): 203–234.

Hellman, Joel S., Geraint Jones, and Daniel Kaufmann (2000). "Seize the State, Seize the Day: An Empirical Analysis of State Capture and Corruption in Transition Economies." Paper presented at Annual Bank Conference on Development Economics 2000 conference, Washington, DC.

Kaminski, Marek (1999). "How Communism Could Have Been Saved: Formal Analysis of Electoral Bargaining in Poland in 1989." *Public Choice* 98 (1–2): 83–109.

Kaminski, Marek (2002). "Do Parties Benefit from Electoral Manipulation? Electoral Laws and Heresthetics in Poland, 1989–93." *Journal of Theoretical Politics* 14 (3): 325–358.

Kaufmann, Daniel, and Paul Siegelbaum (1997). "Privatization and Corruption in Transition Economies." *Journal of International Affairs* 50 (2): 419–464.

Kunicová, Jana, and Thomas F. Remington (2005). "Mandates, Parties, and Dissent: The Effect of Electoral Rules on the Parliamentary Party Cohesion in the Russian State Duma, 1994–2003." Unpublished paper, California Institute of Technology and Emory University.

Kunicová, Jana, and Thomas F. Remington (forthcoming). "Mandates, Parties, and Dissent: The Effect of Electoral Rules on the Parliamentary Party Cohesion in the Russian State Duma, 1994–2003." *Party Politics.*

Lancaster, Thomas D., and W. David Patterson (1990). "Comparative Pork Barrel Politics: Perceptions from the West German Bundestag." *Comparative Political Studies* 22: 458–477.

Levitt, Steven D., and James M. Snyder, Jr. (1997). "The Impact of Federal Spending on House Election Outcomes." *Journal of Political Economy* 105 (1): 30–53.

Luong, Pauline Jones (2002). *Institutional Change and Political Continuity in Post-Soviet Central Asia: Power, Perceptions, and Pacts.* Cambridge: Cambridge University Press.

Milanovic, Branko (1999). *Income, Inequality, and Poverty during the Transition from Planned to Market Economy.* Washington, DC: World Bank Publications.

Milesi-Feretti, Gian Maria, Roberto Perotti, and Massimo Rostagno (2002). "Electoral Systems and the Composition of Public Spending." *Quarterly Journal of Economics* 117: 609–657.

Moser, Robert G. (2001). *Unexpected Outcomes: Electoral Systems, Political Parties, and Representation in Russia*. Pittsburgh: University of Pittsburgh Press.

Remington, Thomas F. (forthcoming). "Presidential Support in the Russian State Duma." *Legislative Studies Quarterly*.

Rogowski, Ronald (1987). "Trade and the Variety of Democratic Institutions." *International Organization* 41 (2): 203–223.

Rose, Richard, and Neil Munro (2002). *Elections without Order: Russia's Challenge to Vladimir Putin*. Cambridge: Cambridge University Press.

Samuels, David J. (2002). "Pork Barreling Is Not Credit Claiming or Advertising: Campaign Finance and the Sources of the Personal Vote in Brazil." *Journal of Politics* 64 (3): 845–863.

Shugart, Matthew Soberg (1998). "The Inverse Relationship between Party Strength and Executive Strength: A Theory of Politicians' Constitutional Choices." *British Journal of Political Science* 28: 1–29.

Shugart, Matthew Soberg, and Stephan Haggard (2001). "Institutions and Public Policy in Presidential Systems." In *Presidents, Parliaments and Policy*, ed. Stephan Haggard and Mathew D. McCubbins, 64–102. Cambridge: Cambridge University Press.

Slinko, Irina, Ekaterina Yakovlev, and Evgeny Zhuravskaya (2005). "Laws for Sale: Evidence from Russia." *American Law and Economics Review* 7(1): 284–318.

Smith, Steven S., and Thomas F. Remington (2001). *The Politics of Institutional Choice: The Formation of the Russian State Duma*. Princeton, NJ: Princeton University Press.

Stein, Robert M., and Kenneth N. Bickers (1994). "The Electoral Dynamics of the Federal Pork Barrel." *American Journal of Political Science* 40 (4): 1300–1326.

Stratmann, Thomas, and Martin Baur (2002). "Plurality Rule, Proportional Representation, and the German *Bundestag*: How Incentives to Pork-Barrel Differ across Electoral Systems." *American Journal of Political Science* 46(3): 506–514.

Thames, Frank C. (2001). "Legislative Voting Behavior in the Russian Duma: Understanding the Effect of Mandate." *Europe-Asia Studies* 53 (6): 869–884.

Weingast, Barry R. (1994). "Reflections on Distributive Politics and Universalism." *Political Research Quarterly* 47(2): 319–327.

Wilson, Rick K. (1986). "An Empirical Test of Preferences for the Political Pork Barrel: District Level Appropriations for River and Harbor Legislation, 1889–1913." *American Journal of Political Science* 30 (4): 729–754.

Zapeklyi, A., and P. Kozlov. (2001). *Tret'ia Gosudarsvennaia Duma: anatomicheskii atlas*. Moscow: Tsentr Politicheskoi Informatsii.

Part II

‖‖‖

Individuals

Chapter 6

||||||||||||||||||||||||||||||||||||||||||||||||||||||

Religion and Social Insurance
Evidence from the United States, 1970–2002

Kenneth Scheve and David Stasavage

One of the major puzzles for political economy and a central question in this volume is why some governments adopt policies that intervene heavily to redistribute income from rich to poor and to provide social insurance against adverse events, while other governments do much less in either regard.[1] Existing literature on the political economy of redistribution and the welfare state has identified a number of plausible factors that can influence policy outcomes in this area. These include, among others, prior levels of inequality, labor market structure, issue bundling and coalition politics, constitutional structures, and partisanship.[2] Models produced by economists have also emphasized that countries with otherwise similar economic and political preconditions may nonetheless wind up with widely divergent welfare state outcomes due to learning or expectations mechanisms that generate multiple equilibria.[3] In this chapter, we investigate empirically the argument that religious involvement and social spending can both serve to insure individuals against the effects of adverse life events.[4] Specifically, we argue that social insurance and religious engagement are two alternative mechanisms that limit the costs of adverse life events. As a consequence, religious individuals on average will prefer lower levels of social-insurance provision than will those who are secular. Moreover, if policy outcomes reflect variation in citizens' preferences, then we can also expect that countries with higher levels of religiosity will have lower levels of welfare spending.[5] This hypothesis is consistent with important stylized facts, like the large difference in both social-insurance provision and religiosity between the United States and many European countries. This chapter discusses a wide array of evidence that goes well beyond this simple comparison in support of the hypothesis, drawing on cross-country evidence, variation in policymaking across the U.S. states, and individual-level data on religiosity and attitudes toward social spending.

Our argument emphasizes differences between individuals who are religious, irrespective of their denomination, and individuals who are not religious, rather than emphasizing differences between individuals of different religious denominations. The latter approach has been more prominent in political economy, due to familiarity with Weber's arguments about Protestantism and capitalism, as well as to observations about the links between Christian Democracy and Catholic doctrine. We suggest that a distinct cleavage exists for the politics of social insurance in advanced industrial countries between the religious and the nonreligious, irrespective of denomination. Our predictions regarding religion and social insurance involve three core assumptions.

First, adverse life events involving unemployment, workplace accidents, illness, or retirement income do not only generate monetary costs for individuals; they also generate psychic costs that can involve a loss of self-esteem, stress, or related phenomena.

Second, we assume, consistent with a substantial theoretical and empirical literature in psychology, that religiosity provides some of the same psychic benefits as does being in good health, having a job, or having a sufficient retirement income.

Finally, as discussed in detail later in the chapter, we assume that individuals have a utility function such that monetary costs and psychic costs are not additively separable. More specifically, we assume, again building on recent empirical findings, that the psychological benefits of religion are greater for those with lower incomes. If one made a more restricted assumption that individuals suffer both monetary and psychic costs from adverse events such as job loss, but their utility is additively separable across these two factors, then religion might lower the psychic costs of adverse life events, but it would not influence an individual's demand for state social-insurance provision.

Our argument emphasizes how religious involvement can serve as an alternative to social insurance for individuals to buffer themselves against adverse events. In some cases religious participation will allow individuals to draw on communal material support in times of difficulty. Although these strictly material benefits from religion may be important, we draw on theoretical and empirical work suggesting that religion can also limit the psychic costs of adverse life events. So, for example, if the psychic costs of unemployment involve a loss of self-esteem, then religion may help insulate individuals against this effect, because their self-esteem is linked heavily to their religious engagement. Likewise, if falling ill or suffering a shock to one's retirement income produces stress, then religion may also serve as a buffer against this type of psychic cost. We will discuss how recent theoretical work by psychologists has emphasized that religious individuals may appraise adverse events as being less threatening to their overall self-image, beliefs, or well-being than would be the case for nonreligious individuals.[6] This theoretical work is supported by numerous recent empirical studies linking religiosity to higher levels of subjective well-being and lower incidence of depression.[7] Although earlier studies by psychologists, and in particular Freud's classic contribution on religion, *The Future of an Illusion* (1927), take a more negative view of religiosity, they share a commonality with recent work in emphasizing how religion can function as a buffer against uncontrollable external forces. In choosing the title for his work, Freud was certainly aware of Marx's (1844) description of religion as providing an illusory form of happiness for the people. We should note that another classic psychological portrayal of religion, *The Varieties of Religious Experience,* by William James (1902) took a less negative view of religiosity than that expressed by Freud or Marx, but James too emphasized religion's role as a buffer against external forces. In our study we do not seek to establish whether one should view religion positively or negatively in an overall sense, and our principal theoretical propositions do not depend on which normative conclusion one draws about religion, provided one accepts it can function as a type of insurance.

Under our assumptions, there should be a negative correlation between an individual's degree of religiosity and the extent to which he or she prefers government provision of social insurance. Further, to the extent that policy outcomes reflect individual preferences, there should also be a negative correlation between aggregate levels of religiosity and social-insurance spending. We evaluate these predictions empirically using cross-country, cross-regional, and individual-level data, focusing our attention on presenting evidence from the United States between 1970 and 2002.

Our cross-country evidence on religiosity is drawn from both the

World Values and ISSP surveys and involves questions about both the importance of religion in individuals' lives and time devoted to religious activities. We find that there is a significant negative correlation between religiosity and levels of social spending in the advanced industrial countries. Despite the small sample size, these results remain robust when controlling for a number of other potential determinants of social-spending levels, including the proportion of the population over age sixty-five, differences in the representation of religious denominations, and beliefs about the importance of effort versus exogenous factors in determining individual economic success.

Although these results are strongly suggestive of a link between religiosity and welfare spending, they are subject to the usual limitations of cross-country evidence with a small number of cases. For example, to what extent are there unobserved and thus omitted characteristics of these countries that might cause a spurious correlation between religiosity and social-insurance spending? To begin to address this possibility, in this chapter we evaluate the link between religiosity and policy outcomes in the U.S. states. For some areas of social-insurance policymaking, such as workers' compensation, U.S. states make their own policy decisions or at least have control over significant features of the programs that determine the extent of insurance. Consequently, evaluating the relationship between religiosity and policy outcomes in the U.S. states allows us to conduct a comparative investigation of the determinants of policy outcomes that includes many more observations than in a cross-country analysis of advanced industrial democracies and for which there is arguably less unobserved heterogeneity across cases. Focusing our attention on workers' compensation and unemployment insurance, we find evidence of a significant negative correlation between religiosity and the extent of social-insurance spending in the U.S. states.

To evaluate directly the individual-level prediction that more-religious individuals prefer lower levels of social-insurance provision, we examine the correlation between religious engagement in cross-country survey data for eleven advanced industrial democracies in 1996 and in survey data for the United States from the 1930s to the present, again focusing our attention on U.S. evidence for the contemporary period. We find that individuals who describe themselves as being religious systematically prefer lower levels of government spending on social insurance than do individuals who are more secular.

In the remainder of the chapter, we proceed as follows. First, we present preliminary evidence on the negative correlation between religiosity and the welfare state in advanced industrial countries and then consider several theoretical arguments that might explain this correlation. We consider existing arguments and then lay out our own argument about religiosity, together with the core assumptions on which it depends. Then we conduct initial empirical tests by showing a negative correlation between religiosity and social-insurance policy outcomes using evidence from the U.S. states between 1970 and 2000. Finally, we consider the hypothesis using individual-level data on religiosity and social-spending preferences, again paying particular attention to recent evidence from the United States.

Religion and Social Insurance

It is well known that there are large differences between advanced industrial countries in terms of levels of income redistribution and social-insurance provision. Moreover, it is well documented that there are significant cross-regional differences in social-insurance provision in federal countries in which regional governments have substantial policy autonomy (e.g., the United States). There is far less certainty about the explanations for these differences. Recent literature has not fully examined to what extent differences in degrees of religiosity might help account both for variation in individual attitudes toward social-insurance provision and for the sizable cross-country and cross-regional differences we observe in actual levels of social spending.

Figure 6.1 presents a simple scatter plot of the level of social spending in percentage of GDP for twenty OECD countries (average 1990–98), plotted against one measure of religiosity from the World Values Survey. Social spending here includes state provision of unemployment benefits, health spending, and retirement benefits. The horizontal axis corresponds to the average response in each country to the question "How important is God in your life?" with 1 corresponding to "not at all" and 10 corresponding to "very." As can be seen, there is a striking negative correlation between the degree of religiosity and levels of social spending. This negative correlation remains even if one drops potential extreme cases like the United States or Sweden. Although figure 6.1 is visually striking, it of

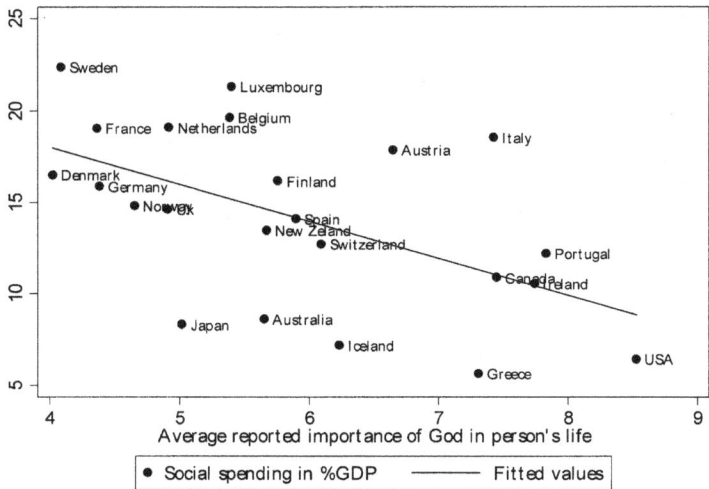

Fig. 6.1. Religiosity and social spending.

course does not tell us why we would expect to observe a negative correlation. In what follows we review existing arguments that may shed light on this question. We then outline our own argument.

Existing Arguments

There are a number of plausible reasons why religious beliefs and activity might influence individual attitudes toward social insurance. Explanations about religion and redistribution may emphasize differences in attitudes between individuals of different religious denominations, such as Catholic versus Protestant. Alternatively, explanations may emphasize differences in attitudes between people who are religiously active, irrespective of denomination, and those who do not hold religious beliefs.

Theories emphasizing the importance of denominational differences are well known in political economy, due in large part to Weber's work on Protestantism and the development of capitalism. This type of theory may also be relevant for understanding social insurance. So, for example, in cases where a religious tradition suggests that worldly success is attributable to individual effort or merit, one might find that believers prefer low levels of social insurance, whereas this would not be the case for members of other religious traditions. One might also suggest that the relative importance of different religious denominations helps determine the types of political parties that form in a country, and these parties themselves lead to different welfare state outcomes. For the case of European countries, it has often been argued that the welfare policies adopted by Christian Democratic parties are influenced by Catholic social teaching and that they differ systematically from the types of welfare policies pursued by Social Democratic parties (Esping-Andersen, 1990). Huber and Stephens (2001) find evidence that Social Democratic governments are associated with a larger public sector, though with fewer transfer payments than Christian Democratic governments. The cross-country empirical results that are discussed later in the chapter suggest, however, that although there is a positive correlation between the percentage of Catholics in a country and levels of social spending, this correlation is generally not statistically significant. Further, the evidence for a significant correlation when considering individual-level data on social-spending preferences is mixed. Finally, the key results regarding the negative correlation between religiosity and social insurance are unaffected by the inclusion of controls for denomination.

Beyond the issue of denominational differences, there are several possible channels through which religiosity, irrespective of denomination, might have an influence on state provision of social insurance. One important possibility is that being religious prompts individuals to become more altruistic, advocating greater spending on the disadvantaged. There is of course a long tradition in different world religions emphasizing charitable works, and we can also observe that religious doctrines about fairness appear to have influenced support of certain groups for the welfare state, such as Christian Democratic parties. However, although religiosity may lead to greater altruism, and consequently greater advocacy of social-insurance provision, for certain groups at certain times, the strong negative correlation between social spending and religiosity in figure 6.1 strongly suggests that religiosity may also have other effects that work in the opposite direction, and our statistical tests further support this view.

Another possible influence of religion on social insurance involves the fact that religion may lead individuals to draw particular inferences about how the economy functions. So, for example, individuals who are religious may be more likely to believe that hard effort will be rewarded with a higher income and that exogenous factors like family background do not represent inherent obstacles to economic success. As a consequence, they will favor less provision of social insurance. Piketty (1995) argues that differing beliefs about the extent to which income is dependent on individual effort are an important determinant of individual attitudes with regard to income redistribution. His argument can also be applied to the case of social insurance. Subsequent empirical evidence has supported this claim, demonstrating that differing beliefs about the determinants of economic success are correlated with individual preferences with regard to income redistribution, and social insurance, and that these beliefs are also correlated with cross-country differences in levels of social spending.[8] Whereas Piketty's model emphasizes how past personal experience influences beliefs about the importance of effort, Benabou and Tirole (2006) have recently suggested that certain individuals may find it useful to maintain a belief that the world is just (in the sense that hard effort is well rewarded) even when faced with contrary evidence. Maintaining a belief in a just world helps people to motivate themselves or their children. Benabou and Tirole also consider a Protestant-ethic extension to their model in which individuals have different beliefs about the likelihood that benefits in an afterlife depend on industriousness during one's lifetime. Drawing on Benabou and Tirole's contribution, one might argue that it is also possible that individuals with religious beliefs (Protestant or other) will have a particularly high propensity to believe the world is just. This does not imply that economic beliefs held by religious individuals will necessarily be inaccurate (it may be the case that nonreligious individuals have more systematically biased beliefs about the economy), but it does suggest a further mechanism through which religion might influence attitudes toward social-insurance provision.

Although there is strong empirical support for the proposition that beliefs about effort play an important role in determining redistributive preferences, the effect of religiosity on social spending does not appear to pass principally through this channel. If we return to the cross-country data used to produce figure 6.1, we find that even when controlling for beliefs about the importance of effort, using a survey response variable involving the importance of effort versus luck in determining economic success, we continue to observe a strong negative correlation between the component of religiosity not correlated with beliefs about effort and the component of social-spending levels not correlated with beliefs about effort. Further empirical tests suggest that the main empirical result that religious individuals prefer less state provision of social insurance is unaffected by the inclusion of this luck/effort variable.

Another possible channel through which religion may affect social-insurance provision is through an issue-bundling effect. If political competition involves both a standard left-right dimension, in which preferences are determined by income, and a second dimension, in which preferences are determined by religious beliefs, then it may be the case that religious individuals who are favorable to social insurance will support political candidates who are less favorable to social insurance but who nonetheless share similar views with regard to the second issue dimension. The second issue dimension could involve questions like whether abortion should be legal and whether homosexual marriage could be legalized (to take two recent examples from the U.S. context) or an issue involving church-state relations. Roemer (2001) has presented a theoretical framework for considering such issue-bundling effects, and in a previous contribution (Roemer, 1998) he provides empirical evidence that policy outcomes involving income redistribution may be affected by religion as a second issue dimension. Arguments about issue bundling suggest that religiosity may be correlated with support for candidates who are unfavorable to social insurance, and hence religiosity may be an important determinant of cross-national variation in levels of social spending. These arguments do not suggest, however, that religious individuals should be inherently less favorable to social-insurance provision.[9] The fact that our empirical tests show a negative correlation of religiosity with both aggregate data on social spending and individual data on social-spending preferences suggests that although religion may influence social insurance through an issue-bundling effect, this is not the only channel through which religion may affect social spending.[10]

The relationship observed in figure 6.1 between religiosity and social spending might also reflect a direct-substitution effect. According to this argument, individuals who are religious are no less demanding of insurance against adverse events than are other people, but because members of religious congregations receive material insurance benefits directly from their churches, they express less demand for social insurance provided by the state. Several recent articles including Hungerman (2005), Chen and Lind (2005), and Dehejia, DeLeire, and Luttmer (2007) have used U.S. evidence to explore whether membership in religious congregations involves a form of monetary insurance in which individuals give monetary contributions and members of congregations who suffer adverse events like unemployment receive tangible benefits from their church. The most direct mechanism for insurance is through charitable spending by churches. Hungerman shows that for members of the U.S. Presbyterian Church, charitable contributions have been negatively corre-lated with levels of state welfare spending. Dehejia, DeLeire, and Luttmer show that the consumption effects of shocks to household income are at-tenuated for members of religious congregations, which is also support-ive of the direct-substitution argument. Although these articles support the idea that religious participation can provide an alternative form of monetary insurance to state-sponsored programs, it seems less likely that these findings also provide an explanation for the gaps in social spending observed in figure 6.1 between highly religious and highly secular coun-tries. The simple reason is that according to the data used by Hungerman, Chen and Lind, and Dehejia, DeLeire, and Luttmer even in a highly reli-gious country like the United States, religious individuals on average give no more than 2 percent of their income to churches. This fact means that in the aggregate the amount of religious giving in the United States pales in comparison with the differences in social-spending levels observed in figure 6.1 between the United States and more secular countries. In order to explain this discrepancy one might suggest that insurance by religious organizations may also involve in-kind payments, such as the provision of subsidized child care. But these payments in-kind might still need to be funded by donations. Even if we assumed that payments in-kind were funded through exchanges of services, so that for example church mem-bers might agree to provide free child care for unemployed members who were seeking jobs, then in order to explain the differences observed in figure 6.1, the value of these services would have to be almost an order of magnitude larger than the direct monetary benefits provided by churches. Moreover, direct evidence of church activity, at least in the United States, is also inconsistent with the direct-substitution argument. For example, using extensive survey data on congregations during the 1990s, a study by Chaves (2004) finds no evidence that U.S. churches provide a "hidden social safety net." In dollar terms, social programs by most congregations are limited and tend to emphasize cultural objectives rather than social insurance. For earlier periods in U.S. history, similar evidence exists. A survey of Protestant church social activities conducted by Douglass and Brunner (1935) suggests the minimal engagement of Protestant churches in social-insurance activities at the time. As an example, in the Chicago area in 1933 the average church spent only $150 on direct relief annually. In sum, though a plausible theoretical mechanism, the direct-substitution argument lacks empirical support for explaining either the cross-country differences in social spending that we observe within the OECD or cross-regional variation in the United States.

One final possibility regarding the link between religion and social insurance is that the relationship is spurious and is due to the fact that both religiosity and social spending are endogenous to a country's level of economic development. The well-known secularization hypothesis suggests that as a country becomes richer, its population will grow less religious. It is also frequently observed that rich countries tend to have larger welfare states, on average, when compared with poor countries, though the theoretical reasons for this are not firmly established. To the extent that both of these hypotheses are accurate, we would expect to observe a negative correlation between religion and social-insurance provision, even if there was no causal relationship between the two variables. In fact, although this argument seems to go some way toward explaining the differences observed between OECD and non-OECD countries, within the sample of high-income OECD countries considered in figure 6.1 the level of economic development (measured in terms of log GDP per capita) is only weakly correlated with either social spending or religiosity.

Our Argument and Its Assumptions

Though we believe that religiosity undoubtedly influences social-insurance spending through several channels, we place particular emphasis on the possibility that religion and social spending are alternative mechanisms of insurance.[11] Government programs like unemployment insurance, workplace-accident insurance, health insurance, and pensions spending help cushion people against the effects of adverse life events, but personal engagement in a religion can also dampen the extent to which people are affected by events like job loss or ill health. In some cases religious participation may bring communal material support involving church funds or services like child care. However, we argue that beyond any purely material benefits, religious engagement can also provide important psychic benefits for individuals who suffer an adverse event. The main cost of social insurance is that it needs to be financed by taxes, and some individuals will inevitably wind up financing collective insurance without needing to draw heavily on its benefits. One of the main costs of religious engagement involves the fact that it draws time away from other activities that people may find pleasurable. If one accepts that religion and welfare state programs have related effects, and that they both have costs, then to the extent that individuals privately insure themselves through religion, they should logically prefer a lower level of insurance by the state.[12]

Our proposition about the effect of religiosity on social insurance involves three core assumptions. First, events like job loss or major sickness not only impose monetary costs on individuals; they also create psychic costs. These psychic costs can involve damage to self-esteem, stress, or the loss of enjoyment from having a network of friends. In a recent contribution, Blanchard and Tirole (2003) have argued that the design of national unemployment insurance ought to take into account the fact that events like job loss involve both monetary and psychic costs. There is abundant empirical evidence to support this proposition. Clark and Oswald (1994) used data from the British Household Panel Study to investigate the correlation of unemployment with subjective measures of individual well-being and with questionnaires frequently used by psychologists to measure "psychological distress." Based on this second set of measures they found that unemployment produced as large an estimated utility loss as did events like divorce or marital separation. Di Tella, MacCulloch, and Oswald (2003) provide further evidence in this regard.

Our second core assumption is that religiosity provides some of the same psychic benefits as does being in a good state in terms of health, employment, or retirement income. There are several reasons why religion may help insure individuals against adverse life events. For one, people who are religious may derive psychic benefits from having a network of friends from their church, mosque, or synagogue, and such associations are likely to provide comfort during times of difficulty in the same way as would friends within the workplace.[13] But this type of psychic benefit should logically exist for any type of collective leisure activity. Religiosity may also have more profound psychic benefits that make it exceptional, if not unique, in influencing the way individuals appraise adverse events like job loss or ill health (Pargament, 1997; Smith, McCullough, and Poll, 2003; Park, Cohen, and Herb, 1990). So, for example, religious individuals may be more likely to judge that such events do not pose challenges to their self-esteem, their overall beliefs, or their life goals, and they may even see adverse events as a challenge offering opportunities for spiritual growth.[14] In an extensive study, Pargament (1997) demonstrates how religiosity also influences the different coping mechanisms that individuals use to confront adverse life events. In making such arguments these authors draw on the theory of stress, appraisal, and coping developed by

Lazarus and Folkman (1984).[15] Lazarus and Folkman define cognitive appraisal as a process through which the person evaluates whether a particular encounter with the environment is relevant to his or her well-being and, if so, in what way (Folkman and Lazarus, 1986, 572). This process could involve a judgment about whether an event poses potential harm to one's self-esteem. Lazarus and Folkman go on to suggest that a range of personality characteristics including values, commitments, goals, and beliefs about oneself and the world helps to define the stakes that the person identifies as having relevance to well-being in specific stressful situations. Although Lazarus and Folkman do not themselves emphasize the importance of religiosity for appraisal, it is not difficult to understand why religious beliefs might have an important influence on this process. These ideas of contemporary psychologists about religion as a buffer against external forces are also consistent with classic work in the field of psychology. So, although Freud (1927) took a negative view of religion, he too emphasized its role in providing individuals with a mental buffer against external forces. Likewise, a less negative portrayal of religion by William James (1902) also emphasized its insurance aspects.

In addition to the strong theoretical arguments, there is clear empirical evidence to support the idea that religion has positive effects on the psychological state of individuals and that it helps in responding to adverse life events. A number of studies have demonstrated that individuals who describe themselves as being religious tend to have higher subjectively measured levels of life satisfaction. This is shown in the study by Ellison (1991), as well as in a second study by Ellison, Gay, and Glass (1989) which demonstrates that religiosity has a positive correlation with subjective life satisfaction even when controlling for levels of sociability. This correlation suggests that the primary psychic benefits of religion involve mechanisms other than simple social support. It is also interesting to note that a number of recent empirical studies have demonstrated that there is a lower incidence of depression in individuals who describe themselves as being religious.[16] This finding applies in particular to what psychologists refer to as intrinsic measures of religiosity as opposed to extrinsic religiosity. Intrinsic religiosity refers to individuals who view religious belief as a goal in and of itself, whereas extrinsic religiosity refers to individuals who may become religious in order to achieve other goals, such as making acquaintances. Although we do not emphasize the difference between intrinsic and extrinsic religiosity in our own empirical work, our empirical measures of religiosity correspond more closely to the intrinsic category.[17] In addition to this empirical evidence, it is important to note that Clark and Lelkes (2004) have shown that individuals who are religious suffer from significantly lower estimated losses in subjective utility as a result of episodes like unemployment. This finding supports our second assumption quite directly. Finally, at least one study has found that people who describe themselves as being religious tend to purchase significantly less life insurance than do nonreligious people, which is also consistent with our assumptions (Burnett and Palmer, 1984).

Our third and final assumption is that individuals have utility functions such that monetary consumption and psychic benefits are not additively separable.[18] More specifically, we assume that the psychological benefits of religion are greater for those with lower incomes. This assumption is important to our argument in that the overall benefits to an individual of consumption and psychological well-being depend on each other, and, therefore, material social insurance that helps with consumption is linked to religiosity that influences psychological well-being. This assumption is consistent with empirical studies indicating higher levels of religiosity generally and religious coping in response to adverse events specifically among the poor, elderly, minorities, and women (see, e.g., Pargament, 1997, p. 156). The recent article by Dehejia, DeLeire, and Luttman (2007) provides further evidence in this regard from the U.S. National Survey of Families and Households. They find evidence that religious involvement may do more for low-income than high-income individuals to attenuate the negative effects on subjective well-being of adverse events like unemployment. This is consistent with our assumption of nonadditive separability, as is the conclusion by Dehejia, DeLeire, and Luttman (2007) that the psychic insurance effect of religion is more clearly observed for African Americans in the United States than for whites.[19]

Religiosity and Policy Outcomes

In figure 6.1, we presented evidence that, consistent with our argument, there is a negative correlation between average levels of religiosity in a country and spending on social insurance in advanced industrial democracies. In Scheve and Stasavage (2006a), we examine this correlation in greater detail. Specifically, we show that it holds for alternative measures of religiosity such as religious attendance; that it is robust to the inclusion of controls for other determinants of social spending such as income inequality, size of the elderly population, trade openness, the presence of majoritarian electoral institutions, real GDP per capita, ethnic heterogeneity, and beliefs about the importance of effort versus luck in determining economic success; and that there is some evidence that the correlation indicates a casual effect.[20]

Although the comparative evidence is strongly suggestive of a link between religiosity and social-insurance spending, it is subject to the usual limitations of cross-country evidence with a small number of cases. To strengthen the empirical case, in this section we evaluate the relationship between religiosity and policy outcomes in the U.S. states between 1970 and 2000. For some areas of social-insurance policymaking, such as workers' compensation, U.S. states make their own policy decisions or at least have control over significant features of the programs that determine the extent of insurance. Consequently, evaluating the relationship between religiosity and policy outcomes in the U.S. states allows us to conduct a comparative investigation of the determinants of policy outcomes that includes many more observations than in a cross-country analysis of advanced industrial democracies and for which there is arguably less unobserved heterogeneity across cases. Focusing our attention on workers' compensation and unemployment insurance, we find evidence of a significant negative correlation between religiosity and the extent of social-insurance spending in the U.S. states.[21]

The dependent variables for this analysis are "Workers' Compensation" and "Unemployment Insurance." Workers' Compensation is equal to each state's real per capita workers'-compensation spending in thousands of 1982 dollars and has a mean of 0.023 and a standard deviation of 0.033. Unemployment Insurance is equal to real per capita unemployment-insurance-compensation spending also in thousands of 1982 dollars and has a mean of 0.061 and a standard deviation of 0.030.[22] Each measure is a state decade average for the 1970s, 1980s, and 1990s, as the unit of analysis is the state observed three times, once for each decade.[23]

We employ two different strategies and sources for measuring religiosity across states. The first, "Religious Attendance," is based on state averages of survey responses about the frequency of church attendance from the General Social Survey (GSS). The GSS data with state-identifying information is available between 1973 and 2002 for all years for which a GSS survey was conducted. We use respondents for 1973–1979, 1980–1989, and 1990–1999 to calculate average state responses to the question "How often do you attend religious services?" with responses coded from o corresponding to "never" to 8 corresponding to "several times a week" for each decade. State averages of Religious Attendance range from 2.9 to 5.8, with an average of 4.0. This variable captures religiosity as revealed by the reported behavior of individuals within a state. The main limitations of this measure are that the GSS sampling frame does not include all states in each decade and that because there is variation across states in the number of individual survey respondents, there is variation across states in the precision of the estimates. Fortunately, the number of missing state-decade observations is modest. Out of a possible 144 observations, we observe Religious Attendance for 116. Nonetheless, we employ a second measure of religiosity available for all observations in part to further evaluate the potential importance of missingness in this variable. To address potential variation in the precision of Religious Attendance across states, we weight our analyses using this variable by the number of individual survey respondents in the state used to calculate the average.

The second measure of state religiosity, "Religious Membership," is equal to the proportion of the population that are members of a church. The data is available for each state for 1971, 1980, and 1990 and each of these years is used to record religiosity for its respective decade.[24] State averages of Religious Membership vary between 0.26 and 0.81, with an average of 0.51. The main limitations of this data are that it does not record membership totals for non-Judeo-Christian denominations, that it is based on self-reports from churches and synagogues, and that religiosity can vary significantly among individuals who fulfill the requirement of belonging to a church. These limitations, however, should not be exaggerated. Judeo-Christian denominations still constitute the great proportion of U.S. citizens who are religious, and clearly membership indicates on average greater religiosity than nonmembership. Moreover, we find this data to be highly correlated with our comparable survey-based measures.[25]

In evaluating whether states with more-religious populations spend less on social-insurance programs, we need to control for other factors associated with the extent of social-insurance provision. These include the following:

"Catholic" is equal to the total number of Catholics as a proportion of the state population. In those specifications in which we use our survey-based measure of religiosity, Religious Attendance, we use a survey-based estimate of the proportion of Catholics, constructed analogously to Religious Attendance. In those specifications employing the Religious Membership variable, we use estimates of the proportion of Catholics in each state from the same membership-data source. As discussed in the previous section, there are a number of reasons why doctrinal differences might lead individuals of different denominations to have different levels of support for social-insurance spending.

"Poverty" is the state poverty rate. This variable is a measure of the overall demand for state insurance and redistributive programs and thus is expected to be positively correlated with each dependent variable. Of course, poorer states may have fewer resources for all public programs, leading to lower spending. Consequently, the overall effect of poverty on each dependent variable is ex ante unclear.[26]

"Unionization" is equal to the percentage of nonagricultural wage and salary employees who are union members, including employees in the public sector. Organized labor strongly supports generous workers'-compensation and unemployment-insurance programs, and thus we expect that states that are more strongly unionized have higher spending levels.[27]

"Democratic Governor" is an indicator variable equal to 1 if the governor of the state is a Democrat and 0 otherwise. Democrats are expected to be associated with greater provision of insurance due to the sources of electoral support for the party.[28]

"Citizen Ideology" is a measure, developed by Berry et al. (1998), based on a combination of the ideological positions of congressional candidates and their public support . The variable increases with the liberalism of the citizens in the state, with the expectation that states with more-liberal citizens will be more likely to implement generous social-insurance policies.[29]

"South" is an indicator variable equal to 1 if the state is in the south and 0 otherwise.[30] Southern states have often been considered to have less-generous social-insurance and welfare systems due to limited electoral competition during important phases of welfare state development (Key, 1949).

"Percent Black" is equal to the percentage of the total state population that is black. A number of studies in both political science and economics have argued that there is less support among individuals for generous social policies and less actual provision of such policies in states with higher concentrations of blacks (see, e.g., Luttmer 2001 and Alesina, Glaeser, and Sacerdote 2001).[31]

"Percent Urban" is equal to the percentage of the total state population living in urban areas. Urban residents may be more likely to be supportive of generous social policies because of differences in both the risks that they face and the availability of alternative, non-state-provided forms of insurance (see, e.g., Rodden 2005). Moreover, urban citizens may be less likely to be religious, making the inclusion of this variable particularly important for estimating the relationship between religiosity and social-insurance provision.[32]

Table 6.1 reports the OLS coefficient estimates and their robust standard errors, adjusted for clustering by state, for the regression of Workers' Compensation and Unemployment Insurance on religiosity and these control variables. For the results reported for Workers' Compensation in the first and second columns, there is a negative and significant correlation between spending and both the attendance and membership measures of religiosity. The magnitude of these estimates is also significant in substantive terms. For the Religious Attendance variable, it implies that an increase in average state attendance by 1 point (roughly the difference between California and Virginia) is associated with a decrease in spending that is about two-thirds the standard deviation of the Workers' Compensation variable. The estimates reported in the third and fourth columns for Unemployment Insurance are more mixed. For the specification using the Religious Attendance variable to measure religiosity, the coefficient estimate is negative but small in magnitude and not statistically significant. However, there is evidence of a significant negative correlation between the Religious Membership variable and unemployment-insurance spending.

The results for the control variables are with some exceptions broadly consistent with previous results reported in the literature. For the Workers' Compensation results in the first and second columns, there is some evidence that poverty, unionization, and democratic control of the governorship are positively correlated with spending, while the percentage of the population that is black is negatively correlated. Perhaps most important for our purposes is that the coefficient estimate for the Catholic variable is actually negative, although not statistically significant. There is not evidence in this data that states with many Catholic voters actually spend more on workers' compensation, as might be predicted based on the idea that Catholic social teachings influence the social policy preferences of adherents. For the Unemployment Insurance variable, there is some evidence that poverty, unionization, urbanization, the percentage of the population that is black, and liberal political ideologies are all positively correlated with spending on unemployment insurance. The results for the Catholic variable are mixed. The coefficient estimate is positive in

TABLE 6.1
Social-Insurance Spending in U.S. States, 1970–2000

Regressor	OLS Estimates			
	Workers' Compensation		*Unemployment Insurance*	
Religious Attendance	−0.021		−0.001	
	(0.006)		(0.004)	
	0.001		0.799	
Religious Membership		−0.082		−0.036
		(0.037)		(0.015)
		0.032		0.017
Catholic	−0.033	−0.037	0.016	0.059
	(0.024)	(0.026)	(0.023)	(0.024)
	0.189	0.160	0.484	0.018
Poverty	0.001	0.001	0.001	0.002
	(0.001)	(0.001)	(0.001)	(0.001)
	0.097	0.386	0.183	0.036
Unionization	0.001	0.002	0.001	0.002
	(0.001)	(0.001)	(0.001)	(0.000)
	0.134	0.033	0.078	0.001
Democratic Governor	0.015	0.019	−0.009	0.003
	(0.006)	(0.008)	(0.009)	(0.006)
	0.026	0.020	0.333	0.581
Citizen Ideology	−0.000	−0.000	0.001	0.001
	(0.000)	(0.000)	(0.000)	(0.000)
	0.621	0.639	0.000	0.004
South	−0.003	0.002	−0.011	−0.004
	(0.009)	(0.011)	(0.006)	(0.006)
	0.784	0.855	0.065	0.532
Percent Black	−0.001	−0.001	0.001	0.000
	(0.000)	(0.000)	(0.000)	(0.000)
	0.014	0.008	0.103	0.110
Percent Urban	−0.000	0.000	0.000	0.000
	(0.000)	(0.000)	(0.000)	(0.000)
	0.238	0.451	0.755	0.101
Decade Fixed Effects	Yes	Yes	Yes	Yes
Standard Error of Regression	0.020	0.026	0.019	0.019
Observations	116	144	116	144

The dependent variable for the results reported in the first two columns is *Workers' Compensation* and in the last two columns is *Unemployment Insurance*. The specifications using the survey measures of religiosity and denomination—the first and third columns—are weighted for the number of respondents used to calculate the state-level measures. For each estimate, its robust standard error clustered by state is reported in parentheses followed by the p-value.

both specifications but statistically significant in only the results reported in the fourth column.

Overall the evidence reported in table 6.1 is consistent with the prediction that more-religious polities are likely to implement less-generous social-insurance policies and, as such, complements the cross-country results discussed earlier. To evaluate the state-level evidence further, we estimated several alternative specifications. First, we considered the possibility that our coefficient estimates for religiosity are biased because we control for a number of factors that may be consequences of religiosity. For example, states that are more religious may have citizens with less-liberal ideologies or may be less likely to have Democratic governors precisely because these things are associated with greater social-insurance spending. Controlling for such factors may attenuate our estimates for the effect of religiosity on spending. We dropped all the control variables except the variable measuring the presence of Catholics and the decade dummy variables. This change in specification did not substantially affect the results.

Second, we considered two strategies for dealing with the possibility that the estimates are biased due to endogeneity and/or omitted variables. This is of particular concern if we want to interpret the partial correlations in the OLS analyses as indicating the causal effect of religiosity on social-insurance spending.

The first strategy is to implement a simple identification strategy using historical levels (1926) of state religiosity and the strength of Protestantism as instrumental variables for current levels of religiosity. These variables are highly correlated with current levels of religiosity, and there is little reason to think that they have an effect on current social-insurance spending except through their correlation with current levels of religiosity, and they thus constitute plausible instruments for current state religiosity.[33] The IV results for the specifications with the Workers' Compensation dependent variable are qualitatively similar to the OLS results reported in table 6.1.[34] The IV results with the Unemployment Insurance dependent variable are stronger than the OLS results for the Religious Attendance measure of religiosity and weaker for the Religious Membership measure, but neither is statistically significant.[35] Overall, the IV results strengthen our confidence of a link between religiosity and spending on workers' compensation and somewhat weaken our confidence of a similar link with unemployment insurance.[36]

The second strategy recognizes the potential limitations of our proposed instruments. Although we are able to verify empirically that the instruments are significantly correlated with our measures of religiosity, and we are able to provide a test evaluating whether the overidentifying assumptions are valid, this does not guarantee that the assumptions necessary for the instruments to be valid hold sufficiently well in our data. For example, it seems possible that there may be unobserved fixed characteristics of the states that are correlated with the spending variables. Because our instruments are measured at only one time, 1926, for each state, they might be correlated with other fixed characteristics of the states not controlled for in our specification, which would violate the exclusion restriction and could significantly bias our IV estimates. An alternative strategy for accounting for potential bias due to an unobserved and thus omitted factor is to control for it using proxy variables. For example, a fixed unobserved factor that might make some states both more religious and spend less on social insurance should be correlated with historical measures of religiosity. By controlling for historical religiosity, specifically 1926 religious membership, we can arguably control for the unobserved factor hypothesized to bias the OLS results in the original specification.[37] We find that adding this variable to the specifications reported in table 6.1 has little effect except to marginally strengthen our evidence of a negative partial correlation between Religious Attendance and Religious Membership and both measures of social-insurance spending.

To further assess the robustness of our results we considered an alternative measure of state social-insurance spending equal to real per capita family assistance in 1982 dollars. It is not clear that this is a good test of our argument because family-assistance spending includes programs such as AFDC/TANF that have a substantial redistributive as opposed to insurance component. It is essential to understand that our argument does not predict a difference between more-religious and more-secular polities on purely static redistributive-spending policies. Consequently, only to the extent that family-assistance programs also provide insurance does this measure offer an opportunity to further test our argument.[38] Employing identical specifications as those reported in table 6.1, we find that Religious Attendance is significantly negatively correlated with spending on family assistance but that Religious Membership is not.

Finally, a couple potential objections to the evidence presented thus far are both related to the time at which the comparative and state evidence was collected. It might be the case that the negative correlation that we observe between religion and social insurance using current data does not hold for earlier periods. Authors like Fogel (2000), McLoughlin (1978), and Chen and Lind (2005) have suggested that religion actually had a positive impact on the development of the U.S. welfare state in the first half of the twentieth century. A related problem is that using current correlations between religiosity and social-insurance provision to investigate causation may be complicated by the presence of policy feedback, the tendency for policies once enacted to reshape the political environment (Hacker and Pierson, 2002; Pierson, 1993). In Scheve and Stasavage (2006b), we present evidence of a negative correlation between state religiosity and early adoption of workers'-compensation programs from 1910 to 1930 in the U.S. states and a negative correlation between state religiosity and workers'-compensation benefit levels for the same period. This evidence suggests that the negative relationship between state religiosity and social-insurance spending is evident for early periods as well and may have played an important role in U.S. welfare state development.

Religiosity and Individual Social-Insurance Preferences

Overall, the country-level and cross-regional evidence suggests that polities that are more religious on average have lower levels of social-insurance spending. The key argument of this chapter is that this relationship is a consequence of religion and welfare state spending being substitute mechanisms for insuring individuals against adverse life events. A key prediction of this explanation is that within countries, individuals who are religious will prefer lower levels of social-insurance provision than individuals who are secular.

In Scheve and Stasavage (2006a), we examine this prediction using international individual-level survey data from the ISSP for eleven advanced industrial democracies in 1996 and find substantial evidence that individuals engaged in more religious activities are significantly less likely to support increased spending on social insurance. In this section, we extend this analysis by evaluating this prediction in greater detail using the General Social Survey (GSS) for the United States from 1973 to 2002. This survey provides us with the opportunity to examine the relationship between religiosity and social-insurance preferences across a greater span of time and with alternative measures of policy preferences.

Theoretically, the dependent variable for this analysis is preferences about the tax level and social-insurance benefit. Ideally, we want to distinguish between individuals who prefer relatively higher taxes and benefits and those who prefer less of both. The GSS has asked a number of relevant questions about social-insurance spending preferences over the past thirty years. Our analysis focuses attention on responses to two questions, one on health spending and one on pension spending, that are especially well suited for our purposes because of the wording of the questions and the number of years in which the questions were asked.[39]

The first dependent variable is based on responses to the following question:

> We are faced with many problems in this country, none of which can be solved easily or inexpensively. I'm going to name some of these problems and for each one I'd like you to tell me whether you think we're spending too much money on it, too little money, or about the right amount . . . improving and protecting the nation's health.

The dependent variable "Health Spending" is set equal to 1 for "too much," 2 for "about the right amount," and 3 for "too little" and thus increases with preferences for more spending. Similarly, the second dependent variable is based on responses to the same question as above but with the ending "social security." The dependent variable "Pension Spending" is coded analogously to Health Spending and as such increases with preferences for more social-security spending. The variable Health Spending was asked to at least a subsample of respondents for all years in which there was a GSS from 1973 to 2002, but the social-security question did not begin to be asked until 1984, and so coverage is from 1984 to 2002 for Pension Spending. Unfortunately, no question is asked for workers'-compensation or unemployment-insurance spending preferences on a consistent basis in the GSS, though we will discuss briefly the results for an employment-assistance question asked much less frequently as well as some other alternative measures of spending preferences available in the GSS.

To measure individual religiosity, we construct the variable "Religious Attendance" based on responses to the question "How often do you attend religious services?" used in the state-level analysis discussed earlier. The variable is coded from 0, corresponding to "never," to 8, corresponding to "several times a week."[40]

In evaluating whether more-religious individuals are less supportive of social spending, we need to control for the other factors likely to affect support for social-insurance spending. These include the following:

- *Income Quartile* ranges between 1 and 4 indicating the quartile of the respondent's family income. To the extent that higher-income individuals are less likely to suffer an adverse event requiring state support or are better able to self-insure for such an event, we can expect them to be less favorable to social spending.

- *Female* is a dichotomous indicator variable equal to 1 for female respondents and 0 for males. This is a standard control variable included in individual analyses, based on the fact that there have been consistent differences observed between males and females for certain policy preferences. Differences could occur either if males and females are socialized to have different preferences or if the variable "Female" here actually proxies for an economic condition, such as greater average income insecurity.

- *Age* is equal to the respondent's age in years. Older individuals should be more likely to favor social spending to the extent that they are more likely to draw on state-provided health or retirement benefits.

- *Black* is a dichotomous indicator variable equal to 1 for individuals who self-identify as black and 0 otherwise. Previous studies have indicated that blacks on average prefer more-generous social-insurance policies. Again, this difference could occur either if blacks are socialized to have different preferences or if the variable "Black" here actually proxies for an economic condition, such as greater average income insecurity.

- *Education Years* is equal to the respondent's highest year in school completed. The variable ranges from 0 for "no formal schooling" to 20 for eight or more years of postsecondary education. Education is often used as a measure of human capital and thus captures an individual's long-run earning potential. Thus, we expect it to have a similar effect on support for social spending as income, with more-educated respondents less favorable of spending. It also may be the case that more-educated respondents may be able to adjust more quickly to adverse shocks, reinforcing the income effect.

- *Unemployed* is a dichotomous indicator variable set to 1 for unemployed respondents and 0 otherwise. Our theoretical argument suggests that those who are currently in the bad state (e.g., unemployed) should have a clear preference for higher social insurance than those who are in the good state (e.g., employed). Of course, given that our primary measures of social-insurance spending preferences are for health and pensions, this variable may only be relevant as another measure of income or overall income insecurity.

- *Catholic* and *Protestant* are dichotomous indicator variables set equal to 1 if the respondent is of the respective denomination and o otherwise. As discussed previously, there are a number of reasons why doctrinal differences might lead individuals of different denominations to have different levels of support for social-insurance spending.

- *Partisanship* ranges from 0, indicating that the respondent considers him- or herself to be a strong Democrat, to 6, indicating the respondent considers him- or herself to be a strong Republican. To the extent that we think partisanship is above all determined by attitudes toward social insurance and redistribution, it would not make sense to enter this variable in the regression, because it would suggest that our dependent variable is essentially an alternative measure of one of our independent variables. However, we nonetheless include this last variable in our second regression to control for several possibilities that may affect our inferences. For example, if religious individuals tend to support Republicans for social policy reasons (e.g., abortion policies), once they decide to vote on the right they may also tend to adopt the attitudes of the political right with regard to social insurance, regardless of their prior economic views. Moreover, a common view in the literature on partisanship is that it is stable and determined relatively early in life. Under this view of partisanship, it is sensible to think about it as an explanatory variable for policy opinions.

Furthermore, we include a set of year dummy variables in each specification estimated in order to account for common shocks that may influence average support for social spending in a given year.

Table 6.2 reports OLS coefficient estimates for the regressions of Health Spending and Pension Spending on religiosity and these control variables. For each dependent variable, there are two specifications reported, one omitting the Partisanship variable and one including it. Across all four specifications, we observe a negative and highly significant correlation between Religious Attendance and the measures of social-spending preferences.

The results for the control variables are generally consistent with expectations. For the dependent variable Health Spending, women and blacks prefer more spending, whereas respondents with higher incomes, Protestants, and Republicans prefer less. Counter to expectations, older respondents prefer lower spending on health. There is no evidence in this data that Catholics, the unemployed, or the more educated are more or

TABLE 6.2
Support for Social Insurance Spending in the United States, 1973–2002

Regressor	Health Spending		Pension Spending	
	Health Spending		*Pension Spending*	
Religious Attendance	−0.011	−0.010	−0.010	−0.009
	(0.002)	(0.002)	(0.002)	(0.002)
	0.000	0.000	0.000	0.000
Income Quartile	−0.006	−0.001	−0.025	−0.020
	(0.004)	(0.004)	(0.004)	(0.004)
	0.089	0.728	0.000	0.000
Female	0.072	0.066	0.117	0.108
	(0.008)	(0.008)	(0.008)	(0.008)
	0.000	0.000	0.000	0.000
Age	−0.002	−0.002	−0.003	−0.003
	(0.000)	(0.000)	(0.000)	(0.000)
	0.000	0.000	0.000	0.000
Black	0.169	0.100	0.199	0.145
	(0.011)	(0.012)	(0.012)	(0.013)
	0.000	0.000	0.000	0.000
Education Years	−0.001	0.001	−0.030	−0.029
	(0.001)	(0.001)	(0.001)	(0.001)
	0.544	0.374	0.000	0.000
Unemployed	0.033	0.026	−0.011	−0.013
	(0.021)	(0.021)	(0.026)	(0.025)
	0.122	0.218	0.669	0.609
Catholic	0.018	0.014	0.092	0.095
	(0.014)	(0.014)	(0.014)	(0.014)
	0.196	0.296	0.000	0.000
Protestant	−0.056	−0.032	0.035	0.053
	(0.012)	(0.013)	(0.012)	(0.013)
	0.000	0.010	0.005	0.000
Partisanship		−0.044		−0.032
		(0.002)		(0.002)
		0.000		0.000
Year Fixed Effects	Yes	Yes	Yes	Yes
Standard Error of Regression	0.583	0.577	0.596	0.591
Observations	23,383	22,987	22,851	22,486

The dependent variable for the results reported in the first two columns is *Health Spending* and in the last two columns is *Pension Spending*. For each estimate, its robust standard error is reported in parentheses followed by the p-value.

less likely to support health spending than other respondents. For Pension Spending, women, blacks, Catholics, and Protestants prefer more spending, whereas richer and more-educated respondents and Republicans prefer less. Again surprisingly, older respondents prefer lower spending, and there is no evidence that the unemployed have systematically different policy preferences.

Among these results, the estimates for the Catholic and Protestant variables merit further discussion. Since both measures are included, the coefficients indicate the policy preferences of each group compared to a mixed baseline group from other faiths and the nonreligious. Substantively, perhaps the more interesting question is whether there are differences between the groups. There are, and despite the fact that the sign for the Protestant variable switches across the two specifications, the differences are consistent across all specifications—Catholics prefer more spending than Protestants. This result has a number of possible interpretations. As discussed earlier, it could be the result of differences in doctrine between Catholics and most Protestant denominations. Alternatively, it may simply indicate differences in economic risk across members of the groups that are not measured by our control variables. Scheve and Stasavage (2006b) find similar differences between Catholics and Protestants for 1930s U.S. survey data and discuss both these possibilities. Although both interpretations are possible, systematic differences in economic risks between Catholics and Protestants seem much less plausible for the contemporary period in the United States as opposed to the 1930s. Finally, it is worth emphasizing that the differences found between Catholics and Protestant when employing U.S. survey data are not replicated in the our comparative analyses using ISSP data from eleven countries (see Scheve and Stasavage 2006a).

In addition to adding the partisanship measure, we estimated several alternative specifications. First, we consider a number of potentially important omitted variables. We added a measure recording whether or not the respondent was a member of a union, a measure indicating the size/urbanness of the place in which the respondent lived, and a measure of the importance that the respondent places on effort versus luck in determining economic success. The inclusion of these additional variables did not substantially change either the magnitude or statistical significance of the coefficient estimate for religiosity in either the Health Spending or Pension Spending analysis.

Second, we consider the possibility that religiosity may not be completely exogenous to an individual's policy opinions. We are particularly concerned with the possibility that there may be unobserved factors that lead individuals both to become more religious and to prefer less social insurance. As discussed earlier, one simple approach to deal with this problem is to attempt to identify a proxy variable that is correlated with the unobserved factor. In the context of the GSS data, one possibility is the religiosity of each respondent's parents. We added a variable recording parents' religious attendance to the specifications in table 6.2 and found qualitatively similar results.[41]

Third, we consider alternative measures of social-insurance spending preferences. There are very few questions that are asked consistently in the GSS that arguably capture social-insurance spending preferences. One possibility is responses to a question that has the exact same wording as for Health Spending and Pension Spending but the spending category is "welfare." This variable was asked in all the GSS surveys from 1972 to 2002. It is not clear that this is a good test of our argument because welfare spending may be interpreted as spending on programs that have a substantial insurance component (e.g., unemployment insurance, health spending, and pensions) or it may be interpreted as primarily about spending programs that provide redistributive transfers to the poor. As discussed earlier, our argument does not predict a difference between the religious and secular on purely static redistributive spending policies. Consequently, only to the extent that the term "welfare" is associated with programs with a significant insurance program targeted broadly does the question offer an opportunity to further test our argument. We replicated the analysis in table 6.2 for the "welfare" question and did find a significant negative correlation between religiosity and preferences for more spending. This is consistent with the main argument of the chapter.[42]

Fourth, one potential objection to our analysis is that the negative correlation that we observe between religiosity and social-insurance preferences in contemporary data does not hold for earlier periods. This might be the case if the correlation was a result of religious individuals supporting Republicans for social-policy reasons (e.g., abortion policy) and then adopting the attitudes of the political right with regard to social insurance, regardless of their prior economic views. In this case, religiosity and social-insurance preferences are negatively related only because of how the issues are bundled in contemporary American politics. Our controls for partisanship go some way in accounting for this possibility in our analysis. However, further evidence can be marshaled by looking at historical data. For example, the health-spending question was asked in the 1970s, before the coalition between fiscal-policy and social conservatives had been substantially strengthened by the Reagan presidency and Newt Gingrich's "Contract with America." If we limit our analysis to only the 1970s, the results are substantially the same. More dramatically, Scheve and Stasavage (2006b) report a significant negative correlation between religious participation and support for social-insurance spending for individual survey data in the 1930s.

Conclusion

We have argued that the literature on the political economy of social-insurance provision should take greater consideration of religiosity as a factor determining welfare state spending outcomes. If social insurance and religious engagement are two alternative mechanisms that limit the psychic costs of adverse life events, then we can expect individuals who are religious, irrespective of denomination, to be less demanding of social insurance by the state. Our empirical results show that this prediction holds up both when considering variation in levels of religiosity and welfare state spending across countries and regions, as well as when considering differences in individual attitudes within countries. Our argument clearly presents a highly stylized view of how choices regarding religion and social insurance are made, but we believe it may nonetheless shed light on the large variations in religiosity and welfare state spending observed between different polities.

NOTES

1. In addition to presenting new empirical evidence on religiosity and social insurance in the United States between 1970 and 2002, this chapter also draws on the theoretical discussion and empirical results presented in Scheve and Stasavage (2006a, 2006b).

2. Iversen and Soskice (2001), Moene and Wallerstein (2001), Esping-Andersen (1990), Huber and Stephens (2001), Meltzer and Richard (1981), Swank and Steinmo (2002), Franzese (2002), Swenson (2002), Mares (2004), Roemer (1998, 2001), and Luttmer (2001). See also the contributions in Pierson (2001).

3. See Benabou (2000), Piketty (1995), Benabou and Tirole (2006), Cervellati, Esteban, and Kranich (2004), and Alesina and Angeletos (2005).

4. This argument builds on an emerging political-economy literature on the possible insurance function of religion. See Clark and Lelkes (2004), Gill and Lundsgaarde (2004), Dehejia, DeLeire, and Luttmer (2007), Gruber (2005), Gruber and Hungerman (2005), Hungerman (2005), Chen (2004), Chen and Lind (2005). We thank Devesh Kapur for pointing out to us the potential insurance effects of religion.

5. Contesting this assumption is a recurring theme in this volume. We think that policy is at least somewhat responsive to voter preferences and believe our empirical analysis supports this view. This assumption does not require redistributive policymaking to be fully consistent with Meltzer and Richard (1981) and thus does not necessarily contradict the arguments in several of the contributions in this volume highlighting factors that limit democratic redistributive policymaking.

6. See in particular Pargament (1997) and Smith, McCullough, and Poll (2003) who draw on the theory of appraisal developed by Lazarus and Folkman (1984).

7. Park, Cohen, and Herb (1990), Smith, McCullough, and Poll (2003), James and Wells (2003), Ellison, Gay, and Glass (1989), Pargament (1997).

8. Piketty (1996), Alesina, Glaeser, and Sacerdote (2001), Alesina and La Ferrara (2005), and Alesina and Glaeser (2004).

9. In order to produce this prediction one would need to suggest not only that issue bundling occurs but also that individuals are subject to a cognitive-dissonance mechanism that prompts them to adopt beliefs about redistribution that are in opposition to their individual economic interest. Even this version of the argument, however, does not suggest the partial correlation between individual religiosity and social-insurance preferences controlling for partisanship that we present later in the chapter.

10. See Lee and Roemer (this volume) for further discussion of how there may be multiple pathways for religious commitments to influence social-policy outcomes that work simultaneously with issue bundling.

11. Scheve and Stasavage (2006a, 2006b) include formalizations of the argument, building on models of social insurance by Wright (1986), Moene and Wallerstein (2001), and Iversen and Soskice (2001), and readers are referred to those articles for further details and description.

12. This hypothesis continues to hold even if individuals are assumed to be partially altruistic, following Atkinson's (1990) approach for modeling altruism.

13. These benefits would be distinct from the material benefits of a network emphasized earlier.

14. The classic model on the economics of religion, by Azzi and Ehrenberg (1975), focuses on the role of expected afterlife benefits for religious individuals, but the current psychological literature does not place the same emphasis on the afterlife as an expected benefit.

15. See the review of appraisal theories by Scherer, Schorr, and Johnstone (2001).

16. See Park, Cohen, and Herb (1990); Smith, McCullough, and Poll (2003); and James and Wells (2003).

17. Allport and Ross (1967) constructed the original Religious Orientation Scale which has been used in a variety of modified forms to measure intrinsic and

extrinsic religiosity. Pargament (1997), pp. 59–67, provides an interesting critique of the idea of dividing religiosity between an intrinsic and an extrinsic variant.

18. Cervellati, Esteban, and Kranich (2004) provide an example of a model of redistributive politics in which utility from income and from a psychic benefit are not additively separable. The assumption of nonadditive separability also constitutes the more general way to model utility from multiple goods or sources and, as such, is a relatively less restrictive modeling assumption than additive separability.

19. The discussion in this section assumes that the benefit that individuals derive from religion depends exclusively on their own personal investment of time. Scheve and Stasavage (2006a) relax this restriction by considering the more realistic possibility that there are network externalities in religious commitment —individuals derive more benefit from time devoted to religion when a certain number of other individuals make the same investment. This assumption leads to the possibility of multiple equilibria but does not change the underlying prediction of a negative correlation between religiosity and social insurance.

20. Evidence that the correlation indicates a causal effect is based on an identification strategy employing measures of the degree of state regulation, the extent of state subsidies for religion, and the degree of religious pluralism as instruments for religiosity. See Scheve and Stasavage (2006a) for details.

21. We focus on workers'-compensation programs and unemployment insurance because they satisfy two criteria: they are clearly insurance programs as opposed to primarily redistributive-spending programs, and significant features of the programs are under state control. We will briefly discuss some extensions of our analysis to other spending areas.

22. The source for both of these variables is Besley and Case (2003).

23. Neither measure is available for Alaska and Hawaii, and so both states are omitted from the analysis.

24. The source for this data is Churches and Church Membership in the United States, 1971, 1980, 1990, accessed from the American Religion Data Archive (http://www.thearda.com/).

25. For example, for the states for which we also have survey measures of Catholic membership, the proportion of Catholics in the state using the church-membership data correlates with the survey-based measure at 0.92.

26. The source for this variable is Berry, Fording, and Hanson (2003).

27. The source for this data is www.unionstats.com and was compiled by Barry Hirsch and David Macpherson.

28. The source for this data is the *Book of the States,* various issues.

29. Our version of the Berry et al. (1998) data comes from the revised 1960–2002 citizen-ideology series accessed from the replication data archive at the Interuniversity Consortium for Political and Social Research.

30. The southern states are Alabama, Arkansas, Florida, Georgia, Kentucky,

Louisiana, Maryland, Mississippi, North Carolina, Oklahoma, South Carolina, Tennessee, Texas, Virginia, and West Virginia.

31. The source for this variable is Besley and Case (2003).

32. The source for this variable is "Selected Historical Decennial Census: Population and Housing Counts," U.S. Census Bureau, http://www.census.gov/population/www/censusdata/hiscendata.html.

33. More specifically, the F-test for the excluded instruments adjusted for clustering at the state level is significant at the 0.006 level for the regressions using Religious Attendance to measure religiosity and at the 0.000 level for the regressions using Religious Membership to measure religiosity. Moreover, the Hansen J-statistic for an overidentification test for all instruments has p-values of 0.37, 0.95, 0.52, and 0.99, indicating that across all four specifications, the data do not indicate that we can reject the null hypothesis that the overidentifying assumptions are valid. It is important to emphasize that this test assumes one of the instruments is valid and thus does not unambiguously indicate that the exclusion restriction necessary for a valid instrument holds.

34. In the interest of brevity, the full table of results for the IV regressions are not reported. For the Workers' Compensation regressions, the coefficient estimate for Religious Attendance is −0.017 with a standard error of 0.011, and the coefficient estimate for Religious Membership is −0.105 with a standard error of 0.039.

35. The coefficient estimate for Religious Attendance is −0.012 with a standard error of 0.011, and the coefficient estimate for Religious Membership is −0.013 with a standard error of 0.024.

36. Another robustness test that we conducted also suggested that the empirical evidence that more-religious states spend less on unemployment insurance was not that strong. Adding state unemployment as a control variable to the specification in table 6.1 eliminates the significant negative correlation between Religious Membership and Unemployment Insurance (it does not have a qualitatively important effect on the results for Workers' Compensation). Unemployment is, of course, endogenous to spending on unemployment insurance, and thus adding the variable may bias all the other coefficients, including the estimates for religiosity. Further research using a fully identified system of equations is necessary to assess the importance of this robustness check for our analysis of the link between religiosity and unemployment-insurance spending.

37. See Woolridge (2002) for an extended discussion.

38. An alternative but related issue is the extent to which the spending program is targeted. Targeted programs—say, to the poor but really for any relatively small subset of the population—do not provide insurance for a significant portion of the population, and so, given our argument, we would not expect a negative correlation between religiosity and spending on targeted programs. To the extent that family-assistance spending does not fit the category of relatively universal insurance, it is a less than ideal test of our argument.

39. Note that the GSS provides the U.S. data for the ISSP. Consequently, it is possible to examine our hypothesis in the GSS data using the same questions that we employed in the ISSP analysis. We conducted this analysis in two different ways. First, using factor analysis, we constructed the dependent variable combining responses to three questions asking individuals whether they would like to see more or less government spending on unemployment benefits, health care, and pensions. This variable replicates the dependent variable in Scheve and Stasavage (2006a). Second, we analyzed responses to each question separately. We found a robust and substantively significant negative correlation between religiosity and spending preferences in all cases except for the analysis of responses to the unemployment-benefits question. We focus the presentation in this section on alternative questions measuring social-insurance policy preferences because these questions are available for many more years and because testing the argument on alternatively worded questions is useful for evaluating the robustness of the result.

40. The results are qualitatively similar if we code answers to this question as dichotomous measures indicating monthly or weekly attendance.

41. Under somewhat different assumptions, we dichotomized the Religious Attendance variable, based on whether attendance was at least monthly, and estimated a treatment effects regression using parent religiosity in the selection equation and again found a robust negative correlation between religiosity and social-spending preferences.

42. Note that for questions that are even more explicitly about redistribution, the correlation between religiosity and spending preferences is substantially attenuated. For example, in the GSS data, there is a question on spending on the poor for which the magnitude of the coefficient estimate is less than half that reported in the regressions in table 7.2. Further, the estimate is only marginally statistically significant in the specification without the partisanship measure and not significant at conventional levels in the specification with the partisanship measure. Again, because this question is arguably much more about relatively targeted redistribution, this null result is not inconsistent with our argument about the effect of religiosity on social-insurance preferences. For discussion of further results using alternative policy-preferences measures, see also the discussion at the beginning of this section.

REFERENCES

Alesina, Alberto, and George-Marios Angeletos. 2005. Fairness and Redistribution. *American Economic Review* 95(3): 960–980.

Alesina, Alberto, and Edward Glaeser. 2004. *Fighting Poverty in the U.S. and Europe.* Oxford: Oxford University Press.

Alesina, Alberto, Edward Glaeser, and Bruce Sacerdote. 2001. Why Doesn't the U.S. Have a European Style Welfare State? *Brookings Papers on Economic Activity* 2001/2: 187–254.

Alesina, Alberto, and Eliana La Ferrara. 2005. Preferences for Redistribution in the Land of Opportunities. *Journal of Public Economics* 89(5–6): 897–931.

Allport, G., and J. Ross. 1967. Personal Religious Orientation and Prejudice. *Journal of Personality and Social Psychology* 5: 432–443.

Atkinson, Anthony. 1990. Income Maintenance for the Unemployed in Britain and the Response to High Unemployment. *Ethics* 100(3): 569–585.

Azzi, Corry, and Ronald Ehrenberg. 1975. "Household Allocation of Time and Church Attendance." *Journal of Political Economy* 83(1): 27–56.

Benabou, Roland. 2000. Unequal Societies: Income Distribution and the Social Contract. *American Economic Review* 90: 96–129.

Benabou, Roland, and Jean Tirole. 2006. Belief in a Just World and Redistributive Politics. *Quarterly Journal of Economics* 121(2): 699–746.

Berry, William, Richard Fording, and Russell Hanson. 2003. Reassessing the "Race to the Bottom" in State Welfare Policy: Resolving the Conflict Between Individual-Level and Aggregate Research. *Journal of Politics* 65 (May): 327–349.

Berry, William, Evan J. Ringquist, Richard C. Fording, and Russell L. Hanson. 1998. Measuring Citizen and Government Ideology in the American States, 1960–93. *American Journal of Political Science* 42 (January): 327–348.

Besley, Timothy, and Anne Case. 2003. Political Institutions and Policy Choices: Evidence from the United States. *Journal of Economic Literature* 41 (March): 7–73.

Blanchard, Olivier, and Jean Tirole. 2003. Contours of Employment Protection. Unpublished paper, MIT and IDEI, Toulouse.

Burnett, John, and Bruce Palmer. 1984. Examining Life Insurance Ownership through Demographic and Psychographic Characteristics. *Journal of Risk and Insurance* 51(3): 453–467.

Cervellati, Matteo, Joan Esteban, and Laurence Kranich. 2004. Redistributive Taxation with Endogenous Sentiments. Unpublished paper, Pompeu Fabra, Barcelona.

Chaves, Mark. 2004. *Congregations in America*. Cambridge, MA: Harvard University Press.

Chen, Daniel. 2004. Club Goods and Group Identity: Evidence from Islamic Resurgence during the Indonesian Financial Crisis. Unpublished paper.

Chen, Daniel, and Jo T. Lind. 2005. The Political Economy of Beliefs: Why Fiscal and Social Conservatives/Liberals Come Hand-in-Hand. Unpublished paper.

Clark, Andrew, and Orsolya Lelkes. 2004. Deliver Us from Evil: Religion as Insurance. Unpublished paper, DELTA, Paris.

Clark, Andrew, and Andrew Oswald. 1994. Unhappiness and Unemployment. *Economic Journal* 104: 648–659.

Dehejia, Rajeev, Thomas DeLeire, and Erzo F. P. Luttmer. 2007. Insuring Consumption and Happiness through Religious Organizations. *Journal of Public Economics* 91(1–2): 259–279.

Di Tella, Rafael, Robert MacCulloch, and Andrew Oswald. 2003. The Macroeconomics of Happiness. *Review of Economics and Statistics* 85(4): 793–809.

Douglass, H. Paul, and Edmund deS. Brunner. 1935. *The Protestant Church as a Social Institution.* New York: Harper and Brothers.

Ellison, Christopher. 1991. Religious Involvement and Subjective Well-Being. *Journal of Health and Social Behavior* 32: 80–99.

Ellison, Christopher, David Gay, and Thomas Glass. 1989. Does Religious Commitment Contribute to Individual Life Satisfaction? *Social Forces* 68(1): 100–123.

Esping-Andersen, Gøsta. 1990. *The Three Worlds of Welfare Capitalism.* Princeton, NJ: Princeton University Press.

Fogel, Robert. 2000. *The Fourth Great Awakening and the Future of Egalitarianism.* Chicago: University of Chicago Press.

Folkman, Susan, and Richard Lazarus. 1986. Appraisal, Coping, Health Status, and Psychological Symptoms. *Journal of Personality and Social Psychology* 50(3): 571–579.

Franzese, Robert. 2002. *Macroeconomic Policies of Developed Democracies.* Cambridge: Cambridge University Press.

Freud, Sigmund. 1927. *The Future of an Illusion.* New York: Norton.

Gill, Anthony, and Erik Lundsgaarde. 2004. State Welfare Spending and Religiosity: A Cross-National Analysis. *Rationality and Society* 16(4): 399–436.

Gruber, Jonathan. 2005. Religious Market Structure, Religious Participation, and Outcomes: Is Religion Good for You? NBER Working Paper 11377.

Gruber, Jonathan, and Daniel M. Hungerman. 2005. Faith-Based Charity and Crowd Out during the Great Depression. NBER Working Paper 11332.

Hacker, Jacob, and Paul Pierson. 2002. Business Power and Social Policy: Employers and the Formation of the American Welfare State. *Politics and Society* 30(2): 277–325.

Huber, Evelyne, and John Stephens. 2001. *Development and Crisis of the Welfare State: Parties and Policies in Global Markets.* Chicago: University of Chicago Press.

Hungerman, Daniel M. 2005. Are Church and State Substitutes? Evidence from the 1996 Welfare Reform. *Journal of Public Economics* 89: 2245–2267.

Iversen, Torben, and David Soskice. 2001. An Asset Theory of Social Policy Preferences. *American Political Science Review* 95: 875–893.

James, Abigail, and Adrian Wells. 2003. Religion and Mental Health: Towards a Cognitive-Behavioural Framework. *British Journal of Health Psychology* 8: 359–376.

James, William. 1902. *The Varieties of Religious Experience.* New York: Simon and Schuster.

Key, V. O. 1949. *Southern Politics in State and Nation.* New York: Knopf.

Lazarus, Richard, and Susan Folkman. 1984. *Stress, Appraisal, and Coping.* New York: Springer.

Luttmer, Erzo. 2001. Group Loyalty and the Taste for Redistribution. *Journal of Political Economy* 109(3): 500–528.

Mares, Isabela. 2004. Economic Insecurity and Social Policy Expansion: Evidence from Interwar Europe. *International Organization* 58(4): 745–774.

Marx, Karl. 1844. *Contribution to the Critique of Hegel's Philosophy of Right.* Deutsch-Französische Jahrbücher.

McLoughlin, William G. 1978. *Revivals, Awakenings, and Reform: An Essay on Religion and Social Change in America, 1607–1977.* Chicago: University of Chicago Press.

Meltzer, Allan, and Scott Richard. 1981. A Rational Theory of the Size of Government. *Journal of Political Economy* 89: 914–927.

Moene, Karl, and Michael Wallerstein. 2001. Inequality, Social Insurance, and Redistribution. *American Political Science Review* 95: 859–873.

Pargament, K. 1997. *The Psychology of Religion and Coping.* New York: Guilford.

Park, Crystal, Lawrence Cohen, and Lisa Herb. 1990. Intrinsic Religiousness and Religious Coping as Life Stress Moderators for Catholics versus Protestants. *Journal of Personality and Social Psychology* 59(3): 562–574.

Pierson, Paul. 1993. When Effect Becomes Cause: Policy Feedback and Political Change. *World Politics* 45(4): 595–628.

Pierson, Paul, ed. 2001. *The New Politics of the Welfare State.* Oxford: Oxford University Press.

Piketty, Thomas. 1995. Social Mobility and Redistributive Politics. *Quarterly Journal of Economics* 110: 551–584.

Piketty, Thomas. 1996. Mobilité Economique et Attitudes Politiques Face à la Redistribution. CEPREMAP Working Paper, Paris.

Rodden, Jonathan. 2005. Red States, Blue States, and the Welfare State: Political Geography, Representation, and Government Policy around the World. MIT Working Paper.

Roemer, John. 1998. Why the Poor Do Not Expropriate the Rich: An Old Argument in New Garb. *Journal of Public Economics* 70: 399–424.

Roemer, John. 2001. *Political Competition.* Cambridge, MA: Harvard University Press.

Scherer, K. R., A. Schorr, and T. Johnstone. 2001. *Appraisal Processes in Emotion.* Oxford: Oxford University Press.

Scheve, Kenneth, and David Stasavage. 2006a. Religion and Preferences for Social Insurance. *Quarterly Journal of Political Science* 1(3): 255–86.

Scheve, Kenneth, and David Stasavage. 2006b. The Political Economy of Religion and Social Insurance in the United States, 1910–1939. *Studies in American Political Development* 20: 132–159.

Smith, Timothy, Michael McCullough, and Justin Poll. 2003. Religiousness and Depression: Evidence for a Main Effect and Moderating Influence of Stressful Life Events. *Psychological Bulletin* 129(4): 614–636.

Swank, Duane, and Sven Steinmo. 2002. The New Political Economy of Taxation in Advanced Capitalist Democracies. *American Journal of Political Science* 46(3): 642–655.

Swenson, Peter A. 2002. *Capitalists against Markets.* Oxford: Oxford University Press.

Woolridge, Jeffrey M. 2002. *Econometric Analysis of Cross Section and Panel Data.* Cambridge, MA: MIT Press.

Wright, Randall. 1986. The Redistributive Roles of Unemployment Insurance and the Dynamics of Voting. *Journal of Public Economics* 31: 377–399.

Chapter 7

IIIIIIIIIIIIIIIIIIIIIIIIIIIIIIIIIIIIIIIIIIIIIIIIIIIIIIIII

Moral Values and Distributive Politics
An Equilibrium Analysis of the 2004 U.S. Election

Woojin Lee and John Roemer

> Democrats are assaulting our basic values. They attacked
> the integrity of the family and parental rights. They ig-
> nored traditional morality. And they still do.
> —1984 platform of the Republican Party

The Republican Party, whose economic policies are perhaps in the economic interest of the top 15 percent of the wealth distribution, is supported by approximately one-half of the U.S. electorate. President George
W. Bush, during his first term, made quite clear what his economic policies are—from tax cuts that benefit primarily the very rich, engendering
large deficits, to abolition of the inheritance tax and privatizing Social
Security.

In contrast, the policies of the Democratic Party are not left-wing; they
are moderate. It would seem that, if voters were rational and concerned
largely about the economic issue, the Democratic Party would receive the
vast majority of the vote. Why is this not the case?

Many explanations can be offered, but we believe the three most likely
explanations are the following:[1]

- Cognitive errors and false consciousness. Voters make cognitive errors concerning economic policy or the theory that maps policies
  into economic outcomes. They may not connect taxation with the
  supply of government goods and services. Or voters may be unsure

how efficiently the government converts tax revenues into the public good. This can be viewed as a case of not understanding the mapping from *policies* to *outcomes*.[2] What voters are concerned with are economic outcomes (their consumption of various goods, and perhaps others' consumption—we do not assume voters are entirely selfish); what they do not understand is how policies engender outcomes, i.e., the theory of the economy. "False consciousness" might be one description of this phenomenon. But false consciousness also applies to another phenomenon, which is distinct from this one— the belief by poor people that rich people deserve their earnings and that it would be unjust to redistribute through taxation.

- Imperfect representation. Politicians represent the wealthy. Bartels (2002), Gilens (2003), and Jacobs and Page (2003) have shown that politicians reflect the preferences of the wealthy, not the average voter. One mechanism, of several, may be that political parties, under a regime of private funding, represent their contributors. Thus, the political competition between Democrats and Republicans may be one between two parties each of whom represents the wealthy, which would skew the equilibrium economic policies to the right.
- Policy bundling. Other issues, besides the economic issue, are of importance to voters, and the support for the Republican Party may be in part due to the bundling of the economic issue with these other issues. Important noneconomic issues are race, gun control, abortion, gay marriage (family values), and foreign policy. Thus, the Republicans may have crafted a program with a large constituency, *in spite of* their economic position.

It is not our aim in this chapter to examine the relative importance of these three possible explanations for the vitality of the Republican Party. We focus on the third explanation and take the U.S. presidential election of 2004 as an example. In particular, we study the importance of religious and/or moral-value issues.

The "American exceptionalism" literature, dating back to Alexis de Tocqueville's *Democracy in America*, emphasizes that moral Protestantism (in particular, that of evangelicals), together with racial division, has always had an unusually powerful influence on U.S. political culture.[3] For the period 1972–1992, we have demonstrated the importance of the race issue in U.S. politics (Lee and Roemer 2006). Today, however, the "values" issue may be more important, although the race issue and the values issue are often interlinked, as can be seen in the case of the Ku Klux Klan movement in the 1920s and the prevalence of racially segregated religious schools.[4]

In this chapter, we study the electoral consequence of the moral-values issue in the 2004 presidential election by distinguishing what we call the policy bundle effect (PBE) from the moral Puritanism effect (MPE). Our model provides a theoretical explanation for the "what's the matter with Kansas" problem (Frank 2005).

There are at least two distinct ways in which the influence of values on equilibrium political outcomes might occur. First, because the Republican Party is identified with a traditionalist stance on moral values, some voters who desire a large public sector may nevertheless vote Republican because traditionalist morality is important for them. We call this effect the *policy bundle effect.* Second, it may be the case that those who subscribe to a traditionalist morality take economic conservatism to be part of that view, in the sense that they view the state as, for instance, usurping the role of the individual and/or family. Indeed, some evangelicals are said to oppose taxation on the grounds that talents to persons are God given, and their fruits should therefore not be redistributed. We call this effect the *moral Puritanism effect.*

The next section carries out an econometric analysis of the 2004 election. Then we describe our model and the method of decomposition that we will employ. Finally, we summarize our numerical computation results and conclude. The ANES variables used in this chapter are defined in the appendix.

Econometric Analysis of the 2004 Election Data

In our empirical analysis and numerical computation, we use an advance release of the 2004 ANES pre-post study. The sample consists of a new cross-section of respondents that yielded 1,212 face-to-face interviews in the preelection study; 1,066 of these respondents later provided a face-to-face interview in the postelection study. Data collection was conducted by the Survey Research Center at the University of Michigan.[5]

We first construct four persistent issues in U.S. politics—the ideal size of the public sector, the issue of moral values, the race issue, and the issue of libertarianism—and four contemporary issues of the 2004 election—the approval on the Iraq war, the Bush tax cut, the Social Security reform, and the school voucher. For every opinion variable in the ANES 2004 which takes the value of j ranging from k to $k+n$, where k is an integer and n is a positive integer, we convert it into

$$\frac{j-(k-1)}{n+2}.$$

Thus, every converted value lies *strictly* between 0 and 1.

The four persistent issues in U.S. politics are constructed in the following way. For the preference of the public sector, we take the average of the following three variables (see the appendix for their definitions): (1) *spending*, (2) *job*, and (3) *health*. For the moral-values issue, we take the average of the following four groups of variables: (1) women's role in the society (*womenrole, workingmom,* and *womenhome*), (2) attitudes on abortion (*abortion*), (3) attitudes on homosexuals (*homo_nodiscrimination, gaymarriage*), and (4) attitudes on traditionalism and modernism (*tradition_important, newlifestyles_important*). For the race issue, we take the average of two variables: (1) *aidtoblacks*, and (2) *blackfavor*. Finally, the issue of libertarianism was measured by the attitude toward big government (*biggovt*).

The four contemporary issues are, on the other hand, constructed from the corresponding questionnaires in the ANES: *iraqwarissue, taxcutissue, ssreform, schoolvouchers*. These are issues specific to the 2004 election.

We take the actual vote share of the 2004 election as the observed vote share and take as the *population* citizens voting for either party D or party R. Estimating the observed policy position of the two parties is tricky; announced size of the public sector or announced stance on the moral-values issue are rarely observable, although we know which party takes a more conservative stance on each of these issues. The ANES 2004 provides information on the public perception about the position of the presidential candidates and the two parties on several variables, such as *spending, job, women's role, abortion*. We take the mean values of these variables for each candidate (party) as the candidates' (parties') position on these issues; if voters are perceptive, this assumption is not unreasonable. We then take the average of the candidate position and the party position as the *observed party position* on specific policy issues.

Regarding the size of the public sector, only two variables (*spending* and *job*) have observed party positions. We take the average of the observed positions of these two variables to be the observed party policy on the size of the public sector. Regarding the moral-value issue, again only two variables (*womenrole* and *abortion*) have observed party positions. We take the average of the observed positions of these two variables to be the observed party policy on the moral-values issue.

We first ran a probit regression to see the salient determinants of the voting pattern in the 2004 election. The dependent variable is the dummy variable indicating whether the respondent voted Republican, and the independent variables are the four persistent election issues, the four temporary issues, and demographic variables such as age, education, household income, and so on. Table 7.1 shows the results. The first column reports the regression coefficients, and the second column reports the coefficients in terms of marginal effects.

We first observe that out of the four persistent issues, the size of the public sector, the moral-values issue, and the race issue are highly salient in determining the voting pattern. This finding may suggest that the most desirable model should consider a model of political competition with three policy issues; the current limitation on the computation time forbids us to pursue this model.[6] Thus, for this chapter we choose the moral-values issue, rather than the race issue, as the second policy issue.

Not surprisingly, several contemporary issues, such as the approval for the Iraq war, are highly salient in determining the outcome in the 2004 election. We focus on the persistent issues rather than temporary issues in our analysis because we are more interested in the long-run pattern of American politics. We assume that the contemporary issues do not affect the policy positions of the two parties on the two persistent issues on which we focus.

Table 7.2 examines the determinants of the two issues on which we focus. We notice from the first column that the preferred size of the public sector is negatively correlated with the conservative stance on the moral-values issue. In other words, the more conservative a voter is on the moral-values issue, the less liberal he or she is on the size of the public sector. But at the same time, we notice that this effect is different across party identifications. Republicans, for instance, have a very strong negative effect (third column), whereas Democrats have no statistically significant effect (second column).

The fourth column examines the determinants of the stance on the moral-values issue. As we expect, it is negatively correlated with the thermometer feelings on feminists and homosexuals and is positively correlated with religiosity. At the same time, we notice that it is also positively correlated with antiblack feelings, although the coefficient is marginally

TABLE 7.1
Probit Regressions for the Republican Vote Share

	(1)voteR	(2)voteR
publicsize	−2.729**	−1.071**
	(2.92)	(2.92)
moralvalue	3.475*	1.364*
	(2.51)	(2.51)
raceissue	2.902*	1.139*
	(2.52)	(2.52)
biggovt	0.595*	0.233*
	(2.17)	(2.17)
iraqwarissue	7.347**	2.884**
	(6.71)	(6.71)
taxcutissue	3.014**	1.183**
	(4.10)	(4.10)
ssreform	0.422**	0.166**
	(2.69)	(2.69)
schoolvouchers	0.171	0.067
	(1.09)	(1.09)
environmentissue	−0.754	−0.296
	(1.03)	(1.03)
age	−0.009	−0.004
	(0.87)	(0.87)
educatio	−0.033	−0.013
	(0.34)	(0.34)
income_hh (10k)	0.042	0.017
	(0.99)	(0.99)
blackdummy	−1.902**	−0.590**
	(3.83)	(3.83)
femaledummy	−0.046	−0.018
	(0.18)	(0.18)
marrieddummy	−0.157	−0.062
	(0.58)	(0.58)
uniondummy	−0.166	−0.066
	(0.51)	(0.51)
usparentsdummy	0.559	0.220
	(1.55)	(1.55)
family_military	−0.405	−0.156
	(1.35)	(1.35)
unemployeddummy	0.452	0.172
	(1.31)	(1.31)
pastfinancial	0.202	0.079
	(1.23)	(1.23)
futurefinancial	−0.477+	−0.187+
	(1.96)	(1.96)
pasteconomy	0.275	0.108
	(1.56)	(1.56)
futureeconomy	0.152	0.060
	(0.73)	(0.73)
religiosity	0.452	0.177
	(0.51)	(0.51)
Constant	−7.291**	
	(4.70)	
Observations	411	411

Absolute value of z statistics in parentheses
+ significant at 10%; * significant at 5%; ** significant at 1%

significant. Thus, what we observe as the stance on moral values incorporates part of racism. There are two possible interpretations. First, our constructed variable on the moral-values issue may be impure in that it contains other elements than moral values. Second, it may be the case that the moral-value issue that Republicans have emphasized may not be truly related with morality; it may be a political cover or a code word for politically unacceptable issues, such as racism. We do not think that there is an easy way of solving this problem.

The Model

A. The Model of Political Equilibrium

We model the 2004 presidential election as a political competition between two parties who compete on a two-dimensional policy space, which in our application will be the *size of the public sector* and the *policy toward moral values.* The model of political competition employed here is that of *party unanimity Nash equilibrium with endogenous parties* (PUNE) as defined in Roemer (2001, chap. 13) and Roemer, Lee, and van der Straeten (2007). Unlike the model of Downs, in our model, parties will generically propose distinct policies in equilibrium. The following is a brief review of the concept of party unanimity Nash equilibrium (PUNE).

The PUNE model attempts to explain observed political equilibria in general elections with single or multidimensional policy spaces. The *data* of the model are (1) a set of *voter types, H;* (2) a *probability distribution* of the voter types, **F**, describing the composition of the polity; (3) a *policy space, T,* over which political competition takes place between parties; and (4) a *utility function* which describes, for every voter type, its preferences over policies, $v(t;h)$. Thus, the data are summarized by a tuple $(H,\mathbf{F},T,v)$. For each probability measure **F**, we will denote the associated distribution function by F and its density by f. (Do not confuse the distribution function F with the probability measure **F**.) We fix the number of parties, exogenously, to be two.

The equilibrium will then consist in a tuple (D,R,τ^D,τ^R), where (1) (D,R) is a partition of the set of voter types into *party memberships* or *constituencies, that is,* $D \cup R = H$, $D \cap R = \varnothing$; ; and (2) $\tau^J \in T$ is the equilibrium platform of party J, for $J = D,R$. (There will be no confusion if we refer

TABLE 7.2
Determinants of Stance on the Size of the Public Sector and Moral Values

	(1) All publicsize	(2) Democrats publicsize	(3) Republicans publicsize	(4) All moralvalue
biggovt	−0.077**	−0.050*	−0.089**	0.004
	(5.91)	(2.37)	(5.05)	(0.51)
moralvalue	−0.337**	−0.124	−0.431**	
	(4.58)	(1.03)	(3.79)	
antiblackaffect	−0.000	−0.002	0.000	0.001+
	(0.26)	(1.55)	(0.49)	(1.92)
therm_poor	0.002**	0.001*	0.001+	0.001**
	(4.13)	(2.29)	(1.75)	(2.68)
therm_feminists	0.001**	0.001**	0.000	−0.001**
	(4.01)	(2.78)	(0.43)	(6.53)
therm_homosexuals	−0.001+	−0.001	−0.000	−0.001**
	(1.89)	(1.38)	(0.92)	(8.25)
therm_southerners	−0.001*	0.000	−0.001*	0.000
	(2.18)	(0.05)	(2.19)	(1.39)
age	−0.001+	−0.001	−0.001	0.001**
	(1.79)	(1.33)	(1.38)	(4.08)
education	−0.006	−0.000	−0.015*	−0.008**
	(1.30)	(0.01)	(2.37)	(3.30)
income_hh (10k)	−0.005*	−0.003	−0.003	−0.001
	(2.48)	(0.98)	(1.13)	(1.25)
blackdummy	0.014	−0.004	0.039	−0.019+
	(0.76)	(0.15)	(0.88)	(1.79)
femaledummy	0.002	−0.022	0.028	−0.020**
	(0.13)	(1.14)	(1.50)	(2.90)
marrieddummy	0.022	0.017	0.029	0.022**
	(1.57)	(0.79)	(1.37)	(3.06)
uniondummy	0.003	0.007	0.005	−0.000
	(0.26)	(0.36)	(0.22)	(0.04)
unemployeddummy	0.017	0.027	0.015	0.004
	(1.22)	(1.10)	(0.66)	(0.46)
pastfinancial	−0.024**	−0.020*	−0.014	0.005
	(3.58)	(2.03)	(1.10)	(1.26)
futurefinancial	0.005	0.009	−0.002	−0.003
	(0.58)	(0.68)	(0.11)	(0.50)
pasteconomy	−0.032**	−0.012	−0.024+	0.010*
	(3.64)	(0.77)	(1.90)	(2.03)
futureeconomy	−0.007	0.009	0.000	0.004
	(0.82)	(0.69)	(0.01)	(0.75)
religiosity	−0.021	−0.092	0.111+	0.233**
	(0.49)	(1.46)	(1.82)	(10.00)
trust	−0.032**	−0.043*	−0.007	−0.007
	(2.63)	(2.20)	(0.38)	(1.01)
constant	0.768**	0.688**	0.845**	0.390**
	(14.59)	(8.21)	(9.12)	(16.37)
Observations	594	231	239	720
R-squared	0.39	0.22	0.36	0.52

Robust t statistics in parentheses
+ significant at 10%; * significant at 5%; ** significant at 1%

to a *party* and its *constituency* by the same variable, for example, R for Republican.)

It is important to note that constituencies are endogenous: they are engendered by the data of the model. Thus, the formation of parties and the policies ultimately proposed are the consequence of voter preferences. Of course, the model does not endogenize everything: the number of parties is taken as given, the policy space is given, and the fact that parties contain the factions described below is also given.

For our application, a voter's type will be an ordered pair $h = (\theta, \rho)$, where $\theta \in [0,1]$ is the voter's ideal size of the public sector (which we sometimes call, for short, his or her "tax rate"), and $\rho \in [0,1]$ is his or her position on the moral-values issue. The policy space T is a set of ordered pairs $\tau = (t,r)$, which we may take to be the unit square, where t is a party's policy on the size of the public sector and r is its policy on the values issue.

We assume that the utility function of the polity is a weighted Euclidean distance function $v : T \times H \to \mathbf{R}$:

$$v(t,r;\theta,\rho) = -(t-\theta)^2 - 2\beta(t-\theta)(r-\rho) - \gamma(r-\rho)^2 \qquad (1)$$

where $\gamma > 0$. We also impose the condition $\gamma > \beta^2$ to ensure that the utility function is concave. For a reason that will be explained later, we assume that the utility functions v are cardinally measurable and unit-comparable.

Note that in vector notation, this function is identical to

$$v(t,r;\theta,\rho) = -(t-\theta, r-\rho) \begin{bmatrix} 1 & \beta \\ \beta & \gamma \end{bmatrix} \begin{bmatrix} t-\theta \\ r-\rho \end{bmatrix} \qquad (2)$$

where

$$\begin{bmatrix} 1 & \beta \\ \beta & \gamma \end{bmatrix}$$

is a weight matrix. We refer to γ as the *relative salience of the issue of moral values* and assume it is positive. The off-diagonal term β, on the other hand, is an interaction term, which can be either positive or negative. (If β is zero, then the utility function is separable.) This term measures how much the voter's evaluation of changes in one issue depends on the expected level of another issue. To see this, suppose we fix t at a certain

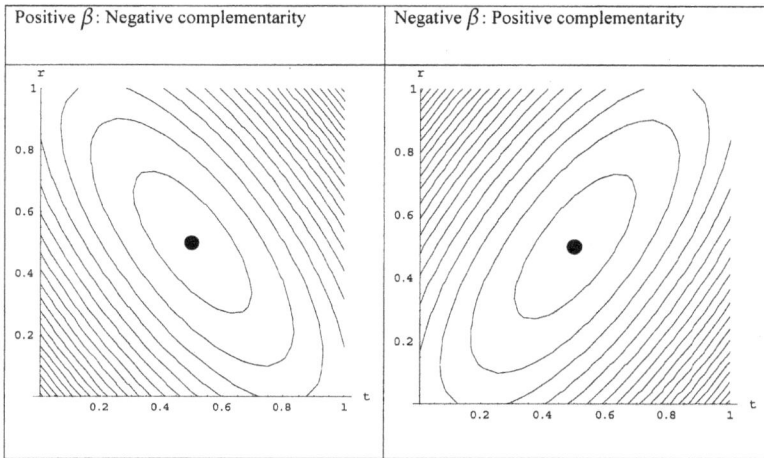

Fig. 7.1. Patterns of complementarity and the shapes of indifference curves.

level, $\bar{t}$, and choose r for each voter that maximizes his or her utility; call it $\hat{r}(\bar{t};\theta,\rho)$. Then it can be shown that

$$\hat{r}(\bar{t};\theta,\rho) - \rho = -\frac{\beta}{\gamma}(\bar{t} - \theta).$$

Thus, if β is negative, then we have positive complementarity between the two issues. If it is positive, then we have negative complementarity. (See figure 7.1.) Whether the utility function exhibits positive or negative complementarity is an empirical matter, which cannot be determined a priori.

Given two policies (τ^D, τ^R) proposed by the two parties, we define $\varphi(\tau^D, \tau^R)$ as the fraction of the polity who prefer the policy τ^D to the policy τ^R. In our model, if the policies are distinct, then the set of voters indifferent between two policies will always have F-measure zero.

A party possesses *entrepreneurs* or *organizers,* and *members* or *constituents.* The members of a party are citizens who, in equilibrium, prefer that party's policy to the policy of the other party. The entrepreneurs are professional politicians who make policy in the party. Think of them as a very small group of individuals who are not identified as citizens characterized by a type. (Their type is irrelevant.) We will assume that the organizers of the Democratic and Republican parties are each divided into two factions, an Opportunist faction and a Militant faction. The Opportunist faction wishes, in the party competition game, to propose a policy that will maximize the party's vote share, or probability of winning. The Militant faction wishes to propose a policy that will maximize the average welfare of the party's constituency. In another interpretation, the Militants are those politicians who are concerned with representing the party's core or base, and the Opportunists are those concerned with appealing to swing voters.

The proposal that parties consist of bargaining factions captures the view that parties have conflicting goals: to represent constituencies and to win office, or, more generally, to maximize vote share. Mathematically, the virtue of the factional model of parties is that it engenders the existence of political equilibria when policy spaces are multidimensional.

Without loss of generality, we could postulate a third faction in each party: a Reformist faction, whose members desire to maximize the average expected welfare of the party's constituency. As is shown in Roemer (2001), the set of equilibria will not change with this additional faction: in an appropriate sense, the Reformists are a "convex combination" of the other two factions. Therefore, we have dispensed with this faction, and also with having to define the probability of victory, which would be essential were we to have to discuss expected utility of voters, something of concern to Reformists. We mention the Reformists because postulating their existence adds an important element of realism to the model, although, it turns out, it does not alter the model's equilibria. Thus, from the formal viewpoint, we may ignore Reformists.[7]

The idea of PUNE is that parties compete against each other *strategically*, as in Nash equilibrium, and factions *bargain* with each other, inside parties. At an equilibrium, each party's platform is a best response to the other party's platform in the sense that it is a *bargaining solution* between the party's factions, given the platform proposed by the other party.

Suppose the members of a party consist of all citizens whose types lie in the set $J \subset H$. We define the *average welfare function* for this party as a function mapping from T to the real numbers defined by

$$V^J(\tau) = \int_{h \in J} v(\tau;h) d\mathbf{F}(h). \quad (3)$$

That is, $V^J(\tau)$ is just (a constant times) the average utility of the coalition J at the policy τ. (For equation (3) to make sense, we must assume that the utility functions v are unit-comparable.)

Suppose the two parties propose policies τ^D and τ^R. Define

$$\Omega(\tau^D, \tau^R) = \{h \in H \mid v(\tau^D, h) > v(\tau^R, h)\}. \quad (4)$$

Then the share of the polity who (should) vote for the D policy is

$$\varphi(\tau^D, \tau^R) = \mathbf{F}(\Omega(\tau^D, \tau^R)). \quad (5)$$

Definition: A *party unanimity Nash equilibrium* (PUNE) *for the model* $(H, \mathbf{F}, T, v)$ is (a) a partition of the set of types $H = D \cup R$, possibly ignoring a set of measure zero; and (b) a pair of policies (τ^D, τ^R) such that
(1a) Given there is no policy $\tau \in T$ such that

$$V^R(\tau) \geq V^R(\tau^R) \text{ and } \varphi(\tau^D, \tau) \leq \varphi(\tau^D, \tau^R)$$

with at least one of these inequalities strict;
(1b) Given τ^R there is no policy $\tau \in T$ such that

$$V^D(\tau) \geq V^D(\tau^D) \text{ and } \varphi(\tau, \tau^R) \geq \varphi(\tau^D, \tau^R)$$

with at least one of these inequalities strict;
(2) for $J = D, R$, every member of coalition J prefers policy τ^J to the other policy, that is,

$$h \in J \Longrightarrow v(\tau^J, h) \text{ for } J' \neq J.$$

Condition (1a) states that, when facing the policy τ^D, there is no feasible policy that would increase both the average welfare of party R's constituents and the vote fraction of party R. Thus, we may view policy τ^R as being a *bargaining solution* between party R's two factions when facing the opposition's policy, as the Militants' desire to maximize the average welfare of constituents and the Opportunists desire to maximize vote share. All we employ here is the assumption that a bargain must be Pareto efficient for the two players in the bargaining game. Condition (1b) similarly states that policy τ^D is a bargaining solution for party D's factions when facing the policy τ^R. Condition (2) states that the endogenous party memberships are stable: each party member prefers his or her party's policy to the other parties' policies.

There are two "free" parameters in this equilibrium concept: one might think that the relative strength of the Militants with respect to the Opportunists in a party is an important variable in determining where on the mini-Pareto frontier of the factions the bargaining solution lies. There is one such parameter for each party D and R. Thus, we can expect that, if there is an equilibrium, there will be a two-parameter manifold of equilibria, where the elements in this manifold are associated with different pairs of relative bargaining strengths of the pairs of factions in D and R. This indeed turns out to be the case, as we will see later.

With differentiability, we can characterize a PUNE as the solution of a system of simultaneous equations. Denote by $\nabla_J \varphi(\tau^D, \tau^R)$ the gradient of the function φ with respect to the policy τ^J. Denote by ∇V^J the gradient of V^J. Then, we can write the necessary conditions for a PUNE where τ^D and τ^R are interior points in T as

(1a) there is a nonnegative number x such that

$$-\nabla_D \varphi(\tau^D, \tau^R) = x \nabla V^D(\tau^D) \quad (6)$$

(1b) there is a nonnegative number y such that

$$\nabla_R \varphi(\tau^D, \tau^R) = y \nabla V^R(\tau^R) \quad (7)$$

Condition (1a) says that the gradients of the vote-share function and the average welfare function for party D point in opposite directions, and so, assuming local convexity, there is no direction in which the policy of the party can be altered so as to increase both the party's vote share and the average welfare of the party's constituents. Thus, conditions (1a) and (1b) correspond exactly to the conditions (1a) and (1b) in the definition of PUNE.

Our next task is to characterize PUNE as a system of equations, which requires us to formulate precisely the party constituencies. Denote the set of types who prefer a policy $\tau^D = (t^D, r^D)$ to policy $\tau^R = (t^R, r^R)$ by $\Omega(\tau^D, \tau^R)$, and compute that

$$\Omega(\tau^D, \tau^R) = \begin{cases} \{(\theta, \rho) \in H \mid \rho > \psi(\tau^D, \tau^R, \theta) \text{ if } \beta(t^D - t^R) + \gamma(r^D - r^R) > 0 \\ \{(\theta, \rho) \in H \mid \rho > \psi(\tau^D, \tau^R, \theta) \text{ if } \beta(t^D - t^R) + \gamma(r^D - r^R) < 0 \end{cases} \quad (8)$$

where

$$\psi(\tau^D, \tau^R, \theta) = \frac{(t^R - t^D) + \beta(r^R - r^D)}{\beta(t^D - t^R) + \gamma(r^D - r^R)} \theta$$

$$+ \frac{((t^D)^2 - (t^R)^2) + \gamma((r^D)^2 - (r^R)^2) + 2\beta(t^D r^D - t^R r^R)}{2\beta(t^D - t^R) + 2\gamma(r^D - r^R)} \qquad (9)$$

We will specify the values of the policies t and r so that larger t means more liberal on the economic issue and larger r means more conservative on the values issue. Thus, at equilibrium, we will expect that $t^D > t^R$, $r^D > r^R$, and $\beta(t^D - t^R) + \gamma(r^D - r^R) < 0$. For an equilibrium with this characteristic, it follows from that the constituency D will be precisely

$$D = \{(\theta, \rho) \in H \mid \rho < \psi(\tau^D, \tau^R, \theta)\}, \quad (10)$$

for these are the types who will prefer policy τ^D to τ^R. R, of course, comprises the remaining types (except for a set of measure zero). See figure 7.2.

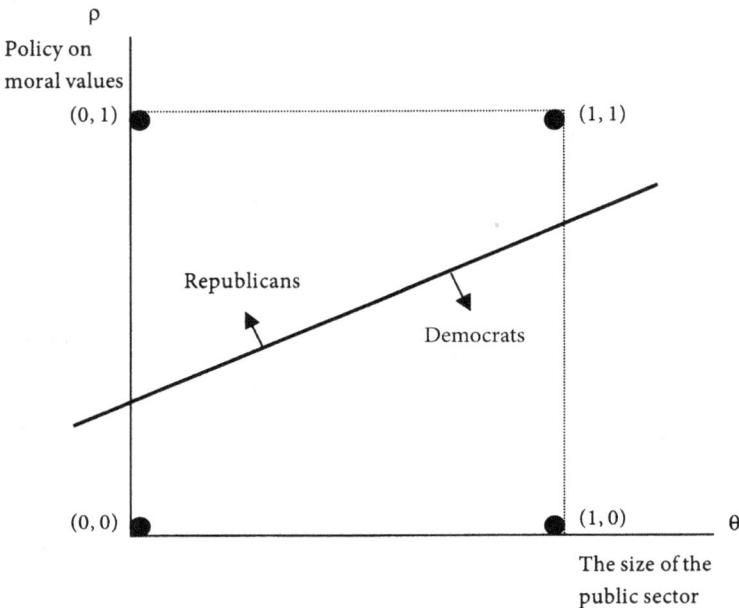

Fig. 7.2. Hypothetical voter separation.

Thus, we can write,

$$\varphi(\tau) = \int_{-\infty}^{\infty} \int_{-\infty}^{\psi(\tau,\theta)} dF(\theta,\rho), \quad (11)$$

where the inside integral is over ρ and the outside integral is over ρ. Similarly, we can write,

$$V^D(\tau^D) = \int_{-\infty}^{\infty} \int_{-\infty}^{\psi(\tau^D,\tau^R,\theta)} v(\tau^D;\theta,\rho) dF(\theta,\rho), \quad (12)$$

$$V^R(\tau^R) = \int_{-\infty}^{\infty} \int_{\psi(\tau^D,\tau^R,\theta)}^{\infty} v(\tau^R;\theta,\rho) dF(\theta,\rho) \quad (13)$$

Now we substitute these expressions into the first-order conditions (6) and (7), and we have fully modeled PUNE—that is, condition (2) of the definition of PUNE holds by construction.

The first-order conditions now comprise four equations in six unknowns—the four policy unknowns of the Left and Right parties, and the two Lagrange multipliers x and y. If there is a solution, there will (generically) be, therefore, a two-parameter family of solutions. As we described earlier, the points in this family or manifold can be viewed as corresponding to equilibria associated with different relative bargaining strengths of the pairs of factions in the parties D and R.

In general, there are many equilibria of the model. But in the empirical work that we have carried out over the past five years, it is heartening to learn that these equilibria are quite concentrated in the policy space (in all the important applications). Thus, we do not lose much predictive power by virtue of the multiplicity of equilibria.

That multiplicity, which is two-dimensional (regardless of the dimension of the policy space), is due to our not specifying the relative bargaining strengths of the internal factions within the parties. In other words, if we could specify what those bargaining strengths were, we could pin down a unique equilibrium. Indeed, at any PUNE, we can compute the associated relative bargaining powers of the Opportunists and Militants in each party. We model the bargaining game within the parties as a Nash bargaining game with threat points. The details of the game and the computation of bargaining powers are presented in Roemer (2001, chap. 8) and Roemer, Lee, and van der Straeten (2007, chap. 2). The relative bargaining power of the Militants in the Democratic Party at PUNE (τ^D,τ^R) is given by

$$\frac{x(V^D(\tau^D) - V^D(\tau^R))}{\varphi(\tau^D, \tau^R) + x(V^D(\tau^D) - V^D(\tau^R))}, \quad (14)$$

where x solves equation (6), and the relative bargaining power of the Militants in Republican Party is given by

$$\frac{y(V^R(\tau^R) - V^R(\tau^D))}{1 - \varphi(\tau^D, \tau^R) + y(V^R(\tau^R) - V^R(\tau^D))}, \quad (15)$$

where y is the solution of equation (7).

Unfortunately, we do not have good data on these relative bargaining strengths. (Indeed, there probably is no formal bargaining game taking place within parties; our model is meant to capture the idea that the setting of policies by parties reflects both vote-maximizing and constituency-representing aims.) One way that we can refine the set of equilibria is to fit the model to the observed data in various ways, for instance, by restricting ourselves to equilibria that generate the *observed* vote shares for a particular election. This essentially eliminates one degree of freedom from the equilibrium set.

We have recently completed an analysis of how the race issue affected the degree of income taxation in the United States, during the period 1972–1992 (Lee and Roemer 2006). Along with Karine van der Straeten, we have extended this analysis to three other countries—the United Kingdom, Denmark, and France (Roemer, Lee, and van der Straeten 2007). In this analysis, we posited either two or three parties, as was appropriate for the particular country, and a two-dimensional policy space, consisting of the economic issue and the race or immigration issue. In each country, we chose model parameters based on empirical data and then conducted some counterfactual calculations to understand the degree to which the race/immigration issue affects the equilibrium on the economic issue. In all cases, we conclude that the effect is significant. In the United States, we compute that the income tax rate would be approximately ten percentage points higher were racism absent from American voters' worldviews.

Our work on this problem illustrates the tractability of the PUNE model—indeed, its capacity to track extremely closely the electoral experience in these countries. We conclude from this work that the conceptualization of parties as consisting of bargaining factions appears to be a fertile one, at least in the pragmatic sense of producing a model that tracks reality well, without having to postulate many exogenous parameters to achieve a good fit of model to data.

B. The Policy Bundle (PB) and Moral Puritanism (MP) Effects

The two counterfactual experiments are carried out in the following way. The first counterfactual experiment is done by assuming that *the issue of moral values (r) is not an issue* in the election (thus, parties compete over the single issue of the size of the public sector, t), although voters continue to possess the same joint distribution described by $F(\theta,\rho)$. (In actual calculations, we set $\bar{r} = \varphi^{obs} r_D^{obs} + (1 - \varphi^{obs}) r_R^{obs}$.) Thus, it continues to be the case, in this counterfactual contest, that voters' views on values will affect the political equilibrium *indirectly* through their effect on preferences about the size of the public sector. If we call t^J an equilibrium public-sector size for party J in the full model and t_I^J an equilibrium public-sector size for party J in this counterfactual, then the difference $t_I^J - t^J$ is exactly a measure of the policy-bundle effect.

The second counterfactual experiment is then carried out by estimating a counterfactual distribution of voter preferences for public-sector size. The point here is to estimate what the effect would be on the equilibrium concerning the economic issue if the strong correlation between the values issue and the economic issue that characterizes Republican voters were reduced. We have seen that Republican voters' views on the size of the public sector were highly correlated with their views on the values issue, whereas there was no similar significant correlation for Democratic voters. We therefore estimate what the distribution of preferences about the size of the public sector would have been, if the views of Republican voters on the public sector were to have had the same correlation with the values issue as is observed on average in the entire population. Call this counterfactual distribution the *value-weak distribution for the public sector*; it is a new joint distribution $G(\theta,\rho)$. We now run a second unidimensional election—again, where the only political issue is the size of the public sector—where we take the distribution of voter types to be given by G. We again fix the value of r to be the average value in the population. The results of this election will be sterilized of both the policy-bundle and the moral Puritanism effects. If we summarize the economic policies of the PUNEs in this election by t_{II}^J then we say that the total effect of moral

Policy space

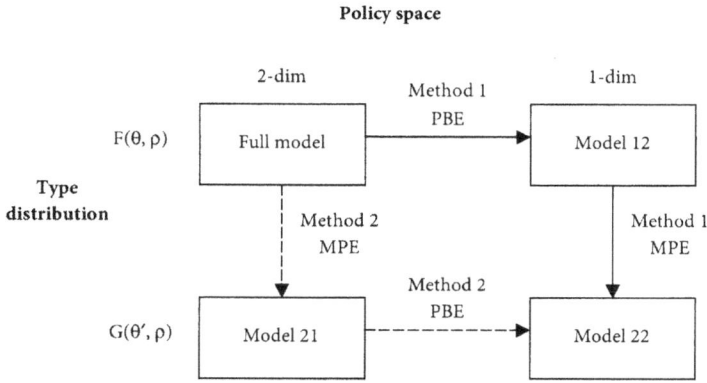

Fig. 7.3. Decomposition of total effects into PBE and MPE.

values on public-sector size is $t_{II}^J - t^J$, and the effect of moral Puritanism is $t_{II}^J - t_I^J$. That is,

$$\text{Total effect}(t_{II}^J - t^J) = \text{PB effect}(t_I^J - t^J) + \text{MP effect}(t_{II}^J - t_I^J).$$

The order of decomposition is not unique, however. Consider the following third experiment. Suppose we assume that the joint distribution is given by $G(\theta,\rho)$ and run a two-dimensional election with this counterfactual distribution. If we call $t_{II'}^J$ an equilibrium public-sector size for party J in this counterfactual, then the difference $t_{II'}^J - t^J$ is exactly a measure of the moral Puritanism effect, and the difference $t_{II}^J - t_{II'}^J$ is a measure of the policy-bundle effect. We call the decomposition method according to the first order "Method 1" and that according to the second order "Method 2." Because the order of decomposition is arbitrary, we take the average of the effects obtained from the two methods. Figure 7.3 illustrates the two methods of decomposition schematically.

Numerical Computation

Our main variables, θ and ρ, lie strictly between 0 and 1. Thus, in the numerical computation, we will assume that the distribution of voter types is given by a five-parameter bivariate Beta distribution specified in Gupta and Wong (1985). More specifically, the joint probability density function of the bivariate Beta distribution we use is given by

$$f(h_1,h_2) = \left[\prod_{j=1}^{2} g(h_j;a_j,b_j) \right] \left[1 + \lambda \prod_{j=1}^{2} (2G(h_j;a_j,b_j) - 1) \right] \quad (16)$$

where

$$g(h_j;a_j,b_j) = \frac{1}{b(a_j,b_j)} (h_j)^{a_j-1}(1-h_j)^{b_j-1} \mathbf{I}_{[0,1]}(h_j)$$

is a univariate Beta density, $G(h_j;a_j,b_j)$ is the distribution function of $g(h_j;a_j,b_j)$, and $a_j > 0, b_j > 0, |\lambda| \leq 1$. It has been shown that the parameter λ is proportional to the coefficient of correlation between h_1 and h_2. We denote the distribution function of f by F. Gupta and Wong (1985) derive the following formula for joint moments of the bivariate Beta distribution:

$$E(h_1^{n_1} h_2^{n_2}) = \prod_{i=1}^{2} E(h_i^{n_i})$$

$$+ \lambda \prod_{i=1}^{2} E(h_i^{n_i}) \left\{ \frac{2B(2a_i+n_i,b_i)}{a_i B(a_i,b_i) B(a_i+n_i,b_i)} * {}_3F_2 \left(\begin{matrix} a_i, 1-b_1, n_1+2a_i \\ a_i+1, n_i+2a_i+b_i \end{matrix} \middle| 1 \right) - 1 \right\},$$

where

$${}_pF_q \left(\begin{matrix} x_1,...,x_p \\ y_1,...,y_p \end{matrix} \middle| z \right) = \sum_{n=1}^{\infty} \frac{\prod_{i=1}^{p} \frac{\Gamma(x_i+n)}{\Gamma(x_i)}}{\prod_{i=1}^{q} \frac{\Gamma(y_i+n)}{\Gamma(y_i)}} \frac{z^n}{n!}$$

is the hypergeometric function. This formula allows us to compute the means and the variances of the two marginal distribution functions and the covariance between the two variables. Thus,

$$Eh_i = \frac{a_i}{a_i+b_i}, \quad (17)$$

$$Var(h_i) = \frac{a_i b_i}{(a_i+b_i)^2 (a_i+b_i+1)} \quad (18)$$

and

$$Cov(h_1,h_2) = \lambda \prod_{i=1}^{2} \frac{a_i}{a_i+b_i} \left\{ \frac{2B(2a_i+1,b_i)}{a_i B(a_i,b_i) B(a_i+1,b_i)} * {}_3F_2 \left(\begin{matrix} a_i, 1-b_i, 1+2a_i \\ a_i+1, 1+2a_i+b_i \end{matrix} \middle| 1 \right) - 1 \right\}.$$

$$(19)$$

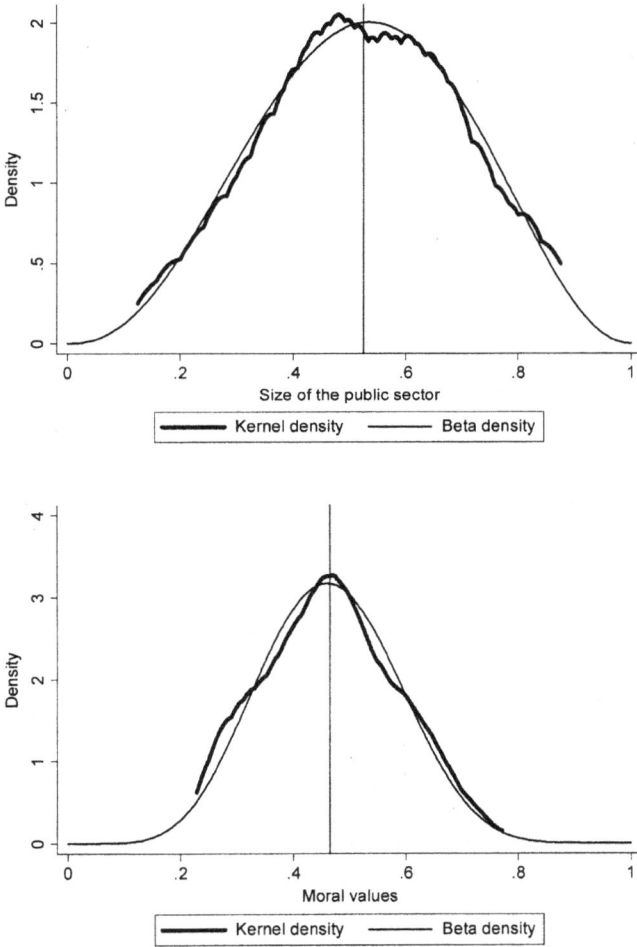

Fig. 7.4. Marginal densities of voter types: nonparametric and parametric. We use the optimal bandwidth suggested by Silverman in drawing the kernel densities.

By comparing them with the empirical means, variances, and covariance, we can determine the values of $(a_1, b_1, a_2, b_2, \lambda)$.

Figure 7.4 shows the estimated beta densities and a nonparametrically estimated densities (a kernel method with the Silverman's optimal bandwidth). As is clear from the figure, the fit is extremely good. Using a nonparametric joint density in numerical computations is possible but

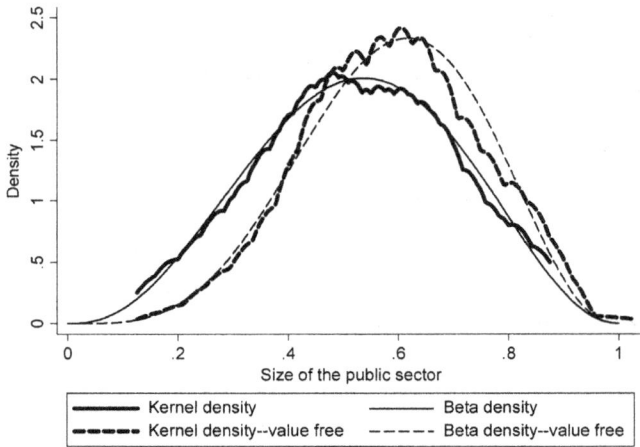

Fig. 7.5. Counterfactual distribution of value-weak preference for the public sector.

extremely expensive in terms of the computation time required; thus, we use the Beta distribution.

We also computed the density of the *value-weak preference for the public sector*. As is shown in figure 7.5, the Beta fit is not bad for the counterfactual distribution as well.

We do not know the empirical values of γ and β. Thus, we varied the value of γ from 0.8 to 1.6, and for each value of γ we chose the value of β that minimizes $j(t_{obs}^D, t_{obs}^R, R_{obs}^D, R_{obs}^R) - j_{obs}$. The values of β's computed in this way are all negative; thus, the utility function exhibits positive complementarity. (See figure 7.1 again.)

Out of the four models described in figure 7.3, two of them are two-dimensional models (i.e., the full model and model 21), and the other two are one-dimensional models (i.e., model 12 and model 22). For the full model and model 21, we use equations (6) and (7), which form a system of four equations in six unknowns (the four policy variables and the two Lagrange multipliers). Consequently, we can expect to find a two-manifold of solutions in these models if there are any solutions. We started the computation by (randomly) choosing a pair of r^D and r^R (with $r^D < r^R$); we solve the four equations for t^D, t^R, x, and y for the chosen values of r^D and r^R. In the computation we checked whether (1) the root found by the computer satisfies the four first-order conditions, (2) the indifference curves of party factions are indeed tangent to each other for both parties, and (3) x and y are nonnegative. For the two counterfactual models, we (randomly) choose a pair of t^D and t^R solving the two equations

$$-\frac{\P j(t^D,t^R,r_{obs},r_{obs})}{\P t^D} = \frac{\P V^D(t^D,r_{obs})}{\P t^D} \text{ and } \frac{\P j(t^D,t^R,r_{obs},r_{obs})}{\P t^R} = \frac{\P V^R(t^R,r_{obs})}{\P t^R}$$

for x and y, while checking whether $x^3 \emptyset$ and $y^3 \emptyset$ hold.

For the two-dimensional models, we run the program until it finds at least sixty PUNEs. For the one-dimensional models, we did three hundred random samplings, which usually finds 100–150 PUNEs. Running the two-dimensional models is more time-consuming than running the one-dimensional models.

We did not use all these PUNEs in computing our decomposition effects. We adopted the following procedure. First, out of the sixty PUNEs in the full model, we selected those whose (equilibrium) vote share is within 10 percent of the observed vote share. Then we computed the average bargaining powers of these equilibria. Finally for the other three models, we chose those equilibria whose bargaining powers are close to the average bargaining powers of the selected equilibria in the full model. This means that we are controlling for the effect of a change in bargaining powers. As we view the relative bargaining powers of the factions as our missing data, it seems to us that this makes good sense. This does not mean that we think the actual bargaining powers would not change. It means that we are interested in the pure effects of MPE and PBE, not the combination of these effects and the effect of a change in bargaining powers.

Figure 7.6 illustrates the equilibrium values of PUNEs for the full model for a particular value of (γ, β). The big rectangles denote the observed policies of the two parties, and the big dots represent the average equilibrium policies of the two parties. The midsized dots represent the ideal policies of the militants in the two parties, and the smallest dots represent the individual PUNEs. In general, D policies are scattered on the southeast corner, and R policies are scattered on the northwest corner.

Table 7.3 shows the results for all different combinations of (γ, β) and their decompositions according to the two methods described in the preceding section. The average policies are the averages of the policies of the two parties.

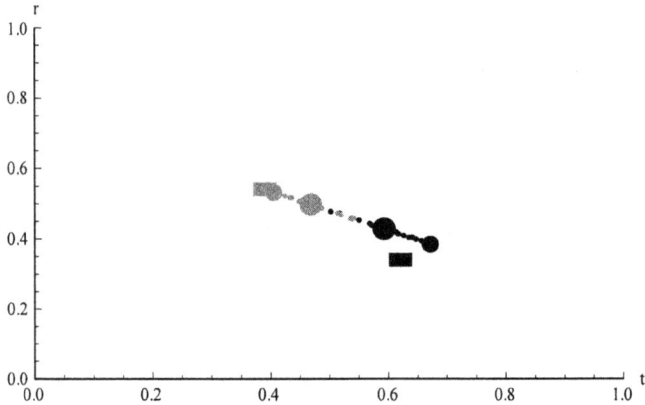

Fig. 7.6. PUNEs ($\gamma = 1.4$; $\beta = -0.60$). Rectangles denote the observed policies of the two parties; midsized dots represent the ideal policies of the militants in the two parties; bigger dots represent the average equilibrium policies of the two parties; smallest dots represent PUNEs; the dark color is for Democrats, and the light color is for Republicans; the horizontal axis is the size of the public sector and the vertical axis is the moral-value issue.

First, we note that the equilibrium policies are differentiated between the two parties. When $(\gamma,\beta) = (1.4,-0.6)$, for instance, the Democratic Party proposes $t^D = 0.59$, and the Republican Party proposes $t^R = 0.47$.

The effect of moral values on redistribution in the United States is small if γ is low, and it is large if γ is high. This is not surprising because γ measures the relative salience of moral values. If $(\gamma,\beta) = (1.4,-0.6)$, we predict that the Republican Party would have proposed $t^R = 0.57$, absent the issue of moral values. Due to the existence of the values issue, however, the Republican Party was able to propose $t^R = 0.47$; thus, the effect of values on the size of the public sector is about 21 percent ($0.10/0.47$) for the Republican Party. This is about 56 percent of the standard deviation of the distribution of ideal points of the tax rate. The effect of values on the size of the public sector for the Democratic Party is also large. Absent the moral-values issue, we predict party D would have proposed $t^D = 0.68$; due to the existence of moral values, it proposed $t^D = 0.59$. If $(\gamma,\beta) = (0.8,-0.21)$, on the other hand, the effect of the values issue on the size of the public sector is about 24 percent of the standard deviations of

TABLE 7.3
PUNEs and the Decomposition Effects

$(\gamma = 0.8; \beta = -0.21)$

	Full	Model 12	Model 21	Model 22	Observed
BPD	0.339	0.265	0.275	0.262	NA
BPR	0.308	0.348	0.334	0.307	NA
tD	0.594	0.551	0.605	0.622	0.62
tR	0.475	0.423	0.505	0.519	0.39
RD	0.438	NA	0.461	NA	0.34
RR	0.485	NA	0.487	NA	0.54
tAVE	0.533	0.495	0.561	0.576	0.502
φ	0.486	0.566	0.583	0.543	0.485

	Democratic Policies		
	Method 1	Method 2	Average
PBE	−0.043	0.017	−0.013
% s.d.	−24.042	9.708	−7.167
MPE	0.071	0.011	0.041
% s.d.	39.775	6.025	22.9
PBE/TOT × 100	−152.809	61.705	−45.552
MPE/TOT × 100	252.809	38.295	145.552

	Republican Policies		
	Method 1	Method 2	Average
PBE	−0.052	0.014	−0.019
% s.d.	−29.168	7.638	−10.765
MPE	0.096	0.03	0.063
% s.d.	53.548	16.74	35.144
PBE/TOT × 100	−119.645	31.330	−44.158
MPE/TOT × 100	219.645	68.671	144.158

	Average Policies		
	Method 1	Method 2	Average
PBE	−0.037	0.015	−0.011
% s.d.	−20.761	8.091	−6.335
MPE	0.080	0.029	0.055
% s.d.	44.830	15.979	30.404
PBE/TOT × 100	−86.256	33.614	−26.321
MPE/TOT × 100	186.256	66.386	126.321

$(\gamma = 1.2, \beta = -0.57)$

	Full	Model 12	Model 21	Model 22	Observed
BPD	0.262	0.243	0.267	0.216	NA
BPR	0.267	0.316	0.258	0.227	NA
tD	0.571	0.525	0.641	0.603	0.62
tR	0.474	0.395	0.567	0.518	0.39
RD	0.442	NA	0.437	NA	0.34
RR	0.492	NA	0.478	NA	0.54
tAVE	0.524	0.469	0.605	0.562	0.502
φ	0.510	0.584	0.471	0.534	0.485

(continued)

TABLE 7.3 (*continued*)

	Democratic Policies		
	Method 1	Method 2	Average
PBE	−0.046	−0.039	−0.042
% s.d.	−25.379	−21.501	−23.44
MPE	0.078	0.071	0.074
% s.d.	43.244	39.366	41.305
PBE/TOT × 100	−142.06	−120.354	−131.207
MPE/TOT × 100	242.06	220.354	231.207

	Republican Policies		
	Method 1	Method 2	Average
PBE	−0.079	−0.049	−0.064
% s.d.	−44.038	−27.426	−35.732
MPE	0.122	0.092	0.107
% s.d.	68.176	51.565	59.870
PBE/TOT × 100	−182.439	−113.622	−148.03
MPE/TOT × 100	282.439	213.622	248.03

	Average Policies		
	Method 1	Method 2	Average
PBE	−0.055	−0.042	−0.049
% s.d.	−30.596	−23.692	−27.144
MPE	0.094	0.081	0.088
% s.d.	52.301	45.397	48.849
PBE/TOT × 100	−140.965	−109.155	−125.060
MPE/TOT × 100	240.965	209.155	225.060

($\gamma = 1.4$, $\beta = -0.6$)

	Full	Model 12	Model 21	Model 22	Observed
BPD	0.379	0.320	0.338	0.338	NA
BPR	0.360	0.254	0.250	0.237	NA
tD	0.593	0.214	0.656	0.679	0.62
tR	0.470	0.479	0.578	0.571	0.39
RD	0.428	NA	0.424	NA	0.34
RR	0.496	NA	0.475	NA	0.54
tAVE	0.530	0.541	0.612	0.617	0.502
φ	0.492	0.452	0.431	0.413	0.485

	Democratic Policies		
	Method 1	Method 2	Average
PBE	0.021	0.023	0.022
% s.d.	11.759	12.769	12.264
MPE	0.065	0.063	0.064
% s.d.	36.362	35.353	35.858
PBE/TOT × 100	24.437	26.535	25.486
MPE/TOT × 100	75.563	73.466	74.514

TABLE 7.3 (*continued*)

	Republican Policies		
	Method 1	Method 2	Average
PBE	0.010	−0.007	0.001
% s.d.	5.386	−4.182	0.602
MPE	0.092	0.109	0.100
% s.d.	51.205	60.773	55.989
PBE/TOT × 100	9.517	−7.389	1.064
MPE/TOT × 100	90.483	107.389	98.936

	Average Policies		
	Method 1	Method 2	Average
PBE	0.011	0.005	0.008
% s.d.	6.028	2.573	4.300
MPE	0.076	0.082	0.079
% s.d.	42.538	45.993	44.266
PBE/TOT × 100	12.412	5.298	8.855
MPE/TOT × 100	87.588	94.703	91.145

$(\gamma = 1.6, \beta = -0.75)$

	Full	Model 12	Model 21	Model 22	Observed
BPD	0.273	0.284	0.291	0.286	NA
BPR	0.296	0.222	0.227	0.199	NA
tD	0.574	0.623	0.648	0.673	0.62
tR	0.475	0.498	0.583	0.577	0.39
RD	0.437	NA	0.423	NA	0.34
RR	0.494	NA	0.470	NA	0.54
tAVE	0.526	0.555	0.614	0.619	0.502
φ	0.506	0.432	0.432	0.416	0.485

	Democratic Policies		
	Method 1	Method 2	Average
PBE	0.050	0.024	0.037
% s.d.	27.529	13.587	20.558
MPE	0.050	0.075	0.062
% s.d.	27.762	41.704	34.733
PBE/TOT × 100	49.789	24.574	37.181
MPE/TOT × 100	50.212	75.426	62.819

	Republican Policies		
	Method 1	Method 2	Average
PBE	0.023	−0.006	0.008
% s.d.	12.852	−3.600	4.626
MPE	0.079	0.109	0.094
% s.d.	44.222	60.674	52.448
PBE/TOT × 100	22.518	−6.308	8.105
MPE/TOT × 100	77.482	106.308	91.895

(*continued*)

TABLE 7.3 (*continued*)

| | Average Policies | | |
	Method 1	Method 2	Average
PBE	0.029	0.005	0.017
% s.d.	16.009	2.943	9.477
MPE	0.064	0.087	0.076
% s.d.	35.722	48.788	42.255
PBE/TOT × 100	30.946	5.691	18.319
MPE/TOT × 100	69.054	94.309	81.682

the distribution of ideal points of the tax rate for the Republican Party and 16 percent for the Democratic Party.

When we decompose the total effect into the two effects that we suggested earlier, we notice that the moral Puritanism effect is generally positive, regardless of whether the value of γ is low or high. The policy-bundle effect, on the other hand, is positive if the issue of moral values is sufficiently salient ($\gamma = 1.4:1.6$), and it is negative if it is not salient ($\gamma = 0.8:1.2$).

Figure 7.7 shows the equilibrium voter separation for the four models that we described in figure 7.3, juxtaposed on the contour plots of the beta densities. For brevity, we illustrate the equilibrium voter separation for two extreme parameter values of (γ,β). Each straight line in these figures demarcates the types who, at equilibrium, vote Republican from the types who vote Democratic. The space of the plots in figure 7.7 is (θ,ρ). Those types "below" a line are Democrats, and those "above" are Republicans. To be precise, each line is the graph of equation (9) above for one of the elections. (Note that ψ is a linear function of θ in equation (9).) For each pair of parameter values, the first panel shows the voter separation for the full model and model 12, and the second panel shows the voter separation for model 21 and model 22. The beta density in the first panel is that with the actual preference for the size of the public sector, and the beta density in the second panel is that with the counterfactual value-weak preference for the size of the public sector. A perfectly vertical voter separation line would correspond to pure class politics: Republican and Democratic voters would precisely correspond to those who desired small and large public sectors, respectively. In both panels, the flatter separation curves are those for the two-dimensional models (i.e., the full model and model 21), and the steeper ones are those for the one-dimensional models (i.e., model 12 and model 22). Thus, the presence of the issue of moral values makes U.S. politics less class-oriented.

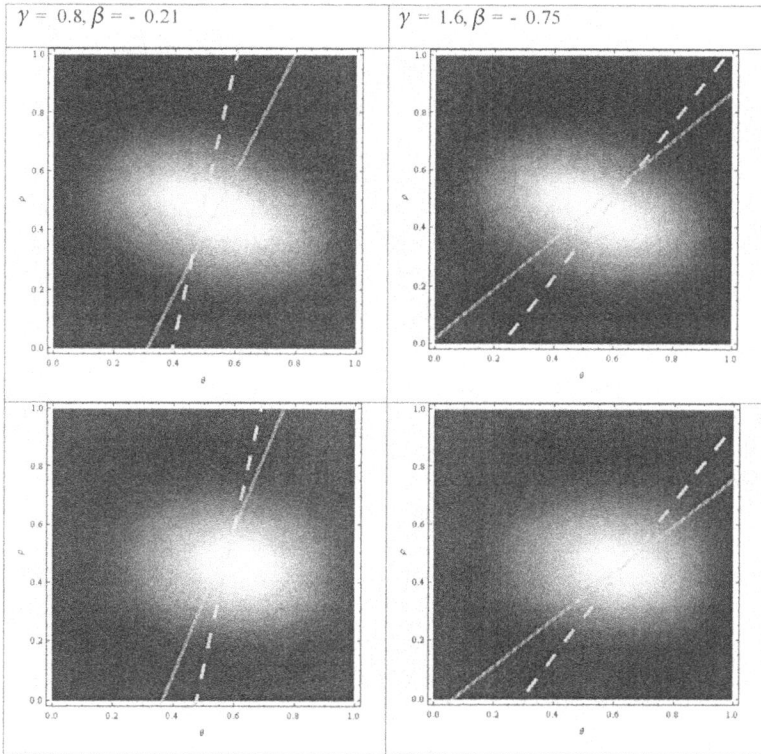

Fig. 7.7. Equilibrium voter separation—full and counterfactuals. In each column, the first panel is based on the actual distribution $F(\theta,\rho)$, whereas the second panel is based on the counterfactual distribution $G(\theta',\rho)$. In both panels, the flatter line is the voter separation line when the policy space is two dimensional, whereas the steeper line is the voter separation line when the policy space is one-dimensional. All separation lines are evaluated at the average equilibrium policies.

Conclusion

There has been much useful work in political science that is relevant to the question that we pose. Almost all of this work, however, has been de-scriptive, in the sense that it searches for *correlations* between voter pref-erences and observed political outcomes. A multiple regression is only, after all, a correlation.

No statistical exercise of correlation, regardless of its sophistication, can answer adequately the kind of counterfactual question in which we are interested. For when we ask, "Why can the Republican Party propose an extremist economic policy and receive half the votes?" we are in fact asking, "What difference from the present reality would force the Republican Party to propose a much less extremist economic policy to remain a political player?" Questions such as this cannot be answered by observing correlations; they require a model of the social mechanism that connects voter views to political outcomes. The venue is party competition, and hence, we believe, a full model of party formation and competition is needed to analyze the problem.

We briefly comment on future research that might use the PUNE model to study the relative importance of the three bulleted explanations in our introduction. The procedure will again be to compute equilibria of the model under various counterfactual assumptions.

Ideally, we would define the set of voter types H as having many dimensions, which would be necessary to characterize voter preferences about many issues—say, the economic issue, the "values" issue, the "race" issue, and foreign policy. One question we are concerned with is whether the most important secondary issue, insofar as explaining the conservative economic policy of the Republican Party is concerned, is the race issue or the values issue—or, more generally, whether one of these issues is important at all. For the period 1972–1992, we believe that we have demonstrated the importance of the race issue (Lee and Roemer 2006). Today, as we have said, the values issue may be more important. To study this question, we would specify a three-dimensional space of voter types, enabling us to represent voter preferences on the economic issue, the race issue, and the values issue. We would then conduct counterfactual experiments of the following sort: How would the equilibrium change if *race were not an issue* in the election? How would it change if *values were not an issue* in the election? Recall that by a change in the equilibrium, we mean a change in party constituencies and party policies.

We note that our procedure is more sophisticated than simply estimating, from the NES data, the *relative salience* of these issues for voters: we posit a full equilibrium model that explains how party constituencies would change, and consequent party policies would change, were these issues to disappear from the electoral arena. The results of this kind of general-equilibrium computation are not related in any obvious way to the relative salience that these issues have for voters. It may be that the issue with larger salience has less effect on the equilibrium positions on the economic-policy dimension than the third issue, because of the nature of correlation of voter views on the three issues.

Appendix: ANES 2004 Pre-Post Study Variables Used in This Chapter

Variables	Definitions
spending	Some people think government should provide fewer services even in areas such as health and education in order to reduce spending. Suppose these people are at one end of a scale, at point 1. Other people feel it is important for the government to provide many more services even if it means an increase in spending. Suppose these people are at the other end, at point 7. And of course, some other people have opinions somewhere in between, at points 2, 3, 4, 5, or 6. Where would you place yourself on this scale? (Rescaled into 0–1)
job	Some people feel the government in Washington should see to it that every person has a job and a good standard of living. Suppose these people are at one end of a scale, at point 1. Others think the government should just let each person get ahead on their own. Suppose these people are at the other end, at point 7. And, of course, some other people have opinions somewhere in between, at points 2, 3, 4, 5, or 6. Where would you place yourself on this scale? (Order reverted and then rescaled into 0–1.)
health	There is much concern about the rapid rise in medical and hospital costs. Some people feel there should be a government insurance plan which would cover all medical and hospital expenses for everyone. Suppose these people are at one end of a scale, at point 1. Others feel that all medical expenses should be paid by individuals through private insurance plans like Blue Cross or other company-paid plans. Suppose these people are at the other end, at point 7. And, of course, some other people have opinions somewhere in between, at points 2, 3, 4, 5, or 6. Where would you place yourself on this scale? (Order reverted and then rescaled into 0–1.)
publicsize	average of spending, job, and health
womenrole	Recently there has been a lot of talk about women's rights. Some people feel that women should have an equal role with men in running business, industry, and government. (Suppose these people are at one end of a scale, at point 1.) Others feel that a woman's place is in the home. (Suppose these people are at the other end, at point 7.) And, of course, some other people have opinions somewhere in between, at points 2, 3, 4, 5, or 6. (Rescaled into 0–1.)
workingmom	"A working mother can establish just as warm and secure a relationship with her children as a mother who does not work." Do you AGREE (1), NEITHER AGREE NOR DISAGREE (3), or DISAGREE (5) with this statement? (Order reverted and then rescaled into 0–1.)

Variables	Definitions
womenhome	"It is much better for everyone involved if the man is the achiever outside the home and the woman takes care of the home and family." Do you AGREE (1), NEITHER AGREE NOR DISAGREE (3), or DISAGREE (5) with this statement? (Order reverted and rescaled into 0–1.)
abortion	There has been some discussion about abortion during recent years. Which one of the opinions on this page best agrees with your view? You can just tell me the number of the opinion you choose. 1. By law, abortion should never be permitted. 2. The law should permit abortion only in case of rape, incest, or when the woman's life is in danger. 3. The law should permit abortion for reasons other than rape, incest, or danger to the woman's life, but only after the need for the abortion has been clearly established. 4. By law, a woman should always be able to obtain an abortion as a matter of personal choice. (Order reverted and then rescaled into 0–1.)
homo_nodiscrimination	Do you FAVOR (1) or OPPOSE (5) laws to protect homosexuals against job discrimination? (Order reverted and then rescaled into 0–1.)
gaymarriage	Should same-sex couples be ALLOWED to marry, or do you think they should NOT BE ALLOWED to marry? 1. Should be allowed 3. Should not be allowed 5. Should not be allowed to marry but should be allowed to legally form a civil union [VOL] (Reclassified as "should be allowed" (1) and "should not be allowed" (3 & 5) and then rescaled into 0–1.)
newlifestyles_problem	"The newer lifestyles are contributing to the breakdown of our society." Do you AGREE STRONGLY (1), AGREE SOMEWHAT (2), NEITHER AGREE NOR DISAGREE (3), DISAGREE SOMEWHAT (4), or DISAGREE STRONGLY (5) with this statement? (Order reverted and then rescaled into 0–1.)
tradition_important	"This country would have many fewer problems if there were more emphasis on traditional family ties." Do you AGREE STRONGLY (1), AGREE SOMEWHAT (2), NEITHER AGREE NOR DISAGREE (3), DISAGREE SOMEWHAT (4), or DISAGREE STRONGLY (5) with this statement? (Order reverted and then rescaled into 0–1.)
moralvalue	Average of womenrole, workingmom, womenhome, homo_nodiscrimination, gaymarriage, newlifestyles_problem, and tradition_important
aidtoblacks	Some people feel that the government in Washington should make every effort to improve the social and economic position of blacks. (Suppose these people are at one end of a scale, at point 1.) Others feel that the government should not make any special effort to help blacks because they should help themselves. (Suppose these people are at the other end, at point 7.) And, of course, some other people have opinions somewhere in between, at points 2, 3, 4, 5, or 6. Where would you place yourself on this scale? (Rescaled into 0–1.)
blackfavor	Some people say that because of past discrimination, blacks should be given preference in hiring and promotion. Others

Variables	Definitions
	say that such preference in hiring and promotion of blacks is wrong because it gives blacks advantages they haven't earned. What about your opinion—are you FOR (1) or AGAINST (5) preferential hiring and promotion of blacks? (Rescaled into 0–1.)
raceissue	Average of aidtoblacks and blackfavor
therm_whites (blacks, poor, feminists, homosexuals, southerners etc.)	I'd like to get your feelings toward some of our political leaders and other people who are in the news these days. I'll read the name of a person (a group of people) and I'd like you to rate that person (group) using something we call the feeling thermometer. Ratings between 50 degrees and 100 degrees mean that you feel favorable and warm toward the person (group). Ratings between 0 degrees and 50 degrees mean that you don't feel favorable toward the person (group) and that you don't care too much for that person (group). You would rate the person (group) at the 50 degree mark if you don't feel particularly warm or cold toward the person (group). If we come to a person whose name you don't recognize, you don't need to rate that person. Just tell me and we'll move on to the next one.
antiblackaffect	thermometer feeling toward the respondent's own race minus thermometer feeling toward blacks
bible	Which of these statements comes closest to describing your feelings about the Bible? You can just give me the number of your choice. 1. The Bible is the actual word of God and is to be taken literally, word for word. 2. The Bible is the word of God but not everything in it should be taken literally, word for word. 3. The Bible is a book written by men and is not the word of God. (Order reverted and then rescaled into 0–1.)
pray_often	People practice their religion in different ways. Outside of attending religious services, do you pray SEVERAL TIMES A DAY (1), ONCE A DAY (2), A FEW TIMES A WEEK (3), ONCE A WEEK OR LESS (4), or NEVER (5)? (Order reverted and then rescaled into 0–1.)
religiosity	Average of pray_often and bible
biggovt	You might agree to some extent with both, but we want to know which one is closer to your own views. ONE, we need a strong government to handle today's complex economic problems; or TWO, the free market can handle these problems without government being involved. (Rescaled into 0–1.)
iraqwarissue	Do you APPROVE (1) or DISAPPROVE (5) of the way George Bush is HANDLING THE WAR IN IRAQ? (Rescaled into 0–1.)
taxcutissue	As you may recall, President Bush signed a big tax cut a few years ago. Did you FAVOR (1) or OPPOSE the tax cut (5), or is this something you haven't thought about (3)? (Rescaled into 0–1.)
ssreform	A proposal has been made that would allow people to put a portion of their Social Security payroll taxes into personal retirement accounts that would be invested in private stocks and bonds. Do you FAVOR (1) this idea, OPPOSE (5) it, or NEITHER FAVOR NOR OPPOSE it (3)? (Rescaled into 0–1.)

Variables	Definitions
schoolvouchers	Do you FAVOR (1) or OPPOSE (5) having the government give parents in low-income families money to help pay for their children to attend a private or religious school instead of their local public school? (Rescaled into 0–1.)
environmentissue	Some people think it is important to protect the environment even if it costs some jobs or otherwise reduces our standard of living. (Suppose these people are at one end of the scale, at point number 1.) Other people think that protecting the environment is not as important as maintaining jobs and our standard of living. (Suppose these people are at the other end of the scale, at point number 7. And of course, some other people have opinions somewhere in between, at points 2, 3, 4, 5, or 6.) (Rescaled into 0–1.)
trust	Generally speaking, would you say that most people CAN BE TRUSTED (1) or that you CAN'T BE TOO CAREFUL (5) in dealing with people? (Order reverted and rescaled into 0 & 1.)
pastfinancial	We are interested in how people are getting along financially these days. Would you say that you (and your family living here) are BETTER off (1) or WORSE off (5) than you were a year ago or JUST ABOUT THE SAME (3)? (Order reverted and rescaled into −1,0,1.)
futurefinancial	Now looking ahead, do you think that a year from now you (and your family living here) will be BETTER OFF (1) financially, WORSE OFF (5), or JUST ABOUT THE SAME (3) as now? (Order reverted and rescaled into −1,0,1.)
pasteconomy	Now thinking about the economy in the country as a whole, would you say that over the past year the nation's economy has gotten BETTER (1), stayed ABOUT THE SAME (3), or gotten WORSE (5)? (Order reverted and rescaled into −1,0,1.)
futureeconomy	What about the next twelve months? Do you expect the economy, in the country as a whole, to get BETTER (1), stay ABOUT THE SAME (3), or get WORSE (5)? (Order reverted and rescaled into −1,0,1.)
age	age
education	Education: 1. 8 grades or less and no diploma or equivalent; 2. 9–11 grades, no further schooling; 3. High school diploma or equivalency; 4. More than twelve years of schooling; 5. Junior or community-college-level degree; 6. B.A.-level degrees; 7. Advanced degree, including LLB.
income_hh	Income of the household (in $10,000)

NOTES

We thank Joon-Jin Song for his advice on the bivariate Beta distribution used in this chapter.

1. See Putterman (1997) and Shapiro (2003) for many other explanations.

2. Roemer (1994) studies the strategic role of party ideology when voters are uncertain about the theory of the economy and parties argue for theories of the economy. In his model, the theory of the economy is the function that maps policies into economic outcomes, and each voter has a prior probability distribution

over possible theories of the economy; after parties announce their theories of the economy, each voter constructs a posterior distribution over such theories.

3. Seymour Martin Lipset (1996), a leading contemporary advocate of American exceptionalism, argues that from colonial times to the present, a particular set of religious values and ideological emphases have distinguished Americans. Among these ideological tendencies, two are especially distinctive: (1) a streak of conservative moralism that fuels recurring crusades for social reform, and (2) meritocratic individualism that supports the spirit of capitalism, antistatist attitudes, and a market economy.

4. For a good review on religion and politics in the United States, see Wald (2003). Mendelberg (2001) and Roemer, Lee, and Van der Straeten (2007) discuss the role of the race card in U.S. politics.

5. After we completed this chapter, the full version of ANES 2004 was released. According to the official web page of the National Election Studies, however, the major difference between the full version and the advance version is that the full version includes non-survey-question variables and corrects for some errors in the advance version. We corrected the errors of the advance release here, so that the dataset we use contains the same survey-question variables as the full version.

6. As will be explained in the next section, our full model requires solving a number of integral equations simultaneously. In the case of a two-dimensional policy space, we need to solve four integral equations, each of which requires evaluating double integrals. If the policy space were three-dimensional, however, we would need to solve six integral equations, each of which requires evaluating triple integrals. Because of the curse of dimensionality, computational time for triple integrals is much longer than that for double integrals.

7. The reader may be puzzled that adding the Reformist faction does not change the equilibrium set. Adding this faction does change something, however: the interpretation of the bargaining powers of the factions associated with particular equilibria. Thus, we do not say that Reformists do not matter; it is just that they do not matter for the present analysis.

REFERENCES

Bartels, Larry M. 2002. "Economic inequality and political representation." Unpublished paper, Russell Sage Foundation.

Frank, Thomas. 2005. *What's the Matter with Kansas?* New York: Metropolitan Books.

Gilens, Martin, 2003. "Public opinion and democratic responsiveness: Who gets what they want from government?" Unpublished paper, UCLA.

Gupta, A., and C. Wong. 1985. "On three and five parameter bivariate beta distributions." *Metrika* 32: 85–91.

Jacobs, Lawrence, and Benjamin Page. 2003. "Who influences U.S. foreign policy over time?" Unpublished paper, Northwestern University.

Lee, Woojin, and John Roemer. 2006. "Racism and redistribution in the United States, 1972–1992: A solution to the problem of American exceptionalism." *Journal of Public Economics* 90: 1026–1052.

Lipset, Seymour. 1996. *American Exceptionalism: A Double-Edged Sword.* New York: Norton.

Mendelberg, Tali. 2001. *The Race Card: Campaign Strategy, Implicit Messages and the Norm of Equality.* Princeton, NJ: Princeton University Press.

Putterman, Louis. 1997. "Why have the rabble not redistributed the wealth? On the stability of democracy and unequal property." In *Property Relations, Incentives and Welfare*, ed. John Roemer. London: Macmillan.

Roemer, John. 1994. "The strategic role of party ideology when voters are uncertain about how the economy works." *American Political Science Review* 88 (2): 327–335.

Roemer, John. 2001. *Political Competition.* Cambridge, MA: Harvard University Press.

Roemer, John, Woojin Lee, and Karine Van der Straeten. 2007. *Racism, Xenophobia, and Distribution: Multi-Issue Politics in Advanced Democracies.* Cambridge, MA: Harvard University Press.

Shapiro, Ian. 2003. *The State of Democratic Theory.* Princeton, NJ: Princeton University Press.

Silverman, Bernard. 1986. *Density Estimation for Statistics and Data Analysis.* New York: Chapman and Hall.

Wald, Kenneth. 2003. *Religion and Politics in the United States.* Lanham, MD: Rowman and Littlefield.

Chapter 8

||||||||||||||||||||||||||||||||||||||||||||||||||||||||||

Giving the People What They Want?
Age, Class, and Distribution in the United States

Christopher Howard

Democratic societies are rife with inequalities. Some of these inequalities are so deep, persistent, or consequential that they provoke disbelief and outrage. How could any nation with some semblance of political equality allow key resources to be distributed so unevenly among its members? Surely, most people would not accept such inequalities, so the answer must lie elsewhere, such as the design of institutions or the disproportionate power of interest groups.

Of course, inequalities that provoke outrage in one person may seem unremarkable, perhaps even legitimate, to another person. Powerful minorities may not have to "rig the game" in order to win more benefits, lower taxes, or less regulation from democratic governments. The majority may, at times, agree with such policies. In chapters 6 and 7 of this volume, we saw how religious and moral values could diminish the public's appetite for economic redistribution. This chapter offers additional evidence that self-interest, narrowly construed, does not determine the level of public support for social policies. In particular, I will analyze the relationship between public opinion and the distribution of government benefits across age and income lines in the United States.

It is easy to see why distributive conflicts in the United States could arise among different age groups. The United States devotes a hefty share of public spending to the elderly through Social Security, Medicare, and Medicaid. The national government spends almost twice as much on these three programs as on all of national defense (U.S. Census Bureau 2006). Accounting for a wider range of programs, the U.S. Congressional Budget Office (2000) has calculated that the national government spends four times as much on senior citizens as on children—even though there are twice as many children in the country as senior citizens. The nonpartisan Urban Institute, using a somewhat different method, puts the spending gap closer to three-to-one. Either way, the disparity is large and growing; in 1960, by contrast, the national government spent almost as much on children as on the elderly (Carasso, Steuerle, and Reynolds 2007). The tilt in favor of senior citizens is more pronounced than in other affluent democracies. Lynch (2001) has estimated that the ratio of elderly to nonelderly social spending is two to three times larger in the United States than in the average European nation.[1]

Distributive conflicts across income lines should likewise be pronounced. Income inequality is higher in the United States than in Europe or Canada. Among the countries tracked by the Luxembourg Income Study, only Mexico and Russia have more inequality than the United States.[2] By any number of indicators, inequality has grown in recent years. In 1975, the lowest quintile of U.S. households had 4.3 percent of national income, while the top quintile had 43.6 percent. By 2005, those shares were 3.4 and 50.4 percent, respectively. The Gini index of income inequality, whose values range from 0 to 1, increased from 0.40 to 0.47 during this same period. At the start of the twenty-first century, affluent Americans controlled a larger share of national income than they had in decades (DeNavas-Walt, Proctor, and Mills 2006).

Both of these developments have elicited much concern at the elite level. One reason is that neither appears likely to diminish anytime soon. Spending on older Americans is projected to grow substantially as the baby-boom generation ages. The recent expansion of Medicare to cover prescription drugs will make the trend more pronounced. The Bush tax cuts of 2001–2003, which were skewed so heavily toward the affluent, are expected to aggravate inequality for years to come. A more fundamental reason is that both trends strike observers as unfair and unsustainable. Admittedly, these are not usually the same observers; moderates and conservatives are more concerned about the age bias in spending, while liberals worry more about inequality. What unites them is a sense that some fundamental piece of the social fabric is being torn apart.

The message from both camps is unambiguous, often passionate. Lawrence Kotlikoff, an economist best known for his work on "generational accounting," has argued that the "intergenerational transfer represented by Social Security and Medicare 'has now gone way beyond what could be rationalized as an antipoverty program. What we are dealing with now is the expropriation of billions of dollars every year from young workers to finance the ever-rising consumption by greedy geezers'" (quoted in Pearlstein 1996). Pete Peterson, former Commerce Secretary under Richard Nixon and now president of the fiscally conservative Concord Coalition, has been openly critical of politicians' unwillingness to rein in the cost of Medicare and Social Security. "With faith-driven catechisms that are largely impervious to analysis or evidence, and that seem removed from any kind of serious political morality, both political parties have formed an unholy alliance—an undeclared war on the future. An undeclared war, that is, on our children" (Peterson 2004: xxvii). "Shame on us," writes syndicated columnist Robert Samuelson, addressing the baby-boom generation. "We are trying to rob our children and grandchildren, putting the country's future at risk. . . . On one of the great issues of our time, the social and economic costs of our retirement, we have adopted a policy of selfish silence" (Samuelson 2007). As chairman of the Federal Reserve Board, Alan Greenspan testified before Congress that continued growth of Social Security, Medicare, and Medicaid threatened the living standards of future generations.[3] Book titles such as *The Coming Generational Storm, Generations Apart: Xers vs. Boomers vs. the Elderly,* and *Young v. Old: Generational Combat in the 21st Century* convey a clear sense of conflicting priorities between young and old (Kotlikoff and Burns 2004; MacManus 1996; Thau and Heflin 1997).

Prominent liberals are less troubled by these trends. They believe that most proposals to cut or privatize Social Security, for example, are unnecessarily drastic. Modest changes to benefits and eligibility will suffice.[4] Moreover, if public spending currently tilts too far in favor of the elderly, their answer is not to spend less on older Americans. The right way to achieve a better balance is by spending more on individuals and families during their working years (Borosage and Hickey 2001; Greenstein and Skocpol 1997; Skocpol 2000).

The more pressing problem for liberals is inequality. While incomes have stagnated for millions of Americans, the rich have grown decidedly richer. The economic tides have been "lifting the yachts [and] swamping the rowboats" (Burtless and Smeeding 1995). The U.S. economy increasingly operates on winner-take-all principles (Frank and Cook 1995). Growing inequality threatens the social compact in which prosperity is shared by all (Sanger 1997); it is part of the "great unraveling" of American society (Krugman 2004). Prominent liberals increasingly refer to conservative fiscal policies as weapons of "class warfare" against less affluent citizens (Emanuel 2004; Greenstein quoted in Francis 2003; Kuttner 2004). They note that inequality is not simply the price Americans have to pay for a vibrant economy. Other nations' economies generate considerable inequalities, which are then tempered by government taxes and transfers. Public policies in the United States do less to reduce inequality than public policies elsewhere (Hacker et al. 2004; Kenworthy 1999; Kenworthy and Pontusson 2005).[5]

Analysts have offered numerous reasons for greater spending on the elderly and growing inequality, some of them demographic and some economic. Those reasons are beyond the scope of this chapter. The central question here concerns the politics of distribution. The prevailing political explanation is that senior citizens and the affluent have much greater influence on policymaking than their numbers would suggest. The elderly are more likely to vote and contribute to campaigns than the nonelderly. Individuals who receive Social Security and Medicare are more likely to vote, contribute, express interest in politics, and contact public officials than recipients of means-tested social programs, most of whom are not elderly. The elderly often participate precisely because of their interest in Social Security and Medicare. Older Americans are also more likely to belong to interest groups (Campbell 2003; Verba et al. 1993).[6] The best-known group is the AARP, which has been described as the "800-pound gorilla sitting on the legislative process," the "enforcer of an insatiable and all but invincible gray lobby," and the "most potent force in American politics" (Rep. Bill Thomas, R-CA, quoted in Fritz 2001: 1A; Schurenberg and Luciano 1988: 128; Birnbaum 1997: 123).[7] The affluent may not have an organization quite like the AARP, but their voices are heard clearly because all the standard forms of political participation are directly related to income as well as age (Page and Simmons 2000; Verba, Schlozman, and Brady 1995). Elected officials will therefore be reluctant to push income redistribution. In short, powerful minorities in U.S. politics have succeeded in shaping policies to serve their interests.

This line of reasoning assumes that public policy would look much different if Americans who were not elderly or not affluent had greater influence. This chapter will test that assumption by listening to what ordinary Americans think. Rather than examine the congruence between aggregate public opinion and public policy (Monroe 1998; Page and Shapiro 1983), I will analyze the congruence between the opinions of specific groups and public policy (Gilens 2004). In particular, I will compare attitudes toward important features of social policy along age and income lines, using evidence from the General Social Survey (GSS) and other national polls.[8] If, for instance, support for Social Security is significantly higher among the elderly than the nonelderly, then the age bias in social spending might reflect the interests of a powerful minority. On the other hand, if support for Social Security transcends age lines, then heavy spending on the elderly might be acceptable to most Americans, and distributive conflicts would not be deeply felt.

As we shall see, U.S. policies toward the elderly and the rich are fairly consistent with public opinion toward social spending and income redistribution.[9] What the elderly want from social policy is close to what the nonelderly want as well. And although support for redistribution from rich to poor does vary inversely with income, lower-income citizens are not exactly clamoring for government action, and their views have not changed in recent decades despite growing inequality. In short, the people who would appear to have the most to lose from heavy spending on the elderly and from growing inequality do not seem terribly bothered by either one.

Old, Middle, and Young

Limited government is a hallmark of the United States, and one common explanation for this is national values. Put simply, Americans want less government than Europeans or Canadians, and they get it (King 1973; Ladd 1994; Lipset 1996). Although Americans do want less government than do their European counterparts in some areas, there is substantial agreement concerning senior citizens. In the most recent Role of Government survey conducted by the International Social Survey Program (ISSP 1999), 87 percent of Americans agreed that government should "provide a decent standard of living for the old." Slightly larger majorities in Europe and Canada agreed with this view.[10] Asked whether government should spend more or less on retirement pensions, half of Americans said "more" and only 10 percent said "less." Their support was greater than in Canada, comparable to Germany, and just a little below Norway and Sweden.

The strong showing for the United States is an early indication that divisions across age lines may not be that large. In the ISSP survey, Americans aged sixty-five and older were slightly *less* likely to agree that government had a responsibility to provide for the old (84 percent) than were Americans aged thirty-five to sixty-four (86 percent) and those aged eighteen to thirty-four (89 percent). The results of the spending question were similar. Forty-eight percent of the Old and Middle groups wanted the government to spend more on Social Security, compared to 56 percent of Young adults. Nine percent of the Old wanted to spend less, compared to 11 percent of the Middle and 8 percent of the Young. This is evidence of generational consensus, not conflict.

These results could be atypical. Americans responded to the ISSP survey in 1996, a year of peace and prosperity. Perhaps they felt unusually generous that year. Pollsters asked the same question about government responsibility for the elderly in 1985, 1990, and 2002.[11] If we pool these responses, the results are virtually identical to those mentioned above. The only major change, surprisingly enough, was declining support among seniors. In 1985, 90 percent of the elderly said that government should provide them with a decent standard of living. By 2002, their support had dropped to 73 percent. Younger adults, in contrast, were still quite supportive (89 percent) in 2002. Signs of a generation gap have started to appear, but it is exactly the opposite of what a simple model of self-interest (i.e., "greedy geezers") would predict.

Since 1984, the General Social Survey has asked Americans, "Are we spending too much, too little, or about the right amount on Social Security?" Pooled results from 1984 to 2004 reinforce the general pattern described here (table 8.1). Over half of younger (60 percent) and middle-aged adults (58 percent) thought that too little was being spent on Social Security. Less than half (47 percent) of older Americans felt the same way. In this case, the generation gap has grown smaller over time. Nevertheless, in every single survey, the Young were more likely than the Old to think that too little was being spent on Social Security.[12]

In case readers are wondering if attitudes toward Social Security are polarized within the Young and Middle groups, the answer is no. Less than 10 percent of young or middle-aged adults thought that spending on Social Security was too large. The overwhelming majority thought that spending on Social Security was too low or about right. Nor is there evidence that Americans under the age of sixty-five have a blanket preference for more spending. Younger adults were much more likely to say that too little was spent on Social Security than on defense, foreign aid, highways, welfare, or improving conditions for African Americans.

The generational consensus extends beyond Social Security. In 2000 and 2002, the National Election Studies asked Americans if the budget surplus should be used to protect Social Security and Medicare. Eighty

TABLE 8.1
Support for Social Policy, by Age

Policy	Young	Middle	Old
Govt should provide decent standard of living for the old (1985–2002)	89.1%	89.4%	83.6%
We're spending too little on Social Security (1984–2004)	59.5	58.0	46.8
Govt should help pay medical bills (1984–2004)	55.9	49.4	43.3
We're spending too little on health (1980–2004)	67.5	70.1	60.8
Support national health insurance (1972–2004)	45.0	42.6	44.2
Govt should provide decent standard of living for unemployed (1985–96)	54.3	48.8	58.9
More govt spending on unemployment benefits (1985–96)	27.9	27.7	26.4
Govt should provide childcare for everyone who wants it (2002)	51.3	38.8	20.3
We're spending too little on assistance for childcare (2000–2004)	63.2	61.6	51.1
Govt should do everything possible to improve standard of living for poor (1984–2004)	33.0	28.2	25.0
We're spending too little on assistance to the poor (1984–2004)	69.6	64.7	56.1

Notes: Young = 18–34, Middle = 35–64, and Old = 65+; all figures refer to the percentage of each group agreeing with each question. Different questions are asked in different years.
Source: Author's calculations based on data from the General Social Survey for all questions except national health insurance, which is from the National Election Studies.

percent of those under the age of sixty-five and almost 90 percent of those over sixty-five agreed. A 2002 poll found that Americans under the age of sixty-five were more likely than Americans over the age of sixty-five to say that government was doing too little to help with the costs of long-term care for the elderly (Kaiser Family Foundation 2002).

Perhaps the most surprising example of generational agreement involves the recent Medicare prescription-drug benefit. This was one of the few domestic spending initiatives to pass during the George W. Bush administration, and its ten-year price tag ($400 billion? $500 billion? more?) is staggering. At a time when the economy was weak and the budget surplus was vanishing, surely here was a proposal that would pit young against old. Nevertheless, in a survey conducted right before the 2000 elections, more adults under the age of sixty-five than over sixty-five favored a general proposal to guarantee prescription-drug coverage to everyone on Medicare.[13] This survey was before details of any plan were made public; people were responding to the principle of coverage. In 2003, as legislators debated specific proposals in Congress, a larger share of the elderly than nonelderly said there were so many problems with these proposals that no bill should be enacted.[14] Shortly after President Bush signed the drug bill into law, a CNN/USA Today/Gallup poll found that the elderly were less likely to support it than the nonelderly.[15] U.S. officials did not promise to spend even more money on older Americans just because the elderly wanted them to.

Conceivably, Social Security and Medicare may enjoy broad approval because all Americans expect to grow old and collect benefits some day. In that case, we might expect support for these programs to increase with age; their self-interest should come into sharper focus as they approach retirement. And yet, young adults support Social Security every bit as much as middle-aged adults (table 8.1). If you asked a room composed solely of twenty-five-year-olds whether we spend too much or too little on Social Security, you would get virtually the same answers as another room of fifty-five-year-olds. Moreover, even when polling organizations ask questions pitting young against old, they have trouble finding signs of generational conflict. A 1999 Los Angeles Times survey asked if grown children should be expected to support their parents. A majority of respondents aged eighteen to forty-four said they should, compared to only a quarter of those over the age of sixty-five. Few members of either group (13 and 15 percent) agreed that "older people should be encouraged to retire early to make room for younger, more energetic workers."[16] In a separate survey, only 12 percent of adults under the age of thirty-five concurred that "senior citizens generally get more than their fair share of benefits, and that is unfair to young people."[17]

So far, it is hard to see much opposition among the nonelderly toward policies that benefit the elderly. To understand why the United States spends so much on the elderly relative to younger groups, perhaps we should examine policies aimed at individuals during their working years. One possibility is that Americans, regardless of age, offer stronger support for retirement pensions than for policies like unemployment benefits and child care. In the Role of Government survey discussed previously, Americans were much less likely than Europeans to agree that government should provide a decent standard of living for the unemployed. A second possibility is that support for these latter policies declines with age. The elderly may exhibit more narrow self-interest than younger adults, and the lack of consensus may explain why government does less for the nonelderly.

National surveys offer evidence that both of these possibilities are true. Table 8.1 displays answers to a number of questions about social policies. The first questions relate to income support for the elderly, the next to health, then unemployment, child care, and poverty. For each policy, there is usually one question about the proper role of government and one about spending. The two questions are conceptually distinct: one could believe that government ought to help the unemployed and that unemployment benefits were too high or too low. Some of these questions have been posed regularly for years; others, such as the one about child care, are more recent. Wherever possible, I have pooled answers from several years in order to give a general portrait of public opinion at the end of the twentieth century.[18] The figures refer to the percentage of each age group that agrees with the statements in the first column.

When it comes to the proper role of government in social welfare, providing a decent standard of living for seniors is literally the only thing that unites most Americans. Almost nine out of ten adults endorse this role. In contrast, Americans basically split fifty-fifty over whether government should help pay medical bills and whether it should provide a decent standard of living for the unemployed. Most Americans do not think that government should provide child care for everyone who wants it, nor do they think that government should do everything possible to improve the standard of living for the poor. Most Americans do not favor national health insurance. Regardless of age, Americans make a big distinction between helping the elderly versus the nonelderly.

Answers to the spending questions are a bit more ambiguous (table 8.1). A greater number of Americans seem to think that too little is being spent on helping the poor, paying for child care, and paying for health care than the number who think that too little is being spent on retirement pensions. This pattern holds true for the Young, Middle, and Old groups, and it seems to indicate that Americans want to close the spending gap between the elderly and nonelderly. Another interpretation, also plausible in my view, is that many Americans want more spending but not necessarily by government. When polls ask about more spending for Social Security or more spending on unemployment benefits, it is clear that government action is involved. When polls ask if "we" are spending too little on health or child care or poverty, respondents might or might not be thinking about government spending. They might be thinking instead about spending by individuals, companies, or charities. Given that many more people say "we" are spending too little on those needs compared to how many say government should be responsible for meeting those needs, it is not easy to claim that Americans want to alter the mix of public spending between the elderly and nonelderly in a significant way.

Differences in opinion are more evident in policies aimed at the nonelderly (table 8.1). Nevertheless, with one partial exception, those differences do not amount to much. There is virtually no gap with respect to national health insurance or spending on unemployment benefits. The elderly are slightly more likely than the nonelderly to think that government should provide for the unemployed. The nonelderly are somewhat more likely to think that government should help people with their medical bills and provide for the poor. Likewise, the nonelderly are more likely to think that additional money should be spent on health, child care, and poverty—though for the reasons just mentioned, it is not obvious that they all want government to do the spending. In no case are the elderly fundamentally at odds with the nonelderly.

The exception is child care. Young adults are much more likely than senior citizens to believe that government should provide child care (51 percent versus 20 percent). Middle-aged adults fall in between (39 percent). No other policy in table 8.1 features such a large difference in opinion. What makes this case different, I suspect, is that the current elderly grew up in a time when most parents did not pay for child care. Mothers, aunts, and grandmothers stayed home with their kids. Questions about parenting highlight these generational differences. Two-thirds of the elderly believe that preschool children will suffer if their mother works, compared to a little more than one-third of young adults. Almost three-quarters of the elderly believe that families are better off if "the man is the achiever outside the home and the woman takes care of the home and family." Roughly 30 percent of young adults and 40 percent of middle-aged adults agree with them.[19] Over time, differences in opinion should narrow as the population consists of more and more adults who grew up when paid child care was more acceptable. Currently, however, senior citizens do not believe that government should play a major role in child care, and even young adults are divided on the issue.

True, the elderly receive a larger share of social spending in the United States than in many other nations. The elderly are also more politically active than other groups of Americans. It seems logical to attribute these spending patterns to political influence. The problem with this reasoning is that Americans who are not elderly have very similar policy preferences to Americans who are elderly.[20] Based on survey results, the elderly do not seem to have power over social policy in the sense of making the rest of the country do something that they would not otherwise do (Dahl 1957).

Have-Lots, Haves, and Have-Nots

Although Americans may feel as strongly as Europeans about helping the elderly, they are clearly less interested in income redistribution. In the 1996 Role of Government survey, less than half of Americans said that government should be responsible for reducing income differences between rich and poor. Between two-thirds and three-quarters of Britons, Germans, Italians, Norwegians, and Swedes thought their governments should redistribute income (ISSP 1999).[21] The gap between the United States and Europe was even larger in a 1999 survey devoted specifically to inequality (ISSP 2002). What is not clear, however, is whether these aggregates conceal interesting variations and, in particular, whether some Americans feel more warmly than others toward income redistribution.[22]

We would expect support for redistribution to vary inversely with income. Of course, we might have expected support for social policies to vary more by age than it actually did, so there could be surprises here as well. In fact, less-affluent Americans are more disposed toward redistribution. For ease of presentation, I combined the twenty-plus income categories in the General Social Survey into just five, based on the cut-off points for income quintiles in the general population.[23] As table 8.2 shows, support for redistribution drops steadily as income increases. Lower-income citizens were more than twice as likely as upper-income citizens to support income redistribution circa 2000. The gap was even greater circa 1980.

TABLE 8.2
Support for Redistribution, by Income

Income category	1978–82	1998–2002
Lower	38.4%	34.5%
Lower-middle	28.8	28.3
Middle	22.7	23.6
Upper-middle	17.9	19.6
Upper	10.4	16.0
TOTAL	27.9	26.9

Notes: The differences across categories in both time periods are statistically significant ($p < .01$). For the exact question wording, see note 22; for explanation of the income categories, see note 23.
Source: General Social Survey, various years.

Although these differences are statistically significant, their political significance is less clear. Less than 40 percent of the poor want government to redistribute income, compared to 10–15 percent of the rich. Either way, it is a minority view. Even if we focus on the poorest of the poor, those with family incomes of less than $10,000, only 40 percent say they want government to redistribute income. Shifting from income categories to subjective class position makes no difference. At the end of the twentieth century, less than a third of Americans who called themselves lower class or working class thought that government should reduce income differences between rich and poor. The contrast with Europe is stark. In the Role of Government survey, two-thirds of lower- and working-class Britons and three-quarters of lower- and working-class Swedes favored government redistribution of income (ISSP 1999). Table 8.2 also indicates that Americans' support for redistribution has changed little in recent decades, despite growing inequality.[24] Public officials in the United States are not exactly ignoring the voices of the disadvantaged when they hesitate to promote redistribution.

Yet a recent study suggests that changes in public opinion have been occurring. We just have not been looking in the right places. Osberg and Smeeding (2005) forgo the usual questions about government responsibility and redistribution from rich to poor. Instead, they use questions from ISSP surveys about what individuals in certain occupations do earn and should earn in order to construct measures of acceptable inequality. One of their most important insights is distinguishing among three types of inequality. The first type—and the one reflected in virtually every opinion survey on the subject—reflects acceptable differences between high and low incomes. In addition, the authors examine acceptable gaps between high and average incomes and between average and low incomes. They discovered that the acceptable ratio of high to low incomes was the same in the United States in 1999 as it was in 1987 (table 8.3). What has changed is the acceptable ratio of high to average incomes. It has dropped in recent years, from 2.7 to 2.0, indicating that Americans are becoming less tolerant of disparities in the top half of the income distribution. What has changed even more is the acceptable ratio of average to low incomes; it has increased from 2.4 to 3.3 in a little more than a decade. Americans thus appear to be growing more tolerant of inequality in the lower half of the income distribution.

The United States is not alone in this regard. The same trends can be observed in the United Kingdom, Germany, and Australia (table 8.3). In

TABLE 8.3
Acceptable Inequality in Four Nations

	1987	1999
United States		
Max.-Min. ratio	6.7	6.7
Max.-Mean ratio	2.7	2.0
Mean-Min. ratio	2.4	3.3
United Kingdom		
Max.-Min. ratio	5.6	6.7
Max.-Mean ratio	2.7	2.1
Mean-Min. ratio	2.0	3.3
Germany		
Max.-Min. ratio	4.8	6.0
Max.-Mean ratio	2.4	2.0
Mean-Min. ratio	1.9	2.9
Australia		
Max.-Min. ratio	3.8	5.0
Max.-Mean ratio	2.1	1.8
Mean-Min. ratio	1.7	2.7

Source: Osberg and Smeeding (2005), tables 3 and 5.

all these countries, citizens tolerated a wider gap between average and high incomes than between average and low incomes in 1987. By 1999 the pattern had reversed, and citizens were tolerating higher gaps between average and low incomes than average and high incomes.

In the United States, these attitudes parallel trends in income inequality. Practically all of the increase in inequality in recent decades has occurred in the upper half of the income distribution. Between 1975 and 2005, the ratio of household income at the eightieth percentile to the fiftieth percentiles grew from 1.73 to 1.99. In other words, one now needs twice as much income as the average citizen in order to be considered among the wealthiest 20 percent of Americans. The ratio of household income at the ninety-fifth to fiftieth percentiles grew even faster, from 2.74 to 3.61, as the very rich distanced themselves from the middle class. In the lower half of the distribution, the ratio of incomes between the fiftieth and twentieth percentiles was literally unchanged during this period (DeNavas-Walt, Proctor, and Mills 2006). Frankly, those of us who study social policy are not accustomed to thinking about redistribution without thinking about the poor. Ordinary Americans appear to understand just where inequality is growing and want to reverse those trends.

Shifting our focus from public opinion to public policy, we do see officials paying less attention to problems felt by people in the lower half of the income distribution and more attention to problems in the upper half. One milestone of the past two decades was the historic 1996 welfare-reform law. It imposed new time limits on welfare recipients and replaced an entitlement program (Aid to Families with Dependent Children) with a block grant (Temporary Assistance for Needy Families), while cutting benefits for the means-tested Food Stamps and Supplemental Security Income programs. The aim was clearly to reduce assistance to the poor. The failure of the Clinton health plan in 1993–94 meant that millions of the working poor remained uninsured. At roughly the same time, policymakers were creating new social programs for the middle class. The poor and near-poor were not formally excluded, but the benefits of these programs have been concentrated among middle- and upper-middle-income individuals.

Take for example the Child Tax Credit (CTC), which was enacted in 1997. The CTC functions like a family allowance, administered through the tax code. It has grown rapidly since its enactment and cost an estimated $46 billion in 2005. Over a third of the benefits went to families earning between $40,000 and $75,000 (a reasonable approximation of the middle class), and another third of the benefits went to those earning over $75,000. The CTC effectively negates much of the redistributive impact of the Earned Income Tax Credit, which has been targeted at families with below-average incomes since 1975 (U.S. Congress 2006). True, the government also created a new health insurance program for low-income children in 1997, called SCHIP, but it is very small. The government spends ten times as much each year on the Child Tax Credit compared to SCHIP.

New social regulations have helped the middle class more than the poor and near-poor. Take for example the Family and Medical Leave Act (FMLA) of 1993. The FMLA was the first nationwide parental-leave law in U.S. history. However, because it only guaranteed unpaid leave, it has been harder for less affluent parents to make use of it. The so-called CO-BRA regulations (1986) were designed to make private health insurance more portable. The law allows individuals to continue coverage when between jobs—providing they pay the full monthly premium, including whatever portion their former employer used to pay (and providing they had health insurance in the first place). Like parental leave, COBRA is more exclusive in practice than it is on paper.[25] These new policies, along with growing tax benefits for employer pensions, employer health insurance, and homeowners, do not benefit many have-nots in American society. They help Americans with well-paying jobs and fringe benefits.

By the same token, a number of existing programs aimed squarely at the middle and upper-middle classes have grown substantially in recent decades. Adjusted for inflation, the value of various tax subsidies for homeowners has doubled since 1980 and now totals over $100 billion in lost income tax revenues each year. Who gets these subsidies? Primarily taxpayers earning over $100,000. The tax incentives for companies that offer health and pension benefits cost over $200 billion combined, and they have grown even faster than those for housing. Most of the employees who benefit are white-collar professionals and unionized factory workers, not low-wage workers in retail or service jobs. Such policies do little to reduce the gap between rich and poor, but they do help people in the middle (Howard 2007). These trends in policymaking parallel trends in public opinion noted by Osberg and Smeeding.

Conclusion

My reading of opinion polls shows that distributive conflicts along age and income lines are much more evident among elites than ordinary Americans. Critics like Kotlikoff, Peterson, and Samuelson, as well as advocacy groups like Americans for Generational Equity, the Concord Coalition, and Third Millennium, have been adept at publicizing their views about generational equity. They have published numerous books and articles, been quoted often in the national media, and testified before Congress. They have been much less successful at attracting grassroots support, and for good reason. There just are not that many buyers for what they are selling. Seniors care very much about Social Security and Medicare and show it through a variety of political acts. They are backed by millions of Americans who are not elderly and who share their concerns. Anyone who appears to diminish the government's role in caring for the elderly is likely to face a cool reception outside the Beltway, as President Bush learned the hard way while trying to sell Social Security privatization to the public.

The challenge facing those who worry about growing inequality is a little different. There does appear to be a market for policies that close the gap between middle-class Americans and the rich. The biggest tax expenditures are financed through the income tax system, which remains one of the most progressive sources of revenue in the United States. Income taxes paid by the upper-middle class and the rich are essentially used to subsidize the pensions, health care, and housing of the middle and upper-middle classes. To the extent that the affluent shoulder the income tax burden, these same policies also have the effect of reducing inequality between rich and poor. The problem is that so few of the poor and near-poor benefit materially from this redistribution. Collecting taxes from the rich and burying the money in an abandoned coal mine would have a similar effect—less inequality, but no improvement in the lives of the least advantaged. The challenge, as I see it, is building a constituency for public policies that address both poverty and inequality. Such policies could still benefit the middle class as long as they offered something substantial to the millions of Americans who are struggling to join the middle class.

Although this chapter has analyzed some of the ways that public opinion is related to important distributive outcomes in the United States, many questions remain to be explored. Most of the evidence cited here points to congruence between public opinion and the basic contours of U.S. social policy; that does not mean that public opinion was the major influence on the creation or subsequent development of key social programs. Originally, the public might have been indifferent toward or ignorant of certain social programs but over time came to embrace them. Alternatively, public officials and interest groups might have deliberately shaped public opinion in favor of spending on the elderly and against redistribution from rich to poor. Neither the sources of public opinion nor the precise causal relationship between public opinion and public policy has been identified in this chapter. Doing so would probably require detailed case studies, such as the one contained in chapter 11. For now, though, we can see why certain distributive outcomes that favor the few over the many persist in the United States: most Americans seem to accept them.

NOTES

This chapter builds on Christopher Howard, *The Welfare State Nobody Knows: Debunking Myths about U.S. Social Policy* (Princeton University Press, 2007), especially chapters 6 and 10. I would like to thank Elisabeth Moss Thomson and Klaus Schultz for research assistance on this project.

1. When Lynch added educational spending to social insurance, the ratio of

elderly to nonelderly spending in the United States was more similar to that of other nations.

2. Data from the Luxembourg Income Study can be accessed at http://www.lisproject.org/.

3. See, e.g., Greenspan's comments to the House Budget Committee on March 2, 2005 (http://www.msnbc.msn.com/id/7066201/).

4. The February 2005 issue of the *American Prospect* contains a number of relevant articles about Social Security.

5. Compared to other affluent democracies, the United States also has unusually high rates of poverty. During the 1990s, poverty was more than twice as common in the United States, regardless of whether one compared the entire population, children, or the elderly. Similar to inequality, public policies were less effective in reducing poverty in the United States than in other countries (Smeeding, Rainwater, and Burtless 2001).

6. Campbell shows that this is a relatively new phenomenon, fueled in large part by the expansion of Medicare and Social Security, which gave the elderly more resources and a larger stake in the outcome of policy debates.

7. In an oft-cited speech, demographer Samuel Preston declared, "In a modern democracy, public decisions are obviously influenced by the power of special interest groups, and that power in turn is a function of the size of the groups, the wealth of the groups, and the degree to which that size and that wealth can be mobilized for concerted action. In all of these areas, interests of the elderly have gained relative to those of children" (Preston 1984: 445–46). For a similar view, see Vogel 1999.

8. The GSS includes a much larger number of relevant questions than the National Election Studies, which has been used in other studies of age differences in social policy (Rhodebeck 1993).

9. For evidence that public opinion influences the general direction of public policy in the United States, see Burstein 2003; Erikson, MacKuen, and Stimson 2002; and Page and Shapiro 1983.

10. Not surprisingly, given the near unanimity in these other countries, gaps in support among age groups were very minor.

11. The GSS data were accessed at the Survey Documentation and Analysis website at the University of California–Berkeley (http://sda.berkeley.edu:7502/).

12. Since 1984, the National Election Studies (NES) has asked Americans whether spending on Social Security should be increased, decreased, or kept the same. The wording is quite close to that used by the GSS, and the results are quite similar as well. In 2002, for instance, 57 percent of younger and middle-aged adults thought that spending on Social Security should be increased, compared to 50 percent of the elderly. In 1984 the figures were 54, 52, and 43 percent, respectively.

13. The gap was 87 percent to 79 percent. The NewsHour with Jim Lehrer/

Kaiser Family Foundation/Harvard School of Public Health, *National Survey on Prescription Drugs* (September 2000), available online at http://www.kff.org/rxdrugs/3065-index.cfm.

14. Kaiser Family Foundation/Harvard School of Public Health, *Medicare Prescription Drug Survey* (September 2003), available online at http://www.kff.org/medicare/3374toplines.cfm.

15. This poll can be found online at http://www.pollingreport.com/health2.htm.

16. Results from this poll (#431) are available online at http://www.latimes.com/news/custom/timespoll/la-statsheetindex.htmlstory.

17. "Young Americans and Social Security," a public-opinion study conducted for the 2030 Center by Peter D. Hart Research Associates (July 1999), available online at http://www.2030.org/pdf/report1.pdf.

18. This seems like a reasonable strategy considering that the elderly/nonelderly spending ratios were very similar in 1980 and 1993, the two end points of Lynch's study (2001).

19. These questions were taken from the General Social Survey. In another poll, respondents were asked if they "absolutely had to choose" between "working for the rights of women and preserving traditional family values." Every age group sided with traditional family values, and support increased with age. Three-quarters of the elderly agreed, compared to two-thirds of adults aged thirty to sixty-four and a little over half of adults aged eighteen to twenty-nine (Kaiser Family Foundation 2002).

20. These findings are consistent with earlier studies of public opinion at the national (Ponza et al. 1988) and local (Logan and Spitze 1995) levels.

21. The ISSP surveys are probably the single best source of cross-national data regarding public opinion on social policy. The World Values Study, by contrast, asks relatively few questions about the proper role of government or specific government programs, and did not ask some of the general questions about inequality in the United States.

22. Question wording can have a large impact on the public's views about redistribution. In 1996, for example, pollsters asked Americans whether it was the responsibility of government "to reduce the differences in income between people with high incomes and those with low incomes." There were five possible answers, ranging from "agree strongly" to "disagree strongly," with a middle position of neither agreeing nor disagreeing. One-third (32.6 percent) of Americans agreed or agreed strongly that government should have this responsibility. That same year, a different set of pollsters asked Americans a two-sided question about income redistribution, indicating arguments for and against. Respondents had the option of placing themselves on a seven-point scale, with 1 being the highest level of support. If we equate support with answers 1 and 2, then a little over one-quarter

(28.4 percent) of Americans were in favor. If we equate support with answers 1–3, then the number jumps substantially (44.6 percent).

The Role of Government survey, administered that same year, gave respondents just four options, ranging from "definitely should be a government responsibility" to "definitely should not," with no middle position. Framed that way, income redistribution received even higher support (48.0 percent saying that it definitely or probably should be government's responsibility). Because I am curious to see if attitudes have changed, I will work with the question asked over the longest stretch of time, which uses the seven-point scale of support. And I will equate support with the first two points on this scale because those numbers were closer to those produced when only five responses were offered. In short, I suspect that most of the people answering "3" on the seven-point scale are closer to no preference than true support and that many of the people forced to agree or disagree would say "neither" if given the chance. All the questions discussed in this paragraph were accessed through the General Social Survey (http://sda. berkeley.edu:7502/).

23. For the 1998–2002 period, the income thresholds were the following: Lower (family income less than $24,000), Lower-Middle ($24,000–41,000), Middle ($41,000–61,378), Upper-Middle ($61,378–91,700), and Upper (over $91,700). For the 1978–82 period, the income thresholds were less than $10,000, $10,000–17,000, $17,000–25,000, $25,000–35,000, and over $35,000.

24. In 1985, 35 percent of lower-class and working-class Americans agreed or agreed strongly that government should reduce income differences. In 1996, support was virtually unchanged at 37 percent (ISSP 1993, 1999). For evidence that many of the poor did not embrace redistribution in the 1970s, see Hochschild 1981. For one explanation of why so few Americans support redistribution, see Alesina and Glaeser 2004.

25. The use of social regulation to promote parental leave, health insurance, and employment of the handicapped (through the 1990 Americans with Disabilities Act) may mean that we need to rethink the distribution of benefits between the elderly and nonelderly. The spending ratios devised by Lynch (2001) may not reveal the full story. On the other hand, there are also substantial regulations governing company-based retirement pensions in the United States.

REFERENCES

Alesina, Alberto, and Edward L. Glaeser. 2004. *Fighting Poverty in the U.S. and Europe: A World of Difference*. New York: Oxford University Press.

Birnbaum, Jeffrey H. 1997. "Washington's Second Most Powerful Man." *Fortune* (May 12): 122–26.

Borosage, Robert L., and Roger Hickey (eds.). 2001. *The Next Agenda: Blueprint for a New Progressive Movement*. Boulder, CO: Westview.

Burstein, Paul. 2003. "The Impact of Public Opinion on Public Policy: A Review and an Agenda." *Political Research Quarterly* 56 (1): 29–40.

Burtless, Gary, and Timothy Smeeding. 1995. "America's Tide: Lifting the Yachts, Swamping the Rowboats." *Washington Post* (June 25): C3.

Campbell, Andrea Louise. 2003. *How Policies Make Citizens: Senior Political Activism and the American Welfare State*. Princeton, NJ: Princeton University Press.

Carasso, Adam, C. Eugene Steuerle, and Gillian Reynolds. 2007. *Kids' Share 2007: How Children Fare in the Federal Budget*. Washington, DC: Urban Institute.

Dahl, Robert A. 1957. "The Concept of Power." *Behavioral Science* 2 (3): 201–15.

DeNavas-Walt, Carmen, Bernadette D. Proctor, and Robert J. Mills. 2006. *Income, Poverty, and Health Insurance Coverage in the United States: 2005*. Washington, DC: U.S. Census Bureau.

Emanuel, Rep. Rahm. 2004. "Middle Class Squeeze." *Congressional Record* 150, 101 (July 20): H5985.

Erikson, Robert S., Michael B. MacKuen, and James A. Stimson. 2002. *The Macro Polity*. New York: Cambridge University Press.

Francis, David R. 2003. "Partisan Lines Harden in Debate over Tax Cuts." *Christian Science Monitor* (March 31): 21.

Frank, Robert H., and Philip J. Cook. 1995. *The Winner-Take-All Society*. New York: Free Press.

Fritz, Sara. 2001. "AARP Told to Back Reform of Social Security." *St. Petersburg Times* (February 15): 1A.

Gilens, Martin. 2004. "Public Opinion and Democratic Responsiveness: Who Gets What They Want from Government?" Paper presented at the 2004 annual meeting of the American Political Science Association, Chicago.

Greenstein, Stanley B., and Theda Skocpol (eds.). 1997. *The New Majority: Toward a Popular Progressive Politics*. New Haven, CT: Yale University Press.

Hacker, Jacob, Suzanne Mettler, Dianne Pinderhughes, and Theda Skocpol. 2004. *Inequality and Public Policy*. Washington, DC: American Political Science Association. Accessed online at http://www.apsanet.org/imgtest/feedbackmemo. pdf.

Hochschild, Jennifer. 1981. *What's Fair? American Beliefs about Distributive Justice*. Cambridge, MA: Harvard University Press.

Howard, Christopher. 2007. "The Haves and the Have-Lots." *Democracy: A Journal of Ideas* (4): 48–58.

International Social Survey Program (ISSP). 1993. *Role of Government I, 1985*. Computer file and codebook. Koeln, Germany: Zentralarchiv fuer Empirische Sozialforschung.

International Social Survey Program (ISSP). 1999. *Role of Government III, 1996*.

Computer file and codebook. Koeln, Germany: Zentralarchiv fuer Empirische Sozialforschung.

International Social Survey Program (ISSP). 2002. *Social Inequality III, 1999.* CD-ROM. Madrid, Spain: Analisis Sociologicos Economicos y Politicos, S.A.

Kaiser Family Foundation. 2002. *A Generational Look at the Public: Politics and Policy* (October). Accessed online at http://www.kff.org/kaiserpolls/.

Kenworthy, Lane. 1999. "Do Social Welfare Policies Reduce Inequality? A Cross-National Assessment." *Social Forces* 77 (3): 1119–39.

Kenworthy, Lane, and Jonas Pontusson. 2005. "Rising Inequality and the Politics of Redistribution in Affluent Countries." *Perspectives on Politics* 3 (3): 449–71.

King, Anthony. 1973. "Ideas, Institutions and the Policies of Governments: A Comparative Analysis." *British Journal of Political Science* 3 (3): 291–313 and (4): 409–23.

Kotlikoff, Lawrence J., and Scott Burns. 2004. *The Coming Generational Storm: What You Need to Know about America's Economic Future.* Cambridge, MA: MIT Press.

Krugman, Paul. 2004. *The Great Unraveling: Losing Our Way in the New Century.* New York: Free Press.

Kuttner, Robert. 2004. "The Hidden Issue of Class." *Boston Globe* (July 21): A15.

Ladd, Everett Carll. 1994. *The American Ideology: An Exploration of the Origins, Meaning, and Role of American Political Ideas.* Storrs, CT: Roper Center for Public Opinion Research.

Lipset, Seymour Martin. 1996. *American Exceptionalism: A Double-Edged Sword.* New York: Norton.

Logan, John R., and Glenna D. Spitze. 1995. "Self-Interest and Altruism in Inter-generational Relations." *Demography* 32 (3): 353–64.

Lynch, Julia. 2001. "The Age-Orientation of Social Policy Regimes in OECD Countries." *Journal of Social Policy* 30 (3): 411–36.

MacManus, Susan A. 1996. *Young v. Old: Generational Combat in the 21st Century.* Boulder, CO: Westview.

Monroe, Alan D. 1998. "Public Opinion and Public Policy, 1980–1993." *Public Opinion Quarterly* 62 (1): 6–28.

Osberg, Lars, and Timothy Smeeding. 2005. "'Fair' Inequality? An International Comparison of Attitudes to Pay Differentials." Unpublished manuscript (June 17). Accessed online at http://www-cpr.maxwell.syr.edu/faculty/smeeding/.

Page, Benjamin I., and Robert Y. Shapiro. 1983. "Effects of Public Opinion on Policy." *American Journal of Political Science* 77 (1): 175–90.

Page, Benjamin I., and James R. Simmons. 2000. *What Government Can Do: Dealing with Poverty and Inequality.* Chicago: University of Chicago Press.

Pearlstein, Steven. 1996. "Older and Out to Spend: A Reason for Declining Savings?" *Washington Post* (October 2): C1.

Peterson, Peter G. 2004. *Running on Empty: How the Democratic and Republican Parties Are Bankrupting Our Future and What Americans Can Do about It.* New York: Farrar, Straus and Giroux.

Ponza, Michael, Greg J. Duncan, Mary Corcoran, and Fred Groskind. 1988. "The Guns of Autumn: Age Differences in Support for Income Transfers to the Young and Old." *Public Opinion Quarterly* 52 (4): 441–66.

Preston, Samuel H. 1984. "Children and the Elderly: Divergent Paths for America's Dependents." *Demography* 21 (4): 435–57.

Rhodebeck, Laurie A. 1993. "The Politics of Greed? Political Preferences among the Elderly." *Journal of Politics* 55 (2): 342–64.

Samuelson, Robert J. 2007. "Entitled Selfishness: Boomer Generation Is in a State of Denial." *Washington Post* (January 10): A13.

Sanger, David E. 1997. "'Parting Benediction' by Lonely Liberal." *New York Times* (January 9): B8.

Schurenberg, Eric, and Lani Luciano 1988. "The Empire Called AARP." *Money* (October): 128.

Skocpol, Theda. 2000. *The Missing Middle: Working Families and the Future of American Social Policy.* New York: Norton.

Smeeding, Timothy, Lee Rainwater, and Gary Burtless. 2001. "U.S. Poverty in Cross-National Context." In Sheldon Danziger and Robert Haveman, eds., *Understanding Poverty*, pp. 162–89. New York and Cambridge, MA: Russell Sage Foundation and Harvard University Press.

Thau, Richard D., and Jay S. Heflin. 1997. *Generations Apart: Xers vs. Boomers vs. the Elderly.* Amherst, NY: Prometheus Books.

U.S. Census Bureau. 2006. *Statistical Abstract of the United States: 2007.* Washington, DC: Government Printing Office.

U.S. Congress, Joint Committee on Taxation. 2006. *Estimates of Federal Tax Expenditures for Fiscal Years 2006–2010.* Washington, DC: Government Printing Office.

U.S. Congressional Budget Office. 2000. *Federal Spending on the Elderly and Children.* Available online at http://www.cbo.gov/showdoc.cfm?index=2300&sequence=0.

Verba, Sidney, Kay Lehman Schlozman, and Henry E. Brady. 1995. *Voice and Equality: Civic Voluntarism in American Politics.* Cambridge, MA: Harvard University Press.

Verba, Sidney, Kay Lehman Schlozman, Henry E. Brady, and Norman H. Nie. 1993. "Citizen Activity: Who Participates? What Do They Say?" *American Political Science Review* 87 (2): 303–18.

Vogel, Ronald J. 1999. *Medicare: Issues in Political Economy.* Ann Arbor: University of Michigan Press.

Part III

Coalitions

Chapter 9

||||||||||||||||||||||||||||||||||||||||||||||||||||||

Good Distribution, Bad Delivery, and Ugly Politics

*The Traumatic Beginnings of
Germany's Health Care System*

Peter A. Swenson

"Will America copy Germany's mistakes?" asked Gustav Hartz, a noted German critic of his country's national health insurance system in a 1935 issue of the *New York State Medical Journal* (Hartz 1935). The answer was made public soon. By the time of publication, President Franklin Roosevelt had already decided against including health insurance in the Social Security Act. Medical leaders whom he summoned to advise him on the matter had vehemently advised against it; bad news from Germany was one reason. FDR's top medical adviser, the internationally renowned Yale neurosurgeon Harvey Cushing, had written to eminent German doctors for their views. They confirmed his suspicions. Surgeon and friend Friedrich Müller gave a mixed but overall discouraging picture and recommended that Cushing consult a highly popular book by the Leipzig surgeon Erwin Liek, the system's harshest critic and sometimes called the father of Nazi medicine (Müller to Cushing, 20 December 1934).

After reading Liek's *The Doctor and His Mission* (1926), Cushing wrote to the right-wing surgeon with high praise for his book, declaring in words that Liek himself could have penned that under national health insurance "the doctor will slowly and progressively deteriorate and . . . our beloved profession will come to be manned by an inferior type of people." Patients would suffer. To Cushing's relief, FDR quickly backpedaled on health insurance, and hence the surgeon expressed his wish to the president of the American Medical Association (AMA) that doctors across America reward FDR with their votes in the 1936 presidential election (Cushing to Liek, 26 January 1935; Cushing to Bierring, 15 August 1936).

Calling it Bolshevik and worse—*German*, for example—organized medicine in America rudely rejected compulsory health insurance and therefore the offer of a massive new flow of fees. If European experience was any indication, some relief from the economic distress of the Depression was what they could have expected. British doctors did well after Lloyd George's legislation of 1911, and this contributed to the British Medical Association's sanguine views. In Germany, even though doctors' criticism was strident and their rhetoric raw, they had recently defended their income with more success than the vast majority of their fellow citizens. Nevertheless, the AMA dug in its heels, although American doctors' income had plummeted along with that of most other fellow citizens. Better than health insurance, Cushing's friend and AMA president Walter Bierring wrote in 1934, would be to reduce the number of graduating medical students by half. Do not increase demand; reduce supply, he counseled (Bierring 1934).

Raising demand through compulsory health insurance, many doctors thought, would jeopardize the quality of medical care in America. That message had already been coming through from the enemy land ever since America had girded for war with Germany in 1917. Speaking from personal experience abroad, prominent Chicago surgeon Edward Ochsner repeatedly confirmed American doctors' fears; his conclusions about Germany resonated with what they saw or heard about scattered capitalist-, labor-, and government-sponsored third-party payment arrangements in America. FDR adviser Cushing was one of Ochsner's appreciative readers (Ochsner 1920, 1934; Cushing to Ochsner, 30 November 1934). Then there was Metropolitan Life's formidable insurance expert Frederick Hoffman, who possibly did more than anyone to spread the bad word about Germany (Hoffman 1919; Numbers 1978, 78). In sum, these observers claimed, if the United States followed Germany, the intimate doctor-patient relationship, essential to good diagnosis and improvement, would be destroyed by compulsion and regimentation. The moral fiber of doctor and patient alike would fray. Partisan and patronage politics would hijack the medical system and poison it with rank incompetence. Government-provided health care would waste vast resources. Medical progress would slow. The health of Americans would, if anything, decline.

Health would be better served, the American reactionaries thought, with public health measures and, above all, revived economic growth. They hastened to report morbidity and mortality statistics that showed Americans, with their higher standard of living, to be more robust than Germans and Britons. More money going into doctors' pockets would not buy better health. Part of the sentiment behind this view stemmed from elite doctors' assessment of the low quality of medicine practiced by many physicians across the country. As Cushing thought, and told FDR, insurance practices would attract and reward even worse (Cushing to Roosevelt, 1 February 1935).

Meanwhile, reports from German doctors indicated, the insurance system demoralized the profession and brought wholesale degradation of clinical practice. A system not of their own making—indeed a system thrust on them by German politicians in alliance with both capitalist and labor interests—was forcing doctors to deliver a high and rising volume of what they knew were often worthless services and medications to defend their income from economizing measures and competition from a surplus of doctors admitted into insurance practice. Despite insurance coverage, German citizens were turning increasingly to alternative medical practitioners, and paying out of pocket, dismayed as they were by the assembly-line treatment they received from regular practitioners working on a fee-for-service basis.

Leading American proponents of national health insurance could only feebly respond to doctors' warning signs about the quality of health care in Germany. For on the question of medical quality, the American medical establishment enjoyed close to a monopoly of certified expertise about what was good and bad medicine, especially now, after rapid turn-of-the-century advances in medical science and therapeutic practice had rescued the status of "regular" medicine from its nineteenth-century doldrums. To be sure, there was also a widely discussed crisis in American medicine, but unlike Germany's, it largely concerned providers' costs, not their quality and respect (Falk, Rorem, and Ring 1933).

Skirting the issue of what health insurance would do to the quality of medicine, liberal public health experts, economists, and other reformers directed attention to the economic devastation to individuals from the period's high and rising health costs, especially for chronic and acute ailments, and income loss from illness-related disability. Social insurance revenue, they hoped, was needed to redistribute resources from the healthy and gainfully employed to the sick; wealthier and therefore usually healthier citizens would subsidize the poor and infirm. But organized medicine met these distributional arguments head on with cold denial, claiming (with rather feeble evidence) that low-income Americans got all the care that was medically necessary. Private practitioners who charged according to sliding fee scales, backed up by free public and charitable dispensaries, did the job that needed doing.

That was the state of things in Germany and the United States during a decisive formative passage in both their systems: venomous conflict in Germany about the perverse impact of compulsory health insurance on the medical system and an impasse in the United States caused by doctors fearing what they had heard about Germany. From the 1930s onward, organized medicine helped push America forth on a different track that would be hard to change: toward a mostly voluntary, private, employment-based, often collectively bargained group insurance system. Because of this, we can reasonably speculate that the flow of bad news from Germany in the 1920s and 1930s helps answer the frequently asked question, "Why is there no guaranteed health insurance in the United States?"

Capital, Labor, and Medicine in the Shaping of the German System

Historical knowledge about Germany's health care system also illuminates a larger question of the way conflicts over the distribution of the costs and benefits of health care play themselves out with complex and shifting relations among three major social forces: capital, labor, and medicine. Though locked in separate battles of their own, capital and labor could still join forces in politically brokered alliances against medicine. As one American medical critic of health insurance warned in 1920, "the Doctor" —if not vigilant—could become "a mere tool of Capital, Labor and the Politicians, to be used and cast aside as fits their fancy" (quoted in Rosen 1983, 112–13).

This critic may well have known something about Germany. From the beginning, Germany's system for organizing the public funding and delivery of health care gave capital and labor direct control over its operation. Likewise, they enjoyed direct influence over the system's evolution. German health care was, therefore, "corporatist" in the extreme. Over time it became even more so. Corporatism refers primarily to the official delegation of public policy making and administrative authority to organized private interests. In European corporatist arrangements, the quasi-public officialdom of labor, employer, agricultural, and other interest associations often spend enormous state resources, all the while acting, as intended, with considerable autonomy from constitutionally and juridically regulated electoral, parliamentary, and bureaucratic processes.[1] Additionally, corporatism refers to quasi-governmental macroeconomic policymaking through collective bargaining of income distribution within and between classes—for example, in highly centralized and inclusive systems of collective bargaining between organized employers and the wage and salaried classes.

The German health care system was, and remains, highly corporatist in both senses: health policy making and administration by organized private interests and relatively encompassing collective bargaining over income determination by those same interests. For example, German labor unions and employers jointly manage the statutory health insurance funds that remunerate their members' providers for medical, dental, surgical, and hospital services. Capital and labor, through the funds, enjoy legally guaranteed representation on public bodies that make critical decisions about what medical, dental, and surgical services qualify for insurance reimbursement to providers. The corporatist system even metes out financial penalties to doctors who engage in what are regarded as excessive drug prescribing.

Also, through the health insurance funds they control, labor and capital must collectively bargain with organized providers over the terms of physicians' and hospitals' remuneration. Independent office-based physicians who wish to engage in insurance practice are required to join regional associations (*kassenärztliche Vereinigungen*) that perform legally prescribed roles, among them collective bargaining with the funds. Doctors cannot strike, and insurance funds cannot collectively lock out doctors. Instead, when intractable disputes occur, the state steps in to resolve them with compulsory arbitration.

These compulsory medical associations collectively bargain a fixed budget to reimburse all ambulatory services over a set period of time. Then the aggregate prospective payment is *transferred over to the regional medical association*. The association, in turn, undertakes the massive administrative task of processing and paying doctors' bills, on a fee-for-service basis, out of this budget for services rendered during the period (for details, see Stone 1980; Behagel 1994). In principle, by giving doctors' unions the job of bill payment out of a limited budget, the law shifts an incentive onto doctors to establish what are unnecessary and uneconomical medical services and then to advocate ways of reducing them.

As we will see, organized medicine in Germany pushed for this unique and remarkable system—compulsory organization and bargaining, collective prospective reimbursement, administrative responsibility for individual fee disbursement, and assumption of economic risks that would create an incentive to control cost-ineffective doctoring—at a crucial turning point in German politics. They got what they wanted, in December 1931, in an unusual agreement with organized labor, brokered at the highest level of German parliamentary and bureaucratic politics. The agreement deeply antagonized big industry and agriculture, powerful social forces already at war with the last Weimar government, which enjoyed substantial parliamentary support. Indeed it gave these conservative forces one more reason to search for an authoritarian alternative and thereby pave the road to the Nazi dictatorship.

Through its telling, the evolution of the German health care system from 1883 into the 1930s illuminates how good health care distribution could generate bad (but expensive) delivery and give rise to some very ugly medical politics. The repercussions were great in Germany, of course, but also not insignificant across the Atlantic. Reformers in the United States, none of them highly respected clinicians and medical researchers, could not credibly extol the German system's results, while its manifest failures only stiffened the American reactionaries' resolve.

The Origins of "Bismarckian" Health Insurance

The core corporatist features of Germany's current health care system —introduced in 1931, drastically revised by the Nazi government, but in large part reinstated across all of West Germany by 1955—emerged within the framework of the health insurance law passed in 1883. Otto von Bismarck, the founder and first chancellor of the Wilhelmine Empire in 1871, normally gets credit for the law. The *Gesetz betreffend die Krankenversicherung der Arbeiter* was the world's first compulsory system of national health insurance, restricted however to industrial wage earners until middling-income groups were brought in against strong medical opposition during the 1920s. Bismarck, it is usually said, intended to construct a social insurance system to forge a bond of loyalty between the worker and the authoritarian state, and thus intended to take the wind out of the rising socialist labor movement's sails.

Germany's leading capitalists did not oppose the legislation, and in fact their early support validates recent historiography that questions the primacy of Bismarck's antisocialist motives (Hennock 1998, 68–69; Kähler 1994, 455). Close to industrialists—an industrialist himself (lumber and paper)—Bismarck may have mouthed the argument mostly to persuade Emperor Wilhelm I, who was rattled by assassination attempts by socialists, of the need for social insurance. In fact, in 1883, industrialist Henry Axel Bueck did not believe that social insurance would do much to change the political mood of the working class. Twenty years later, Bueck, now the leader of Germany's most powerful capitalist organization, saw his prediction fully confirmed. Workers were as militant as ever. But that did not mean that Bueck thought the law to have been a mistake. On the contrary, he wrote that "with worker insurance the German Reich has with incomparable boldness and most tenacious endurance accomplished a work of civilization [*Kulturarbeit*] of the highest order, which will for all time . . . bring it renown" (Bueck 1905, 791).

Clearly German industrial capitalists had other reasons for support. Recent research on Germany's early social insurance concludes that because of their various managerial interests the leadership of German heavy industry supported early development of the modern welfare state in its first few decades, even though all its details did not come out to their satisfaction (Breger 1982, 1994; Kleeberg 2003, 108–11; Mares 2003). In the case of industrial accident insurance, industrialists were even out ahead of Bismarck. As one industrialist said, "Who was it after all that introduced the whole accident insurance idea? It was we, and without us the whole legislation would not have gotten underway!" (Breger 1994, 46).

Doctors could not have missed the fact that the design of health insurance was in part created for capitalists, if not directly by them. One aspect favorable to capitalists even disappointed Bismarck—because it conflicted with his simultaneous state-building objectives—moving him to scorn it as a "changeling" (*untergeschobenes Kind*) (Rothfels 1927, 55; Tennstedt 1977b, 23). For this and other reasons, the law's real father was the formidable civil servant and devout Lutheran social reformer Theodor Lohmann. Lohmann decidedly favored building big industrial employers' existing company sickness funds into the new system. Most notable was the arrangement at the steel and engineering colossus, Friedrich Krupp A.G., which dated from 1837. Later, in 1855, the Krupp fund introduced limited "self-management" (*Selbstverwaltung*)—or at least co-management of company funds by workers. Lohmann, who took charge of crafting the legislation, saw in such arrangements the possibility, practiced by other industrialists with far greater sincerity than Krupp did, of forging a mutually beneficial corporate bond between capital and labor, and so to uplift as well as pacify capitalist society (Vossiek 1937, 16–18, 26–28; Lohmann, letter to Friedrichs 1874).

Bismarck, by contrast, had favored a more administratively centralized system, a more direct link between worker and state that largely bypassed the employer. In part because of his fiscal ambitions, he envisaged workers drawing tax-funded pensions and other entitlements from a single payer, the state. He did not have in mind payments from autonomously managed multiple payers handling payroll contributions that would not pass through the Reich treasury.

Bismarck's disappointment may well have contributed to his famous observation on the legislative process that "whoever knows how laws and sausages come into being can no longer sleep soundly at night." Many doctors lost sleep after getting a taste of the finished product, as well as subsequent amendments into the 1920s. The 1883 law allowed companies with over fifty workers to maintain their existing funds or start up new company funds (*Betriebskrankenkassen*). These funds were to enjoy complete freedom to contract as they pleased with individual doctors over their fees and other conditions of employment. The law did not spell out the role of doctors and thus failed to guarantee their status as solo practitioners against the economic might of big capitalists. Furthermore, the law did not guarantee collective bargaining with medical organizations and arbitration of conflicts so that medical interests might be protected.

The law required smaller firms, and those not wishing to form their own funds, to enroll their workers in multiemployer local funds (*Ortskrankenkassen*) that also contracted with doctors on terms dictated by the market and organizational clout. Large firms could elect to enlist their employees in these local funds, but they rarely chose to do so for managerial and economic reasons.[2] Mine operators retained their preexisting compulsory benefit funds (*Knappschaftskassen*), and small-scale artisanal trades could set up funds on a guild basis (*Innungskrankenkassen*). Agricultural funds (*Landkrankenkassen*) were set up in accordance with law passed in the 1920s.

In all cases, workers contributed two-thirds of the contributions to the funds in which they were enrolled, and employers contributed one-third.

Contributions were calculated as a proportion of a legislatively defined basic wage. Funds dispensed sick pay (*Krankengeld*) and paid providers for medical, dental, and other service benefits from doctors who contracted with the funds. The law set standard minimum service benefits (*Regelleistungen*), but the funds retained freedom to offer supplementary benefits (*Mehrleistungen*). Family coverage was the most important of the voluntary extras. Funds were free to set contributions higher than the statutory minimum if necessary to pay for supplemental benefits.

While the legislation created the theater for unending trench warfare between physicians and the insurance funds, it also pitted capital and labor against each other. Both company and local funds were, according to the 1883 law, to be co-managed by workers and employers. For their self-management councils, workers and employers elected representatives in proportion to their contributions, 2:1. However, in practice, big employers dominated the company funds in their relations with doctors. The law had reserved for them the chairmanship of co-management committees and therefore the routine administration of the company funds. Thus, workers played only a limited advisory role in the company funds.

In the case of the local funds, however, Lohmann had unintentionally made it possible for workers to establish labor union officials in executive positions, which occurred across the board as soon as the unions gave up their initial boycott around 1890. Because employers received only one-third minority representation—and probably because, as smaller enterprises, their interests differed somewhat from the interests of the big company funds—the company and local funds assumed dramatically different positions on important aspects of the system's evolution. That organized labor discovered it could dominate and therefore recruit large numbers of personnel into the local fund system is what, no doubt, caused the industrialist Bueck to criticize Lohmann in private, even though he praised compulsory social insurance in general.

The local funds intensely resented the fact that the larger companies' funds could usually offer better benefits and services (e.g., for dependents), even for lower contributions, than the local funds. The company funds' administrative costs were lower, in part because they did not have to construct new buildings or hire much extra executive and administrative staff. Also, for various reasons, they could hold necessary financial reserves at cheaper cost. But the local funds complained that the main advantage of the company funds lay in risk selection: larger employers hired healthier workers and discharged others (Hauptverband deutscher

Krankenkassen 1924, 8). Smaller firms tied to the local funds had less freedom to select for risks in hiring workers—and little interest anyway, because payment of benefits came out of a common pool. Thus, it became their long-run ambition to abolish the employer-controlled portion of the system so as to absorb their revenues and members into a more egalitarian and economical package.

The company funds fired back, however, that the local funds were more expensive largely because they were unable to monitor lax, abusive, and fraudulent behavior by members and the physicians they turned to. A severe problem, they reasonably claimed (see the Leipzig funds' experience in 1931, discussed later), was doctors' raking of fees with a high volume of unnecessary medical services—"overdoctoring," "busywork," and "mass production" (*Überarztung, Vielgeschäftigkeit, Massenbetrieb*). In the more intimate company arrangement, it was supposed, members were motivated and able to keep an eye on one another's waste and abuse, especially feigned illness and other malingering (*Simulantentum*). This monitoring apparently had been one of Lohmann's justifications for building company funds into the system (Schwenger 1934, 78–80). The company funds also were better able to keep matters under control through selective contract arrangements with physicians that the local funds proved unable to maintain against doctor strikes. But both systems suffered from politically fatal cost problems for which doctors, in the end, had to accept partial responsibility.

The Interests Organize

Conflict between capital and labor within the insurance fund system, as well as other rivalries in the non-medical camp, gave powerfully organized doctors significant leverage to influence developments over the years from the 1890s into the 1930s. Unified, doctors gained much of what they wanted against fragmented enemies.

Initially, however, there seemed to be little need to summon their resources for a fight. It took more than a decade and a half after passage of the health law before doctors mobilized on a national basis. What finally triggered national action was perceived abusive treatment they suffered at the hands of the local multiemployer funds once they became dominated in the 1890s by Social Democratic trade unionists. Organizational escalation thus began in 1894 when socialists assembled the funds they controlled into a national organization, the *Hauptverband deutscher Krankenkassen*, to coordinate policies and strategies vis-à-vis relations with doctors, bureaucrats, and politicians.

One of the most prominent Social Democratic movers and shakers in medical politics during this phase was Friedrich Landmann, a doctor himself. In his 1898 publication, *The Solution to the Doctor Question*, Landmann announced his conviction that fellow physicians and chemical companies were massively swindling the insurance funds with useless treatments and medications. Considering the rudimentary state of therapeutic medical knowledge and the unprincipled concoction and marketing of drugs, Landmann had a respectable argument. For most illnesses, the best therapy was rest, good food and hygiene, clean air, and time for the body's natural healing power to take its course. Heavily influenced by nineteenth-century therapeutic skepticism—the break with heroic medicine of the past—Landmann thought patients were probably better served on the whole by homeopathic and natural healers than by the *Schulmediziner*, not because they were more effective but because they were cheaper. And less dangerous.

Furthermore, Landmann argued, workers were best cared for if the relatively few carefully selected doctors they could consult were hired on salaries—indeed *good* salaries—to serve on a restricted and exclusive panel (no private, independent practice on the side). Useless medical therapies were to be tightly controlled, thus making more funds available for sick leaves, bed rest, and rehabilitation on the therapeutic side and for public health and hygiene measures, including education, on the preventive side. Thereby, workers' meager salaries were also better taken care of (Landmann 1892, 1898; Möller 1910, 115–20, 127–50; Tennstedt 1977a, 15–19; Plaut 1913, 62, 80–90).

Landmann advanced therapeutic as well as economic reasoning for a restrictive form of what Americans called "contract practice," which was vilified by physicians on both sides of the Atlantic. Landmann was personally involved in two bitterly contested efforts in 1898, closely watched by German doctors across the country. Local funds in the towns of Barmen and Remscheid were trying to dissolve their current arrangements with physicians and set up restrictive contract practices. The tough resistance that local physicians summoned became a *cause célèbre* for doctors all across Germany. They had little doubt that if Landmann proved successful locally, his therapeutic heterodoxy would hitch a ride around the rest of the country on the juggernaut of socialism, laying waste to doctors' prestige and careers.

Spurred by the Barmen and Remscheid conflicts, in the year 1900, German doctors organized themselves in the city of Leipzig under the leadership of Hermann Hartmann, in the *Verband der Ärzte Deutschlands zur Wahrung ihrer wirtschaftlichen Interessen*. By 1904, this "Leipziger Verband"—later (and here) called the "Hartmannbund," after its founder—had grown in leaps and bounds, taking the health insurance system by storm with well-coordinated strikes (Plaut 1913, 90–98; Neuhaus 1986, 299–313; Huerkamp 1985, 285–96). The doctors' main objectives were, first, "organized free choice of physician"—a closed-shop system in which insured patients could choose any area physician belonging to and agreeing to terms of employment approved by the Hartmannbund. Conflict over this near-holy principle continued into the Weimar period (Hayek 1927). Also, organized medicine demanded payment on a fee-for-service basis (*Einzelleistungshonorierung*), also a matter of deep significance to doctors and great consequence in political developments to come.

Members of the Hartmannbund were required to seek approval from the organization, on a case-by-case basis, before accepting contracts that were not already officially negotiated with a fund or association of funds. Costs of violations were fines, expulsion, and worst of all perhaps, professional and social ostracism. Doctors readily surrendered to this hierarchical authority no doubt in part because of the high-handed treatment they reportedly received from Social Democratic fund managers (Möller 1910). Doctors' relations with the labor-dominated local funds were of course far more status infected than their relations with the employer-dominated company funds. University-trained middle-class professionals found it galling to have to submit to the hierarchical authority of a man trained to be a machinist or carpenter, and perhaps taught manners by a father even lower down the scale. Quite possibly the insurance boss was a reader of Marx, certainly not of Virchow or Ehrlich.

The Hartmannbund's main tools of resistance were as militant as those of its class enemy in industrial conflict with their own bosses: strikes of blacklisted funds, centrally controlled strike benefits, and a national employment bureau. One primary goal was the same too: collective bargaining between the funds and local units of the Hartmannbund. The vast majority of strikes, sometimes citywide in scope, as in Cologne, Leipzig, Munich, and Gera, almost always achieved at least partial success (Neuhaus 1986, 300). Very often success rode in with the arrival of state authorities demanding an end to hostilities.

By contrast, the silence of the historical record indicates that conflicts with the company funds were less dramatic, or at least less notorious for their smaller size, even if the employer funds pursued similar objectives. An all-out defensive mobilization against big business might well have been a tactical and strategic failure. Panel doctors working for big firms were generally paid well for good working conditions, and therefore they could probably not be pulled into a strike against their employers. Some even joined a separate organization friendly to their capitalist employers. Also, big employers were busy fighting their own propaganda battle with organized labor against efforts to unify and centralize the health system. They had little incentive to join forces with the local funds. For example, during the second big Cologne strike of 1909 against the local funds, the company funds offered no support. Doctors would have been unwise to attack the capitalist-controlled funds and give them reason to join forces with labor against them (Plaut 1913, 108; Neuhaus 1986, 296).

Even if doctors seem to have trod gingerly in their relations with the company funds, they nevertheless stimulated a capitalist counterorganization across Germany. Once again, Krupp was central. Its company health insurance fund had served as a model for the legislation; now it provided the core personnel for the organization of the some thirty-five hundred company funds across the country, making them a major political force in social policy for years to come (Schwenger 1934, 53). Key figures were Otto Heinemann and, notably, his son Gustav, the future Social Democratic Party (SPD) leader and president of the Federal Republic (1969– 1974). Gustav served in the late 1920s as a key legal expert to the *Reichsverband* and, writing in that capacity in the organization's journal (*Die Betriebskrankenkasse*), brought on himself blistering and insulting criticism from Karl Haedenkamp of the doctors' Hartmannbund.[3]

The senior Heinemann took over the Krupp company fund in 1903 and the following year co-founded and directed a regional organization of large company funds in Rheinland-Westfalia (*Verband der rheinisch-westfälischen Betriebskrankenkassen*). The purpose was to coordinate neighboring funds in their purchasing relations with providers to bring costs under control ("25 Jahre Verband rheinisch-westfälischer Betriebskrankenkassen" 1929, 265–71). Hospitals were one part of the problem, but the more difficult task was to confront an increasingly well-organized and defiant medical profession. In short, they sought to defend their favored solutions to the "doctor question." Broken down into its components, the *Arztfrage* posed three questions: whether to deal with doctors as employees or autonomous professionals; individually or collectively; and on a salary, capitation, or fee-for-service basis.

In the company fund view, doctors' demands for autonomy, collective bargaining, and fee-for-service payment were an intolerable intrusion on employers' managerial prerogatives to contract over terms of payment with a limited and exclusive panel of physicians on an individual basis (Thomsen 1996). What doctors called free choice by patients, *freie Arztwahl*, the funds called *Arztzwang*, or forced employment of doctors. Funds, not patients, should have unlimited free choice of doctors, employers thought; workers could then choose from among the ones the company fund recruited. Also, instead of fee-for-service medicine, the company funds favored payment by salary or per-patient capitation. Their capitalist managers believed that paying fee-for-service, like paying workers piece rates, made sense only if the goods or services delivered could be inspected and rejected when, made in great haste, they were of insufficient quality. But quality control was not possible for medical treatment. Quality in services was best assured through careful hiring of quality servants (Walther 1998; Thomsen 1996).

Within a short time after 1904, associations of company funds formed in other regions to deal with the doctors' Hartmannbund. These regional associations' need for coordination gave rise to the national organization in 1907, mainly to assert the separate and distinct interests of the company funds in legislative politics. At this level, however, the issues were not the ones that inflamed relations between company funds and doctors but rather conflicts between company funds and the socialist-dominated local funds. In short, it was about the political defense of the company fund system ("25 Jahre Betriebskrankenkassenverband" 1932, 305–17).

Until then, the national policy arena had been dominated by the local funds' national organizations, especially the *Hauptverband deutscher Krankenkassen*. Controlled by Social Democratic trade unionists, this national organization asserted many of the same interests as the company funds, like Krupp's. But the Social Democrats also aggressively pushed for centralization and unification of the social insurance system in general, and the health insurance system in particular. In other words, the *Hauptverband* called for the ultimate dissolution of the company funds and absorption or their members—a better risk pool—into the local funds. In the meantime, the labor movement did all it could to promote regulations that hindered the formation of new company funds.

In 1907, to counter the socialists' centralizing designs, big employers put together a national confederation of company funds (*Verband zur Wahrung der Interessen der Deutschen Betriebskrankenkassen*, later renamed the *Reichsverband der Betriebskrankenkassen*). This organization, also headquartered in the Krupp company town of Essen, was directed of course by Krupp's Heinemann. Within a short time the *Reichsverband* succeeded in fully neutralizing all sympathies in the Reich bureaucracy for the idea of greater benefits equality and administrative efficiency through centralization. Their effective, aggressively distributed counterpropaganda proffered two related arguments. First, workers paid lower company fund contributions for better benefits. Second, even Social Democratic workers resisted their absorption into the larger multiemployer local funds.

In resisting centralization the capitalists' company funds allied with other key allies from the German working class. These were the Catholics' Center Party (*Zentrum*) and its closely allied organization of Christian trade unions. Although vastly outnumbered, these were still hardy competitors to the Social Democratic unions, with deep regional roots (for example in Bavaria), and as we will see, they were key players in medical politics. They in turn set up their own competing national association of local insurance funds that they managed to dominate, the *Zentralverband der deutschen Ortskrankenkassen*.

In short, organized medicine in Weimar Germany faced off against a complex array of divided opponents. On the burning *Arztfrage*—whether and how payers should exercise managerial control over medical professionals—their opponents were largely in agreement. All favored, on the whole, individual rather than collective contracting, reasonable limitations on patients' choice of physician, and payment by capitation or salary, not on a fee-for-service basis. But despite that unity, on most of these issues doctors firmly held their ground against capital and labor.

Because of doctors' success in collective bargaining, achieved with their aggressive strike and boycott tactics—and the *deus ex machina* of compulsory state arbitration—they only displaced conflict and strengthened the resolve of their opponents on another burning issue: *whether and how to control the number of new physicians allowed into insurance practice.* Too many doctors, performing too many services for fees, were bankrupting the system and degrading medical practice. Competing over patients, doctors indulged them with unnecessary prescriptions for useless or even harmful and addictive drugs (*Gefälligkeitsverschreibungen*) and certifications of illnesses (*Gefälligkeitszeugnisse*) to qualify workers for days off with sick pay. For the extra fees they merrily applied electrical devices for all manner of expensive treatments that lacked evidence of efficacy from clinical testing: for example, Roentgen treatment of tuberculosis with obsolete machines that were weak and relatively harmless—or worse, up-to-date and strong, and therefore a threat to the very tissue that the tuberculosis was attacking ("Fragen der Zeit" 1930, 287).

Throughout much of the insurance system, fee-for-service prevailed, and fee reduction was not a viable option until well into the Depression. So "doctor reduction" (*Arztabbau*) to reduce competition over patients came to be a logical and for some of the players a preferred solution. The politics surrounding this burning issue played a key role in the shaping of the system imposed in 1931 and later reinstalled after the Nazi catastrophe was over.

Between Capital and Labor: Medicine's Answer to the Doctor Question

During the last three years of Weimar democracy, conflicts between the three main economic interest groups in German medical politics, and divisions within them, made unpredictability a certainty. Capital, labor, and medicine struggled with and against one another to reconcile quality, economy, and equality. The choices of electoral politicians, attempting to broker workable agreements among the interests, steered developments violently away from one imperfect solution toward the next. It so happened that a Catholic (Center Party) politician, Heinrich Brüning, came to dominate that process. In the end, he chose, for better or worse, to please the medical profession, satisfy labor, and antagonize capital.

At the center of Weimar democracy, and especially its social politics, was the Center Party (*Zentrum*), whose electoral constituency was both proletarian and bourgeois. Because of Catholic social reformism's independent position between capital and labor it was only logical that class antagonists in the Reichstag, attempting to work together in majority coalitions, could accept Heinrich Braun, leader of the Catholic's Center Party, to serve as Reich Minister of Labor between 1920 and 1928. The Social Democrat Rudolf Wissel interrupted the party's control of social policy for about two years. Adam Stegerwald, leader of the Christian unions and Prussian minister of welfare, then took over the Ministry of Labor between 1930 and 1932.

At the helm in this period was Chancellor Brüning, who had served as executive director, Stegerwald's right-hand man, of the interconfessional Christian labor confederation between 1920 and 1930. In 1930, after dissolving the Reichstag, Reich president Paul von Hindenburg chose Brüning to serve as chancellor of the Reich. Now Stegerwald was Brüning's right-hand man.

These were fateful choices for the German health care system. First, in July 1930, Brüning and Stegerwald tried their hands at bringing capital and labor together against medicine to deal with the fiscal crisis of the health insurance system. When that failed miserably, they took a 180-degree turn and brokered a new alliance between labor and medicine. The deal, worked out in negotiations at the Imperial Labor Ministry in July and October 1931, met with the powerful capitalists' and agrarians' profound indignation. Passed into law in December 1931, it was soon abrogated by the Nazi regime, but it was resuscitated largely intact after World War II to become the basis of the German system today.

Capital and Labor against Medicine: The 1930 Presidential Emergency Decree

The Great Depression, with Brüning's political brokerage, brought capital together with both branches of the labor movement against the German medical profession. Brüning's predecessor government, the Grand Coalition led by Social Democrat Hermann Müller (with party colleague Wissel responsible for social insurance in the Ministry of Labor) had sought calmer relations with the doctors, and with their truce came a historical first: the Hartmannbund's first declaration of goodwill toward health insurance in 1929—almost half a century after Bismarck (Mayer 1929; "Sitzung des Verbandsausschusses" 1930, 98).

But because of the Depression, truculence quickly followed truce, and labor returned to what proved to be a futile war with medicine. Chancellor Brüning, facing crushing pressure from organized capitalists to trim social insurance charges, responded with emergency legislation perceived by doctors as a frontal assault on their profession (Neebe 1981, 78–89). Local sickness funds controlled by the socialist and Christian unions stood side by side with the big industrialists' company funds behind a presidential decree of 26 July 1930, proposed to President Paul von Hindenburg by Brüning. Hindenburg signed the emergency legislation into law without a Reichstag vote; having been dissolved by him earlier, it would not have been able to challenge it, if so disposed, until after a new general election.

The Hartmannbund's Haedenkamp railed that Brüning's decree amounted to a declaration that doctors were unfit to fulfill their duties properly without external guardianship (*Entmündigung*). Nothing less than a total "system change" was under way, bringing with it a "narrowing of doctors' citizenship rights." While doctors bewailed injury to their "status honor," medicine's critics scorned the medical profession's "victim mentality" (Haedenkamp 1930, 661–62; Thomsen 1996, 98). Thus began a furious war of unified payers against unified providers over four main features of the decree: control of malingering by medical examiners, cost shifting onto patients, pressure for more cost-effective clinical practice, and reduction of the number of doctors admitted into insurance practice.

Control of Malingering. More of a symbolic than real immediate threat to doctors was a new legal requirement that the insurance funds hire medical examiners (*Vertrauensärzte*) to review all certifications by insurance practitioners' of their patients' inability to work and therefore qualification for sick pay. Postdiagnostic exams (*Nachuntersuchungen*), it was thought, would force many workers on "sick vacation" back to the workplace. The funds had already gathered compelling evidence of this malingering from various experiments: a great many workers simply returned to work rather than show up when ordered for reexamination.

Although many funds already had such examiners, and sometimes required routine reexamination, physicians' resistance to the practices rendered them less than systematic and effective. Now that they were to be compulsory, the Hartmannbund declared war on the measure and forbade members to apply for or accept examiner jobs without the association's permission ("Kampf der Aerzte gegen die Reichsnotverordnung" 1930, 214). The political impact, if not the medical one, of this action was clear. Along with doctors' individual and collective reactions to other aspects of the emergency decree, it helped persuade the reformers that the legislation was not going to work.

Cost Shifting. Another major economizing measure in Brüning's first decree targeted unhealthy workers, not doctors, for the biggest economic hit, a substantial cut in their sick pay. Furthermore, workers were now to pay a ten-Pfennig fee for each doctor visit and a fifty-Pfennig co-payment for each prescription. Fewer patients, it was hoped, would seek medical attention and certifications of illness for trivial problems. In one way, the fees proved a great success. For example, the city of Leipzig watched its caseload sink from around 200,000 to 170,000 in the third quarter of 1930, and then to 130,000 in the fourth.

Among the organizations involved, only the Hartmannbund complained. Doctors blasted the legislation for sacrificing their own, not just patients', well-being. But the health funds noted very quickly the "astonishing result" that total expenditures on physicians' fees did not budge and that the financial health of the funds would not rebound. For example, Leipzig's consolidated local fund found that its doctors' fees remained flat at about one million Reichsmarks despite its steeply declining caseload. In other places, reportedly, expenses even went up ("Fragen der Zeit" 1931a, 59–60; "Fragen der Zeit" 1931b, 70). The conclusion: to make up for a declining caseload, doctors simply increased the services that they performed on remaining patients.

Capital joined with labor in bemoaning doctors' ability to rescue themselves economically at everyone else's expense with the rush to perform more services. By seeking "safety in numbers" (*Flucht in die Menge*) through "out-of-control doctoring" (*uferlose Verarztung*), the capitalists' company funds found, doctors were able to defend their incomes with enormous success ("Freie Arztwahl" 1930, 65; "Aerztetagung" 1931, 157; Wolff 1997, 129). Socialists agreed. But, according to Julius Moses, the most prominent of socialist doctors and, therefore, a defender of health insurance,

> Every doctor who sees reality as it is, and openly expresses it—namely that there is no academic profession that recovered economically so fast after the war and inflation . . . as the medical profession—is a "traitor" for saying the truth. . . . Whoever says it openly, whoever doesn't chime in with cries of woe that all doctors are suffering, they are "lacking in professional consciousness" and "undermine the prestige of the doctor"; they are ostracized and boycotted. . . . Not even in theology is such an unshakeable belief in dogma demanded as it is from certain medical circles regarding the belief in [protection of] economic interests as an ethical principle ("Fragen der Zeit" 1931b, 70).

Moses, a victim of Theresienstadt in 1942, was of course regarded by organized medicine as one of the worst traitors of all.[4]

Thus, with the fee-for-service remuneration system, which they had so successfully imposed, doctors were able to evade the laws of supply and demand, which normally enforce falling income on stable numbers of competitive suppliers in depressed markets. Notably, organized medicine's favored explanations for the perverse outcome blamed patients for their "demandingness" (*Begehrlichkeit*), the insurance system for cultivating this trait, and low fees for forcing doctors against their will to indulge them. Finally, feebly, they blamed a rising morbidity rate. Only rarely did doctors blame themselves. One exception blamed physicians' "lack of self-respect" for their softness toward pushy patients ("Reichsausschuß" 1931, 385; "Reform der Krankenversicherung" 1930, 163; Beierast 1931, 69). Outside critics of the medical profession of course charged doctors with what today might be called "supplier-induced demand." Greedy doctors, not needy patients, were the problem.

Cost-Effective Medicine. Defending themselves rather ably from economic privation through individual action, doctors also took collective action against other threatening aspects of Brüning's decree. One of these made it the legal obligation of insurance funds to monitor and enforce "economical treatment and prescription practices" (*wirtschaftliche Behandlungs- und Verordnungsweise*). This had only been vaguely exhorted before. Furthermore, cost-effective medicine was now more specifically defined to exclude "unnecessary" medical, dental, and surgical care.

Since passage of the insurance code in 1911—a first step in institutionalizing medical conflict resolution—doctors and funds had been called on in principle to pursue the economical practice of medicine. In 1923, the insurance funds, bureaucrats, and politicians attempted in vain to construct institutional means to develop guidelines for control of clinical practice. All it accomplished was an infuriated medical profession. Now, the threat of real enforcement was in the air. Individual physicians could now be sued for damages if found in violation of regulations—should they ever be formulated. Also, collective contracts could be abrogated if the contracting medical association resisted remedies to systemic problems. If doctors struck in response, the insurance bureaucracy could allow funds to substitute cash payments for service benefits, leaving patients to seek and pay any doctors they chose at any rate. This measure potentially doomed doctors' strikes over control issues to failure.

As in 1923, physicians vehemently rejected the idea that they should be held responsible for waste, even if there was no hiding the fact that their excessive and unnecessary practices were widespread. In 1926 Erwin

Liek had already confirmed for all, in lurid detail and purple prose, all the worst suspicions held by the insurance funds, labor ministry officials, and many doctors. But in his best-selling book, *The Doctor and His Mission*, and a subsequent one, *Social Insurance's Damages* (Liek 1926, 1928), Liek laid blame primarily at the feet of the insurance system for the moral degeneration of the profession and the German people alike.

Doctors probably worried too much about this humiliating aspect of the 1930 decree. More than anything else it proved to be a symbolic and therefore politically threatening challenge to their claim to status and power, based as it was on a putative monopoly of therapeutic knowledge. Just what exactly constituted economical and necessary clinical practice, of course, could hardly be legislated in the Reichstag. The insurance funds had no powerful incentive or resources to apply existing (shaky) therapeutic science, or to generate new knowledge about clinical efficacy, to that end. The law did propose the creation of an overarching corporatist agency to deliberate how to organize and pay for cost-effective medicine, but it never got off the ground.[5]

Controlling the Doctor Surplus. By far the most controversial measure in the emergency decree of July 1930 called for a slow but deliberate reduction, through attrition, in the number of physicians entitled to receive remuneration from the insurance funds. Since 1924, all funds were in principle required to hire or process the bills of no more than one registered contract physician for every one thousand members. Thus, for example, the 250,000 members of various local funds in a district were to have access to 250 regionally organized doctors. Companies that had not yet caved under medical pressure for "organized free choice" among doctors, and therefore still contracting with closed panels, operated under similar constraints. Hence, for example, a large company fund with twenty thousand members had to contract individually with at least twenty physicians.

In practice, efforts to slim down met with intense opposition from the Hartmannbund and achieved little success. Over the years, doctors even succeeded in preventing funds from gaining reductions with a decline of employment in a company or district. This problem became acute during the Depression, when firms suffered major drops in demand. In effect, physicians had achieved a system of permanent tenure for individual practitioners through manipulation of the complex negotiation and arbitration processes written into the insurance code. A kind of protective common law had evolved through negotiations in local admission and contract committees consisting of physician and fund representatives and through state arbitration when the parties could not agree.

Especially in the Depression, this corporatist administrative law system guaranteed, from the insurance funds' standpoint, that too many doctors were chasing too few paying patients. For example, a company with twenty thousand workers could lay off five thousand of them but still be saddled with twenty doctors trying to maintain fee income through more intensive doctoring of fewer patients. Thus, the company funds were the most fervent advocates of "doctor reduction."

The 1930 decree now, decisively, called for bringing the system back into balance by requiring the funds to replace only two out of every three doctors who departed due to retirement, death, or other reason. Over time, funds were thereby allowed to bring their ratios back down to 1:1000. This was radical surgery even if it was slow. The Hartmannbund leadership sounded alarm at the prospect, over the long haul, of ten thousand fewer positions in insurance practice when, currently, there were no more than about thirty-five thousand registered. And there were more doctors on the march, because politicians, not doctors, controlled the universities. The numbers take one's breath away: between 1925 and 1932 the number of medical students *tripled*. In 1931 doctors in training numbered eighteen thousand or so, and twenty-five thousand more (!) were expecting entry into medical school in 1932 (Titze 1984, 104–7; Kater 1986, 56–60; Thomsen 1996, 129, 184). The system was drowning, nobody doubted, in a "glut of doctors" (*Aerzteschwemme*).

From a sheer economic standpoint, organized doctors already admitted into insurance practice should at least have loudly welcomed the new, more restrictive admission rules. And indeed, there was disagreement and vocal protest in response to the Hartmannbund's fight against restrictions (Jacobs 1929; Thomsen 1996, 32–33). Fewer doctors would mean less frenetic churning of fees for useless services to achieve a target income. They might even be able to get fees increased without economic damage to the funds. Indeed, it was not impossible to find doctors who would speak for shrinking the competition. One physician enlisted by the company funds declared that fewer prescriptions would be good for the health of their members—not just for the finances of the insurance funds. A problem, he noted, was the excessive prescription of pain relievers among other "more or less poisonous substances . . . whose effects over the long term we know very little" (Tröscher 1930, 273–74).

But although many insurance physicians saw a benefit in doctor reduction of the kind being proposed, official pronouncements belied that support. The Hartmannbund could not advocate that solution, even if it made economic and therapeutic sense. There were two reasons: organizational and political. First, in the 1920s, the Hartmannbund's leadership feared that endorsing restrictions would so antagonize and discourage unemployed doctors, many of whom were members, that they would break ranks and scab for the insurance funds. The funds would then be able to let collective contracts lapse, bust the doctors' unions, and return to restrictive contract practice. As Haedenkamp put it, young doctors would be driven into the arms of the socialist funds. Years of hard work would be destroyed (Thomsen 1996, 34). As we will soon see, Brüning's next major move, responding to Hartmannbund pressure, promised to rescue the medical leadership from this conundrum.

Over time, the reasoning became as much political as organizational. The politics of medicine in Weimar Germany was not just about how to organize the system to reconcile costs, coverage, and quality. It was also, pure and simple, about ideology, and increasingly the worst kind. By 1931, the cancer of Nazism had spread well into the medical profession where the immune response was weakest: among medical students and large numbers of young unemployed physicians. Indeed, because universities were continuing to hand out many thousands of new medical degrees every year, *a rising number of doctors were clamoring loudly for access to a declining caseload.* Though unemployed, the "young doctors" (*Jungärzte*) joined the Hartmannbund in large numbers and became an increasingly noxious and disruptive presence. Nazi MDs recently socialized in the poisonous politics of medical school, and organized in their special Nazi association, ferociously attacked the organization from within for its collaboration in a health insurance system controlled by capital—and, worse, labor—including its joint gate-keeping admission committees. This was a betrayal of all that Nazism stood for (Hubenstorf 2002/2003, 208–9).

The huge and growing doctor surplus made the 1930 answer to the doctor question politically untenable. Unemployed doctors had gained a powerful source of support: a small but influential number of radicalized doctors in the Reichstag. And these were gaining support within a parliament with a shrinking middle. Indeed, according to the Social Democratic funds, there was now a clear Reichstag majority sympathetic to overturning all restrictions on entry into insurance practice.

To moderate Weimar politicians like Brüning and Stegerwald, with their ears open to the local funds' complaints, doctors had proven themselves economically unsupportable and clinically irresponsible. Now many of them were proving to be a political menace to the shaky democracy by bankrupting the social security system. So Brüning sought a solution that might at least stave off disaster by enlisting organized medicine's support. In exchange, a few things had to give, including doctor reduction. Swept away with that ambition was capital's support.

Labor and Medicine against Capital: The 1931 Emergency Decree

Seeking a way out of the quagmire, Brüning changed course radically in 1931 and brought labor—Christian as well as Social Democratic—once again to a détente with medicine. By backpedaling on control of the doctor surplus, he moved forward toward reconciliation. In a deal brokered by Brüning and hammered out in the offices of the Reich Labor Ministry in October 1931, the labor fund officials and the Hartmannbund leadership agreed on a substantial loosening of the 1930 admission regulations. *From now on, funds had to lower their sights and permanently accept a doctor-member target ratio of 1:600.* This revision was incorporated into a new presidential emergency decree signed by President Hindenburg in December 1931.

On this revision, according to the *Deutsche Krankenkasse*, the mouthpiece of the Social Democratic local funds, labor sided with medicine because the burgeoning medical proletariat, "dynamite in the foundations of the state" (*Sprengpulver im Staatsgefüge*), was too dangerous to be ignited ("Der kassenärztliche Dienst" 1931, 1107). Ominous signals from the Reichstag, according to one Brüning supporter, probably Social Democratic local fund leader Helmut Lehmann, wrote of "a very strong majority in the Reichstag and in the current government for almost unlimited admission of the young doctors to insurance practice." In sum, the capitalists' passive wait-and-see approach, their gamble that no government would ever dare to throw open the admission gates, was "too flimsy (*billig*) to be taken seriously" ("Die Neuregelung" 1931, 1274; Tennstedt 1977b, 132n. 64).

In the deal, the Hartmannbund leadership accepted another major change: *a substantial across-the-board cut in the standard fee schedule.* But in the bargain they hastened to gain something far more important—a radical restructuring of the system to the medical association's profound organizational advantage and an enormous threat to the capitalists' company funds. First of all, the reform introduced *compulsory membership of all insurance doctors in new regional associations that the Hartmannbund leadership could quickly dominate.* The company funds now had to give up all hope of working collaboratively with physicians through a separate medical association (Gibbon 1912, 35). More important, and also in line with principles adopted at the Hartmannbund's Cologne convention of June 1931, the legislation imposed on all insurance funds *a legal obligation to bargain collectively, on a regional basis, with these new medical associations.* The labor funds had already accepted collective bargaining with the doctors' associations in practice; now the capitalists' funds would have to negotiate with the doctors' unions, just as they did with labor unions.

It is logical to think that by getting agreement for compulsory collective bargaining and doctors' associations, Haedenkamp consciously and ingeniously maneuvered organized medicine into a position where it could pursue an economically rational admissions policy that was also consistent with organizational survival. From now on, if the medical associations agreed to the restrictive policy that the funds had been clamoring for, the funds could no longer simply turn around and legally exploit a reserve pool of unemployed young doctors now feeling betrayed by the Hartmannbund for accepting restrictions. That is to say, the funds would no longer have the potential to bust the regional doctors' unions because the unions enjoyed permanent legal status and an exclusive—corporatist—right to be negotiated with.

The emergency decree of 1931 brought one other and even more radical departure from current practice. *Collectively, doctors were now to shoulder official responsibility for pursuing cost-effective practices.* A collective incentive to do this was built into the compulsory bargaining process. Collective bargaining between doctors and funds was now to produce negotiated or arbitrated settlements on a district basis over fixed budgets for ambulatory services. In other words, the funds and medical associations were to settle on a collective prospective capitation fee (*Gesamtpauschale*) —calculated to fall or rise more or less in step with workers' income. The funds would then hand over the budget amount to the compulsory regional medical associations, which would then distribute fees for individual services performed by their members out of this budget (Ritter 1931, 603–5). The supposed genius of this arrangement—which made the rest of the deal easy to swallow for the labor-dominated funds—was that if too many services were performed by their members, the doctors' associations would have to lower the fee per service. Reluctance to lower fees would give organized medicine an incentive to find ways to impose cost-effective clinical practice. Now it would be doctors' role alone to bring about a new, cost-effective medical order.

As early as 1900, German doctors had tossed around the rather intriguing idea of having their associations monitor and control members' unsound clinical practices to work within a budget. The Social Democratic local funds, having rejected the idea back then, had approved of the idea in principle in 1928 and formally adopted it at their Nuremberg convention in 1929. Now, in 1931, the politically pivotal Christian labor unionists, an increasingly radicalized constituency to which Brüning was tightly beholden (Neebe 1981, 243–44n. 44), agreed. Both saw the advantages of handing over to doctors themselves, on a collective basis, the responsibility for controlling the nature and volume of medical services billed for in insurance practice in order to stay within their budget. In Social Democratic insurance executive Helmut Lehmann's probably overoptimistic words, it would bring "a thoroughgoing protection of the funds against uneconomical treatment methods" (Lehmann 1932, 8, 16–18).

Capitalists protested loudly, and in vain, against the clever, complicated, and radical transformation of the health care system. Heinemann suspected a political and therefore more ominous motive behind this elaborate and radical transformation of the system. At work behind this "peculiar alliance of interests" (*eigenartige Interessenverbundenheit*) he saw the Social Democratic unionists' unshakeable long-term goal of absorbing company fund members into a unified system of local funds. Haedenkamp, too, he believed, harbored his own "delusional dream of centralization and collectivism" and was therefore "openly conducting the business" of the Social Democratic insurance funds, known for their ambition of forming compulsory collective bargaining "as a first step toward the unitary fund system" ("Herr Dr. med. Haedenkamp" 1932, 141–43).

Hostilities between capital and the medico-labor alliance flared again, as they had in the winter of 1930, when the the capitalists' Heinemann accused Haedenkamp of "distortion of the facts," "immeasurable exaggeration," and "cheap propaganda of the vilest nature" for his criticisms of the company funds' protests. In response to one of the doctor's diatribes, Heinemann blasted Haedenkamp for thinking that he can "dress down prominent health fund officials like stupid schoolboys [*wie dumme Jungen abkanzeln*]" ("Aenderung in der Krankenversicherung" 1930, 198; "An den Herrn Schriftleiter der 'Aerztlichen Mitteilungen'" 1931, 1). One of these officials was Heinemann's son, future *Bundespräsident* Gustav Heinemann. Things had come a long way since the turn of the century, when socialists like Friedrich Landmann and the labor-dominated local funds were doctors' worst enemy.

Aftermath: Nazi Doctors

The doctor-labor agreement of October 1931 became the foundation of a decree imposed the following December against the will of Germany's major capitalist interests. The system it set up became the foundation of Germany's postwar health care system. Reich president Paul von Hindenburg signed it at the urging of Center Party chancellor and former Christian trade unionist Heinrich Brüning. Brüning, it seems, was caught between labor—especially his own increasingly radicalized branch of it —and capitalists. By choosing to forge a medico-labor alliance, he helped shred the tolerance of many right-wing industrial elites for the failing democratic order.

In the end, Brüning's legislation did nothing to appease many of Germany's doctors. For one thing, it had no time to achieve a calming effect. Large numbers of physicians had already begun migrating politically in a rightward direction away from their traditional political home, the DNVP (*Deutschnationale Volkspartei*), whose core constituencies were increasingly doctors' enemies: heavy industry and agriculture. (Haedenkamp himself had served as a DNVP member of the Reichstag from 1924 to 1928.) Indeed, after Hitler seized power, many doctors became Hitler's willing allies, administrators, and executioners in caring for the new patient, *das Volk*, and its body, *der Volkskörper*. One of them was Haedenkamp and the entire staff of the Hartmannbund, which moved from Leipzig to Berlin to run the new *Kassenärztliche Vereinigung Deutschlands* (KVD). Shortly after Hitler seized power in 1933, Haedenkamp wrote, "Never in the past has the medical profession been so closely tied to the will and the objectives of the state as today" (Haedenkamp 1933, 8).

The proportion of doctors who fell in line is astonishing: by 1936, over 30 percent of non-Jewish physicians had become Nazi Party members; in the course of the Nazi dictatorship, the figure hovered around 45 percent (almost 50 percent of male physicians). Corresponding membership levels for the SA were 21 and 26 percent. The SS claimed roughly 4 percent of doctors in 1936 and 7 percent in following years. No other professional group in Germany was so well represented (Rüther 1997, 166–67; Kater 1987, 311; Kater 1989, 54–88).

Were one forced to sort through the contributory causes and choose the single most important contributory factor that turned German doctors into enemies of democracy and, less directly, psychologically predisposed them to become tools of a criminal regime, one would have to point to Germany's compulsory national health care system. Recent historical research suggests as much (Kater 1986; Thomsen 1996). Doctors even blamed the insurance system for the German public's declining faith in regular medicine's therapeutic superiority. Behind the rising economic success of quackery (*Kurpfuscherei*), Liek and others thought, was workers' dissatisfaction with the impersonal and mechanical mass delivery of services by doctors bustling to earn fees (Timmerman 2001).

But more directly infuriating for doctors was the direct role that national health insurance accorded to capital and labor in the mission to ensure that Germans received quality medical care while economizing on its costs. Because institutionalized incorporation of these organized class interests routinely rode roughshod over physicians (they felt), Weimar democracy itself became tainted. After all, it had been secured early on by the cross-class Stinnes-Legien agreement of 1918 and the resulting, if not terribly successful, corporatist *Zentralarbeitsgemeinschaft* (Central Commission of Industrial Employers and Workers). According to this corporatist system of cross-class collaboration, business and labor leaders would collaborate on the major social insurance problems of the day (Feldman and Steinisch 1985, 34, 46, 53, 80–81, 201, 210–11).

Even Haedenkamp came under fire from the growing extremist wing of the medical profession for his attempts to work with the social insurance system. Speaking through the party's newspaper, *Völkischer Beobachter*, Nazi doctors blasted away at Haedenkamp and the Hartmannbund for its 1931 collaboration with labor (Haedenkamp 1931, 692). But once Hitler came to power, Haedenkamp went straight to work for the new regime. There were no protests to be heard from him about Nazi eugenics: on behalf of the Hartmannbund, he had called for systematic forced sterilizations in 1932 in the name of "racial hygiene"—before Hitler took power. He retained the top leadership role in the Nazi health system. He helped craft the first *Reichsärzteordnung*, the new and separate legal code for the medical profession, turning it into anything but a free, individualistic

—and ethnically inclusive—enterprise dedicated to doing no harm. (He survived de-Nazification and remained a top medical leader until his death in 1955 [Schwoch 2001; Hubenstorf 2002/2003, 213].)

As regards the unsolved doctor surplus, the Nazi regime now gave Haedenkamp the freedom to proceed with impunity in doctor reduction. He helped fashion the guidelines for firing married female doctors and blocking women's entry into medical study and insurance practice. As for the Jews, his was a direct role in expelling them from the health care system. Jews had constituted no less than half of Berlin's doctors in early 1933, and 60 percent of its doctors practicing insurance medicine. By 1934, none of them could engage in insurance practice. By 1938, they were excluded from medical practice altogether, except as nonlicensed caregivers for other Jews. That was the final solution to the surplus doctor question.

Now that Hitler's Germany was shutting all Jews out of medical practice, American organized medicine began, around 1938, refusing to license émigrés trained abroad, many of them from Germany and Austria. Jewish doctors in large numbers were seeking refuge on the other side of the Atlantic. But American physicians had an oversupply problem too. And they used another argument as well: *the quality of medical education abroad was often inferior* (Kohler 1997).

Conclusion: Distributional Politics Are Not Entirely about Distribution

The fiscal strain on the German welfare state from the Great Depression and the unchecked flood of doctors onto the medical market converged in Germany to create a perfect storm of clashing economic interests. The clash of interests gave rise to a most hideous politicization of medicine. But it also gave rise, as postwar German health care indicates, to a highly unique health care system that was not unworkable and—despite inevitable flaws in practice—even somewhat fair and rational in design.

This German story shows that alignments as well as conflicts of labor's and capital's distributional interests, inflamed and brokered by politicians, can drive the politics of welfare state development. Comparative historical analysis of welfare state development suggests that this might be a general pattern (Swenson 2002). But the German story shows that the *quality* of welfare policy, not just its distributional implications, can also play a powerful role. Certainly in the case of health insurance, the question of quality takes on deep importance. Here, doctors can hold their own against labor and capital. Because the public credits them with superior knowledge about illness and health, physicians can exercise influence over medical politics to an extent far out of proportion to their numbers or resources relative to capital and labor.

The politics of medicine and health insurance in Germany and the United States in the 1930s also show that in the realm of social policy-making, the distributional rhetoric of fairness and justice does not necessarily trump in the democratic game. Reactionaries hold their own with other powerful rhetorics. They often appeal, of course, to the inviolability of property acquired from work and savings—and to the unfairness of taxation to serve the idle and prodigal. But this argument has only a limited democratic reach. Another rhetoric of reaction, elegantly dissected by Albert Hirschman—against the futility, perversity, and jeopardy of reform —enjoys a much broader democratic appeal (Hirschman 1991). Reactionaries throughout history, like Erwin Liek in Germany and his devotees Harvey Cushing and Edward Ochsner in America, routinely assert the futility and even counterproductivity of our efforts to aid the poor. Those efforts put other social values in jeopardy. Money goes to waste. Entitlement to assistance breeds dependence and perpetuates poverty. The moral hazards of insurance bring professional degradation and cultural decay.

In the case of medical care in the 1920s and 1930s, there were *pieces of truth in parts of these arguments*, which gave them credibility to politicians and voters. Thus, the arguments endowed relatively few people with immense power far out of proportion to their numbers. In Germany, the arguments aided the Nazis in their war on the democratic welfare state. In America, the arguments, backed by evidence from Germany, helped block the passage of national health insurance for years to come.

NOTES

The author would like to thank the Max Planck Institute for Research on Societies for supporting the research for this chapter, and Lina Daly, Sigrun Kahl, Karl Ulrich Mayer, and Mark Schlesinger for their helpful comments on draft versions. All translations from German sources are the author's own.

1. Thus, corporatist representation of interests deviates from the individualistic one-person-one-vote system of electoral representation, which segments representation by geography (electoral districts), not economic function.

2. In 1931 there were 3,519 company funds with 2,843,000 members, for an average of about 800 members per fund. There were 2,101 local funds with about 13,000,000 members, or about 6,000 members per fund on average.

3. Throughout the Weimar years of his remarkable and circuitous political career, Gustav Heinemann, unlike Haedenkamp, remained a committed democrat. Initially an activist in the liberal German Democratic Party (DDP), which dissolved, he made a brief attempt to create a viable cross-confessional reform party. In the end he voted for the Social Democrats in 1933, protesting Hitler. A co-founder of the Christian Democratic Union (CDU) in 1945, he broke with the party in 1952, mostly over foreign policy, and eventually found his way into the SPD. As a Social Democrat, he was elected to the presidency of the Federal Republic.

4. A practicing physician in Berlin, Moses chaired the *Verein Berliner Kassen-ärzte* (Berlin Association of Contract Physicians) and published its journal *Der Kassenarzt* (*The Contract Physician*). From 1922 on, he was member of the Social Democratic Party executive council.

5. The *Hauptausschuß für Krankenversicherung* was to seat representatives of the peak organizations of employers, workers, funds, and doctors and be chaired by the Labor Minister. Its tasks, among other things: "To establish principles and guidelines for the administration of sickness insurance in general, especially for economy and simplicity, for prevention and elimination of abuses and defects."

REFERENCES

"25 Jahre Betriebskrankenkassenverband." 1932. *Die Betriebskrankenkasse* 25:13 (10 July).

"25 Jahre Verband rheinisch-westfälischer Betriebskrankenkassen." 1929. *Die Betriebskrankenkasse* 22:23 (10 December).

"Aenderung in der Krankenversicherung." 1930. *Die Betriebskrankenkasse* 23:16 (25 August).

"Aerztetagung," 1931. *Die Betriebskrankenkasse* 24:13 (10 July).

"An den Herrn Schriftleiter der 'Aerztlichen Mitteliungen.'" 1931. *Die Betriebskrankenkasse* 24:1 (10 January).

Behagel, Katrin. 1994. *Kostendämpfung und ärztliche Interessenvertretung: Ein Verbandssystem unter Streß*. Frankfurt: Campus.

Beierast, W. 1931. "Mehr Disziplin und Selbstachtung." *Ärztliche Mitteilungen* 32:4 (24 January).

Bierring, Walter. 1934. "The Family Doctor and the Changing Order." *Journal of the American Medical Association* 102 (June 16).

Breger, Monika. 1982. *Die Haltung der industriellen Unternehmer zur staatlichen Sozialpolitik in den Jahren 1878–1891*. Frankfurt: Haag and Herchen.

———. 1994. "Der Anteil der deutschen Grossindustriellen an der Konzeptualisierung der Bismarckschen Sozialgesetzgebung." In Lothar Machtan, ed., *Bismarcks Sozialstaat*. Frankfurt: Campus.

Bueck, Henry Axel. 1905. *Der Centralverband Deutscher Industrieller 1876–1901, Volume 2*. Berlin: Deutscher Verlag.

Cushing, Harvey, letter to Bierring, Walter. 15 August 1936. Series I, Folder 175. Harvey Cushing Papers, Sterling Library, Yale University.

Cushing, Harvey, letter to Liek, Erwin. 26 January 1935. Series II, Folder 196. Harvey Cushing Papers, Sterling Library, Yale University.

Cushing, Harvey, letter to Ochsner, Edward H. 30 November 1934. Series II, Folder 194. Harvey Cushing Papers, Sterling Library, Yale University.

Cushing, Harvey, letter to Roosevelt, Franklin. 1 February 1935. Series II, Folder 196. Harvey Cushing Papers, Sterling Library, Yale University.

Falk, I. S., C. Rufus Rorem, and Martha D. Ring. 1933. *The Costs of Medical Care: A Summary of Investigations on the Economic Aspects of the Prevention and Care of Illness*. Chicago: University of Chicago Press.

Feldman, Gerald, and Irmgard Steinisch. 1985. *Industrie und Gewerkschaften 1918–1924: Die Überforderte Zentralarbeitsgemeinschaft*. Stuttgart: Deutsche Verlags-Anstalt.

"Fragen der Zeit." 1930. *Die Betriebskrankenkasse* 23:23 (2 December).

———. 1931a. *Die Betriebskrankenkasse* 24:5 (10 March).

———. 1931b. *Die Betriebskrankenkasse* 24:6 (25 March).

"Freie Arztwahl." 1930. *Die Betriebskrankenkasse* 23:6 (25 March).

Gibbon, I. G. 1912. *Medical Benefit: A Study of the Experience of Germany and Denmark*. London: P. S. King and Son.

Haedenkamp, Karl. 1930. "Notverordnung!" *Ärztliche Mitteilungen* 31:31 (2 August).

———. 1931. "Parteipolitische Angriffe auf den Hartmannbund." *Ärztliche Mitteilungen* 32:34 (22 August).

———. 1933. "Das neue deutsche Ärzteblatt." *Deutsches Ärzteblatt* 63.

Hartz, Gustav. 1935. "Will America Copy Germany's Mistakes?" *New York State Medical Journal* 35:5 (March 1).

Hauptverband deutscher Krankenkassen. 1924. *Bericht über den 28. deuschen Krankenkassentag am 27. u. 28. July 1924*. Berlin: Verlagsgesellschaft deutscher Krankenkassen.

Hayek, Hermann v. 1927. *Freie Arztwahl und Sozialversicherung*. Munich: Verlag der Aerztlichen Rundschau Otto Gmelin.

Hennock, E. P. 1998. "Social Policy under the Empire: Myths and Evidence." *German History* 16:1.

"Herr Dr. med. Haedenkamp." 1932. *Die Betriebskrankenkasse* 25:6 (25 March).

Hirschman, Albert O. 1991. *The Rhetoric of Reaction: Perversity, Futility, Jeopardy.* Cambridge, MA: Belknap.

Hoffman, Frederick. 1919. *Failure of German Compulsory Health Insurance: A War Revelation.* Newark, NJ: Prudential Press.

Hubenstorf, Michael. 2002/2003. "'Deutsche Landärzte an die Front!': Ärztliche Standespolitik zwischen Liberalismus und Nationalsozialismus." In Christian Pross and Gotz Aly, eds., *Der Wert des Menschen: Medizin in Deutschland 1918–1945.* Berlin: Hentrich.

Huerkamp, Claudia. 1985. *Der Aufstieg der Ärzte im 19. Jahrhundert.* Göttingen: Vandenhoeck and Ruprecht.

Jacobs, Carl. 1929. *Arzttum in Not: Betrachtungen über die Krisis im Ärztestand.* Leipzig: Vogel.

Kähler, Kristian. 1994. "Zur Entwicklung der sozialpolitischen Geschichtsschreibung in den 1950er Jahren." In Lothar Machtan, ed., *Bismarcks Sozialstaat.* Frankfurt: Campus.

"Kampf der Aerzte gegen die Reichsnotverordnung." 1930. *Die Betriebskrankenkasse* 23:17 (10 September).

"Der kassenärztliche Dienst im Rahmen einer Gesamtreform der Krankenversicherung." 1931. *Deutsche Krankenkasse* 18:40 (1 October).

Kater, Michael. 1986. "Physicians in Crisis at the End of the Weimar Republic." In Peter D. Stachura, ed., *Unemployment and the Great Depression in Weimar Germany.* London: Macmillan.

———. 1987. "Medizin und Mediziner im Dritten Reich: Eine Bestandsaufnahme." *Historische Zeitschrift* 244.

———. 1989. *Doctors under Hitler.* Chapel Hill: University of North Carolina Press.

Kleeberg, John M. 2003. "From Strict Liability to Workers' Compensation: The Prussian Railroad Law, the German Liability Act, and the Introduction of Bismarck's Accident Insurance in Germany, 1838–1884." *International Law and Politics* 36:53.

Kohler, Eric D. 1997. "Relicensing Central European Refugee Physicians in the United States, 1933–1945." Museum of Tolerance Online: Multimedia Learning Center, http://motlc.wiesenthal.com/site/pp.asp?c=gvKVLcMVIuG&b=395145 (accessed June 8, 2007).

Landmann, Friedrich. 1892. *Anleitung zur Verminderung der Arzneikosten bei den Krankenkassen: Für den Gebrauch der Kassenvorstände*, 2d edition. Elberfeld: Selbstverlag.

———. 1898. *Die Lösung der Arztfrage.* Elberfeld: Selbstverlag.

Lehmann, Helmut. 1932. *Ärzte und Krankenkassen*, 5th edition. Berlin: Verlagsgesellschaft deutscher Krankenkassen.

Liek, Erwin. 1926. *Der Arzt und seine Sendung: Gedanken eines Ketzers.* Munich: J. F. Lehmanns.

Liek, Erwin. 1928. *Die Schäden der sozialen Versicherungen und Wege zur Besserung*. Munich: J. F. Lehmanns.

Lohmann, Theodor, letter to Friedrichs, Rudolf. 5[–16] October 1874. In Lothar Machtan, ed., *Mut zur Moral: Aus der privaten Korrespondenz des Gesellschaftsreformers Theodor Lohmann*. Bremen: Temmen.

Mares, Isabela. 2003. *The Politics of Social Risk: Business and Welfare State Development*. New York: Cambridge University Press.

Mayer, Ernst. 1929. "Freie Arztwahl und Massenproblem." *Ärztliche Mitteilungen* 11:13 (30 May).

Möller, Wilhelm. 1910. *Die Herrschaft der Sozialdemokratie in der deutschen Sozialversicherung*. Berlin: Reichsverband gegen die Sozialdemokraten.

Müller, Friedrich, letter to Cushing, Harvey. 20 December 1934. Series II, Folder 196. Harvey Cushing Papers, Sterling Library, Yale University.

Neebe, Reinhard. 1981. *Großindustrie, Staat und NSDAP 1930–1933*. Göttingen: Vandenhoeck and Ruprecht.

Neuhaus, Rolf. 1986. *Arbeitskämpfe, Ärztestreiks, Sozialreformer: Sozialpolitische Konfliktregelung 1900 bis 1914*. Berlin: Duncker and Humblot.

"Die Neuregelung der Beziehungen zu den Aerzten." 1931. *Deutsche Krankenkasse* 18:45 (5 November).

Numbers, Ronald L. 1978. *Almost Persuaded: American Physicians and Compulsory Health Insurance, 1912–1920*. Baltimore, MD: Johns Hopkins University Press.

Ochsner, Edward H. 1920. "Compulsory Health Insurance: A Modern Fallacy." *Journal of the Michigan State Medical Society* 19 (1920).

———. 1934. *Social Insurance and Economic Security*. Boston: Bruce Humphries.

Plaut, Theodor. 1913. *Der Gewerkschaftskampf der deutschen Ärzte*. Karlsruhe: Braun.

"Reform der Krankenversicherung." 1930. *Die Betriebskrankenkasse* 23:14 (25 July).

"Reichsausschuß." 1931. *Ärztliche Mitteilungen* 32:22 (30 May).

Ritter, G. 1931. "Gedanken über eine Reichspauschale als Gemeinlast der Krankenkassen." *Ärztliche Mitteilungen* 32:30 (25 July).

Rosen, George. 1983. *The Structure of American Medical Practice 1875–1941*. Philadelphia: University of Pennsylvania Press.

Rothfels, Hans. 1927. *Theodor Lohmann und die Kampfjahre der staatlichen Sozialpolitik*. Berlin: Esmittler and Son.

Rüther, Martin. 1997. "Ärztliches Standeswesen im Nationalsozialismus 1933–1945." In Robert Jütte, ed., *Geschichte der deutschen Ärzteschaft: Organisierte Berufs- und Gesundheitspolitik im 19. und 20. Jahrhundert*. Cologne: Deutscher Ärzte-Verlag.

Schwenger, Rudolf. 1934. *Die deutschen Betriebskrankenkassen*. Munich and Leipzig: Duncker and Humblot.

Schwoch, Rebecca. 2001. *Ärztliche Standespolitik im Nationalsozialismus: Julius Hadrich und Karl Haedenkamp als Beispiele*. Husum: Matthiesen Verlag.

"Sitzung des Verbandsausschusses." 1930. *Die Betriebskrankenkasse* 23:9 (10 May).

Stone, Deborah A. 1980. *The Limits of Professional Power: National Health Care in the Federal Republic of Germany*. Chicago: University of Chicago Press.

Swenson, Peter A. 2002. *Capitalists against Markets: The Making of Labor Markets and Welfare States in the United States and Sweden*. New York: Oxford University Press.

Tennstedt, Florian. 1977a. "Ärzte, Arbeiterbewegung und die Selbstverwaltung in der gesetzlichen Krankenversicherung." *Jahrbuch für Kritische Medizin* 2 (Special Volume 17).

————. 1977b. *Soziale Selbstverwaltung: Geschichte der Selbstverwaltung in der Krankenversicherung*, Band 2. Bonn: Verlag der Ortskrankenkassen.

Thomsen, Peter. 1996. *Ärzte auf dem Weg ins "dritte Reich": Studien zur Arbeitsmarktsituation, zum Selbstverständnis und zur Standespolitik der Ärzteschaft gegenüber der staatlichen Sozialversicherung während der Weimarer Republik*. Husum: Mattiesen Verlag.

Timmerman, Carsten. 2001. "Constitutional Medicine, Neoromanticism, and the Politics of Antimechanism in Interwar Germany." *Bulletin of the History of Medicine 75*.

Titze, Hartmut. 1984. "Die zyklische Überproduktion von Akademikern im 19. und 20. Jahrhundert." *Geschichte und Gesellschaft* 10.

Tröscher, Dr. med. [no first name]. 1930. "Volksgesundheit und Notverordnung." *Die Betriebskrankenkasse* 23:22 (25 November).

Vossiek, Wilhelm. 1937. *Hundert Jahre Kruppsche Betriebskrankenkasse 1836 bis 1936*. Berlin: Verlag für Sozialpolitik, Wirtschaft und Statistik.

Walther, Peter. 1998. *Betriebskrankenkassen von der Reichsversicherungsordnung bis zur Machtergreifung*. Aachen: Shaker Verlag.

Wolff, Eberhard. 1997. "Mehr als nur materielle Interessen: Die organisierte Ärzteschaft im Ersten Weltkrieg und in der Weimarer Republik 1914–1933." In Robert Jütte, ed., *Geschichte der deutschen Ärzteschaft: Organisierte Berufs- und Gesundheitspolitik im 19. und 20. Jahrhundert*. Cologne: Deutsche Ärzteverlag.

Chapter 10

||||||||||||||||||||||||||||||||||||||||||||||||||||||||

Democracy and Distributive
Politics in India

Pranab Bardhan

To most theorists of democracy in the West, India is an embarrassing anomaly and hence largely avoided. By most theoretical stipulations India should not have survived as a democracy: it is too poor, its citizens are largely rural and uneducated, its civic institutions are rather weak. It is a paradox even for those who believe in a positive relationship between economic equality or social homogeneity and democracy: its wealth inequality (say, in land distribution, and even more in education or human capital) is high, and its society is one of the most heterogeneous (in terms of ethnicity, language, caste, and religion) in the world.

Yet this country, with the world's largest electorate (it is now larger than the electorate in North America, Western Europe, and Japan combined), keeps lumbering on decade after decade as a ramshackle, yet remarkably resilient, democratic polity.[1] Of course, depending on the defining features of democracy the depth of Indian democracy may be rather limited. It is useful to keep a distinction between three general aspects of (liberal) democracy: (a) some basic minimum civil and political rights enjoyed by citizens, (b) some procedures of accountability in day-to-day administration under some overarching constitutional rules of the game, and (c) periodic exercises in electoral representativeness. These aspects are of varying strength in different parts of India. In general the performance in much of the country over the past half a century has been really impressive in terms of (c), some pitfalls and electoral malpractices notwithstanding. If uncertainty about the outcome of elections, giving the opposition some chance of winning office, is key to a polity's minimum democratic character,[2] then India comes off in flying colors, at least in the past three decades or so. If, however, you care as much or more about (a) and (b), then India's performance has been somewhat mixed, satisfactory in some respects but not in others. Also, except in three or four states in India, all these aspects of democracy are weaker at the local village or municipality level than at the federal or provincial levels.

There are several ways in which the historical and social origins of democracy in India are sharply different from those in much of the West, and the indigenous political culture has fundamentally reshaped the processes of democracy. These differences are reflected in the current functioning of democracy in India and its impact on distributive politics, making it somewhat difficult to fit the Indian case to the canonical cases in the usual theories of democracy. In the rest of this chapter we point out some of these differences (as well as similarities) and spell out their effects, particularly in terms of economic reform, governance, and distributive policies and transfers.

A.

Whereas in Europe democratic rights were won over continuous battles against aristocratic privileges and arbitrary powers of absolute monarchs, in India these battles were fought by a coalition of groups in an otherwise fractured society against the colonial masters. Even though part of the freedom struggle was associated with ongoing social movements to win land rights for peasants against the landed oligarchy, the dominant theme was to fight colonialism. And in this fight, particularly under the leadership of Gandhi, disparate groups were forged together to fight a common external enemy, and this fight required strenuous methods of consensus building and conflict management (rather than resolution) through co-opting dissent and selective buyouts. Long before Independence the Congress Party operated on consensual rather than majoritarian principles. The various methods of group bargaining and subsidies and "reservations" for different social and economic categories that are common practice in India today can be traced to this earlier history. This context has also meant that in India, unlike in much of the West, democracy has been reconciled with multiple layers of nationality, where a pan-Indian nationalism coexists with assertive regional nationalisms in the same citizenry.

B.

Unlike in Western Europe, democracy came to India before any substantial industrial transformation of a predominantly rural economy and before literacy was widespread, which seriously influenced the modes of political organization and mobilization, the nature of political discourse and the individual's relation to the public sphere, and the excessive economic demands on the state. Democratic (and redistributive) aspirations of newly mobilized groups outstripped the surplus-generating capacity of the economy, demand overloads sometimes even short-circuiting the surplus-generation process itself. In my book *The Political Economy of Development in India* (Bardhan [1984] 1998) I described the political equilibrium underlying a broad pattern of economic deadlock in India, which in spite of recent deregulations and liberalizations and the higher growth rates in the past two decades, has persisted in some basic features. This deadlock is generated by the usual collective action problems for large and heterogeneous coalitions in pulling together in their long-run collective interest, yielding more easily to short-run particularistic compromises in the form of sharing the spoils of the system to the detriment of long-run public investment, particularly in improving India's creaking infrastructure (power, ports, railways, roads, irrigation, and the like), which acts as a severe bottleneck for private investment and growth. With national elections sometimes taking place before the usual five-year period (due to unstable political coalitions) and the state elections held on a rolling basis across states on a cycle disconnected with the national elections, at any given time some important election somewhere is never too far, preoccupying the minds of politicians with short-run expediencies, and the need for long-run commitments in policy gets shortchanged.

In catering to these short-run demands a large part of public resources get frittered away in the form of implicit or explicit subsidies, galloping amounts of what are called nondevelopment expenditures (mainly salaries, pensions, and debt servicing), and largely politicized mismanagement of capital in the bloated public sector and overregulation of the private sector. The fiscal deficit of the central and state governments taken together in 2003–4 was about 10 percent of GDP[3] (up from 7.5 percent in 1980–81), while public investment declined from 8.4 percent of GDP to 5.6 percent in the same period. Public investment in infrastructure as a proportion of GDP has declined significantly, and the hoped-for private investment to fill the gap has not materialized (largely on account of anticipated political problems of recovery of user fees and tolls, and frequent political interventions in regulatory institutions), except in some sectors like telecommunication, civil aviation, and ports.

The central government budgetary subsidies (explicit subsidies like those for food, fertilizer, petroleum, and interest rate and implicit subsidies in the form of unrecovered costs of public provision of goods and services that are not public goods) as a proportion of the fiscal deficit of the central government amount to nearly 90 percent. According to estimates by the National Institute of Public Finance and Policy two-thirds of these budgetary subsidies are what they call "nonmerit" (largely accruing to the relatively rich). Apart from their inequity, they are also inefficient. For example, a large part of the money lavished on subsidizing fertilizer, water, and electricity would have been much better spent (in terms of both promoting agricultural growth and reducing environmental damage from the resultant overextraction of groundwater and overuse of chemicals) instead in public investment in irrigation and watershed management. But the lobby of middle and large farmers is much too strong, and very few politicians can or want to take them on. Even left political parties (which largely represent public-sector office workers and unionized industrial labor) find it easier to enter essentially "logrolling" arrangements with them. These problems are, of course, familiar from pork-barrel politics in many democracies, but they are more acute in a country of such extreme heterogeneity reflected in a bewildering crisscross of interest alignments, and much less affordable at India's level of extreme poverty and appalling infrastructure. When the surplus generated in the system is small and the claimants on the public fisc are too many, the common-pool problem is particularly severe.

The collective action problem has become more acute in the past three decades as more newly mobilized groups started asserting themselves and as the massive countrywide organization of the Congress Party, which used to coordinate transactional negotiations among different groups and leaders in different parts of the country, fell into disarray. One reason for the decline of the party is the erosion of the mechanisms of intraparty democracy since the 1970s, as a result of which the organizational channels of demand articulation and conflict resolution got clogged. The lack of inner-party democracy in all major parties in India in recent years has led to a proliferation of small and regional parties; as ambitious politicians found it more difficult to rise through the usual channels and ladders inside a national party, they staked their claims from outside by forming their own parties and strategically used their support for advancing their personal and regional or group agendas.

C.

In the evolution of democracy in the West the power of the state was gradually hemmed in by a civil society dense with interest-based associations. In India groups are based more on ethnic and other identities, although the exigencies of electoral politics have somewhat reshaped the boundaries of (and ways of aggregating) these identity groups (thus, two subcastes in the population may not accept food or marriage connections with each other, but they coalesce into a generic caste group for electoral purposes). This situation has also meant a much larger emphasis on group rights than on individual rights.[4] A perceived slight of a particular group (in, say, the speech or behavior of a political leader from another group) usually causes much more of a public uproar than crass violations of individual civil rights, even when many people across different groups are to suffer from the latter. There is a distinctly low sense of public outrage (except among a handful of urban liberals) when the state violates an individual's freedom of expression, the police routinely beat up or torture a suspect, or the authorities ban a book or film on the alleged ground that it might offend the sensibilities of some group.

The issues that catch public imagination are the group demands for preferential treatment (like reservation of public-sector jobs) and protection against ill treatment. This is not surprising in a country where the self-assertion of hitherto subordinate groups in an extremely hierarchical society takes primarily the form of a quest for group dignity and protected group niches in public jobs.[5] More on this later.

D.

In Western history, expansion of democracy gradually limited the power of the state. In India, on the other hand, democratic expansion has often meant an *increase* in the power of the state. The subordinate groups often appeal to the state for protection and relief against the tyrannical ways of dominant groups in their localities. With the decline of hierarchical authority in the villages and with the moral and political environment of age-old deference to community norms changing, the state has moved into the institutional vacuum thus left in the social space. For example, shortly after Independence popular demands for land-reform legislation (for the abolition of revenue intermediaries, for rent control and security of tenure), however tardy and shallow it may have been in implementation, brought the state into the remotest corners of village society. In more recent days, with the progress of the state-supported Green Revolution, in matters of loans, tubewells, fertilizers, seeds, agricultural extension, land records, and the like, the state is implicated in the texture of everyday village life in myriad ways.

With the advantage of numbers in electoral politics as hitherto backward groups get to capture state power, they are not too keen to weaken it or to give up the loaves and fishes of office and the elaborate network of patronage and subsidies that come with it.[6] This propensity serves as a major political block to the (largely elite-driven) attempts at economic liberalization of recent years. Not merely fiscal consolidation is particularly difficult at the state government level where these groups are dominant (with serious underpricing of water and electricity, overmanning of the public payroll, and a long-standing refusal to tax the better-off farmers), but some of the remaining obstructive industrial regulations (for example, in the matter of getting electricity or water connection and land registration in starting a factory) are in the jurisdiction of these governments. Of course, economic reforms are not generally popular in India, as they are often perceived to benefit mainly the rich.[7] Even ruling politicians who support reforms play them down during election time; a party that initiates some economic reforms is quick to oppose them when out of power. The electorate does not seem to mind such time-inconsistency; in several elections (both national and provincial) those who believe reforms do not help them have voted against whichever is the ruling party. The anti-incumbency sentiment (which is likely to be a reaction to inept or corrupt governance and failed delivery of public services) has merged with a general grievance about the perceived inequity in the effects of reforms carried out by ruling parties.

Jenkins (2000), however, has pointed out that the Indian political system has clever, if sometimes clandestine, ways of diffusing resistance to reform. He correctly points out how reformers in a government may enjoy some autonomy in the context of the great malleability and fragmentation in the Indian interest-group structure, how accommodations arranged through informal political networks mediate conflicts between winners and losers, and how particular reform measures generate a chain reaction of demand for more reform from within. He cites cases of "back-door reforms" in public-sector companies and of some pro-business state governments deliberately looking the other way as some of the rigid labor laws are violated. It is not clear, however, how such "reform by stealth" can be sustained in the long run. As suggested by the foregoing discussion of the staggering burden of subsidies and public debt and the continuing fiscal crisis endangering the prospect of any massive and much-needed improvement in the public infrastructure, the changes to which Jenkins refers are as yet not substantial and purposive enough to break the basic political logjam in the macroeconomy.

Beyond the direct economic consequences of short-run distributive politics are the consequences for democratic governance. The diminishing hold of elite control and the welcome expansion of democracy to reach the lower rungs of the social hierarchy have been associated with a loosening of the earlier administrative protocols and a steady erosion of the institutional insulation of the decision-making process in public administration and economic management. These changes have affected not just the ability to credibly commit to long-term decisions but the whole fabric of governance itself. It is now common practice, for example, for a low-caste chief minister in a state to proceed, immediately upon assuming office, to transfer away top civil servants belonging to upper castes and get pliant bureaucrats from his or her own caste. Some of the new social groups coming to power are even nonchalant in suggesting that all these years upper classes and castes have looted the state, and now it is their turn. If in the process they trample on some individual rights or some procedural aspects of democratic administration, the institutions that are supposed to kick in to restrain them are relatively weak. Highly corrupt politicians are regularly reelected by their particular ethnic or local constituencies (which they nurse assiduously even while fleecing the rest of the system). Personal extravagance at state expense by particular ethnic leaders is often a source of community pride for historically disadvantaged groups.

This state of affairs is part of a fundamental tension between the participatory and procedural aspects of democracy in India: the unfolding of the logic of populist democracy has itself become a threat to democratic governance. Kaviraj (1995, 119) has described the situation as a strange Tocquevillian paradox: "democratic government functioned smoothly in the early years after 1947 precisely because it was not taking place in a democratic society; as democratic society has slowly emerged, with the spread of a real sense of political equality, it has made the functioning of democratic government more difficult." Some people are not too worried by these difficulties, and they regard them as part of the initial necessary turmoil of democratic movement forward and group self-assertion. The writer V. S. Naipaul (1997, 39), who is fascinated by the "million mutinies" in contemporary India, says, "When people start moving, the first loyalty, the first identity, is always a rather small one. . . . When the oppressed have the power to assert themselves, they will behave badly. It will need a couple of generations of security and knowledge of institutions and the knowledge that you can trust institutions—it will take at least a couple of generations before people in that situation begin to behave well."

I wish I could share in this optimistic belief in democratic teleology. The breakdowns in democratic governance and economic management structures are not easy to repair, and there are irreversibilities in institutional decay. Besides, in India's multilayered social structure, by the time one self-aware group settles down and learns to play by the institutional rules, other newly assertive groups will come up and defy those rules, often in the name of group equity.

E.

In the theories of democracy, socioeconomic cleavages are often regarded as obstacles to the functioning of democracy. John Stuart Mill ([1861] 1951, 486) considered free institutions as "next to impossible in a country made up of different nationalities." In *The German Ideology,* Marx and Engels also traced the persistence of German absolutism to divisions among the social classes in the Germany of their time. In the last chapter of *The Political Economy of Development in India* (Bardhan [1984] 1998), I offered a somewhat contrary hypothesis: the Indian experience seems to suggest that the very nature of socioeconomic heterogeneity may make the divided groups somewhat more interested in the procedural usefulness of democratic processes. In a country with an extremely heterogeneous society and the elements of even the dominant political coalition quite diverse, and most important, where no individual group is by itself strong enough to be able to hijack the state, there may be some functional value of democracy as a mutually accepted mode of transactional negotiations among contending groups and as a device by which one partner in the coalition may keep the demands of other partners within some moderate bounds.[8] I would not, however, go to the other extreme of Lijphart's claim (1996) that India is actually an impressive example of his brand of "consociational" democracy. Although India, after Independence, has always been ruled by some form of political coalition (sometimes even within the same ruling party), I doubt if it conforms to at least two important criteria of power-sharing democracies, one relating to proportionality in political and civil-service representation and the other to minority veto powers.

F.

Democracy, at least in theory, is associated with the supremacy of the "rule of law" (as opposed to rule by persons). To this day this concept is rather alien in much of Indian political culture, in spite of what the pious statements in the Indian Constitution (or judicial activism in many remarkable instances of public-interest litigation against abuses of power) may suggest. The law as actually enforced is often not above elected politicians. In many states the institutional independence of the police and the criminal-justice system is quite eroded, leading to criminalization of politics in parts of the country. Some of the criminal elements have figured out that once elected on a ruling-party ticket they can neutralize the police, who will not press the criminal charges against them with any alacrity. Police officers are often rewarded, for example, with plum postings, if they do the elected politicians' bidding. The National Police Commission forcefully pointed out these problems in its eight-volume reports in 1979 and 1981–82, without making much headway in taking action. The politicization of police and civil administration was the institutional background of the state-abetted pogrom in Gujarat in 2002. The participation of the urban middle classes in this pogrom in a state where capitalism is more advanced than in most other states has led some commentators to point to the unorthodox combination of economic liberalism and political illiberalism. This combination is contrary to the traditional idea of middle classes promoting liberal values, but it is not unfamiliar to readers of Karl Polanyi or observers of the Latin American political scene over decades.

Even in noncriminal aspects of social life, democratic participants often accept benefits from a politician's decisions as personal favors to them as individuals or as members of a favored group, rather than as part of their constitution-protected rights. The political process is a way of linking up with powerful patrons who act as elected "godfathers" (this is akin to the way Christian Democrats used to function in Sicily or some political bosses used to in Chicago). The emphasis is not on impersonal procedures of accountability but more on politically legitimized ways of manipulating the network of patronage distribution.

This is, of course, to be expected in a society where individuals' community bonds are stronger than their role as citizens, where they are sometimes better protected against all kinds of hazards by their community than by the impersonal forces of a distant and corrupt state. After all, the rule of law means little for the weaker sections of society when these laws in the way they are formulated (even in some industrial democracies, with their vaunted rule of law, the laws themselves, when they are made, are "for sale" to the highest corporate or special-interest contributors to the legislators) or enforced, have at best weak links to the politicians' promises on the basis of which electoral mobilizations take place. The judicial process is massively clogged and corrupt in India, and the poor often feel that the law is just another "stick" with which the resourceful rich can beat them. In contrast, the community arbitration processes[9] can sometimes provide some measure of protection for the weak against the strong; as long as all parties belong to the same moral community, there are usually some accepted limits to and symbolic sanctions against the kind of ruthless exercises of power that sometimes accompany the cut-throat impersonality of the legal system. On the other hand, community arbitration can often be highly oppressive (as, for example, in the case of *jat* or *rajput* caste panchayats in North Indian villages severely punishing young people contemplating intercaste marriages), and the state may be the only, though clumsy and heavy-handed, protector of the disadvantaged minority.

In Indian democracy the legislative process is often relegated to a second order of importance, giving short shrift to the deliberative process in the legislature that John Stuart Mill and other theorists of democracy valued so much. More often than not the legislature becomes an arena for slogan-mongering, shouting matches, and a generous display of the theater of the absurd. Sometimes breathtakingly radical pieces of legislation on complex issues get passed without much discussion, with their potential opponents reasonably confident that they will be able to undermine the laws at the enforcement stage.

On many controversial issues the opposing parties do not try to resolve them in legislative deliberations but quite literally go to the streets

for this purpose. They (including the ruling party) concentrate on organizing mass rallies and counterrallies and a show of strength in popular
mobilization, in the process bringing normal life in the cities and towns
to a standstill for the day. Contrary to what happens in most democracies,
Indian political leaders, who should be spending time debating in the legislature, think first of a general strike or *bandh* to register their protest
and flex their muscles of mobilization, taking pride in how their followers
have paralyzed the daily life of a city. By and large India is less of a legislative or deliberative democracy and more one of popular mobilization.
This usually means short-run populist measures or patronage distribution
are at a political premium, not long-gestation attempts at structural transformation of the constraints in the lives of most people.

In a recent book Chatterjee (2004) has distinguished between the legally
constituted domain of civil society (where the elite wants to maintain the
structure of constitutionality and modernity) and the mobilized, if somewhat contingent, terrain of what he calls "political society" of the poor
in the Indian cities, where an entire subculture of paralegal arrangements
has been recognized and administered by the state. Some of these poor
people live as squatters on public land, travel ticketless on public trans-
port, regularly steal water and electricity from public connections, and in
other ways encroach on and reconstitute the public space. The logic of
political mobilization and of social-welfare claims drives the government
agencies to look away from some of the pilfering and even provide some
public services to these people "on a case-to-case, *ad hoc*, or exceptional
basis, without jeopardizing the overall structure of legality and property"
(ibid., 136). These paralegal arrangements do not quite belong to the terrain of relations between the state and the demand of its citizens asserting
their rights. Chatterjee considers these negotiations between the state and
political society as part of "the encounter between modernity and democracy" (51), where the elite pursuit of modernity is seriously compromised
by the compulsions of popular sovereignty or legitimacy.

I am, however, not persuaded that the rule of law is such an inescap-
ably elitist project. Its absence actually hurts many of the marginalized
groups: ask the street vendor who has to pay protection money to the local goons or the small shopkeeper or petty producer who has to pay the
corrupt policeman or inspector. Some of the development projects that
require eviction of squatters have the potential of expanding job prospects for the poor. That the government or the private contractors often
get away with reneging on the commitments to adequately rehabilitate the

oustees[10] is a failure of the mechanisms of accountability, but the development project itself is not necessarily an elite conspiracy. Political connivance at the large-scale stealing of electricity in some slums that in the end makes the general supply of electricity unviable or unreliable renders the livelihoods of many poor producers elsewhere more precarious. Short-run populist mobilization is not a sure safeguard for the long-run health of democracy.

G.

In the electoral process the Indian masses, particularly the poor and the socially disadvantaged, take a much more participatory role than their counterparts do in advanced industrial democracies. John Stuart Mill emphasized the aspects of moral education flowing from democracy, but in India the more important impact of democracy has been on the political awakening and enhancement of group self-esteem. Democracy has clearly brought about a kind of social revolution in India. It has spread out to the remote reaches of this far-flung country in ever-widening circles of political awareness and self-assertion of hitherto subordinate groups. These groups have increased faith in the efficacy of the political system, and they vigorously participate in larger numbers in the electoral process. In the National Election Study carried out by the Centre for the Study of Developing Societies, the percentage of respondents who answered positively to the question "Do you think your vote has effect on how things are run in this country?" went up between 1971 and 1996 from 45.7 percent to 57.6 percent for "backward caste" groups (designated as OBC in India), from 42.2 percent to 60.3 percent for the lowest castes (designated as scheduled castes), 49.9 percent to 60.3 percent for Muslims, and from 48.4 percent to 58.7 percent for all groups taken together.

The increased faith in politics is not, however, matched by faith in politicians. The Indian electorate is often regarded as reflexively anti-incumbent, particularly in contrast with the electorate in the United States. Although, as I noted before, some of the anti-incumbency may be related to the government's failure to deliver basic social services, for an extremely poor country like India the electorate does not *in general* punish the politicians for the continual scourge of poverty, unemployment, disease, and illiteracy which afflicts the lives of the common people. It is possible that endemic poverty is regarded by common people as a complex phenomenon with multiple causes, and they ascribe only limited responsibility to the government in this matter. The measures of government performance are rather noisy, particularly in a world of illiteracy and low levels of civic organization and formal communication on public issues. As I indicated before, a perceived slight in the speech of a political leader felt by a particular ethnic group will usually cause much more of an uproar than if the same leader's policy neglect keeps thousands of children severely malnourished in the same ethnic group.

The same issue of group dignity comes up in the case of reservation of public-sector jobs for backward groups which, as I said before, fervently catches the public imagination of such groups, even though objectively the overwhelming majority of the people in these groups have no chance of ever landing those jobs, as they and their children largely drop out of school by the fifth grade. Even when these public-job quotas mainly help the tiny elite in backward groups, as a symbol and a possible object of aspiration for their children, they ostensibly serve a valuable function in attempts at group upliftment, even though it is a divisive and inefficient way of achieving that objective.

Particularly in North India there seems to be a preoccupation with symbolic victories among the emerging lower-caste political groups; as Hasan (2000) points out with reference to BSP, a politically successful party of the oppressed castes in Uttar Pradesh, these groups seem less concerned about changing the economic-structural constraints under which most people in their community live and toil. Maybe this is just a matter of time. These social and political changes have come to North India rather late; in South India, where such changes took place several decades back, it may not be a coincidence that there has been a lot more effective performance in the matter of public expenditures on pro-poor projects in health, education, housing, and drinking water. This difference reflects the fact that in South India there has been a long history of social movement against exclusion of lower castes from the public sphere, against their educational deprivation, and so on in a way that is more sustained and broad-based than in North India. One may also note that the upper-caste opposition to social transformation is somewhat stronger in North India, as demographically upper castes constitute in general a larger percentage of the population than has been the case in most parts of South India. So new political victories of lower castes in North India get celebrated in the form of defiant symbols of social redemption and recognition aimed at solidifying their as yet tentative victories, rather than in committed attempts at changing the economic structure of deprivation.

Although the electorate does not seem to penalize politicians for their endemic poverty, economists cannot help noticing that they are less forgiving when there is a sharp and concentrated *deterioration* in their economic condition. Sen (1983) has commented on the political sensitivity of democracies to the threat of famine, but to me the more commonplace sensitivity in India is the electorate's high degree of inflation sensitivity. It is a common presumption that a double-digit annual inflation rate, if it continues for some time, will be politically intolerable in India, and politicians of all parties universally support a conservative monetary policy to avoid this danger (even when the government stocks of food and foreign exchange are huge). The poor tend to make the government directly responsible for inflation and expect it to stop inflation in its tracks even at the expense of cutting budgetary programs on (physical and social) infrastructure which would have helped the poor in the long run—as they say, contra Keynes, in the *short* run "we are all dead," when the country is poor (and incomes are largely unindexed in the face of high inflation).

H.

For a large federal democracy, India, by constitutional design, differs from the classical case of U.S. federalism in some essential features. Not merely is the federal government in India constitutionally more powerful vis-à-vis the states in many respects (including the power to dismiss state governments in extreme cases and to reconstitute new states out of an existing state in response to movements for regional autonomy), but it has also more obligation, through mandated fiscal transfers, to help out poor regions. In classical federalism the emphasis is on restraining the federal government through checks and balances; in India it is more on regional redistribution and political integration. Stepan (1999) has made a useful distinction between "coming-together federalism" as in the United States, where previously sovereign polities gave up a part of their sovereignty for efficiency gains from resource pooling and a common market, and "holding-together federalism" as in multinational democracies like India (or Spain or Belgium), where compensating transfers keep the contending nationalities together.

Economic integration of regional markets is a distant goal in India, largely unachieved even in more than fifty years of federalism. There are many restrictive regulations on the free flow of goods across the state boundaries. Even though the Essential Commodities Act of 1955, which enabled the federal and state governments to impose controls on production and trade of a wide range of commodities and thus segment the Indian market, has now been largely repealed, many restrictive regulations (for example, the Maharashtra Cotton Monopoly Procurement Scheme, authorizing the state government to acquire all raw cotton produced in the state) remain. Although attempts are being made to replace the state sales taxes with a destination-based value-added tax, some of the entry taxes hindering interstate trade remain. There are also strong regional movements for reserving public-sector jobs for the so-called sons of the soil.

As I mentioned before, the government at the center is increasingly dependent on the support of powerful regional parties, which has obvious implications for the politics of redistributive federalism. Political leaders at the center who are key to the survival of a coalition government there often have agendas that are primarily oriented to their own state. Take for example the Ministry of Railways at the center, which presides over one of the largest railway systems in the world and is *the* largest commercial employer in India. A major part of the minister's agenda in several recent governments has been to provide jobs for people in his or her own state and add railway connections at great cost to remote locations in local constituencies, apart from keeping passenger fares below cost, often at the expense of system-wide efficiency and the gaping long-term investment needs of this vital infrastructural sector.

Regional parties also negotiate support in exchange for additional fiscal transfers to particular states. A significant part of the central transfers to the states has always been discretionary (like the numerous central-sector and centrally sponsored schemes earmarked for objectives like poverty alleviation), not linked to revenue-raising efforts by the state governments. The state governments also enjoy a great deal of autonomy in domestic borrowing to cover fiscal deficits, even though formally such borrowing requires authorization by the central government. More than half of the borrowings by the state governments now are spent in covering current expenditures, pushing them toward a debt trap. The state governments also act frequently as a guarantor of bonds issued by the state-owned enterprises, generating staggeringly large contingent liabilities. And then because current revenues, transfers, and borrowings are frequently not enough, the central government often has to bail out fiscally distressed states, creating perverse incentives for them not to keep their fiscal house in order. As the logic of economic reform and increased competition leads to increased regional inequality, one of the toughest political-economy issues in the coming years will be how to resolve the tension between the demands of the better-off states for more competition and those of the populous backward states (which a weaker center can ill afford to ignore politically) for redistributive transfers.

In this chapter I have elaborated on some of the main differences in the origins and current functioning of Indian democracy compared to the canonical models of democracy in the West and on the way these differences shape the nature of distributive politics. Democracy has brought about a veritable social revolution in India, a country of extreme social inequality, but some of the consequences for governance and economic reform have not always been wholesome. The Indian polity has yet to resolve the tension between the procedural and participatory aspects of democracy, between the institutions of insulation necessary for credible long-term policy commitments and the need for public accountability and mobilization in a country long ruled by hierarchical and heavy-handed authorities distant from the people.

NOTES

1. India is an obvious outlier in the empirical rule cited in Przeworski (1999): the expected life of democracy in a country with per capita income under one thousand dollars (in 1985 Purchasing Power Parity) is about eight years.

2. This definition, for example, is suggested in Przeworski (1999).

3. India's ratio of public debt to revenue is one of the highest in the world, and yet most macroeconomic indicators are relatively stable, primarily because most of the debt is not in foreign currency and the domestic debt market is sheltered by capital account controls. But the long-term risks of such a situation are large. The recently legislated Fiscal Responsibility and Budget Management Law is a step in the right direction, but political pressures to postpone its effective implementation are substantial.

4. One of the early leaders who carried in him the tension between individual and group rights was B. R. Ambedkar, who was a constitutional lawyer and a founding father of the Indian Constitution, but who was also a major spokesman of an oppressed caste group.

5. One of the triumphant slogans of BSP, a major party mobilizing the historically oppressed low castes in North India, used to be, "*vote se lenge PM/CM, arakshan se SP/DM*" (we'll take the offices of the Prime Minister and the Chief Minister through votes; we'll take through reservation the offices of the Superintendent of Police and the District Magistrate).

6. In some sense this is familiar in the history of American municipal politics in big cities, where one after another hitherto disadvantaged ethnic group captured the city administration and distributed patronage.

7. For some evidence of public opinion on this question, see the survey results of the Lokniti-CSDS team after the 2004 elections (Suri 2004). It is not, however, obvious that people always have a clear understanding of what is meant by economic reforms. If reforms mean reduction of subsidies, thus raising the user charges for many publicly provided goods and services or loss of jobs in some old firms or occupations as a result of increased competition, one can see why people involved will be opposed. But if it were to be made clear that a higher electricity price means the ability of the public utility to provide less-erratic power supply and fewer power cuts, or if more competition means the rise of new firms expanding employment opportunities, or if deregulation means loosening the grip of corrupt inspectors over small enterprises, some of this opposition may melt away.

8. For a similar argument about the persistence of democracy in another extremely heterogeneous country, Papua New Guinea, see Reilly (2004).

9. Even in the Western judicial system the trial by jury is a recognition of the role of the community in the judicial process.

10. In a recent judgment on the Narmada dam, the Indian Supreme Court has ruled that rehabilitation of people displaced by the Sardar Sarobar project has to be completed one year before the submergence of their villages.

REFERENCES

Bardhan, P. [1984] 1998. *The Political Economy of Development in India.* New Delhi: Oxford University Press.

Chatterjee, P. 2004. *The Politics of the Governed: Reflections on Popular Politics in Most of the World.* New York: Columbia University Press.

Hasan, Z. 2000. "Representation and Redistribution: The New Lower Caste Politics of North India." In F. R. Frankel, Z. Hasan, R. Bhargava, and B. Arora, eds., *Transforming India: Social and Political Dynamics of Democracy.* New Delhi: Oxford University Press.

Jenkins, R. S. 2000. *Democratic Politics and Economic Reform in India.* Cambridge: Cambridge University Press.

Kaviraj, S. 1995. "Democracy and Development in India." In A. K. Bagchi, ed., *Democracy and Development*. New York: St. Martin's.

Lijphart, A. 1996. "The Puzzle of Indian Democracy: A Consociational Interpretation." *American Political Science Review* 90(2): 258–68.

Mill, J. S. [1861] 1951. *Utilitarianism, Liberty, and Representative Government*. New York: E. P. Dutton.

Naipaul, V. S. 1997. Interview. *India Today* 22: 26–39.

Przeworski, A. 1999. "Minimalist Conception of Democracy: A Defense." In I. Shapiro and C. Hacker-Cordón, eds., *Democracy's Value*. Cambridge: Cambridge University Press.

Reilly, B. 2004. "Ethnicity, Democracy and Development in Papua New Guinea." *Pacific Economic Bulletin* 19(1): 46–54.

Sen, A. K. 1983. "Development: Which Way Now?" *Economic Journal* 93: 745–62.

Stepan, A. 1999. "Federalism and Democracy." *Journal of Democracy* 10(4): 19–33.

Suri, K. C. 2004. "Democracy, Economic Reforms and Election Results in India." *Economic and Political Weekly* 39(51): 5404–11.

Chapter 11

||||||||||||||||||||||||||||||||||||||||||||||||||||||||||

The Political Uses of Public Opinion
Lessons from the Estate Tax Repeal

Mayling Birney, Ian Shapiro,
and Michael J. Graetz

What impact does public opinion have on legislative outcomes in a democracy? In this chapter, we ask this question while examining the surprising case of the repeal of the federal estate tax in 2001. This repeal benefits only a tiny minority of very wealthy Americans: those bequeathing, or inheriting from, estates larger than $1 million. Logically, one might have anticipated, as congressional Democrats did for a long time, that such a regressive measure would provoke a popular backlash. If enacted at all, it would be done in the dead of night or after being buried quietly within a larger bill, like a congressional pay raise. Yet, over recent years, estate tax repeal somehow acquired a populist flavor and became a high priority for mainstream as well as conservative politicians. Beginning in 2000, the House and Senate repeatedly voted to repeal the estate tax in stand-alone measures, as shown in figure 11.1. Although, due to budgetary constraints, the actual repeal that was signed into law in June 2001 was only a temporary one-year repeal,[1] the details of which are shown in table 11.1, the repeated achievement of broad bipartisan support was an astonishing success for repeal advocates. As the battle for a permanent repeal persists, Republicans, at least, continue to view this highly regressive measure as a winning issue with the public.

Our goal in this chapter is to unravel this conundrum and explore its implications for our understanding of how public opinion affects political outcomes. Our investigation is unorthodox in that, in addition to the usual public sources, archival research, and scholarly literature, we engaged in some one hundred interviews, the great majority not for attribution, with

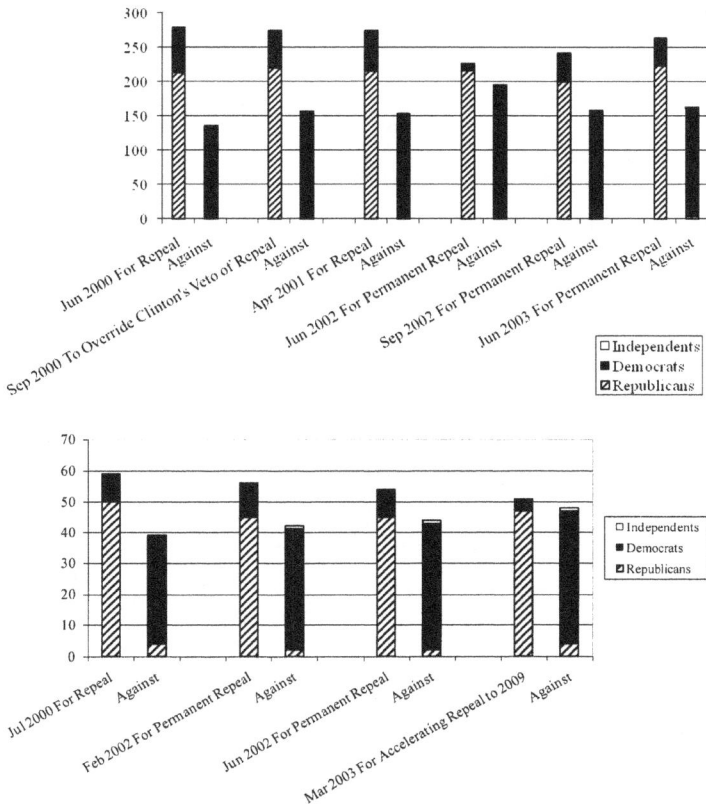

Fig. 11.1. *Top*: House votes on estate tax repeal. *Bottom*: Senate votes on estate tax repeal.

congressmen, senators, political aides, civil servants, journalists, interest-group representatives, analysts, and others with different stakes in the outcome. We find that, although political scientists often view public opinion and interest-group activity as separate influences on the policymaking process, public opinion is in fact a weapon that can be deployed, more or less effectively, by interest groups that are struggling to shape what Congress does. Our case study reveals that interest groups expended great effort to identify the wide-ranging contours of public opinion and used this knowledge to shape politicians' perceptions of public opinion on the issue. Part I of this chapter demonstrates the extent to which the direction of public opinion on the estate tax is open to interpretation—something

TABLE 11.1
Summary of Key Changes to the Federal Estate and Gift Taxes
(Signed into Law in June 2001)

Year	Estate Tax Exemption Level	Top Estate Tax Rate	Gift Tax Exemption Level	Top Gift Tax Rate	Basis for Inherited Assets	State ET Automatic Credit
2002	$1,000,000	56%	$1,000,000	56%	stepped-up	12%
2003	$1,000,000	49%	$1,000,000	49%	stepped-up	8%
2004	$1,500,000	48%	$1,000,000	48%	stepped-up	4%
2005	$1,500,000	47%	$1,000,000	47%	stepped-up	deduction
2006	$2,000,000	46%	$1,000,000	46%	stepped-up	deduction
2007	$2,000,000	45%	$1,000,000	45%	stepped-up	deduction
2008	$2,000,000	45%	$1,000,000	45%	stepped-up	deduction
2009	$3,500,000	45%	$1,000,000	45%	stepped-up	deduction
2010	REPEALED	n/a	$1,000,000	35%	Carry-over	n/a
2011 (law reverts to 2001 law)	$1,000,000	55% (60% for some estates > $10,000,000)	$1,000,000	55%	stepped-up	16%

that was apparently not well understood until recent years—and shows how polls were strategically deployed to "interpret" it for politicians.

Indeed, as discussed in part II, evidence suggests that interest groups even structured their very policy position around their efforts to manage elite perceptions of public opinion on the estate tax. Members of the Family Business Estate Tax Coalition, which in 1995 began to exert pressure to diminish estate taxes, have since become strangely wedded to the repeal stance, even as significant obstacles remain to achieving permanent repeal and readily available reform options might better serve their interests. In part, they seem to fear that, were they to abandon the goal of repeal, they would lose the momentum they have gained from so effectively framing public opinion around principles that are associated with repeal but that are not associated with reform options geared to reducing the estate tax burden. Part II also presents a fuller portrait of how interest groups and political leaders actively shaped politicians' understandings of latent public opinion to serve their own policy goals. Notably, the focus was on convincing politicians that public opinion on this issue could be turned against them in the future, not on changing public opinion itself.

We see the recent successes of interest groups in shaping politicians' perceptions of public opinion as vital to developing broad political support for repeal. In fact, this effort to repeal the tax is the first serious one since the budget surpluses of the 1920s. The timing and persistence of this effort cannot be explained by the reach and rates of the tax alone, as these have been more or less constant for decades, and the estate tax was notably more onerous in the 1970s.[2] Other factors, beyond the actual burden of the tax, contributed to the appeal of repeal in recent years. Undoubtedly, the strength of the economy in 2000 and 2001, the fact that the government was running budget surpluses, demographic changes in the profiles of the wealthiest Americans, and Republican ascendance in Washington made it a propitious time for abolishing the estate tax. Yet these factors still do not explain why estate tax repeal, rather than other longer-standing conservative tax priorities that garner more support from corporate America and supply-side economists, succeeded. When the role of interest groups in shaping elite perceptions of public opinion is also considered, the timing and persistence of the repeal effort begin to make more sense.

I. Interpreting Public Opinion: Principle or Priority?

Starting in the late 1990s, interest groups and political parties employed opinion polling strategically to understand the contours of public opinion on the estate tax. They wanted to know how it varied according to the frameworks, symbols, and principles invoked; with reference to the particular reform or repeal options presented; and in juxtaposition with other priorities. In improving their understanding of these contours, activists could promote to politicians the interpretation that best served their goals. Advocates of repeal were especially active and effective in this regard. With an eye to what such polling revealed to those actively engaged in the debate, in this section we examine the partisan and nonpartisan poll data that was inserted into the public debate on the estate tax. We located, through extensive archival research and interviews with political actors, the publicly released national polling data on the estate tax that dates from 1997 to 2003. This period encompasses the time when estate tax repeal had its greatest momentum on the national stage. In 1997, following the passage of an estate tax reform provision to raise the unified exemption from $600,000 to $1 million, the new goal of many estate tax opponents became estate tax repeal; and both houses of Congress have held floor votes on the issue of estate tax repeal.

Many analysts, and even strong advocates of repeal, reported being surprised by how wide-ranging were the contours of opinion that became apparent. After all, considering that only the wealthiest 2 percent of Americans pay the estate tax and that the estate tax is the most progressive part of the tax code, the vast majority of the public could only lose from estate tax repeal. Yet many polls show that most people support repeal when it is presented as a stand-alone issue—even those least likely to pay the tax and most likely to be beneficiaries of the roughly $30 to $40 billion it raises each year. This amount of revenue boosts the federal budget by 1 to 2 percent, nearly enough to fund, say, the Department of Homeland Security or the Department of Education. Is the explanation that people do not understand their self-interest? There is indeed clear evidence that, in light of misunderstanding and misinformation, many do not. Yet, although this is an important component of the explanation for public support for estate tax repeal, polls show that, even when people are disabused of their illusions on this score, support for repeal remains surprisingly strong. Principled judgments about fairness, which were often primed by question wording, are at least as important as appeals to self-interest. That said, when asked to consider its priorities or the possibility of a higher exemption, the public's verdict typically shifts dramatically, to the extent that the large majority was then found to *support* retaining the estate tax in a reformed version.

Perceived and Misperceived Self-Interest

If we were to impute preferences based on accurately perceived expectations of economic self-interest, those who never expect to pay the estate tax should favor keeping it, given the likelihood that repeal would entail either a relative shift of the tax burden to them or a reduction in services that might benefit them. It would be reasonable to anticipate no more than a modest showing in support of repeal: that small percentage of persons who might realistically risk paying the tax upon death, plus their likely heirs. Yet many polls since the late 1990s have shown widespread public support for estate tax repeal, in the realm of 60 or 70 or 80 percent. Moreover, supporters appear to be spread more or less equally across income groups, contrary to what self-interest would predict.[3]

More sophisticated economic models may impute preferences based on potentially inaccurate perceptions of economic self-interest; and misperceptions certainly do help to explain a good portion of the public support for estate tax repeal. People know very little about estate tax levels and rates and rules, as evidenced by a January 2000 Gallup poll, in which most people (53 percent) admitted that they simply did not "know enough to say" whether the "federal inheritance tax" was too high, too low, or about right. Obtaining accurate information can be difficult, especially when others have an incentive to mislead you. With little background knowledge, many people seem to guess that nearly everyone is taxed at death—a misperception sometimes encouraged by question wording. For example, in a 2003 National Public Radio/Kaiser Foundation/Harvard Kennedy School (hereafter NKK) survey, two-thirds of respondents either thought "most people have to pay" the estate tax (49 percent) or said they did not know (18 percent); and 62 percent of those opposing the estate tax said one reason was because "it affects too many people." Controlling for socioeconomic and demographic factors, and general attitudes toward the tax code, Joel Slemrod (2003) uses results from this survey to estimate that the misconception that most families pay the estate tax "increases the likelihood of favoring abolition by 10.6 percent."[4]

In keeping with this estimate, surveys consistently show that the number of people in favor of repeal drops when respondents are given information on exemption levels or how many people pay. For instance, in the NKK poll, 60 percent of respondents say they want to eliminate the estate tax when the exemption level is not specified. Yet the percentage who favor repeal drops to 48 percent when respondents are asked to consider an estate tax with an exemption of at least $1 million, which is what the actual exemption was slated to be even before the repeal law passed. When asked to consider an estate tax with an exemption of at least $5 million, which was one of the proposed reforms rejected in the Senate, even fewer, 35 percent, still favor repeal.

Precisely how misperceptions about the estate tax change people's views is difficult to say, but it may be through affecting a person's perception of self-interest in repeal or through affecting his or her unselfish evaluation of the social fairness of the tax. In practice, these reasons are entangled because, even provided with correct information, people may misunderstand their own self-interest, and their perceptions of social justice may correspond to their misperceived self-interest. For instance, once given more information about who pays the estate tax, and hearing arguments both for and against repealing it, the percentage of people believing that they or someone in their household would have to pay the tax fell from 37 to 30 percent in a 2002 Greenberg Research poll, and support for repeal correspondingly dropped from 60 percent to 47 percent. Some of the change in views might thus be attributed to a change in respondents' perceptions of self-interest.

Yet more remarkable than the difference made by the presence of correct information is the difference that is *not* made. After all, a full 30 percent of informed people still believed someone in their household would have to pay the estate tax. This result is even more extreme than another often-cited July 2000 Gallup poll showing that 17 percent of informed respondents believe they will personally benefit from estate tax repeal, even after being told that only estates valued at over $1 million would be subject to estate tax. In the 2003 NKK poll, 69 percent of those supporting repeal said a reason was because "it might affect [me] someday." Like stereotypical lottery-ticket holders, Americans' judgments about their likely future wealth seem wildly optimistic.[5]

Principles of Fairness

Despite the important role of evaluations based on self-interest—and confused self-interest—they do not seem to account for the majority of public support for estate tax repeal. A surprisingly high percentage of people—26 percent in the NKK poll—still want repeal even with an exemption of $25 million or more.[6] People's particular judgments about tax fairness are central to accounting for the high support for repeal, and repeal proponents learned to "message" their goal in terms of principles of fairness. We do not discount the possibility that public opinion on the estate tax could also have migrated in recent decades, especially as inflation, demographic changes, social changes, and economic changes have meant that people of more diverse backgrounds would likely come within reach of the estate tax. However, we cannot determine the extent of any such shifts since, with few exceptions, similarly worded poll questions have not been asked over time.[7]

Whatever underlying shifts there may have been in public opinion, our analysis here shows that the dramatic disparities in publicly reported polling results over the past few years depended principally on framing and phrasing rather than timing. For instance, a December 1999 poll by the Democratic Emily's List found that only 37 percent of voters answered "favorable" when asked, "When you hear that George W. Bush wants to eliminate the inheritance tax, is your reaction to that favorable, neutral, or unfavorable?" One month later, a poll by the Republican consultants McLaughlin and Associates found that 79 percent of likely voters approved when asked, "Do you approve or disapprove of abolishing the estate tax, also known as the 'death tax'?" In yet another contrast, a neutral

Gallup poll that was conducted within three days of the McLaughlin poll found that only 41 percent of adults felt that the estate tax was too high when asked, "Thinking about the federal inheritance tax, do you consider this tax too high, about right, too low, or don't you know enough to say?" Though each of the questions is simply worded, they differ by invoking "George W. Bush," delivering negative connotations with the words "abolish" and "death," and encouraging respondents to be comfortable saying they do not know.

The strategic and disciplined use of the term "death tax," rather than "estate tax," has received particular attention as an innovation of repeal proponents. The terminology certainly seems to shift the issue to new ground: as a tax "on death—and not as one on wealth" (Green 2001). At one point in 1999 or 2000, the Republican leadership in fact issued a directive to its membership to use only the term "death tax" to refer to the estate tax. One of the major advantages of the term is that, in contrast to the term "estate tax," it makes the tax sound like it applies to everyone; after all, everyone dies, but few people think of themselves as having "estates." In addition, the term also conjures up an image of government invasiveness during families' most terribly wrenching times. Not surprisingly, people react less favorably to the term. In a 2002 Greenberg Research poll, people rated the "estate tax" at 37.9 on a favorable-feelings scale of 1 to 100, but the "death tax" scored an even lower 31.3. However, as these numbers suggest, the impact of the term on public opinion seems to have actually been relatively modest. To control for the impact of the "death tax" terminology in question wording, the 2002 National Election Survey asked the question in two parallel forms and reported a difference of barely more than two percentage points; 67.8 percent favored "doing away with the estate tax" and 70.0 percent favored "doing away with the death tax" (Bartels 2003b). The 2003 NKK poll found a larger difference, of 6 percent, when it added the phrase "that some people call the death tax" to a question about the estate tax. Yet a March 2001 CBS News/New York Times poll that explained who pays the tax, thus negating any impact the term might have on its perceived scope, showed essentially no difference when it compared the use of the term "estate tax" to "estate/death tax."

More support for repeal was gained through relating it to principles of fairness, which might be firmly and easily evaluated by anyone, regardless of their familiarity with this particular tax. In a representative democracy, people may tend to defer to experts on questions they see as economic, but they are unlikely to do so on moral questions. Speaking about double or triple taxation has been particularly effective.[8] The rhetoric portrays the estate tax in moral rather than financial terms: as an unfair double tax versus as a fair means of preventing extraordinary wealth from altogether escaping tax. In a January 2001 McLaughlin poll, even once informed of the exemption level and rate of the estate tax, 86.9 percent of voters agreed that it was "unfair for the government to tax a person's earnings while it is being earned and then tax it again after a person dies." Note that this question is not a question about the estate tax itself, but the coupling of the estate tax with double taxation implies that the one is the other.

This coupling technique was often used in poll questions and in the public presentation of poll responses to produce the perception of towering opposition to the tax—upward of 70 or 80 percent. It was even used to claim gay and lesbian support for repeal on the grounds that gays and lesbians were denied the benefits of the estate tax's 100 percent spousal deduction.[9] In truth, it is not the estate tax that discriminates against gays and lesbians but, rather, the prohibition of their marrying. Of poll questions that coupled questions about the tax with the unfairness of double taxation, the only result we saw with support of less than 70 percent was a May 2001 McLaughlin poll in which 60 percent of likely voters thought it unfair to apply an estate tax of 40 percent or greater to *billionaires.* McLaughlin conducted this poll specifically to argue that "voters view the estate tax as wrong on principle"; indeed, the sense of unfairness was more widespread among those earning less than forty thousand dollars a year. Figure 11.2 shows results from those questions that ask about the "fairness" of the estate tax or about whether it is "fair" or not—producing results even more dramatic than did another effective framing technique, which was to ask about repeal as a stand-alone issue. Also worth noting is that, regardless of prompting, it appears that people opposed to the tax may have often evaluated the tax with reference to principles of tax fairness. Of those who supported repeal in the 2003 NKK poll, 92 percent say that a reason is because "the money was already taxed once and it shouldn't be taxed again"—which is 18 percent more than the percentage who credit the next most popular reason (that "it might force the sale of small business and family farms").

Indeed, messages that emphasized the burden of the estate tax on family farms and small businesses were also especially resonant, possibly because the American Dream preserves a romantic perception of their bootstrapping spirit; because of a dispassionate recognition that enterprises

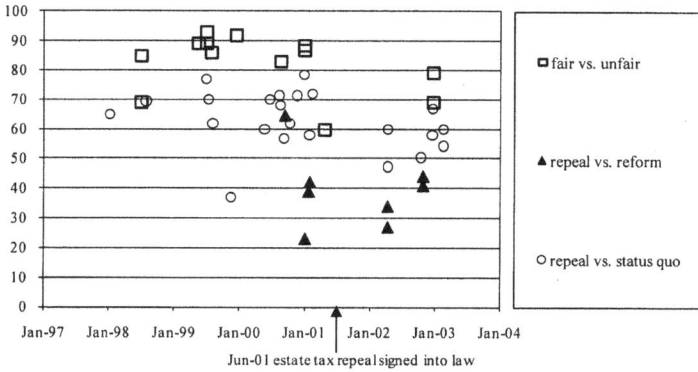

Fig. 11.2. Poll results on estate tax repeal: framing the issue as a question of fairness or a choice between options. This chart includes publicly released national polling data, from 1997 through the end of 2003, in which respondents were asked to evaluate the repeal or the fairness of the estate tax. The pollsters and poll sponsors are identified in the appendix. Data sources include the publications and press releases of the polling organizations and the Roper Center for Public Opinion Research at the University of Connecticut.

are commonly heavy in business assets but low in cash flow; or because so many people have, or have a close family member who has, a small business or farm.[10] In reality, most of the estate tax burden does not fall on family-owned businesses or farms; in 1998, only 1.6 percent of taxed estates held half or more of their value in family-owned business assets, and only 1.4 percent held half of more of their value in farm real estate or assets (Friedman and Lee 2003). Notwithstanding this, the public was more likely to want to repeal the tax for these particular groups than for all people. The message of these findings is clear: it was in the interests of the Republican Party leadership and repeal proponents to try to associate relief for small businesses and farmers with complete repeal, and it was in the interests of the Democratic Party leadership and others who opposed all-out repeal to try to disassociate the two options.

Not all arguments polled by the pro-repeal side proved to be effective at winning public approval. Sociotropic arguments—which tried to trade on public support for what benefits the economy—are one example. A March 2001 poll by three business-school professors, for example, found only one-third of respondents believing that the tax reduces economic growth, almost 40 percent believing it does not, and over a quarter with no opinion (Lantz, Gurley, and Linna 2003). An earlier 1998 poll by the pro-repeal Americans Against Unfair Family Taxation found that 53 percent of respondents believed that the estate tax would hurt the economy; but they and other organizations did not bother to poll the question thereafter. During the late 1990s, proponents of repeal deemphasized arguments about economic effects in favor of appeals to perceptions of self-interest and moral claims about fairness.

Polls were also actively used to understand which messages or frames would most appeal to certain segments of the population. Extremely valuable—and surprising even to many advocates of repeal—was the finding that males and females, people of all age groups, people of all different income levels, and blacks and whites often gave more or less the same responses to many questions. This suggested the potential to enlist unexpected groups in support of the repeal effort. However, responses of people with different profiles did sometimes differ in informative ways. Blacks and Hispanic Americans, for instance, were less convinced than whites and Asian Americans by the argument that "death taxes are unfair to heirs, small businesses, and family farms and should be eliminated"; in one poll, only 48.5 percent of blacks and 55.3 percent of Hispanic Americans agreed with that statement, compared to 66.8 percent of whites and 87.8 percent of Asian Americans.[11] Yet blacks' support for repeal was entirely comparable to whites in response to a question framing estate tax repeal in terms of double taxation.[12] Certainly these numbers made it clear that there was little likelihood of intense hostility from minorities against the move to get rid of the estate tax.

A Matter of Priority

As will be discussed in part II, supporters of the estate tax seem initially to have maintained a sense of false complacency in the face of the repeal effort, expecting that, if only people correctly understood who was subject to the estate tax, nearly everyone would oppose repeal. This belief was way off the mark, as the foregoing evidence makes clear. Eventually realizing that maintaining the existing estate tax was an untenable political position, by 2000 the stance of estate tax supporters was to back a more immediate and permanent reform of the tax—through raising the exemption, lowering rates, and/or excluding farmers and small businessmen—as an alternative to repeal. They struggled even to defend this moderated stance, which they argued for principally on the grounds of the great progressivity of the estate tax. That only the very wealthiest Americans are subject to the tax may appeal to the less wealthy either out of self-interest or on principle, that is, as a desirable outcome. Either way, progressivity clearly convinces some people; and yet this remains only a limited group. Still nearly half of *supporters* of the estate tax explicitly declined to justify their views in these terms in the NKK poll.

Despite the limited appeal of petitions for progressivity, supporters of the estate tax did not promote other principle-based arguments widely. Notably, they found the public unresponsive when the estate tax was defended on the grounds that "America is founded on the notion of equal opportunity for all," and "eliminating the estate tax creates a two-tiered society where some individuals do better than others based on inherited wealth rather than hard work." Although the equality-of-opportunity principle formed the basis of the successful defense of the estate tax in the 1920s, during the only other serious attempt in history to repeal it, the justification scored a disappointing 4.6 on a scale of 0 ("completely unconvincing") to 10 ("extremely convincing") in a 2002 Greenberg poll. In fact, only one of several principled justifications for the estate tax was viewed as "convincing" in that poll, scoring a 6.4. This rather surprising argument was that repeal should be opposed because, as it "has been eliminated and put back in place four times in the past, making estate planning impossible," it would be better to have a "permanent reform that simplifies this tax once and for all and keeps 99 percent of taxpayers exempt." With this discovery, the opponents of repeal now had their own somewhat misleading message for tapping into public frustration with government incompetence.[13]

Ultimately, advocates of retaining the estate tax found that their position received the most support when questions encouraged respondents to consider their priorities rather than their principles, as illustrated in figure 11.2. One way to do this was to pit estate tax repeal against more broadly beneficial tax cuts. For instance, in the 2002 Greenberg poll, supporters of the estate tax rated as most convincing (scoring 7.3) the argument that "we should cut taxes for the middle class by abolishing the marriage penalty and making college tuition and job training costs tax deductible, rather than giving more tax breaks to multi-millionaires." This is consistent with the fact that, in annual Gallup polls from 1997 through

2001, no more than 6 or 7 percent of Americans ever ranked estate tax repeal as their highest tax-cut priority, whereas typically more than 30 percent prioritized "a tax cut for moderate and low-income Americans."

A second way to encourage respondents to voice their priorities was to allow them to choose an option between the two extremes of repealing or maintaining the existing estate tax. For instance, in a February 2002 Gallup poll, after being told that "federal inheritance taxes currently apply only to estates valued at more than $1 million," 55 percent of people wanted to either maintain the existing estate tax or to reform the tax to exempt family farms and small businesses—substantially more than the 39 percent who wanted repeal. The following week, a Bloomberg poll found that 47 percent of people preferred a raised exemption level of $3 million to all-out repeal, slightly more than the 42 percent with opposite preferences. In addition, when people learned more about the estate tax, they seemed more likely to accept it; in 2002, a Greenberg poll found that, after being informed about the existing estate tax and hearing strong arguments for both sides, two-thirds of people, 67 percent, preferred reform to repeal.

Theoretical Perspectives on Interpreting Public Opinion

Public support for estate tax repeal, as expressed in polls, has clearly been responsive to question wording and "framing effects"—to such a degree that what the public truly wants is open to interpretation. This is generally consistent with the way political scientists have long understood public opinion, particularly on policy issues, which is as something less than fully fixed and rational. At one extreme, theorists such as Converse have viewed responses to opinion polling as tantamount to a confusion of "nonattitudes" (Converse 1964). Others, such as Page and Shapiro, have argued that public opinion might be stable and clear on some high-salience policy issues (Page and Shapiro 1992), if not necessarily on issues of lower salience like the estate tax repeal. In the case of the estate tax, public opinion may not obviously favor a particular policy position, but the polling of it reveals identifiable contours. That is, within a given framework—whether one that presents the issue as a principle of fairness or one that presents it as a matter of priority—public opinion does seem to follow roughly consistent patterns. Even the term "death tax" had limited impact on poll results. The relatively robust contours suggest the hypothesis that public judgments, even when hasty and misinformed, may be more responsive to reasons or recognized political symbols (Sears 2001) than to vague associations. They are consistent with those theories that view people as holding a stable core of attitudes, even while their preferences on policy positions are not fixed (Bartels 2003a; Kuklinski and Hurley 1996; Zaller and Feldman 1992).

Yet some of the contours of public opinion on the estate tax are surprising from the standpoints of prevailing political science views. Notably, even though the subject is taxation—the quintessential pocketbook issue—people's preferences are largely based on beliefs that have nothing to do with self-interest. This is in sharp contrast to the well-known economic median voter theorem, which imputes preferences based on self-interest, implying erroneously that we would see just a small percentage of support for estate tax repeal. What we find is consistent with the view of Sears and Funk, who argue that self-interest has little effect on policy judgments unless the personal stakes are substantial and clear (Sears and Funk 1991). Many rational choice models nevertheless treat economic policy positions as reflective of self-interest, though this is not a necessary approach even within a rational choice framework. For instance, a variation on the economic median voter theorem, Downs's theory of rational ignorance, provides an important partial explanation for the extensive support seen. This theory justifies why, given the costs of obtaining correct information, it can be rational to remain ignorant and to base judgments on rough-and-ready shortcuts; thus, sensible individuals might make guesses about the scope of the estate tax that misjudge their self-interest regarding the issue. Indeed, when optimistic misperceptions about future self-interest are taken into account, public opinion on the estate tax becomes somewhat more understandable. These misperceptions favored opponents of the estate tax, as both sides of the debate clearly understood. Still, they remain far from adequate for explaining the high levels of support for estate tax repeal.

Many people were inclined to see the estate tax in terms other than self-interest, and repeal proponents found that an effective strategy was to associate their position with principles of fairness that resonated with those whose support they sought. In doing this, they turned a seeming liability—the low salience of their cause—into a major opportunity. Low salience may have meant, consistent with a dynamic that John Zaller has written about (Zaller 1992), that people were less likely to have thought about the estate tax and less likely to have readily accessible facts and considerations in their mind that might resist arguments, associations, and information presented to them in poll questions. Estate tax defenders also tried to find principled messages that resonated with large majorities of the public, but these were not nearly as successful. Why not? One reason, as discussed further in part II, is that they were generally less organized, less innovative, and on the defensive. They did not invest nearly as much in testing messages and remaking their image. Had they done so, they may have engineered a different outcome consistent with the stable existence of the estate tax since 1916. For instance, to encourage senators to support strategic "message" amendments that pitted the estate tax repeal against spending priorities like prescription-drug benefits, they might have polled this trade-off; but they never did so. The eventual realization that progressivity-based arguments were of limited appeal, along with the discovery that their position could be defended as a once-and-for-all simplification of the tax code, provide evidence that strategic investment in public-opinion research can yield high payoffs.

Yet, at the same time, was there also something inherently more difficult about winning over public opinion for the policy position that they were advocating? In some ways, the supporters of the estate tax did have a particularly awkward position to argue, misconceptions about who pays the tax aside. To begin with, people have high animosity toward taxes as a general category; when asked, in a February 1998 Zogby poll, which one of three taxes they disliked the most, only 7 percent named the estate tax, but 31 percent of people volunteered—without any prompting—that they "hate all taxes." This suggests that it may be much easier to get people to state a position against a tax than it is to get them to state a position for it. In addition, many people seem uncomfortable with "class warfare," as the opposition dubbed it, notwithstanding that the public seems receptive to this argument applied to corporate taxation. Moreover, Americans have very little resentment against the wealthy and, as a whole, believe strongly in the achievability of the American Dream (Hochschild 1996). In the popular imagination, the wealthy are the success stories, like Bill Gates or Oprah Winfrey, the sort of people you want to root for, not resent.

The decision to defend the estate tax on the basis of its progressivity seems to have saddled the supporters of the estate tax with a fundamental liability. They were arguing for an inherently divisible position: that the wealthy should pay higher taxes, to a *degree*. In order for people to agree with them, they needed not only to accept the existence of the estate tax but also to accept that the proposed rates or exemptions represented the right balance between the competing considerations of fairly giving to the poor and fairly taking from the rich. But the "right balance" is always a difficult call, inherently open to compromise and dependent on particular details. Moreover, a progressive outcome can be achieved in any number of ways, begging the question of why it should be sought through an estate tax. Meanwhile, in emphasizing principles of fairness, the other side was advocating an indivisible position, in which a judgment about the right or wrong approach was a straightforward call that could be made on the basis of simple convictions. This innovation of indivisibility was not one taken by supporters of the tax.

Consequently, supporters of the estate tax eventually resorted to framing the tax as a matter of *priority*. This framing allowed them to draw on the flip side of the issue's relatively low salience, which was its relatively low priority in people's minds, turning this to their advantage. Most people were not compelled by the idea of estate tax repeal, and they preferred estate tax reform or other tax reforms. In essence, the reform advocates introduced choices—tapping into a combination of cross-cutting and self-interested preferences—as a defensive maneuver. Inconveniently, but unsurprisingly, this strategy was most effective after respondents were educated about who pays the tax. Better informing the general public, of course, would be an overwhelming task because of the low salience of the issue, but at least in certain districts this might be a conceivable, if daunting, option. That difficulty aside, the main objective of introducing choices and priorities into polling questions was not necessarily to find a practical way to change public opinion at large. In simply yielding favorable polling results, such questions could help take back the mantle of public opinion and pressure legislators and the media with the shift.

The data on public opinion suggests, but ultimately leaves unexplored, some other interesting hypotheses about what might characterize the contours of public opinion on the estate tax or taxes more generally. First, at least in the case of the estate tax, more people responded favorably when presented with arguments about justice in *processes*, such as the principle that double taxation is wrong or that people should be allowed to pass on wealth to their children.[14] Sociotropic arguments about justice in *outcomes*, which tried to link the estate tax to progressivity or to economic growth, did not resonate with as many people. Whether or not this represents a general pattern—or one particular to tax issues, to low-salience issues, to trust in government,[15] to timing, to demographic, or to other conditions—is a good research question. Second, people responded more favorably to justifications that invoked more personal, concrete examples or symbols—such as images of how the estate tax affects family businesses and farmers—than to justifications that were expressed in abstract, numerical terms—such as explanations about how few people would pay the estate tax under an exemption level of $3 million. Indeed, taking this approach to the extreme, Republican strategist Frank Luntz advises in a memorandum, "A compelling story, even if factually inaccurate, can be more emotionally compelling than a dry recitation of the truth" (Luntz 2002). Finally, although it is clear that people dislike taxes in general, the existence of a large minority of the public that consistently desires estate tax repeal raises the question of whether certain types of taxes may be especially likely to make Americans bristle. Is it more offensive to be taxed at death than during life? Is there agreement about what constitutes "confiscatory" tax rates? Is there something inherently more objectionable about taxing assets or legacies—wealth that people may have long owned —than new income flows or transactions?

II. Leveraging Public Opinion for Policy Goals

By actively testing different messages, repeal proponents learned how better to frame their position to appeal to various segments of the population, as we have seen. The objective of these polls was not to be responsive to the public but to learn how to make the public appear responsive to their goals. But how did these results enter into the policymaking process, if at all? Our analysis in this section shows that poll results were leveraged to help change the ideological profile of repeal and bring together a broad coalition around repeal. In conjunction with organized activity, repeated polling was used to generate momentum around repeal, through heightening awareness of the parameters of latent public opinion. This momentum both assured politicians that they need not worry about a potential public backlash and helped to hold the repeal coalition together. In addition, favorable polling results impressed the potential opposition as an intimidating storehouse of political ammunition, compelling additional support in key districts and deterring some of the opposition and competing lobbyists from entering the fight.

Opponents of repeal also eventually tried to do the same for their position, but they were a dollar short and a day late—conducting and releasing their first moderately detailed public poll in 2001, more than a year after repeal had already passed both the House and Senate, when most legislators had already committed to a position. From 1997 through 2003, pro-repeal advocates conducted eleven separate publicly released polls on the repeal or the fairness of the estate tax, compared to only three by defenders of the estate tax. Defenders of the tax also lacked the broad-based membership to claim to represent or influence particular districts. This is not to say that Democratic pollsters did not privately poll the issue and test it with focus groups in earlier years. They did, and because their studies affirmed the low priority of the issue, they reported feeling secure that the repeal issue would not derail their candidates in the short term. Presumably because that was their main concern, whatever other valuable information these polls revealed was not made public or, it seems, applied to developing a strategy for the policy debate over the longer term. In contrast, as elaborated on here, repeal advocates' leveraging of apparent public opinion was relentless, effective, and audacious in the degree to which it aimed to remake the image of estate tax repeal.

From Extreme to Mainstream

In the early 1990s, repeal of the estate tax was a fringe issue of the extreme right, with only a handful of notably conservative co-sponsors in the House and Senate. The orthodox wisdom was that any attempt to repeal the estate tax would be a debacle, an apparent move by shady politicians to do favors for their rich friends, at the expense of ordinary Americans. Yet, by June 2000, some of the most liberal members of the House were co-sponsors of repeal, and sixty-five Democrats had voted for its passage. The situation was similar in the Senate, where the bill passed the Senate 59–39, with the support of nine Democrats. Even some of the most committed advocates of repeal were surprised by the degree of bipartisanship, although they had worked for years to change the image of repeal and to broaden support.

The initial realization that repeal might be politically feasible emerged, for some, only after a 1992 Gephardt-Waxman proposal to expand the estate tax produced a completely unforeseen public-relations fiasco and was hurriedly withdrawn by Democrats.[16] Before then, even some key repeal advocates had assumed that the public and politicians would strongly favor the estate tax. Repeal was initially left out of the 1994 Republican Contract with America, and it moved to the top of the Republican agenda only after successful experiences pursuing estate tax reform united and emboldened, rather than merely assuaged, repeal advocates. The estate tax reforms in 1997 and 1998 raised the exemption levels and created relief for family farms and small businesses. The latter was accomplished through the Qualified Family Owned Business Interests (QFOBI) provision,[17] but this turned out to be so confusing and difficult to apply that many people on both sides of the issue had contempt for its workability. Some early champions of repeal sensed that what had been politically unthinkable in the past might become unstoppable as they learned better how to leverage public opinion, diversify their coalition, and remake the image of repeal.

Even as wealthy families and ideologically conservative groups contributed to the repeal effort, it was the wholesome, hard-working image of farmers and small businessmen that became its face. The key repeal coalitions recruited, as illustrated in figure 11.3, substantial breadth and weight. They were led by the National Federation of Independent Businesses (NFIB), the American Farm Bureau (AFB), the National Association of Manufacturers (NAM), the National Cattleman's Beef Association (NCBA), the Food Marketing Institute (FMI), the Newspaper Association of America (NAA), and the Policy and Taxation Group. Excepting the last group, which was funded by several wealthy families, all these were groups with nationwide chapters or members; and nine coalition members were listed in *Fortune* magazine's "Power 25" Washington interest groups. Their prioritization of estate tax repeal, especially when reform would have exempted nearly all their memberships, is striking considering that relatively few farmers and small businesspersons are affected by

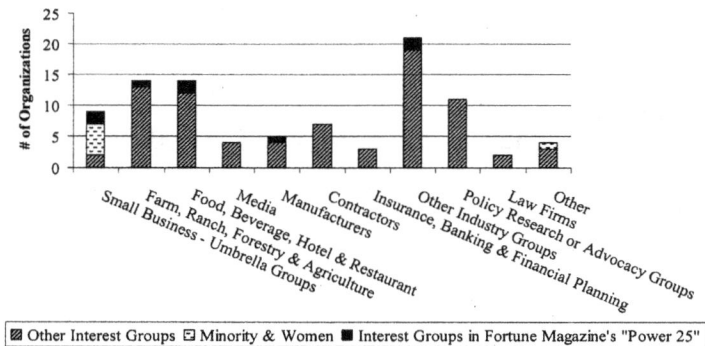

Fig. 11.3. The coalition for estate tax repeal as of January 2002. This nonexhaustive chart includes the seventy-seven members of the American Family Business Estate Tax Coalition, plus other groups that vocally supported repeal of the estate tax.

the tax. This is particularly so because the reform proposals might have been permanent, without the 2010 sunset clause that renders the actual achievement of repeal questionable for most of its supporters.

Just as with most segments of the public, many lay members of these groups misunderstood their self-interest in repeal or viewed the estate tax as unfair; and repeal advocates encouraged these beliefs. A survey in 1996 found more than 60 percent of family-owned businesses reporting that paying estate taxes would limit business growth and threaten their survival, with a third believing the tax liability would require them to sell all or part of their business (Astrachan and Tutterow 1996). Yet the Congressional Research Service estimates that the 1998 estate tax affected 7.5 percent of farm-owner decedents and 4.4 percent of business-owner decedents and that "only a tiny fraction, almost certainly no more than a percent or so, of heirs of business owners and farmers would be at risk of being forced to liquidate the family business to pay estate and gift taxes" (Gravelle and Maguire 2001). Indeed, in an investigative piece for the *New York Times*, David Cay Johnston found that the American Farm Bureau could not direct him to any instance of a farm that had been sold to pay the estate tax, nor could he uncover one on his own reporting (Johnston 2001).

Efforts by repeal advocates to diversify their profile were stimulated and backed by the results of public-opinion polls that claimed overwhelming support for repeal across major demographic and political groups. Their polls and focus groups revealed valuable information about which principles appealed most to whom and which frames were most effective. In addition to promoting specific angles—such as using "death tax" rhetoric or invoking the wholesome image of farmers—repeal advocates promoted framing repeal as a stand-alone issue in polls and congressional roll-call votes. This approach effectively pitted repeal against the status quo. Perhaps unwittingly, neutral polling organizations like Zogby and Gallup repeated and promoted this framing by disproportionately using it in their polling. This occurred even though, by 2000, the estate tax debates in Congress and in the 2000 presidential election campaign were explicitly between repeal and reform, not between repeal and the status quo. Figure 11.4 shows that in the eighteen months prior to the June 2001 repeal of the estate tax, neutral polling organizations used the stand-alone framing that repeal advocates promoted, rather than presenting the choice as between repeal and reform, in seven of the ten poll results they released on estate tax repeal.

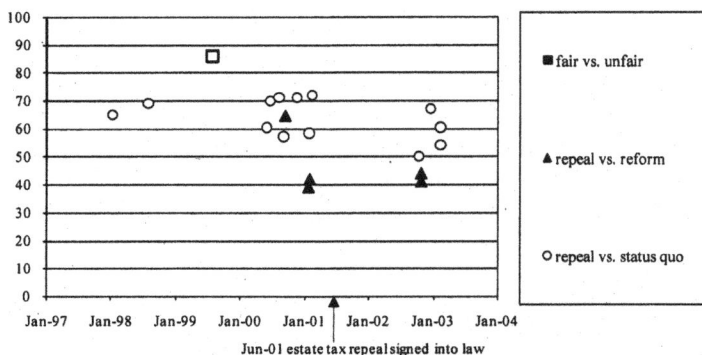

Fig. 11.4. Poll results on the repeal of the estate tax: frames used by neutral poll sponsors. This chart includes publicly released national polling data, published by neutral poll sponsors from 1997 through the end of 2003, in which respondents were asked to evaluate the repeal or the fairness of the estate tax. The pollsters and poll sponsors are identified in the appendix. Data sources include the publications and press releases of the polling organizations and the Roper Center for Public Opinion Research at the University of Connecticut.

Polls were also more directly used as hooks to approach minority organizations or sympathetic politicians. Thus, gay and lesbian support was claimed after the findings of an April 2001 poll showing that 72 percent of likely gays and lesbians believe the tax is discriminatory and that 82 percent would support a law to get rid of it even though they knew that they might not benefit.[18] Claiming widespread public support was a key part of the larger project to diversify the image of repeal, and the coalition became skillful at working with Democrats and interest groups that would not usually be thought of as natural allies for the cause. Frank Blethen, publisher of the liberal-leaning *Seattle Times* and an early key organizer for estate tax repeal, helped to persuade minority newspaper publishers to join the coalition for repeal and furnished local newspapers around the country with free copy-ready political ads against the death tax. The NFIB arranged for unexpected faces like Chester Thigpen, an elegant, eighty-three-year-old, African American man from Mississippi, the grandson of slaves, who had built an environmentally friendly tree-farm business on the same land on which he was born, to testify emotionally against the estate tax. Although he advocated reform, not repeal, his story was repeatedly circulated in the case for repeal. Patricia Soldano of the Policy and

Taxation Group, and the savvy political strategists whom she hired, saw that it was possible and important to garner support from minority business owners, environmentalists, women's business groups, and gays and lesbians.

In addition, knowing that politicians are most sensitive to public opinion associated with their district, repeal advocates used targeted polls to claim the support of spatial, not only demographic or political, constituencies. For instance, in April 2001, McLaughlin published the results of state-level polls on estate tax repeal, and the approval ratings of senators, taken in Iowa, Louisiana, New Mexico, Montana, and South Dakota. These polls were no doubt meant to deliver reinforcement and pressure to Senate Finance Committee chair Charles Grassley (R-IA), Finance Committee ranking member Max Baucus (D-MT), and John Breaux (D-LA), all of whom supported the estate tax repeal and would shortly have the choice of bargaining for it, against other tax cuts, as members of the June 2001 omnibus tax bill conference committee. These polls also targeted Democratic minority leader and repeal opponent Tom Daschle (D-ND), wary repeal supporter Mary Landrieu (D-LA), and the states' other senators.

In addition, members of the coalition operated an "inside-outside" strategy of grassroots mobilization at the district level. The coalition was not only diverse in profile but also spatially diverse enough to deliver a personalized message to elected officials across different types of constituencies. In this case, the NFIB and AFB were an ideal duo, with the NFIB having its strongest influence in the House and AFB having its strongest influence in the Senate, where farmers are overrepresented by virtue of the number of low-population states with farming interests. Coalition groups looked to contacts on the Hill for guidance as to which members of the House or the Senate should be targeted. Then, understanding that "members of our organizations are the best lobbyists," they arranged not only large eruptions of letters and phone calls but also in-person contacts from local civic groups and well-respected and successful local persons. These persons would ideally be "the owner of the local hardware store," the kind of person an elected official "likes to be seen with," or someone he or she has "known for thirty years." Not all of them would pay the estate tax, but these well-regarded individuals—the "grasstops" of the grassroots—caught the attention of members of Congress and contributed to the sense of a citizen uprising by hard-working, dignified, intelligent Americans who were being unfairly victimized.

The public image of repeal was so completely remade that politicians stood to gain, not lose, from associating themselves with the moral high ground it had claimed and its array of all-American supporters. This situation made it even easier for politicians with ideological sympathy for repeal—particularly those who wanted to roll back the progressivity of the tax code—to prioritize the legislation. Other politicians signed on to the bill to please certain constituents, interest groups, fellow representatives, or party leaders, at the same time feeling comfortable not only that there would be no eventual public backlash but that there might well be public approval. "No one is going to lose his seat over supporting repeal," one congressman said to us. Conservative strategist Grover Norquist, borrowing a strategy used by environmental-protection groups, decided to give politicians an added impetus to prematurely fingerprint themselves on the issue by including it in the political "scorecards" published by his group, Americans for Tax Reform. Even those who did not want the estate tax to be repealed but did believe it needed to be significantly reformed understood the power of the image now being associated with repeal. Some of them told us that, even though they both hoped and expected the repeal bill would later be compromised in favor of a reform option, they supported it because they saw it as the only way to put the estate tax back on the agenda. As the bill gained momentum, moderates and Democrats were reassured by the presence of familiar company on the bill's list of sponsors,

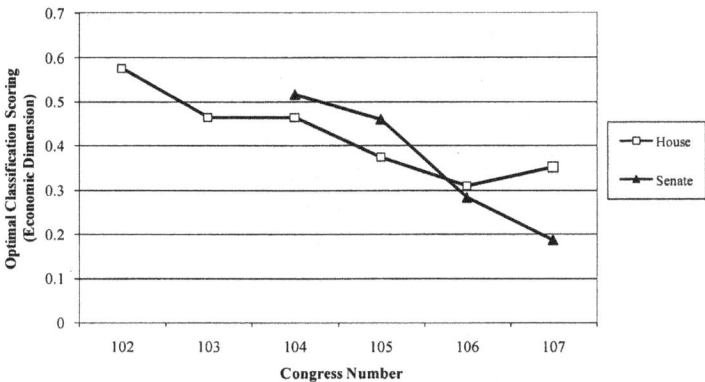

Fig. 11.5. Average ideological position of repeal-bill sponsors. This chart uses the first dimension of Keith Poole's Optimal Classification data, which represents the ranking of legislators on a liberal-conservative dimension based on their past voting records in the chamber. The scoring scale ranges from 1 (most conservative) to −1 (most liberal).

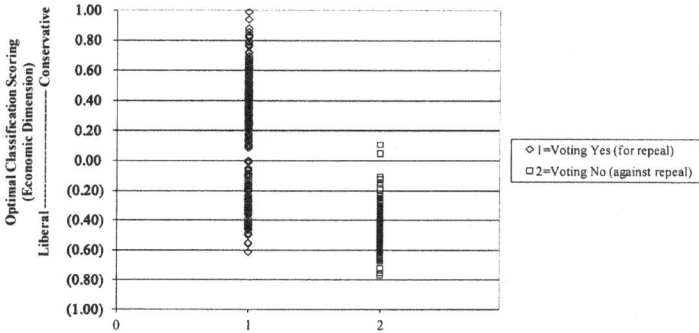

Fig. 11.6. Ideological distribution of legislators voting on HR 8 in the 106th Congress, June 9, 2000, roll-call vote. This chart uses the first dimension of Keith Poole's Optimal Classification data, which represents the rankings of legislators on a liberal-conservative dimension based on their past voting records in the chamber. Sixty-eight legislators with a negative (liberal) OC score voted yes, whereas only two legislators with a positive (conservative) OC score voted no. Thus, the mean OC score of those voting yes is 0.27, whereas the mean score of those voting no is –0.44.

including moderate John Tanner (D-TN), who served as the bill's lead Democratic co-sponsor, and liberal Neil Abercrombie (D-HI), both of whom were frustrated with their party's failure to court small businesses. Surprising to many, repeal was even backed by the congressional black caucus, though not unanimously, apparently to protect the capital accumulation of the first large wave of black entrepreneurs and businessmen.

Led on the Hill by Representative Jennifer Dunn (R-WA) and Senator Jon Kyl (R-AZ), repeal advocates steadily built support across the spectrum. Figure 11.5 charts how dramatically the issue shifted on the ideological spectrum by comparing, across Congresses, the ideological rankings of the average repeal-bill sponsor, using Keith Poole's Optimal Classification (OC) system (Poole 2000). The OC data is a calculation of the liberal-conservative ideological rankings of individual legislators based on their past voting record in the chamber. In the 102nd Congress, only three extremely conservative legislators supported repeal, but by the 106th Congress, the *average* sponsor—of 244 in the House and 47 in the Senate— was a mainstream Republican. Figure 11.6, which uses OC scores to show the distribution of House legislators' votes in June 2000, demonstrates the extraordinary degree to which repeal was rebranded to penetrate deep into the Democratic Party. It gained the support of not only conservative Democrats but also liberal ones who, on most budgetary bills, would not be seen on the side of conservative Republicans.

The Running Room of Public Opinion

The positive public image of estate tax repeal gave its supporters running room that the other side did not have, largely because repeal opponents were hamstrung by a failure to effectively manage their own public image in the eyes of politicians. Initially, supporters of retaining the estate tax paid little attention to changing views about public opinion, instead focusing on countering misinformation and pro-repeal arguments on the Hill. Not until early 2001, years after the repeal effort had begun in earnest, after estate tax repeal had already passed both houses by large majorities, and only after the Democrats lost the White House, did supporters of the estate tax put large resources into recrafting its public image. Only then did they pay for strategic polling and launch a coordinated image-oriented campaign. Yet they had trouble developing a public image that could compete with the repeal advocates' rainbow coalition. Many life-insurance providers were strongly opposed to estate tax repeal, but because their opposition was fundamentally out of a self-interest in their estate-planning and insurance business, it undeniably would "look bad" to take too high profile a stance. So they hesitated about whether and how to take action. Labor organizations were preoccupied with other priorities and uninterested in opposing tax cuts that are, in fact, supported by many of their lay members, actual self-interest aside. Many charitable organizations also were wary of estate tax repeal because they expected repeal to lead to a steep decline in charitable bequests, but not all of them felt free to speak against the repeal for fear of seeming greedy and alienating wealthy donors or board members. Debating their options internally, they too hesitated.

Supporters of the estate tax at last received a public-relations boost in February 2001, when, assisted by a Boston-based group called Responsible Wealth, Bill Gates Sr., George Soros, Steven Rockefeller, and over a hundred other wealthy businessmen, public figures, and philanthropists published a statement opposing repeal. Warren Buffett insisted even more vehemently on the tax's importance in making success dependent on merit rather than inheritance. The unexpected statements caught the public eye, but the supporters of the estate tax still lacked a very compelling image; they appeared to be a collection of the ultrawealthy plus highbrow liberal think tanks. Moreover, despite this public stance, they did not supply significant funding to groups like OMB Watch and Responsible Wealth to run extensive and repeated polls that might dislodge the framing of the issue that was, by then, deeply entrenched into media treatments and politicians' perceptions. The Responsible Wealth statement was shrewdly countered by Black Entertainment Television founder Bob Johnson, who organized some fifty prominent African American businessmen to sign their own syndicated advertisement defending repeal as conducive to capital formation in the black community. In addition, a new group called Disabled Americans for Death Tax Relief emerged to declare the millionaire opponents of repeal "callous and heartless" for denying disabled persons the "full financial help" of their parents. Clearly, supporters of the estate tax were not going to find it easy to create a more appealing public image, but at least now they were battling for it.

Led by Responsible Wealth and OMB Watch, some charitable-sector organizations, insurance-sector representatives, and others joined up in 2001 to coordinate an active, savvier opposition campaign. Their financial investment and organizational resources paled in comparison to the other side, but they were able to make headway, as late in the debate as it was. Among other things, they invested in polling different messages on the estate tax issue and were able to report that, when given choices, the American public preferred reform to repeal by a ratio of two to one. This finding, in combination with a worsening federal budgetary situation, the new priority of a war on terrorism, and the strategic introduction of Democratic proposals to reform the estate tax at last gave some of the cover of public opinion to legislators who wished to vote against permanent repeal. In June 2002, six senators who had previously voted for repeal nevertheless voted against making the repeal permanent.

In contrast, the Republican leadership had been leveraging public opinion to their advantage for years. In both the House and the Senate, Republicans did not miss opportunities to force stand-alone votes, against tradition on tax bills. This was an issue which they clearly saw as politically difficult for many Democrats. They had learned the previous year that a large omnibus tax bill has a sticker-shock problem. Members of Congress can oppose it as simply being too expensive. Moreover, individual members could claim that they supported aspects of the bill but not others, and so—contrary to logrolling logic—were obliged to oppose the whole.

But the message behind one's vote on a stand-alone bill is clear, and many members did not want to be on the record against repeal. Others simply found it difficult to vote no on tax cut after tax cut. This fingerprinting strategy was especially important once the White House changed hands and some Democrats discovered that what they thought of as "free votes" —votes that would ingratiate them with some of their constituents, even as the legislation would assuredly be vetoed by President Clinton—were no longer so. Along with the pressures that had earlier impelled them to support repeal, they now had to confront the public-relations risk of being seen as flip-floppers if they backtracked.

Supporters of repeal had leverage because they could make a credible threat to take the issue public in campaigns against politicians who did not support their bills. They had amply demonstrated their ability to tap into public attitudes in opinion polls, as well as to direct effective district- or state-level agitation by interest groups. In fact, they later made good on some of these threats. For instance, public-relations stunts and death-tax-related ads on the radio, in print, and/or on television were launched against repeal opponents such as Senator Paul Wellstone (D-MN), Senator Patty Murray (D-WA), Senator Jean Carnahan (D-MO), presidential candidate Governor Howard Dean (D-VT), and Senate minority leader Tom Daschle (D-SD). In the ad targeting Daschle, who lost his 2004 re-election bid by a single percentage point, an announcer leverages his vote against repeal to tap into widespread resentment of overtaxation: "You're born. You go to school. You work hard. You raise a family. You pay your taxes. And when you die, the IRS can tax you again, taking as much as 55 percent of everything you've saved for your children. It's called the death tax. And it's wrong. . . . Isn't a lifetime of taxes enough?"[19]

Beyond deterring the opposition to repeal, positive public perceptions of estate tax repeal also played a role in keeping competing tax-cut lobbyists at bay. The apparent popularity that the issue had gained by 2000 encouraged presidential candidate George W. Bush to include it in his proposed tax-cut plan and to mention it frequently in his campaign speeches, to resounding applause. Once in office, his first tax-cut proposal included the same four elements he had pitched in his campaign: income tax rate cuts, marriage-penalty relief, a child tax credit, and estate tax repeal. Enthused by Bush's successful entrance into the White House, Republicans in Congress were ready to be deferential to their new president and his tax-relief package. Long-standing and more broadly beneficial proposals such as a cut in the capital-gains tax or reform of the alternative-minimum tax were sidelined in part because they were less arousing. Also, aware that it would cut a bad public image to provide corporate tax breaks ahead of individual tax relief, the White House ordered corporate lobbyists not to try to put their priorities into this bill, promising them a later bill for corporate tax relief. Thus, although, by itself, public opinion was not sufficient to move estate tax repeal to the top of the agenda, it cleared space for advocates, giving them the running room that others did not have. The estate tax made this "cut," and others, not only because politicians could agree with it or had something to gain from supporting it but also because they had come to believe that it could not hurt them in the eyes of the public.

All or Nothing

By insisting on repeal, rather than aiming for any of a number of estate tax reform options, estate tax opponents had strengthened their tactical hand. First, as we discussed earlier, the public responded most favorably to principled arguments for repeal when considered as a stand-alone issue, so this indivisible stance helped to construct an image of widespread public support. Second, anticipating that they might need to compromise in order to get past the multiple veto points—the House, the Senate, the president, and complex budgetary rules—it may have been prudent to stay with as extreme a position as could be managed, particularly in the years before unified party control was achieved in 2000. Third, the repeal stance was vital for holding together the coalition of interest groups and ideologues driving the legislation. Anything less would have splintered the coalition, because they would have disagreed about what form any reform should take and their sets of interests would have ceased to overlap. Repeal was their least common denominator. Farmers, for instance, would generally have preferred a higher exemption level to address their concerns about the valuation of inherited land, whereas large family businesses would have preferred lower estate tax rates since they are less likely to be fully exempted by a higher exemption level. As will be explained, farmers were also extremely averse to proposals to tie repeal to the implementation of carryover basis, a rule that would subject many a bequeathed asset to larger capital-gains taxes by setting the original purchase value, rather than the market value at the time of inheritance, as the tax basis. Meanwhile, conservative ideologues seemed interested in repeal above all, motivated by the prospect of eradicating an entire tax, and the most progressive one at that.

But especially in 2001 and afterward, the coalition experienced serious centrifugal pressures because some groups, particularly those with large memberships who were doing the legwork, were not necessarily well served by continuing to be wed to repeal. Although legislators had repeatedly voted for an enduring repeal, the June 2001 omnibus bill that did pass included only a one-year repeal in 2010 and then a reinstatement of the estate tax—at 2001 levels—in 2011. Because of a combination of stubborn minority opposition in the Senate and budgetary constraints, it became highly uncertain whether a full and permanent repeal of the estate tax would ever be passed. Any of a number of foreseen and unforeseen obstacles might overwhelm it: the economy has since worsened; the war on terrorism and in Iraq has taken front stage and eaten into the budget; other tax-cut priorities threaten to close out the estate tax repeal; the Democrats won the House and Senate in 2006; and Senate scoring rules make an extension of repeal dramatically more costly, on the books, as 2011 draws closer.

In addition, the risks of staying in the repeal coalition are even higher for those who object to carryover basis, which would be the cheapest rule to implement in conjunction with any repeal. The current law allows the capital appreciation of inherited assets to be based on market value at inheritance, a practice called stepped-up basis, rather than being based on the original purchase value, a practice called carryover basis. But the quid pro quo for the one-year repeal had been the replacement of stepped-up basis with carryover basis, lending momentum to the possibility that the quid pro quo for any permanent repeal might also be carryover basis. Although in practice it can be difficult to capture tax on carryover amounts, this issue was of particular concern to farmers and proprietors of independent newspapers, whose businesses often have few liquid assets but considerable accumulated net worth. Many were strongly opposed to giving up stepped-up basis, even if it meant accepting an estate tax reform rather than repeal, and some thought the issue might split the coalition. The issue in fact led to a split among farmers; as the AFB continued to lead the repeal coalition, another major farm group, the National Farmers Union, whose members are on average less wealthy, began to vocally support a reform option that would immediately raise the exemption to $4 million per person ($8 million per couple) and modestly lower rates.

Once coalition members understood the tradeoffs, why did they not show more interest in the compromise proposals? These included legislation to dramatically and permanently raise the exemption to $5 million or more or to entirely exempt family farms and small businesses from the estate tax while maintaining stepped-up basis. Arguably, their memberships would have much preferred these immediate changes to the risks inherent in pursuing permanent repeal. When questioned about the reasons for their continued allegiance to total repeal in light of these options, some coalition members emphasized the importance of staying unified, pointing out that they had already been much more influential as a whole than they could have been in parts. Some referred to a lack of trust in the Democrats or their reform options, noting that inflation would erode any proposed threshold and that it can be difficult to craft workable devices, as shown by their previous experience with QFOBI. Others alluded to the potential costs of turning on Republican allies on the Hill who would be needed for other legislative priorities.

In addition, some interest-group members emphatically justified their stance with the conviction that the estate tax is morally wrong, suggesting how completely they had embraced the framing in which the pro-repeal forces had invested so much. Although we have no doubt that the actions of organized interests were centrally motivated by other considerations, is it possible that the principle kept their troops fired up and purposeful? Some literature in political psychology suggests that participation in groups tends to move like-minded people to more extreme points in the direction indicated by their predeliberative commitments (Sunstein 2000). If so, glue is perhaps the right metaphor in this regard. Principles and ideologies may help hold together organized groups and perhaps even move members to subordinate individual interests to a common purpose, but they are not sufficient on their own to move political agendas. Perhaps they magnify intensity of cause after commitments have been made for other reasons.

Regardless, standing by the principle of repeal was viewed by coalition members as important for keeping *policymakers* receptive. By premising their message on the idea that the tax is just "wrong," they had generated the appearance of overwhelming public support, built a broad coalition, and shifted politicians' thinking about the estate tax. The issue was viewed less and less as a distributive issue, about which horse-trading and compromise can be acceptable (Miller 1996), and more and more as an issue of moral principle, about which compromise seems inherently hypocritical.

That the pro-repeal coalition could do this with such a highly progressive tax is impressive as well as ironic, given that money is inherently divisible. To compromise now risked weakening their carefully crafted public image and accepting the legitimacy of "splitting the difference." Thus, the need to assure politicians that their stance could resonate with the public, in conjunction with the strategic desire to maintain a unified alliance between diverse interest groups and ideological politicians, may have increased the likelihood of achieving an all-or-nothing outcome, versus a marginal reform.

Perspectives on the Role of Public Opinion in Policy Debates

Public opinion seems to have played a key role, but not a direct role, in the repeal of the estate tax. Aware of the relatively low priority of the estate tax issue in the public eye, most politicians are unlikely to have felt immediate pressure due to public opinion. After all, the public as a whole was not particularly engaged, and the contours of its opinion could be interpreted in support of either reform or repeal. Thus, the dynamic of this debate does not correspond to the dynamic in a thermostatic model of policymaking, in which politicians respond to public opinion with policy changes, at least on higher-salience or priority issues, and public opinion in turn responds to policy change (Wlezien 1995; Page and Shapiro 1992). Still, perceptions of the underlying contours of public opinion did appear to matter for the estate tax outcome.

In particular, politicians were alert to latent public opinion—to use V. O. Key's phrase (Zaller 2003; Key 1961): how the public might view the issue should salience be raised or should active efforts be made to influence their views. Many legislators, wary especially because repeal could be portrayed as a favor to their wealthy friends, were reluctant to act unless there were solid indicators that latent public opinion would not rise up to haunt them. For advocates of repeal, it was critical to manage public opinion to combat the long-standing conventional wisdom on Capitol Hill that supporting estate tax repeal would be costly with voters. They drew adeptly on common misperceptions of self-interest and coupled repeal with principles of fairness to generate the appearance of extremely high support for repeal. Their very position of a hard-line stance on repeal was chosen, and adhered to, after taking into account several factors that included the degree to which that position might resonate with the public. Understanding that politicians feel pressure to create policies that benefit groups with positive social constructions (Schneider and Ingram 1993), repeal advocates also crafted an image as independent farmers, hard-working small businessmen, and entrepreneurial minorities.

Reform advocates struggled to take back the mantle of public opinion. To do so, they relied on the flip side of low salience, which was the issue's low priority in people's minds. Note that although both the low salience and low priority of an issue might contribute to a low overall intensity of public opinion on the issue, the two are distinct concepts and played different roles in this policy debate. The low salience of the issue worked to repeal advocates' advantage because it meant that many people had not given the matter much thought, allowing more scope for careful framing to have effect. The low priority of repeal meant that nearly everyone preferred other tax cuts to repeal, as well as that healthy majorities supported estate tax reform options over repeal.

Each side's opposing claim to represent public opinion was plausible because the contours of public opinion on this issue were so wide. And it may not be unusual that public opinion appears to be quite different depending on which lens is invoked (Jacobs and Shapiro 1995–96; Ginsberg 1984; Lippman 1925). Charged issues are often contentious precisely because there are two highly compelling ways to look at them. For instance, studies have shown that although only 20–25 percent of poll respondents say that that too little is being spent on "welfare," 63–65 percent say that too little is being spent on "assistance to the poor" (Bartels 2003a). How, if at all, people square the tensions in holding these two views simultaneously is a complex matter that activists on neither side of the issue try to resolve. Instead, they advertise the aspect of majority opinion that is favorable to their cause. In the hurly-burly of political conflict, publicized opinion polls are less authentic measures of public opinion than they are rocks that activists throw at one another to signal their reach.

On the estate tax issue, the battle to produce favorable polling results was part of the larger war to manage politicians' perceptions of the lens through which the public would view the issue. Advocates of repeal were especially effective at all aspects of this war. They communicated the framings of public opinion that best served their objectives; diversified the coalition to change their image from privileged to all-American; implied, through coordinating an active inside-outside strategy, that the issue had a reasonably high level of public salience and priority, at least among the "grasstops"; and presented a credible threat that they could, and would, move district-level public opinion on the issue as a last resort. Boosting these efforts was the fact that neutral polling organizations, perhaps unwittingly, disproportionately took up the stand-alone framing promoted by repeal advocates—even though the political options being debated were between repeal and reform, not between repeal and the status quo. In changing how legislators saw the issue on an ideological spectrum, and how legislators thought the public would react to it, advocates changed legislators' calculations of the likely electoral costs and benefits of their positions.

Advocates of repeal may have been especially effective at signaling the latent threat of a public backlash because they invested, over several years, in polling, framing, and "grasstops" organizing. This effort required financial and membership resources, and as reported by people on both sides of the issue, the repeal advocates were advantaged in at least three stages. Wealthy individuals and interest groups were willing to provide seed money to initiate message framing and organize the coalition; they had the money for frequent polls and the organization to coordinate "grasstops" activism; and they had the funds to, in some districts, heighten salience on repeal and turn it into a potent campaign issue. This advantage raises the question of whether those with greater resources have the better ability to claim the mantle of public opinion. If so, it may not be that unusual to see, as we did in this case, great asymmetry in the skillfulness with which intense interests on each side manage their public image. Repeal advocates could credibly threaten to fire up latent public opinion to discipline legislators. This disciplining might take place through either preelectoral rational anticipation, in which legislators change their stance to increase the probability of their reelection, or postelectoral turnover, in which those who stick to unpopular stances are voted out of office (Stimson, Mackuen, and Erikson 1995).

Regardless of which side was more effective, on neither side of the debate did concentrated interests or political leaders try to circumvent public opinion to achieve their objectives. The idea that public opinion matters for policy outcomes stands in contrast to theories that, at the other extreme from the thermostatic model, see public opinions on policy issues as inconsequential. Among these theories are the views that public opinion is irredeemably difficult to interpret (Converse 1964; Schattschneider 1960) or itself the product of manipulation by a "power elite" (Domhoff

2002; Kingdon 1993). Other theories contend that, even if public opinion is viewed as stable and well formed, it still may not matter for lower-salience or lower-priority policy issues; politicians may not expect voters to sanction them, because of cross-cutting preferences over other issues that matter to them (Roemer 1999), strong habitual stability in party or candidate allegiances (Campbell et al. 1960), or other factors. With these ideas in mind, some theorists contend that policy outcomes are determined by the activities of interest groups or politicians who, especially on relatively low-salience issues, can either disregard or manipulate public opinion (Geer 1996; Olson 1971).

What we have observed suggests an alternative theory of political outcomes in which interpretations of latent public opinion can enable or obstruct change, but these interpretations are largely driven by interest-group activity and political leadership. If so, the contours of public opinion, in interaction with organized activity to selectively reveal and perhaps even shape latent opinion, determine how much "running room" policy leaders have to maneuver. If issue advocates can convince politicians that latent public opinion is favorable to their proposal, or at least not against it, they may widen the range of politically acceptable outcomes to encompass their proposal, creating an opening for policy leaders to run with the issue. Gaining adequate running room does not imply that a policy proposal will pass—district pressure from interest groups and the ideological preferences of politicians certainly matter more for giving impetus to legislation—but it would imply that politicians are no longer wary that public opinion could be turned against them regarding it. Systematic studies across issues could help identify which factors, such as low salience or the existence of multiple public-opinion contours, most contribute to large potential running room.

This "running-room" view bears some resemblance to a latitude theory of public opinion, but it is distinct, with different implications. In latitude theory, public opinion may constrain policymakers from pursuing policies outside some zone of acceptability, lest they "suddenly encounter a catastrophic avalanche of protest"; but so long as politicians stay clear of the "electrified fence," public opinion is not a constraint (Diamond 2001). In our view, public opinion does exhibit contours that limit how the public might respond to various framings of the issue, but whether or not politicians have an accurate picture of the contours, as well as whether they assess them as unthreatening or as electrified barriers, depends largely on interest-group and partisan activity. Moreover, there is considerable room for political advantage and maneuver within the contours, and sometimes the chance to alter them. Therefore, unlike in latitude theory, even when public-opinion contours are constant, the potential for public opinion to enter the debate as a constraint, and in which direction, may change dramatically. Given this wide potential for change, when interest groups are interested in gaining support for legislation (as distinct from when they are interested in influencing an election), they may often find it more direct and cost-effective to invest in altering politicians' perceptions of public opinion, rather than in altering public opinion itself.

In the case of estate tax repeal, before repeal advocates refashioned the issue's public image, the conventional wisdom had indeed been that an avalanche of public outrage would blast politicians who supported repeal. Yet the coalition for repeal eventually did such an effective job of convincing legislators that public opinion was on their side, and could reliably be maintained that way, that the conventional wisdom was all but reversed. Many legislators then wondered if it would be acceptable to uphold the estate tax—or if that would contribute to their being branded as tax-and-spend types, as Daschle was by some. At that point, supporters of the estate tax became desperate to ensure that their side still had running room too, which is why it was so important to demonstrate the low priority of the issue in the public eye. Although they have probably not succeeded in spinning the issue to the point that a repeal vote looks very costly—as had so long been assumed would be the case—their efforts at least helped reassure politicians that a vote for reform, rather than repeal, could be rendered as a respectable, safe position.

Thus, the case of estate tax repeal suggests a dynamic in which the impact of latent public opinion may largely depend on interest-group activity, at least on lower-salience issues. This view is distinct from both classic and modern models of policymaking that stress the direct influence of either organized interests or public opinion on politicians. It is compatible with, but still distinct from, views that highlight the influence of political leaders on public opinion, such as Jacobs and Shapiro's study of two high-salience issues, Clinton's health-care-reform initiative and the Republican Contract with America. Jacobs and Shapiro emphasize, similar to what we find, that "crafted talk" is used to make existing policy agendas seem more agreeable to the public (Jacobs and Shapiro 2000). However, whereas in Jacobs and Shapiro's cases political leaders have a read on public opinion and try to use the media as a conduit for communicating their messages *to the public,* in the estate tax case we find that interest groups joined political strategists to serve as critical intermediaries for interpreting public opinion *to politicians.*

In this view of politics, organized interests, as well as politicians, possess substantial potential for political entrepreneurship. In particular, interest groups can help clear and sow the locations of perceived minefields of public opinion. Their potential to be successful in doing so might be higher on lower-salience issues, for which the balance of political organizing may be more likely to be asymmetrical and public opinion less fixed and less well understood. However, since low-salience issues may also be low-priority issues, opponents of a proposal may also have a good deal of potential to be entrepreneurial in countering with alternative frameworks.

The importance that interest groups placed on interpreting public opinion to politicians seems, in the case of the estate tax, to have been one factor contributing to the coalition's strange adherence to total repeal, even when such a stance was contrary to the interests of most of its members. At that point, suddenly changing one's tune was perceived as a public-image risk that outweighed the perceived risk of continuing to pursue an all-or-nothing outcome. Such stickiness is markedly at odds with divide-the-dollar conceptions of politics, in which coalitions are easily split by any new offer, with an infinite number of combinations possible. Although the images of political issues may be audaciously recast, the extent of the running room generated may be linked to the nature of the images, so that they may constrain the likelihood of certain outcomes down the line.

Appendix: Polls on the Repeal or the Fairness of the Estate Tax

The following polls are the basis for figures 11.2 and 11.4. These poll sponsors released national polling data, from 1997 through the end of 2003, in which respondents were asked to evaluate the repeal or the fairness of the estate tax. Data sources include the publications and press releases of the polling organizations and the Roper Center for Public Opinion Research at the University of Connecticut.

Pollster/Poll Sponsor	Poll Completion Dates
Poll Sponsor Is Politically Neutral	
Bloomberg	Mar-01
CBS News & New York Times	Mar-01, Nov-02
Gallup/CNN & USA Today	Jun-00, Feb-01, Nov-02
International Communications Research/NPR & Kaiser & Kennedy	Mar-03
Opinion Dynamics/Fox News	Jan-03
Pew Research Center for the People & the Press	Sep-98, Sep-00
Rasmussen Research Portrait of America Poll	Jul-00
Poll Sponsor Is Democratic or Opposed to Estate Tax Repeal	
Emily's List	Dec-99
Greenberg Quinlan Rosner Research/OMB Watch	May-02
Penn Schoen Berland/Democratic Leadership Council	Feb-01
Poll Sponsor Is Republican or Advocates Estate Tax Repeal	
Luntz Research Companies	Aug-98, Jan-03
Market Strategies/Republican National Committee	Sep-99
McLaughlin & Assoc/Americans Against Unfair Family Taxation	Jun-99, Jul-99, Jan-00, Sep-00, Jan-01, May-01
Tarrance Group with Lake, Snell Perry/Food Marketing Institute	Nov-00
Wirthlin Worldwide	Aug-99

NOTES

Parts of this research overlap with the book on the estate tax repeal by Michael Graetz and Ian Shapiro, *Death by a Thousand Cuts* (2005). The book is written for a general audience and therefore does not undertake systematic analysis of the polling data presented here; nor does it address the political-science literature to which we contribute. An abridged version of this chapter has also appeared in the *National Tax Journal* (September 2006), with more limited theoretical discussion and empirical evidence than appear here. The authors are grateful to research assistants Susannah Camic, Molly Lewis, and Jeffrey Mueller, as well as the politicians, political aides, interest-group representatives, journalists, analysts, and activists who agreed to be interviewed for this project. Thanks are also due to Yale's Institution for Social and Policy Studies and the Carnegie Corporation of New York for financial support of our research.

1. The omnibus tax-reform bills passed by both houses of Congress included a phase-out of the estate tax followed by full repeal. However, the specifics of the phase-out, other tax-cut provisions, and the overall price tags of the omnibus bills differed substantially, so that aspects had to be compromised. During conference committee, behind closed doors, the decision was unexpectedly made to sunset the entire tax cut, including the estate tax provisions, after ten years. This effectively resulted in a one-year repeal.

2. The estate tax burden was greatest in the 1970s, when the exemption rate fell below half a million dollars (in 2001 dollars) and the maximum tax rate rose

as high as 77 percent. In the years after the federal estate tax was enacted in 1916, fewer than 1 percent were subject to it, and sometimes less than 0.5 percent were; and in recent decades, about 2 percent of the population has paid the estate tax. Since the 1930s, the percentage of national wealth held by those who are subject to the estate tax has not changed much. As estimated from estate tax returns themselves, the top 1 percent of Americans are estimated to have held between 20–25 percent of the country's wealth since the 1940s, save for several years beginning in the late 1970s when the figure dropped to around 18 percent. The wealth share of the top 1–2 percent has remained roughly 6 percent of the country's wealth since 1946 (Kopczuk and Saez 2004).

3. Lower-income persons support repeal of the estate tax at nearly the same rate as others. A 2001 McLaughlin poll showed support for repeal from 76 percent of those with annual incomes under forty thousand dollars, compared to 81 percent of those with higher incomes. Joel Slemrod finds a similar result in his analysis of the 2003 NKK survey (Slemrod 2003).

4. The analysis is a linear probability regression that controls for the belief that the current tax system is complex and/or unfair, age, gender, race, education, and income. The only variables that are found to be significant for support of estate tax repeal are misconceptions about who pays and being over age sixty-five (Slemrod 2003).

5. Larry Bartels (2003a) provides further evidence that opinion on the estate tax is largely based on "simple-minded and sometimes misguided considerations of self-interest" that correspond closely to people's "subjective sense of their own tax burden." In a detailed analysis of the 2002 National Election Study survey, he finds that the perception that one's own tax burden is "too high" accounts for about a third of the net support for repeal; and ironically, "this apparent misplaced self-interest is most powerful among people whose own economic circumstances make them least likely to have any positive personal stake in repealing the estate tax" (Bartels 2003b). Note also that the economic and stock-market boom in and around 2000 may have contributed somewhat to people's optimism. Moreover, the shift away from traditional defined-benefit pension plans toward 401(k), defined-contribution, and other individual retirement savings plans means that some people might feel wealthier since they hold their own retirement assets.

6. Although this 26 percent is less than half of the 60 percent of NKK respondents who supported repeal when no exemption level was specified, we cannot conclude that all those whose stance on repeal depended on the particular exemption level are self-interested. Some of them may instead view a higher exemption as more just.

7. No real difference exists in responses to a question about "eliminating the inheritance tax" that was asked, in identical form, by the Pew Research Center in September 1998 and August-September 2000. A ten-percentage-point difference does exist between responses to a question asked, in identical form with a margin

of error of +/−3.1 percent, by McLaughlin and Associates in September 2000 and January 2001. But responses to similar questions asked by Gallup in June 2000 and November 2002 yielded a 10 percent difference in the *opposite* direction.

8. Although it is not precise to characterize the estate tax as equivalent to double taxation, since it captures revenue from many assets that would otherwise entirely elude tax, it is true that the estate tax may also double tax some assets. The claim of double taxation is premised on the belief that the assets in an estate have already been taxed once under the income tax. Repeal opponents claim that the estate tax acts as a backstop to the income tax, covering assets that have escaped taxation, including capital gains, which are passed on at the time of death and are exempt from taxation because of the step up in basis.

9. In an April 2001 memorandum to "Interested Parties," Frank Luntz makes this claim on the basis of a poll of six hundred likely gay and lesbian Americans, in which 97 percent "believe that just like traditional married couples, they too should have the right to pass along their assets to their partner without paying up to 55% in death taxes," 72 percent believe the estate tax is "discriminatory," and 82 percent wanted to see it eliminated.

10. In the 2002 Greenberg Quinlan poll, 36 percent of respondents said they or a family member had a small business and 23 percent said they or someone in their family owned a family farm.

11. These numbers are from an October 2000 Zogby International poll of 2,526 registered voters. Respondents were asked to agree with one of the following statements: "On estate or death taxes: Statement A: Death taxes are unfair to heirs, small businesses, and family farms and should be eliminated. Statement B: Since death taxes affect only a small percentage of small businesses and family farms, the tax process can be easily changed without exempting large estates and businesses."

12. In a September 2000 McLaughlin and Associates poll of one thousand likely voters, respondents were asked, "Do you think it is fair or unfair for the government to tax a person's earnings while it is being earned, and then tax it again after a person dies?"; 87.9 percent of whites and 91.6 percent of blacks considered it unfair.

13. They neglected to mention that every one of these occasions occurred more than a century ago, during times of war or national crisis, when the estate tax was resorted to as an intentionally temporary measure; and in fact, frequent reforms to the estate tax are what have made planning most difficult.

14. In a different context, that of trying to distinguish "easy issue" voters from "hard issue" voters, Carmines and Stimson noted that some people may find it easier to think about processes than outcomes. They differentiate "easy" issues from "hard" issues on the basis of three factors: being "symbolic rather than technical," more likely to "deal with policy means than ends," and "long on the political agenda" (Carmines and Stimson 1980).

15. Stanley Feldman, for instance, hypothesizes that when people have low trust in government, they are more likely to place weight on principles of process justice rather than outcome justice. The reasoning behind this is that the latter depends more heavily on government intervention. However, in the case of the estate tax, this reasoning does not always apply. The idea that repealing the estate tax would lead to more economic growth, for instance, assumed less government intervention (Feldman 2003).

16. See HR 4848, the Long Term Care Family Security Act of 1992, introduced on April 9, 1992, and sponsored by Representatives Waxman and Gephardt, which included a provision that would reduce the unified credit against estate and gift taxes from $600,000 to $200,000.

17. The Qualified Family Owned Business Exemption (QFOBE) was created in 1997 and modified into the Qualified Family Owned Business Interests (QFOBI) deduction in 1998.

18. See note 9.

19. The ad was paid for by the Club for Growth Advocacy, a 527 organization founded in 2001 to "educate the public and lobby for policies that promote economic growth." Twenty-five thousand dollars was dedicated for this particular run, from April 14 to 25 on statewide cable networks.

REFERENCES

Astrachan, Joseph, and Roger Tutterow. 1996. "The Effect of Estate Taxes on Family Business, Survey Results." *Family Business Review* 9: 303–14.

Bartels, Larry M. 2003a. "Democracy with Attitudes." In *Electoral Democracy*, ed. M. B. MacKuen and G. Rabinowitz. Ann Arbor: University of Michigan Press.

———. 2003b. "Homer Gets a Tax Cut: Inequality and Public Policy in the American Mind." Paper presented at the annual meeting of the American Political Science Association, Philadelphia.

Campbell, Angus, Philip E. Converse, Warren E. Miller, and Donald E. Stokes. 1960. *The American Voter*. New York: John Wiley.

Carmines, Edward G., and James A. Stimson. 1980. "The Two Faces of Issue Voting." *American Political Science Review* 74 (1): 78–91.

Converse, Philip. 1964. "The Nature of Belief Systems in Mass Publics." In *Ideology and Discontent*, ed. D. E. Apter. New York: Free Press.

Diamond, Gregory Andrade. 2001. "Implications of a Latitude-Theory Model of Citizen Attitudes for Political Campaigning, Debate, and Representation." In *Citizens and Politics: Perspectives from Political Psychology*, ed. J. H. Kuklinski. New York: Cambridge University Press.

Domhoff, G. William. 2002. "The Power Elite, Public Policy, and Public Opinion." In *Navigating Public Opinion: Polls, Policy, and the Future of American*

Democracy, ed. J. Manza, F. L. Cook and B. I. Page. New York: Oxford University Press.

Feldman, Stanley. 2003. "A Conflicted Public? Equality, Fairness and Redistribution." Paper presented at the Conference on Inequality and American Democracy, Princeton University.

Friedman, Joel, and Andrew Lee. 2003. "Permanent Repeal of the Estate Tax Would Be Costly, Yet Would Benefit Only a Few, Very Large Estates." Washington, DC: Center on Budget and Policy Priorities.

Geer, John. 1996. *From Tea Leaves to Opinion Polls: A Theory of Democratic Leadership*. New York: Columbia University Press.

Ginsberg, Benjamin. 1984. "Polling and the Transformation of Public Opinion." In *The Captive Public*, ed. B. Ginsberg. New York: Basic Books.

Gravelle, Jane G., and Steven Maguire. 2001. "Estate and Gift Taxes: Economic Issues." Congressional Research Service Report RL30600.

Green, Joshua. 2001. "Meet Mr. Death." *American Prospect,* May 21.

Hochschild, Jennifer. 1996. *Facing Up to the American Dream: Race, Class, and the Soul of the Nation*. Princeton, NJ: Princeton University Press.

Jacobs, Lawrence R., and Robert Y. Shapiro. 1995–96. "Presidential Manipulation of Polls and Public Opinion: The Nixon Administration and the Pollsters." *Political Science Quarterly* 110: 519–38.

———. 2000. *Politicians Don't Pander: Political Manipulation and the Loss of Democratic Responsiveness*. Chicago: University of Chicago Press.

Johnston, David Cay. 2001. "Focus on Farms Masks Estate Tax Confusion." *New York Times*, April 8.

Key, V. O., Jr. 1961. *Public Opinion and American Democracy*. New York: Knopf.

Kingdon, J. W. 1993. "Politicians, Self-Interest, and Ideas." In *Reconsidering the Democratic Public*, ed. G. E. Marcus and R. L. Hanson. University Park: Pennsylvania State University Press.

Kopczuk, Wojciech, and Emmanuel Saez. 2004. "Top Wealth Shares in the United States, 1916–2000: Evidence from Estate Tax Returns." *NBER Working Paper Series* (Working Paper 10399).

Kuklinski, James A., and Norman L. Hurley. 1996. "It's a Matter of Interpretation." In *Political Persuasion and Attitude Change*, ed. D. C. Mutz, P. M. Sniderman, and R. C. Brody. Ann Arbor: University of Michigan Press.

Lantz, Keith, A. Lee Gurley, and Kenneth Linna. 2003. "Popular Support for the Elimination of the Estate Tax in the United States." *Tax Notes Today* 99: 1263.

Lippman, Walter. 1925. *The Phantom Public*. New York: Harcourt, Brace and Co.

Luntz, Frank. 2002. "The Environment: A Cleaner, Safer, Healthier America." In *Straight Talk*. Washington, DC: Luntz Research Companies.

Miller, Nicholas. 1996. "Majority Rule and Minority Interests." In *NOMOS XXXVIII: Political Order*, ed. I. Shapiro and R. Hardin. New York: New York University Press.

Olson, Mancur. 1971. *The Logic of Collective Action: Public Goods and the Theory of Groups*. Cambridge, MA: Harvard University Press.

Page, Benjamin I., and Robert Y. Shapiro. 1992. *The Rational Public: Fifty Years of Trends in Americans' Policy Preferences*. Chicago: University of Chicago Press.

Poole, Keith. 2000. "Non-Parametric Unfolding of Binary Choice Data." *Political Analysis* 8: 211–37.

Roemer, John. 1999. "Does Democracy Engender Justice?" In *Democracy's Value*, ed. I. Shapiro and C. Hacker-Cordón. Cambridge: Cambridge University Press.

Schattschneider, E. E. 1960. *The Semi-Sovereign People*. New York: Holt, Rinehart and Winston.

Schneider, Anne, and Helen Ingram. 1993. "Social Construction of Target Populations: Implications for Politics and Policy." *American Political Science Review* 87 (2): 334–46.

Sears, David O. 2001. "The Role of Affect in Symbolic Politics." In *Citizens & Politics: Perspectives from Political Psychology*, ed. J. H. Kuklinski. New York: Cambridge University Press.

Sears, David O., and C. L. Funk. 1991. "The Role of Self-Interest in Social and Political Attitudes." In *Advances in Experimental Social Psychology*, ed. M. P. Zanna. New York: Academic Press.

Slemrod, Joel. 2003. "The Roles of Misconceptions in Support for Regressive Tax Reform." In *Brookings Institution Briefing: Do Misperceptions Guide the Tax Policy Debate?* Washington, DC.

Stimson, James A., Michael B. Mackuen, and Robert S. Erikson. 1995. "Dynamic Representation." *American Political Science Review* 89 (3): 543–65.

Sunstein, Cass R. 2000. "Deliberative Trouble? Why Groups Go to Extremes." *Yale Law Journal* 110 (71): 71–119.

Wlezien, Christopher. 1995. "The Public as Thermostat: Dynamics of Preferences for Spending." *American Political Science Review* 39: 981–1000.

Zaller, John. 1992. *The Nature and Origins of Mass Opinion*. Cambridge: Cambridge University Press.

———. 2003. "Coming to Grips with V. O. Key's Concept of Latent Opinion." In *Electoral Democracy*, ed. M. MacKuen and G. Rabinowitz. Ann Arbor: University of Michigan Press.

Zaller, John, and Stanley Feldman. 1992. "A Simple Theory of Survey Response: Answering Questions versus Revealing Preferences." *American Journal of Political Science* 36 (3): 579–616.

About the Contributors

Pranab Bardhan is Professor of Economics at the University of California at Berkeley and author of *Scarcity, Conflict, and Cooperation.*

Mayling Birney is a Wilsom-Cotsen Post-Doctoral Fellow at the Princeton Society of Fellows and the Woodrow Wilson School of Public and International Affairs.

Daniela Donno is a Ph.D. candidate in the Department of Political Science at Yale University.

Steffen Ganghof is Professor of Comparative Politics at Potsdam University in Germany. He is the author of *The Politics of Income Taxation.*

Michael J. Graetz is Justus S. Hotchkiss Professor of Law at Yale University and author of *Death by a Thousand Cuts: the Fight over Taxing Inherited Wealth* (with Ian Shapiro) and *True Security: Rethinking Social Insurance.*

Christopher Howard is the Pamela Harriman Professor of Government and Public Policy at the College of William and Mary. He is the author of *The Welfare State Nobody Knows: Debunking Myths about U.S. Social Policy* and *The Hidden Welfare State: Tax Expenditures and Social Policy in the United States.*

Jana Kunicová is a consultant with the World Bank, focusing on the issues of public-sector governance and institutional reform in Europe and Central Asia. She has published articles in the *British Journal of Political Science, Party Politics,* and edited volumes.

Woojin Lee is Associate Professor of Economics, University of Massachusetts at Amherst. His most recent book, coauthored with John Roemer and Karine van der Straeten, is *Racism, Xenophobia, and Distribution: Multi-Issue Politics in Advanced Democracies.*

Isabela Mares is Associate Professor of Political Science at Columbia University. She is the author of *The Politics of Social Risk* and of *Taxation, Wage Bargaining and Unemployment*.

Nicoli Nattrass is Professor of Economics and Director of the AIDS and Society Research Unit at the University of Cape Town, South Africa. Her books include *The Moral Economy of AIDS in South Africa*; *Mortal Combat: AIDS Denialism and the Struggle for Anti-Retrovirals in South Africa*; and, with Jeremy Seekings, *Class, Race and Inequality in South Africa*.

John Roemer is Elizabeth S. and A. Varick Professor of Political Science and Economics at Yale University. His most recent books are *Racism, Xenophobia, and Distribution* (coauthored with Woojin Lee and Karine van der Straeten) and *Democracy, Education and Equality*.

Kenneth Scheve is Professor of Political Science at Yale University. He is the author, with Matthew Slaughter, of *Globalization and the Perceptions of American Workers*.

Jeremy Seekings is Professor of Political Studies and Sociology at the University of Cape Town, South Africa. His books include *The UDF: A History of the United Democratic Front in South Africa, 1983–1991* and, with Nicoli Nattrass, *Class, Race and Inequality in South Africa*.

Ian Shapiro is Sterling Professor of Political Science at Yale University, where he also serves as Henry R. Luce Director of the Yale Center for International and Area Studies. His most recent books are *Containment: Rebuilding a Strategy against Global Terror*, *The Flight from Reality in the Human Sciences*, and *Death by a Thousand Cuts: The Fight over Taxing Inherited Wealth* (with Michael Graetz).

David Stasavage is Associate Professor of Politics at New York University. He is the author of *Public Debt and the Birth of the Democratic State: France and Great Britain, 1688–1789*.

Peter A. Swenson is Saden Professor of Political Science at Yale University. He is the author of *Fair Shares: Unions, Pay and Politics in Sweden and West Germany* and *Capitalists against Markets: The Making of Labor Markets and Welfare States in the United States and Sweden*.

Index

2004 presidential election, 186–220; ANES variables, 189, 215–218, 219n5; antiblack feelings, 190–192; Bush tax cut issue, 188; contemporary issues, 188, 190; correlation analyses of, 213–214; Democratic Party, 190, 200–201, 208–212; econometric analysis of, 188–192; Iraq war issue, 188; libertarianism issue, 188, 189; Militant factions, 195–196, 197, 198, 200–201; moral Puritanism effect (MPE), 188, 202–203, 207, 212; moral values issue, 188, 189–192, 202–203, 208, 212, 214; Opportunist factions, 195–196, 197, 198; party unanimity Nash equilibrium (PUNE) model, 192–215; persistent issues, 188–189, 190; policy bundle effect (PBE), 188, 202–203, 207, 208; policy bundling, 187; race issue, 188, 189, 190, 214; Reformist factions, 196, 219n7; Republican Party, 10, 190–192, 201, 208–212; school vouchers issue, 189; size of public sector issue, 188, 189–190, 194, 202–203, 208, 212; social security reform issue, 188; the "what's the matter with Kansas" problem, 188

AARP (formerly American Association of Retired Persons), 224
Abercrombie, Neil, 321
Actuarial Society of South Africa, 105
advanced economies: cuts in entitlement programs, 19; developing economies compared to, 4–5. See also OECD
adverse life events, 149–151, 159–161; costs of, limits to, 149; losses in subjective utility, 162; monetary costs, 150; psychic costs, 150–151, 160; religiosity as alternative to social insurance, 150,
159–160, 170, 177; religiosity as mechanism to cope with, 160–161; to religious individuals, 151; unemployment (*see* unemployment)
AFB (American Farm Bureau), 316, 317, 319, 326
the affluent: American optimism about, 304; politicians and, 187; power/influence in United States, 10–11, 224–225; public spending on, 10; resentment against, 312; share of national income in United States, 222; tax cuts (2001–2003), 222; taxation of, 236
Africa: AIDS in, 100–104, 111; North Africa, 107; South Africa (*see* South Africa); Southern Africa, 100, 101, 103, 104; Sub-Saharan Africa, 8, 103, 107, 109
African Americans. *See* blacks
agrarian welfare regimes, 5, 26–27, 29, 33–34
Aid to Families with Dependent Children, 234
AIDS (Acquired Immunodeficiency Syndrome): Africa, 100–104, 111; Caribbean countries, 8, 100, 111; Global Fund to Fight AIDS, TB, and Malaria, 106–107; India, 100; inequality, 7; Latin America, 8, 100, 111; people getting treatment, percentage, 7; people living with, number, 7; poverty, 7–8, 100–101, 106; South Africa, 100; South Asia, 100; Southeast Asia, 100; Sub-Saharan Africa, 8, 103; UNAIDS (United Nations Programme on AIDS), 7, 113. *See also* HAART; HIV
Allport, G., 178n17
Alvarez, C., 101
AMA (American Medical Association), 245–246
Ambedkar, B. R., 295n4

American exceptionalism, 187–188, 219n3
American Farm Bureau (AFB), 316, 317, 319, 326
American Medical Association (AMA), 245–246
American National Election Studies (ANES): 2004 presidential election data, 189, 215–218, 219n5; "death tax terminology," 305; long term care for the elderly, 226–227; spending on social security, 237n12
Americans Against Unfair Family Taxation, 308
Americans for Generational Equity, 235
Americans for Tax Reform, 320
Ames, Barry, 124
ANES. *See* American National Election Studies
Argentina, 28, 35
Asia. *See* Central Asia; East Asia; South Asia; Southeast Asia
Atlantic Charter (1941), 32
Australia: acceptable inequality, 232–233; religiosity and social spending, *154*; taxation, 76, 84; welfare regime, 23, 28
Austria: center of gravity of the government, 62; centralization of wage-bargaining, 58; employment performance, variables affecting, 68; religiosity and social spending, *154*; taxation, 76, 78–79, 89; welfare regime, 21
Averting the Old-Age Crisis (World Bank), 19
Azzi, Corry, 178n14

Bahujan Samaj Party (BSP), 292, 296n5
Barbados, 32, 33, 34
Bartels, Larry M., 187, 335n5
Baucus, Max, 319
Baur, Martin, 124–125
Belgium: centralization of wage-bargaining, 58; employment performance, variables affecting, 68; payroll taxes, 44; taxation, 76
Benabou, Roland, 156
Berry, William, 165
Beveridge Report (1942), 32, 33
Bicheldei, K. A., 120
Bickers, Kenneth N., 122
Bierring, Walter, 246

Bismarck, Otto von, 250–251, 252
blacks: 2004 presidential election, 190–192, 321, 323; social insurance, 165, 166–167, 172
Blanchard, Olivier, 160
Blethen, Frank, 318
Borzutzky, Silvia, 30
Botswana, 25, 101, 112
Braun, Heinrich, 260
Brazil: *Bolsa Familia* program, 38; HAART coverage, 108, 111, 112; income grants, 38–39; *Previdencia Rural*, 37; public spending, 123–124; welfare regime, 23, 28, 30, 35–36, 37–38, 38–39
Britain: Colonial Development and Welfare Act (1940), 33; health insurance, 246; income redistribution, 231, 232; welfare regime, 28, 32
British Colonial Office, 33
British Empire, welfare regime in, 32–33
British Guiana, 32
British Household Panel Study, 160
British Medical Association, 246
Browne, E., 62
Brüning, Heinrich: Center Party (*Zentrum*), 260; Christian labor confederation/unions, 261, 270; German health care system, 260, 261, 267, 268, 270, 271; Stegerwald and, 261
Brunner, Edmund deS., 158
Bruno, M., 47
BSP (Bahujan Samaj Party, India), 292, 296n5
Bueck, Henry Axel, 251, 253
Buffett, Warren, 322
Burundi, 112
Bush, George W.: economic policies, 186; estate tax repeal, 304–305; Medicare prescription drug benefit, 227–228; Social Security privatization, 235; tax cuts (2001–2003), 188, 222, 324–325

Calmfors, Lars: unemployment and centralization of wage-bargaining, 45, 47, *48*, 49, 57, 64, 66; utilitarian objective function of unions, 51–52
Cambodia, 112
Cameron, D., 47, 57
Campbell, Andrea Louise, 237n6
Canada: centralization of wage-bargaining,

58; employment performance, variables affecting, 68; inequality in, 222; religiosity and social spending, *154*; retirement pensions, 225; taxation, 76, 84

Cardoso, Fernando Henrique, 38

Carey, David, 77, 93n4

Caribbean countries: AIDS, 8, 100, 111; HAART coverage, 108, 109, 111; HAART rollout, 107

Carmines, Edward G., 336n14

Carnahan, Jean, 324

Castles, Francis, 23, 62

CBS News/New York Times poll, 305

Center Party (*Zentrum*), 259, 260–261

Central Asia, 107

centralization of wage-bargaining in OECD countries, 46–49, 56–61; averages for OECD countries, 58; economy-level bargaining, 47; employment, 46–49; extreme centralization, 48, 49, 58; extreme decentralization, 48, 49, 58; firm-level bargaining, 47; industry-level bargaining, 47; intermediate centralization, 48, 49, 56–57, 58, 64; monetary policy, 49; social wage, 55; unemployment, 47–48, 56–61, 63–64; unions, 46; wage moderation, 53, 54

Centre for the Study of Developing Societies, 291

Cervellati, Matteo, 179n18

Chatterjee, P., 290

Chaves, Mark, 158

Chen, David, 157–158, 169

child care/children, public spending on, 222, 227t, 229–230

Child Tax Credit (CTC), 234

Chile, welfare regime in, 19, 23, 28, 30, 35

Christian Democracy, 150, 155

Clark, Andrew, 160, 162

Clark, Mary, 39

class-oriented politics, 212

Clinton, Bill, 324

Club for Growth Advocacy, 337n19

coalition politics: distributive politics, 14–15; economic effects in India, 12–13; institutional change, 11; side payments, 4

COBRA (Consolidated Budget Reconciliation Act of 1985), 234

Communist Party of the Russian Federation (CPRF), 142n6

Concord Coalition, 223, 235

Congress Party (India), 281, 283

Congressional Research Service, 317

Contract with America, 315, 332

Converse, Philip, 310

corporatism: cross-class collaboration, 272; electoral representation compared to, 274n1; Europe, 248–249; German health care system, 248–249, 250, 266, 269, 272

Costa Rica, 36, 39

CPRF (Communist Party of the Russian Federation), 142n6

Croatia, 84, 85

CTC (Child Tax Credit), 234

Cusack, Tom, 62

Cushing, Harvey, 245–246, 247, 274

Daschle, Tom, 319, 324, 332

De Waal, A., 104

deagrarianization, welfare regimes and, 5, 28, 29, 31, 36, 39

Dean, Howard, 324

decommodification, welfare regimes and, 21–22

defamilialization, welfare regimes and, 21–22

Dehejia, Rajeev, 157–158, 162

DeLeire, Thomas, 157–158, 162

democracy, 280–297; in countries with per capita income below one thousand dollars, 295n1; distributive outcomes, 119; fears of, 1–2; HAART, 99, 111, 114; in India, 280–297; inequality, 221; injustice, 2; majorities in, 2; "new democracy," 134, 141; "third wave" of, 1

Democracy in America (Tocqueville), 187–188

Democratic Party: 2004 presidential election, 190, 200–201, 208–212; estate tax repeal, 298, 307, 315, 318, 320–321, 322, 323–324, 326, 327; Militants in, 200–201; moral values issue, 190, 208; Republican Party on, 186; size of the public sector, 190, 202, 208, 212; social insurance, 165, 166–167

democratization: pauperist welfare regimes, 5; welfare regimes, 5, 29, 36–37, 39

demographic outsiders, 60–61

Denmark: centralization of wage-bargaining, 58; dual income tax system (DIT), 81; employment performance, variables affecting, 68; religiosity and social spending, *154*; taxation, 76, 78, 81, 84

developing economies: advanced economies compared to, 4–5; electoral rules, effect of, 8; inequality in, 7; kin and family in, 5; welfare regimes, 4–5

Development and Crisis of the Welfare State (Huber and Stephens), 19

"developmental states," 24

Di Tella, Rafael, 160

Disabled Americans for Death Tax Relief, 323

distributive politics: attention paid to lower *vs.* upper half of income distribution, 234–235; coalition politics, 14–15; divide-a-dollar logic of, 4, 333; electoral rules, 121–126; exogenism of preferences to political processes, 13; fairness and justice, 274; majorities in, 2; in new democracies, 141; questions this book addresses, 2–3; theme of this book, 14–15; theory and reality, mismatch between, 2

DIT. *See* dual income tax system

divide-a-dollar logic, 4, 333

The Doctor and His Mission (Liek), 245, 265

doctors: German health care system, 12, 249–250, 254, 255, 256–260, 261, 263–268, 269–271, 273; influence on medical politics, 274; Jewish, 273

Douglass, H. Paul, 158

Downs, Anthony, 192, 311

downward redistribution, 1–2, 3, 5

Dreijmanis, J., 62

Driffill, John: unemployment and centralization of wage-bargaining, 45, 47, *48*, 49, 57, 64, 66; utilitarian objective function of unions, 51–52

dual income tax system (DIT): Denmark, 81; features, 7, 73, 81–82; Finland, 7, 73, 81; influence, 93n9; Italy, 81, 82, 85–86; Norway, 7, 73, 81; policy learning, 7, 82; stability of, 7; Sweden, 7, 73, 81; tax competition, 85–86

Dunn, Jennifer, 321

Earned Income Tax Credit, 234

East Asia: HAART rollout, 107; welfare regimes, 23–24, 25, 26, 36, 38

Eastern Europe: dual transition from authoritarianism, 118–119; welfare regime, 19

"easy issue" voters *vs.* "hard issue voters," 336n14

economic redistribution: downward redistribution, 1–2, 3, 5; in the South, 24; upward redistribution, 14. *See also* income redistribution

Ehrenberg, Ronald, 178n14

the elderly, 221–231; attitudes toward public spending on childcare, 230; interest in Social Security, Medicare, 224, 225, 235; long term care for, 226–227; power/influence in United States., 10–11, 224–225, 230–231, 237n7; public spending on, 10–11, 221–223, 225–231; welfare regimes worldwide, 25

electoral rules, 121–126; developing economies, 8; effect on distributive politics, 121–126; electoral incentives, 121; legislative behavior, 121, 124; mixed systems, 124–126 (*see also* Russian State Duma); in new democracies, 141; proportional representation (*see* PR); Russian State Duma, 120; single-member districts (*see* SMD)

Ellison, Christopher, 161

Emily's List (www.emilyslist.org), 304

employer health insurance, 235

employer pensions, 235

employment, 56–67; capital movements, exposure to, 64; centralization of wage-bargaining, 46–49; full employment, 20; labor market outsiders, 60; monetary policy, 48, 49–50; nonwage labor costs, 43–44; OECD employment performance, cross-national differences in, 56–67; sensitivity to changes in wages, 55; taxation, 44, 53, 55, 60; wage moderation, 47; welfare states, 51. *See also* unemployment

employment policies, welfare regimes and, 4–5, 28, 29

Engels, Friedrich, 287

Esping-Andersen, Gøsta, 19–25; Bismarckian welfare systems, 25; critiques of, 22–23; decommodification in, 21–22;

defamilialization in, 21–22; development economists compared to, 24; family/kin in, 22; full employment in, 20; labor market policies in, 20, 23; social policies in, 20; three-part typology of welfare regimes, 4, 19–24; unemployment in, 20–21

estate tax, federal, 298–339; 1970s, 301, 334n2; 2011 reinstatement of, 326; animosity toward, 312; carryover basis, 326; as "death tax," 305, 310; as double or triple taxation, 306, 313, 336n8; enactment of, 334n2; equality-of-opportunity principle, 309; as "estate tax," 305; as issue of moral principle, 327–328; as "just wrong," 327–328; misperceptions about, 302–304, 308, 311, 335n5; percentage of population paying, 334n2; phase-out of, 324n1; progressivity of, 302, 309, 312–313, 320; public opinion, 299–300, 304; reform of, 308–309, 325, 326, 329, 336n13; repeal of (*see* estate tax repeal); stepped-up basis, 326; supporters of, 308–310, 312–313, 315, 322–324, 332

estate tax repeal: 2001 law, 298, 300, 326; 2010 sunset clause, 317, 326; advocates of, 329–330; backlash against, 298; beneficiaries of, 298, 301–302; black businessmen, 323; black caucus, 321; charitable organizations, 322; coalition for, 316; competing tax-cut lobbyists, 324–325; Democratic Party, 298, 307, 315, 318, 320–321, 322, 323–324, 326, 327; economic effects, 307–308; fairness issue, 302, 304–308, 311, 313, 315, 328, 333–334; farmers, 306–307, 310, 316–317, 325, 326, 327; fingerprinting strategy favoring, 320, 324; framing of the issue, 323, 330; gays and lesbians, 306, 318, 336n9; Gephardt-Waxman proposal (1992), 315; government incompetence, 309; grassroots mobilization favoring, 319; ideological position of sponsors, 320–323; image of high support for, 328, 332; insurance providers, 322; interest groups, 330; justice in processes *vs.* justice in outcomes, 313; labor organizations, 322; leveraging public opinion for policy goals, 314–322; lower-income persons, 335n3; opponents of, 314–315,

326, 336n8; permanent repeal, 298, 300, 317; persistence of efforts favoring, 300–301; polls on, 333–334; priority among tax cuts, 309–310, 313, 328, 329; public opinion, 13; replacement of stepped-up basis with carryover basis, 326; Republican Party, 298, 307, 323, 327; resources required to achieve, 330; "running-room" model of public opinion, 13–14, 322–325; salience of the issue, 310, 311–312, 313, 315–316, 329; self-interest, 302–304, 309, 311, 335n5; small businesses, 306–307, 310, 316–317, 325, 327; sociotropic arguments favoring, 307–308; as stand-alone issue, 317, 323–324; support for, 302–310, 318, 320–321, 335n3; temporary repeal, 298; timing of, 300–301, 304; total repeal, 325–338, 333; upward redistribution, 14; votes on, 299; wealthy individuals, 330

Esteban, Joan, 179n18

Estonia, 86

Ethiopia, 112

EU (European Union), 88

Europe: corporatism, 248–249; HAART rollout, 107; income inequality, 222, 231; income redistribution, 232

European Commission, 62

European Union (EU), 88

Eurostat, 77, 93n4

Family Business Estate Tax Coalition, 300

Family Medical Leave Act (FMLA, 1993), 234

federal estate tax. *See* estate tax, federal

federalism: "coming-together" *vs.* "holding-together," 293

Feldman, Stanley, 337n15

Ferejohn, John, 122

Finland: centralization of wage-bargaining, 58; dual income tax system (DIT), 7, 73, 81; employment performance, variables affecting, 68; religiosity and social spending, *154*; taxation, 76, 89

FMI (Food Marketing Institute), 316

FMLA (Family Medical Leave Act, 1993), 234

Fogel, Robert, 169

Folkman, Susan, 161

Food Marketing Institute (FMI), 316

Food Stamps, 234

France: centralization of wage-bargaining, 58; employment performance, variables affecting, 68; religiosity and social spending, *154*; taxation, 76, 78–79, 89; unemployment, 44; welfare regime, 21

franchise, downward redistribution and, 1–2

Franzese, Robert, 57, 60

Freud, Sigmund, 151, 161

Friedrich Krupp AG, 251–252, 257, 258

Funk, C. L., 311

The Future of an Illusion (Freud), 151

Gallup polls on estate tax repeal, 304, 305, 309–310, 317, 335n7

Gandhi, Mahatma, 281

Gates, Bill, 74, 312

Gates, Bill, Sr., 322

Gay, David, 161

General Social Survey (GSS): ISSP and, 181n39; National Election Studies (NES) compared to, 237n8; public spending on Social Security, 225, 237n12; public spending on the elderly, 226; religiosity and social-insurance preferences, 170–171; religious attendance, 163–164; social-insurance spending preferences, 176; spending on the poor, 181n42; traditional family values, 238n19; women's rights, 238n19

geographically-targeted spending. *See* pork-barrel politics

George, Lloyd, 246

Georgia, Republic of, 86

Gephardt, Dick, 337n16

German health care system, 245–279; 1883 law, 250, 252–253; 1930 emergency presidential decree, 261–268; 1931 emergency decree, 261, 268–271; administrative costs, 253; administrative responsibilities, 249–251; agricultural funds (*Landkrankenkassen*), 252; antisocialist motives, 251; big business/larger companies, 253–254, 257, 265–266; Bismarck and, 250–251, 252; Brüning and, 260, 261, 267, 268, 270, 271; busywork (*Vielgeschäftigkeit*), 254; capital and labor, conflict between, 254–255, 260, 273; capital and labor, cooperation between, 248, 251–252, 261, 272, 273; capitalists and, 251, 268, 270, 271; capitation/salary (*Gesamtpauschale*), 259, 269; caseloads, 263; Center Party (*Zentrum*), 259; certifications of illness (*Gefälligkeitszeugnisse*), 260, 262; Christian trade unions, 259; co-management of funds, 252, 253; co-payments for prescriptions, 262–263; collective bargaining, 269, 270; company funds (*Betriebskrankenkassen*), 252, 253–254, 256–259, 262, 269, 275n2; compulsory benefit funds (*Knappschaftskassen*), 252; compulsory nature, 250; "contract practice," 255; corporatism, 248–249, 250, 266, 269, 272; cost-effectiveness, 264–265, 269, 272; cost shifting to patients, 262–263; in the Depression, 266, 273; doctors, free choice of, 258; doctors, glut of (*Aerzteschwemme*), 266–267, 273; doctors, Jewish, expulsion of, 273; doctors, reimbursement of, 249–250, 256, 258, 259, 264; doctors, role of, 12, 256–260, 261, 263–268, 269–271; doctors, strikes by, 256–257, 264; doctors, unnecessary prescriptions by (*Gefälligkeitsverschreibungen*), 260, 266; doctors, unnecessary treatment by, 249–250, 254, 255, 260, 264–265, 270; doctors, young/unemployed (*Jungärzte*), 267, 269; fairness and justice, 274; fee-for-service payment (*Einzelleistungshonorierung*), 256, 258, 259, 264; fee schedule, 268–269; fees for doctor visits, 262–263; guild-based funds (*Innungskrankenkassen*), 252; Haedenkamp and, 257, 262, 267, 269, 270–273; Hartmannbund (*Verband der Ärzte Deutschlands zur Wahrung ihrer wirstschaftlichen Interessen*), 256–257, 258, 261, 262, 263, 265, 266, 267, 268–269, 271; Heinemann and, Otto, 257, 259; hospitals, reimbursement of, 249; income determination, 249; insurance reimbursement, 249; insure code (1911), 264; Krupp AG, 257; Landmann and, 255–256; local multiemployer funds (*Ortskrankenkassen*), 252, 253–257, 258–259, 261–262, 275n2; Lohmann and, 251–252, 253; malingering (*Simulantentum*), 254, 262; mass production doctoring (*Massenbetrieb*), 254; medical examiners (*Vertrauensärtze*), 262; medical students, 266, 267; minimum service benefits (*Regelleistungen*), 253; national confederation of company funds (*Reichsverband der Betriebskrankenkassen*), 259; Nazi government, Nazism, 250, 261, 267, 271–273; overdoctoring (*Überarztung*), 254; patients "neediness," "demandingness" (*Bedürftigkeit, Begehrlichkeit*), 264; politicization of medicine, 273; postdiagnostic exams (*Nachuntersuchungen*), 262; postwar system, 273; quackery (*Kurpfuscherei*), 272; regional medical associations, 269–270; self-management (*Selbstverwaltung*), 252; sick pay (*Krankengeld*), 253; smaller firms, 254; Social Democratic Party (SPD), 256, 258, 267, 268, 270; socialists, 255, 263, 271; supplementary benefits (*Mehrleistungen*), 253; United States, influence on, 245–248, 250, 274; Weimar period, 260–261, 267, 272

The German Ideology (Marx and Engels), 287

Germany: acceptable inequality, 232–233; Bundestag, 124–125, 142n1; centralization of wage-bargaining, 58; employment performance, variables affecting, 68; health care system (*see* German health care system); income redistribution, 231; industrial accident insurance, 251; organized labor in, 12; organized medicine in, 11; PR (proportional representation), 124–125; religiosity and social spending, 154; retirement pensions, 225; SMD (single-member districts), 124–125, 142n1; social-insurance programs, 44; taxation, 76, 84, 87, 88, 89–91; welfare regime, 21; welfare state in, 251

Gesetz betreffend die Krankenversicherung der Arbeiter, 250

Gilens, Martin, 187

Gingrich, Newt, 176

Glass, Thomas, 161

Global Fund to Fight AIDS, TB, and Malaria, 106–107

Golden, Miriam, 57

Goodin, R., 22

Goodman, Roger, 25

Grassley, Charles, 319

Greece, 76, 89, *154*

Greenberg Research, 303, 309–310, 336n10

Greenspan, Alan, 223

GSS. *See* General Social Survey

Gupta, A., 203–204

HAART (highly active antiretroviral therapy), 104–117; Botswana, 112; Brazil, 108, 111, 112; Burundi, 112; Cambodia, 112; Caribbean countries, 107, 108, 109, 111; Central Asia, 107; coverage, determinants of, 108–114; democracy, 99, 111, 114; developing countries, 107; Dominican Republic, 112; East Asia, 107; Ethiopia, 112; Europe, 107; global rollout, 107; Haiti, 105; HIV prevalence, 99–100, 109; income distribution, 99; India, 112; inequality, 111–112; international pressure on national governments, 106–107, 114; Latin America, 107, 108, 109, 111; level of development, 114; life expectancy, 104–107; Malawi, 112; Middle East, 107; Nigeria, 112; North Africa, 107; per capita expenditure on health, 109; per capita income, 99, 107, 109, 111; political will, 112–113; Russia, 108, 112; South Africa, 105, 106–107, 108, 112, 113; South Asia, 107; Southeast Asia, 107; Sub-Saharan Africa, 107, 109; Tanzania, 112; Thailand, 112; Uganda, 112; voluntary counseling and testing (VCT), 104, 105; Zambia, 112; Zimbabwe, 112. *See also* AIDS; HIV

Haedenkamp, Karl: German health care system, 257, 262, 267, 269, 270–273; Nazism, 271–272

Hailey, Lord, 33

Haiti, 105

Hall, P., 57

handicapped, employment of, 239n25

Hartmann, Hermann, 256

Hartz, Gustav, 245

Hasan, Z., 292

Haspel, Moshe, 125

health insurance: American Medical Association (AMA), 245–246; Britain, 246; compulsory insurance, 246, 248; employer health insurance, 235; in Germany (*see* German health care system); medical school graduates, 246; organized

health insurance (*continued*)
  opposition to in United States, 245–248; quality of medical care, 246–247; Roosevelt and, Franklin, 245–246; universal health insurance, 2
health spending: public spending on, 227t, 229–230, 239n25; religiosity, 170–177
Heinemann, Gustav, 257, 271, 275n3
Heinemann, Otto, 257, 259, 270–271
highly active antiretroviral therapy. *See* HAART
Hindenburg, Paul von, 261, 262, 271
Hirschman, Albert, 274
Hitler, Adolf, 271, 273, 275n3
HIV (Human Immunodeficiency Virus): inequality, 101, 103–104; level of development, 100–101; life expectancy, 99; per capita income, 103; poverty, 103; prevalence, 99–100, 101–102, 103, 109; South Africa, 101–103; Southern Africa, 101
Hoffman, Frederick, 246
homeowner, tax subsidies for, 235
Hong Kong, 36, 37, 38
Huber, Evelyne, 19, 30, 62, 155
Hungerman, David M., 157–158
Hurricane Katrina (2005), 2

Iceland, *154*
ideologies, 327
Iliffe, John, 101–102
ILO (International Labour Organization), 24, 28, 32
immigrant workers, welfare regimes and, 5, 28, 29–31
import-substitution industrialization (ISI), 35, 37
"Income Distribution and Employment Programme" (ILO), 24
income grants, 38–39
income redistribution: Britain, 231, 232; burying money in an abandoned coal mine, 236; elected officials' reluctance to push for, 224; Europe, 232; Germany, 231; Italy, 231; Norway, 231; state-sponsored, support for, 11; Sweden, 231, 232; taxation, 236; United States, 225, 231–232, 238n22
income thresholds in United States, 239n23
India, 280–297; accountability in day-to-day administration, 280–281, 286; AIDS, 100; anti-incumbency, 291–292; budgetary subsidies, 283, 286; castes, lower, 292–293; castes, upper, 292; civic administration, 288; civil and political rights, 280–281; coalition politics, 12–13; collective action problem, 283; colonialism in, 281; common-pool problem, 283; community arbitration processes, 289; conflict management, 281; consensus building, 281; corruption, 286; criminal justice system, 288; criminalization of politics, 288; democracy in, 280–297; economic deadlock, 282; economic integration, 294; economic reforms, 285–286, 295, 296n7; elections, national, 282; elections, state, 282; electoral representativeness, 280–281; elite control, 286; Essential Commodities Act (1955), 294; faith in politics, 291; farmers, 283, 285; federalism, 293–295; fiscal transfers to states, 294; freedom of expression, 284; governance, 286–287; group rights/privileges/dignity, 13, 284, 285, 291, 292–293; Gujarat pogrom (2002), 288; HAART coverage, 112; individual rights, 284, 286; inflation sensitivity, 293; infrastructure, 281, 282–283, 286, 293; inner-party democracy, 283–284; interest-group capture of democratic politics, 13; law, rule of, 288–291; legislative processes, 289; Maharashtra Cotton Monopoly Procurement Scheme, 294; North India, 292–293; patronage, 290; police, 288; the poor, 290, 291, 292–293; popular mobilization, 290–291; pork-barrel politics, 283; poverty, 291–292, 293; power of the state, 284–285; private sector, regulation of, 282; public debt/deficits, 282–283, 286, 295n3; public investment, 282–283; public-job quotas, 292; public sector, 282; railways, 294; regional inequality, 295; regional parties, 294; short-run demands/measures, 282, 290; socioeconomic heterogeneity, 287–288; South India, 292; state governments, 294–295; taxation, 294; welfare regime, 25
industrial accident insurance, 251
inequality, 231–235; acceptable inequality, 232–233; AIDS, 7; attention paid to

lower *vs.* upper half of income distribution, 234–235; Australia, 232–233; democracies, 221; in developing economies, 7; Germany, 232–233; growth in, 223–224; HAART coverage, 111–112; HIV, 101, 103–104; liberals, 223–224; tax cuts (2001–2003), 222; United Kingdom, 232–233; United States, 222, 224, 232–233; welfare regimes, 35

inheritance tax. *See* estate tax, federal

injustice, democracy and, 2

institutional change, coalition politics and, 11

institutions, political actors and, 119

interest groups: elite perception of public opinion on estate taxes, 300–301; estate tax repeal, 330; interpretation of public opinion, 331, 333; latent public opinion, 332; policy outcomes, 331; political entrepreneurship, 333; public opinion, 299

International Labour Organization (ILO), 24, 28, 32

International Social Survey Program (ISSP). *See* Role of Government survey

Ireland, 76, *154*

ISI (import-substitution industrialization), 35, 37

ISSP (International Social Survey Program). *See* Role of Government survey

Italy: centralization of wage-bargaining, 58; dual income tax system (DIT), 81, 82, 85–86; employment performance, variables affecting, 68; income redistribution, 231; religiosity and social spending, *154*; taxation, 76, 87; welfare regime, 21, 22

Iversen, Torben, 48–51, 56, 57, 60

Jacobs, Lawrence, 187

Jacobs, Lawrence R., 332–333

James, William, 151, 161

Japan, 22, 23, 76, *154*

Jenkins, R. S., 285–286

Johnson, Bob, 323

Johnston, David Cay, 317

Kato, Junko, 79, 93n6

Kaviraj, S., 286–287

Keesings's World News Archive, 62

Kenya, 34

Key, V. O., 328

Kirchhof, Paul, 91, 94n15, 94n16

Kittel, B., 57

Korpi, W., 22

Kotlikoff, Lawrence, 222–223, 235

Kranich, Laurence, 179n18

Krupp AG, 251–252, 257, 258

Kyl, Jon, 321

labor market insiders in OECD, 52, 53

labor market outsiders in OECD: definition, 52; employment, 60; size of, need to reduce, 68; taxation, 51; transfers to, 53, 60–61, 63, 64–66; unemployment, 51, 53, 60–61, 63, 64–66; unions, 45, 61; wage moderation, 54–55

Lancaster, Thomas D., 124, 125

Landmann, Friedrich, 255–256, 271

land reform, welfare regimes and, 5, 26. *See also* deagrarianization

Landrieu, Mary, 319

Lange, P., 57

Latin America: AIDS, 8, 100, 111; HAART coverage, 108, 109, 111; HAART rollout, 107; welfare regimes, 19, 23, 24, 25, 27, 30–31, 36

Latvia, 86

Lazarus, Richard, 161

legislative behavior, electoral rules and, 121, 124

Lehmann, Helmut, 270

Lelkes, Orsolya, 162

Levitt, Steven D., 122–123

Li, V., 101

liberalism/liberals: inequality, 223–224; public spending on the elderly, 223; social insurance, 165, 166–167

libertarianism in 2004 presidential election, 188, 189

Liek, Erwin, 245, 264–265, 272, 274

Lijphart, A., 288

Lind, Jo T., 157–158, 169

Lindert, Peter H., 75

Lipset, Seymour Martin, 219n3

Lohmann, Theodor, 251–252, 253, 254

Long Term Care Family Security Act of 1992, 337n16

Los Angeles Times (newspaper), 228

Lula da Silva, Luiz Inácio, 38, 39

Luntz, Frank, 314, 336n9

Luttmer, Erzo F. P., 157–158, 162

Luxembourg, 76, *154*
Luxembourg Income Study, 22, 222, 237n2
Lynch, Julia, 222, 235n1, 239n25

MacCulloch, Robert, 160
Mair, Peter, 62
Malawi, 112
Malloy, James, 35
Marx, Karl, 1, 151, 287
Mauritius, 32, 34
Mbeki, Thabo, 106
McLaughlin and Associates on estate tax repeal, 304–305, 306, 319, 335n3, 335n7, 336n12
McLoughlin, William G., 169
median voter theory: downward redistribution, 3; economic policy, 1–2; self-interest, 311; simplicity belied, 14
Medicaid, 221
Medicare: interest in among the elderly, 224, 225, 235; prescription drug benefit, 227–228; public spending on, 221, 222–223, 226–227
Meltzer, Allan H., 1, 178n5
Mendoza, E., 62
Mexico, 222
Middle East, 107
Milesi-Ferretti, Gian Maria, 123
Mill, John Stuart, 287, 289, 291
monetary policy: centralization of wage-bargaining, 49; employment, 48, 49–50; unemployment, 49–50, 57; unions, 48, 49–51, 54; wage-bargaining, 48–49; wage moderation, 49, 54, 55–56
moral Puritanism effect (MPE), 188, 202–203, 207, 212
moral values: 2004 presidential election, 188, 189–192, 202–203, 208, 212, 214; class-oriented politics, 212; Democratic Party, 202, 208; "policy bundling" effect of, 10; policy outcomes, 10; racism, 192; Republican Party, 188, 190, 192, 202, 208; traditional family values, 238n19
Moses, Julius, 263, 275n4
MPE (moral Puritanism effect), 188, 202–203, 207, 212
Müller, Friedrich, 245
Müller, Heinrich, 261
Murray, Patty, 324

Naipaul, V. S., 287
Namibia, 101
National Association of Manufacturers (NAM), 316
National Cattleman's Beef Association (NCBA), 316
National Election Studies (NES). *See* American National Election Studies
National Election Survey. *See* American National Election Studies
National Farmers Union, 326
National Federation of Independent Businesses (NFIB), 316, 318, 319
National Institute of Public Finance and Policy (India), 283
National Party (South Africa), 37
National Police Commission (India), 288
Native Administration and Political Development in British Tropical Africa (Hailey), 33
NCBA (National Cattleman's Beef Association), 316
NES. *See* American National Election Studies
Netherlands: centralization of wage-bargaining, 58; employment performance, variables affecting, 68; payroll taxes, 44; religiosity and social spending, *154*; taxation, 44, 76, 89, 90; welfare regime, 21
New York Times (newspaper), 317
New Zealand: religiosity and social spending, *154*; taxation, 76, 89; welfare regime, 23, 32
Newspaper Association of America (NAA), 316
NFIB (National Federation of Independent Businesses), 316, 318, 319
Nigeria, 112
NKK poll on estate tax repeal, 303, 304, 305, 306, 309, 335n6
Nordic countries, 81, 82, 86. *See also* Scandinavia
Norquist, Grover, 320
North Africa, 107
Norway: centralization of wage-bargaining, 58; dual income tax system (DIT), 7, 73, 81; employment performance, variables affecting, 68; income redistribution, 231; register of all personal shareholders, 86; religiosity and social spending, *154*;

retirement pensions, 225; taxation, 7, 73, 76, 81, 86, 89

Ochsner, Edward, 246, 274
OECD (Organization for Economic Co-operation and Development), 43–71, 76–92; average level of government expenditures, 43; cross-national differences in employment performance, 56–67; demographic outsiders, 60–61; early postwar period, 56; employment, 43–44, 46–50, 51, 53, 55, 56–67; labor market insiders, 52, 53; labor market outsiders (*see* labor market outsiders in OECD); monetary policy, 48, 49–51, 54, 55–56; nonwage labor costs, 43–44; public sector growth, 43; social policy expenditures, 4, 5–6, 44–46, 52–53; social spending, 159; social spending as percentage of GDP, 153–154; social wage, 52, 54, 55, 56; taxation, 44, 51, 53, 54, 55, 60, 62–66, 73, 74, 76–92; unemployment, 44, 45, 47–51, 53, 56–66; wage-bargaining, 48–49, 55 (*see also* centralization of wage-bargaining in OECD countries); wage moderation (*see* wage moderation in OECD countries)
OMB Watch, 323
open economies, welfare regimes and, 28
Optimal Classification (OC) system, 321–322
Organization for Economic Co-operation and Development. *See* OECD
Osberg, Lars, 232, 235
Oster, E., 100
Oswald, Andrew, 160

Page, Benjamin, 187
Page, Benjamin I., 310
Palme, J., 22
parental leave, 239n25
Pargament, K., 160
party unanimity Nash equilibrium (PUNE) model, 192–215
Patterson, W. David, 124, 125
pauperist welfare regimes, 5, 26–27, 28, 29
PBE (policy bundle effect), 188, 202–203, 207, 208
pension spending, religiosity and, 170–177
Perotti, Roberto, 123

Peterson, Pete, 223, 235
Pew Research Center, 335n7
Philippines, 25
Piketty, Thomas, 156
Poland, 86
Polanyi, Karl, 288
Policy and Taxation Group, 316, 318–319
policy bundle effect (PBE), 188, 202–203, 207, 208
policy bundling, 187
policy outcomes: congruence between opinions of specific groups and public policy, 224–225; interest groups, 331; mapping from policies, understanding of, 186–187; moral values, 10; public opinion, 298–299, 330–333; religiosity, 9, 149, 162–170
political actors, institutions and, 119
political agendas, advancing, 327
The Political Economy of Development in India (Bardhan), 282, 287
"Political Economy of Income Distribution in Developing Countries" (Princeton series), 24
"Political Economy of Poverty, Equity and Growth" (World Bank), 24
political entrepreneurship, 333
political parties: changes in party constituencies, 214; factional model of, 196; Militant factions, 195–196, 197, 198, 200–201; Opportunist factions, 195–196, 197, 198; platforms as bargaining solution between party factions, 196–197; Reformist factions, 196, 219n7; vote-maximizing *vs.* constituency-representing aims, 201
Poole, Keith, 321
the poor: efforts to aid, 274; income redistribution, attitudes toward, 232; in India, 290, 291, 292–293; public spending on assistance to, 227t, 229–230; taxation, 236; welfare regimes, 28, 35–38. *See also* poverty
pork-barrel politics (geographically targeted spending): in India, 283; Russian State Duma, 119–120; SMD (single-member districts), 8, 122–123
Portugal, 22, 76, *154*
postcommunist countries' transition from authoritarianism, 118–119

poverty: AIDS, 7–8, 100–101, 106; HIV, 103; India, 291–292, 293; social insurance, 165, 166–167; United States, 165, 237n5. *See also* the poor (*under "p"*)

PR (proportional representation): dissent from party leader's votes, 136–141; faction switching, 132, 135; Germany, 124–125; locally based spending, 8; loyalty to the party line, 121, 123; regional biases, 133; in Russian State Duma, 120–121, 129, 132, 135, 136–141; transfer spending, 123

Preston, Samuel, 237n7

principles, political, 327

proportional representation. *See* PR

Przeworski, Adam, 6, 75, 295n1

public opinion, 298–339; altering politicians perceptions of, 332; consistent patterns of, 310–311; elite perception on estate taxes, 300–301; estate tax, 299–300; estate tax, federal, 304; estate tax repeal, 13; framing/phraseology, sensitivity to, 14, 304–308, 310, 317, 329; interest groups, 299; interpretation of, 13, 310–314, 331, 333; latent public opinion, 328, 331, 332; latitude theory of, 331–332; leveraging it for policy goals, 314–322; personal, concrete examples or symbols, 313–314; in policy debates, 328–333; policy outcomes, 298–299, 330–333; politicians' perceptions of, 299; publicized polls as measures of, 329; resources available for influencing, 330; "running-room" model of, 13–14, 322–325, 331–333; salience of the issue, 310, 328; thermostatic model of policymaking, 328; as a weapon, 299

public sector, size of: 2004 presidential election, 188, 189–190, 194, 202–203; Democratic Party, 190, 202, 208, 212; Republican Party, 190, 202, 208, 212

public spending, 221–230; on the affluent, 10; on assistance to the poor, 227t, 229–230; in Brazil, 123–124; on child care/children, 222, 227t, 229–230; on the elderly, 10–11, 221–223, 225–231; geographically-targeted (*see* pork-barrel politics); on health, 227t, 229–230; on Medicare, 221, 222–223, 226–227; on Social Security, 221, 222–223, 225,

226–227, 229, 237n12; in the South, 24; taxation, 73; transfer spending (*see* transfer spending); on unemployment benefits, 227t, 228, 229–230

PUNE model (party unanimity Nash equilibrium), 192–215

Putin, Vladimir, 120, 141–142, 142n2, 142n7

QFOBI (Qualified Family Owned Business Interests), 316, 327, 337n17

Rabesona, Josette, 77, 93n4

race, 2004 presidential election and, 188, 189, 190, 214

racism, income taxes and, 201

Ragin, C., 62

rational ignorance theory, 311

Razin, A., 62

Reagan, Ronald, 176

redistribution: downward redistribution, 1–2, 3, 5; in the South, 24; upward redistribution, 14. *See also* income redistribution

religiosity, 149–185; altruism, 155; American exceptionalism, 219n3; belief in a just world, 156; beliefs about determinants of economic success, 155–156; conservative economic causal beliefs, 10; as coping mechanism for confronting adverse life events, 160–161; denominational differences, 154–155; direct-substitution effect, 157; health spending, 170–177; incidence of depression, 151, 161; individual spending preferences, 170–177, 181n42; intrinsic *vs.* extrinsic, 161; issue-bundling effect, 157; level of economic development, 159; level of life satisfaction, 161; life insurance, purchase of, 162; losses in subjective utility, 162; material/tangible benefits, 157–159; network externalities in religious commitment, 179n19; pension spending, 170–177; policy outcomes, 9, 149, 162–170; psychic benefits, 9, 150–151, 160, 161, 179n18; self-esteem, 151, 160; social insurance, 149–185; social spending, 151–152, 153–154; spending on targeted programs, 180n38; spending on the poor, 181n42; subjective well-being,

151; unemployment, 9; unemployment insurance, spending on, 152, 163, 166, 168, 179n21; urbanization, 166; welfare spending, 149–150; welfare states, 153; workers' compensation, spending on, 152, 163, 166, 168, 170, 179n21

Religious Orientation Scale, 178n17

Remington, Thomas F., 125

Republican Party: 2004 presidential election, 10, 190–192, 201, 202, 208–212; the affluent, 186; Contract with America, 315, 332; on Democratic Party, 186; economic policies, 186–187, 214; estate tax repeal, 298, 307, 323, 324–325, 327; Militants in, 201; moral values issue, 188, 190, 192, 202, 208; policy bundling, 187; size of the public sector, 190, 202, 208, 212

Responsible Wealth, 322, 323

Richard, Scott F., 1, 178n5

Rockefeller, Steven, 322

Roemer, John, 157

Role of Government survey (ISSP): cross-national data on social policy, 238n21; GSS and, 181n39; importance of religion in individuals' lives, 152; income redistribution, 231, 232, 238n22; public spending on the elderly, 225–226; public spending on unemployment benefits, 228

Roosevelt, Franklin, 245–246, 247

Ross, J., 178n17

Rostagno, Massimo, 123

"running-room" model of public opinion, 13–14, 322–325, 331–333

Russia: dual transition from authoritarianism, 118–119; HAART coverage, 108, 112; inequality in, 222; as "new democracy," 134, 141; party system, 132; taxation, 86

Russian State Duma, 126–143; balance of power, 130; dissent from party leader's votes, 136–141; elector hedging, 132–133; electoral nomination, 132–133; electoral parties *vs.* legislative factions, 127–132; electoral rules, 120; faction membership, 142n8; faction switching, 131–132, 135–136, 142n8; federal budget, votes on, 127, 136; independents in, 133, 143n10; informal rules, 134; learning by legislating, 134; "not voting,"

meaning of, 134; partisan structure, 129; party cohesion, 125; pork-barrel politics, 119–120; PR (proportional representation), 129, 132, 133; PR (proportional representation) in, 120–121; Putin and, 120, 141–142, 142n2, 142n7; relationship with executive branch, 128–129; research design, 134–138; research results, 138–141; roll call votes, 143n14; SMD (single-member districts), 120–121, 126, 132–133, 135, 136–141, 142n2; start-up groups ("deputy groups"), 128, 142n5; weakening of, 134

Sachs, J., 47

Samuels, David J., 124

Samuelson, Robert, 223

Samuelson, Robert J., 235

Scandinavia, 90. *See also* Nordic countries

Scharpf, Fritz, 43–44

SCHIP (State Children's Health Insurance Program), 234

Schmitter, P., 57

Sears, David O., 311

secularism, social insurance and, 149

self-interest: estate tax repeal, 302–304, 309, 311, 335n5; level of public support for social policies, 221; median voter theory, 311; misperceptions of, 328; policy judgments, 311; public spending on the elderly, 228; rational choice models, 311; rational ignorance theory, 311; upward redistribution, 14; the "what's the matter with Kansas" problem, 9, 188

Sen, A. K., 293

senior citizens. *See* the elderly

Serbia, 86

Shapiro, Robert Y., 310, 332–333

Silverman, Bernard, 205

Singapore, 25, 26

single-member districts. *See* SMD

Slemrod, Joel, 303

Slinko, Irina, 142n4

Slovakia, 86

SMD (single-member districts), 120–126, 136–142; budget discipline, 122; dissent from party leader's votes, 136–141; electoral hedging, 132; electoral nomination, 132–133; faction switching, 132, 135; Germany, 124–125, 142n1; party

SMD (*continued*)
allegiance, 133; pleasing constituencies, 121; pork-barrel (geographically targeted) politics, 8, 122–123; Putin and, 141–142, 142n2, 142n7; in Russian State Duma, 120–121, 126, 132–133, 135, 136–141, 142n2; transfer spending, 122; in United States, 121–123, 126
Smeeding, Timothy, 232, 235
Smith, Steven S., 125
Snyder, James A., Jr., 122–123
Social Democratic parties, 155
Social Democratic Party (SPD): German health care system, 256, 258, 267, 268, 270; Heinemann and, Gustav, 257, 275n4; Müller and, 261
social insurance, 149–185; altruism, 155; belief in a just world, 156; beliefs about determinants of economic success, 155–156; blacks, 165, 166–167, 172; church membership, 164, 166, 168, 169; Democratic Party, 165, 166–167; denominational differences, 154–155; differences in provision of, 153–154; individual spending preferences, 170–177, 181n42; issue-bundling effect, 157; level of economic development, 159; liberalism, 165, 166–167; poverty, 165, 166–167; religiosity, 149–185; religious attendance, 163–164, 166, 168, 169, 171, 173; secularism, 149; southern states, 165; unemployment insurance (*see* unemployment insurance); unionization, 165, 166–167; United States, 162–170; in United States, 152; urbanization, 165–166; workers' compensation (*see* workers' compensation)
Social Insurance's Damages (Liek), 265
social policy expenditures: on labor market outsiders, 53; reform of, 68; social policy transfers, 53; social services, 53; unions, 5–6, 44–46, 52–53; wage moderation, 67
Social Security: 2004 presidential election, 188; interest in among the elderly, 224, 225, 235; privatization of, 235; public spending on, 221, 222–223, 225, 226–227, 229, 237n12
Social Security Act (1935), 245
social spending: Catholics, 155, 164–165, 166–167, 175; level of economic

development, 159; OECD, 159; religiosity, 151–152, 153–154
social wage: centralization of wage-bargaining, 55; unions, 52, 54; wage-bargaining, 55; wage moderation, 56
Soldano, Patricia, 318–319
The Solution to the Doctor Question (Landmann), 255–256
Soros, George, 322
Soskice, David, 48–51, 56
the South: "developmental states" in, 24; public spending in, 24; redistribution in, 24; taxation in, 24; welfare regimes in, 19, 23–39
South Africa: AIDS, 100; HAART, 105, 106–107, 108, 112, 113; HIV, 101–103; welfare regime, 24–25, 27, 28, 31, 32–33, 34, 37, 38
South Asia, 100, 107
South Korea, 37, 38
Southeast Asia, 100, 107
Southern Africa, 100, 101, 103, 104
southern Europe, welfare regimes in, 22
Spain, 22, 76, *154*
SPD. *See* Social Democratic Party
spending. *See* child care/children; health spending; pension spending; pork-barrel politics; public spending; social spending; transfer spending; unemployment insurance; welfare spending; workers' compensation
Stegerwald, Adam, 261, 268
Stein, Robert M., 122
Steinmo, Sven, 79
Stepan, A., 293
Stephens, John, 19, 62, 155
Stillwaggon, E., 100
Stimson, James A., 336n14
Stratman, Thomas, 124–125
Sub-Saharan Africa, 8, 103, 107, 109
Supplemental Security Income, 234
Swank, Duane, 79
Sweden: center of gravity of the government, 62; centralization of wage-bargaining, 58; dual income tax system (DIT), 7, 73, 81; employment performance, variables affecting, 68; income redistribution, 231, 232; religiosity and social spending, 153–154; retirement pensions, 225; taxation, 76, 89; welfare regime, 21

Switzerland: centralization of wage-bargaining, 58; employment performance, variables affecting, 68; religiosity and social spending, *154*; taxation, 76

Taiwan, 38
Tanner, John, 320–321
Tanzania, 112
taxation, 72–98; above-normal returns to capital, 74–75, 81, 82, 83, 85; of the affluent, 236; animosity toward, 312; Australia, 76, 84; Austria, 76, 78–79, 89; Belgium, 76; burying money in an abandoned coal mine, 236; Canada, 76, 84; capital income, 73, 74, 75–77, 79–80, 81; capital investment, 6–7; cash-flow taxes, 80–81; corporate tax competition, 73–74, 82–88; corporate taxes, 82–83, 84–85, 87–88; country size, 83–84; Croatia, 84, 85; Denmark, 76, 78, 81, 84; differentiated income taxation, 73, 75–79, 88–91, 92; dual income tax system (DIT) (*see* dual income tax system); employment, 44, 53, 55, 60; Estonia, 86; European Union (EU), 88; evangelical opposition to, 188; expenditure/consumption taxes, 74–75, 77, 80–81, 83, 84; Finland, 7, 73, 76, 81, 89; flat income taxes, 80, 81, 86–87, 89; France, 76, 78–79, 89; Georgia, Republic of, 86; Germany, 76, 84, 87, 88, 89–91; Greece, 76, 89; horizontal distribution of tax burden, 6–7, 72, 73; income redistribution, 236; income taxes, 74, 79–82, 82–83, 84–85, 87–88, 201, 236; India, 294; international tax competition, 7; Ireland, 76; Italy, 76, 81, 82, 85, 86, 87; Japan, 76; labor market outsiders, 51; labor taxes, 77; Latvia, 86; left-wing governments/parties, 75, 88–89; Luxembourg, 76; Netherlands, 44, 76, 89, 90; New Zealand, 76, 89; Nordic countries, 81, 82, 86; normal returns to capital, 74–75, 80, 81, 83; Norway, 7, 73, 76, 81, 86, 89; OECD, 44, 51, 53, 54, 55, 60, 62–66, 73, 74, 76–92; payroll taxes, 78; Poland, 86; the poor, 236; Portugal, 76; "progressive" taxes, 78, 80, 81; progressivity of estate tax, 302, 309, 312–313, 320; progressivity of wage taxation, 88–89; public

spending, 73; racism, 201; "regressive" taxes, 78; right-wing governments/parties, 88–89; Russia, 86; Scandinavia, 90; Serbia, 86; Slovakia, 86; in the South, 24; Spain, 76; Sweden, 7, 73, 76, 81, 89; Switzerland, 76; tax structure efficiency, 6–7, 72–73, 75, 77–78; tax subsidies for homeowners, 235; Ukraine, 86; unemployment, 5, 62–66; unfairness of, 274; United Kingdom, 76, 84; United States, 76, 89; vertical distribution of tax burden, 6–7, 72, 73; wage income, 73, 74, 78, 81, 82, 85; wage moderation, 54; welfare states, 72–73, 75, 78
Taylor Committee of Inquiry into a Comprehensive System of Social Security for South Africa, 38
Temporary Assistance for Needy Families, 234
Tesar, L., 62
Thailand, 101–102, 112
Thames, Frank C., 125
thermostatic model of policymaking, 328
Thigpen, Chester, 318
Third Millennium, 235
Tirole, Jean, 156, 160
Tocqueville, Alexis de, 187
trade unions. *See* unions
transfer spending: Christian Democratic governments, 155; to labor market outsiders, 53, 60–61, 63, 64–66; PR (proportional representation), 123; SMD (single-member districts), 122; Social Democratic governments, 155
Traxler, F., 57
Treatment Action Campaign, 107
Trinidad and Tobago, 32

Uganda, 112
Ukraine, 86
UNAIDS (United Nations Programme on AIDS), 7, 113
unemployment: central bank independence, 64; centralization of wage-bargaining, 45, 47–48, 56–61, 63–64; conservative parties, 62; demographic outsiders, 61; France, 44; ideological polarization of the government, 64; individual well-being, 160; labor market insiders, 53; labor market outsiders, 51,

unemployment (*continued*)
53, 60–61, 63, 64–66; left-wing parties,
62; maturation of welfare states, 57, 67;
monetary policy, 49–50, 57; psychic
costs, 151; public spending on unemployment benefits, 227t, 228, 229–230;
religiosity, 9; taxation, 5, 62–66; trade
openness, 64; variables affecting, 48;
wage moderation, 5, 6, 45; welfare
regimes, 20–21; Western Europe, 5
unemployment insurance, religiosity and
spending on, 152, 163, 166, 168, 179n21
unionization: social insurance, 165, 166–
167; United States, 165
unions: centralization of wage-bargaining,
46; demographic outsiders, 61; labor
market outsiders, 45, 61; monetary
policy, 48, 49–51, 54; optimal strategy
for, 44; rational strategy for, 67; social
policy expenditures, 5–6, 44–46, 52–53;
social wage, 52, 54; utilitarian function
of, 51–53; wage moderation, 6, 44–46,
51, 53–54, 61; welfare states, 5–6
United Kingdom: acceptable inequality,
232–233; centralization of wage-bargaining, 58; employment performance, variables affecting, 68; religiosity and social
spending, 154; taxation, 76, 84
United Nations Programme on AIDS
(UNAIDS), 7, 113
United States: American exceptionalism,
187–188; attention paid to lower *vs.*
upper half of income distribution, 234–
235; Catholics in, 164–165, 166–167,
175; center of gravity of the government,
62; centralization of wage-bargaining, 58;
church membership, 164, 166, 168, 169;
class-oriented politics, 212; distributive
conflicts among different age groups,
221–222; employment performance,
variables affecting, 68; German health
care system, 245–248, 250, 274; income
redistribution in, 231–232; income
thresholds, 239n23; inequality in, 222,
224, 232–233; party preferences, 186;
poverty, 165, 237n5; religiosity and social
spending, 153–154; religious attendance,
163–164, 166, 168, 169, 171, 173;
religious giving in, 158; SMD (single-
member districts) in, 121–123, 126;

social insurance, 152, 162–170; taxation, 76, 89; unionization, 165; universal
health insurance, 2; welfare regime, 21
U.S. National Survey of Families and
Households, 162
universal health insurance in United
States, 2
upward redistribution, 14
Urban Institute, 222
urbanization, 165–166

van der Straeten, Karine, 192, 200, 201
Vargas, Getúlio Dornelles, 30
The Varieties of Religious Experience
(James), 151
voting rights. *See* franchise

wage-bargaining in OECD countries:
centralization of (*see* centralization of
wage-bargaining in OECD countries);
monetary policy, 48–49; social wage, 55
wage moderation in OECD countries:
centralization of wage-bargaining, 53,
54; effectiveness of, 67; employment, 47;
labor market outsiders, 54–55; monetary
policy, 49, 54, 55–56; social policies, 51;
social policy expenditures, 67; social
wage, 56; taxation, 54; unemployment, 5,
6, 45; unions, 6, 44–46, 51, 53–54, 61
Wall Street Journal (newspaper), 72
Wallerstein, Michael, 6, 57, 75
Waxman, Henry, 337n16
wealth. *See* the affluent (*under "a"*)
Weber, Max, 10, 150, 154
welfare policy, quality of, 273–274
welfare regimes, 19–42; agrarian regimes,
5, 26–27, 29, 33–34; in Argentina, 28,
35; in Australia, 23, 28; in Austria, 21;
in Barbados, 32, 33, 34; Bismarckian
systems, 25; in Botswana, 25, 37; in
Brazil, 23, 28, 30, 35–36, 37–38, 38–39;
in Britain, 28, 32; in British Empire,
32–33; in British Guiana, 32; in Chile,
19, 23, 28, 30, 35; Confucian regimes,
24; conservative regimes, 21; contributory schemes, 29, 31, 35; in Costa Rica,
36, 39; deagrarianization, 5, 28, 29, 31,
36, 39; decommodification, 21–22; defamilialization, 21–22; defined benefits,
36; democratization, 5, 29, 36–37, 39;

developing economies, 4–5; distributional regimes, 24; in East Asia, 23–24, 25, 26, 36, 38; education, 32; the elderly, 25; electoral competition for votes of nonunionized poor, 28; employment, 20; employment-based welfare, 4–5, 28, 29; factors affecting pace, direction of change, 28–29; family/kin role, 22, 25; "first-stage" *vs.* "second-stage" reforms, 39; in France, 21; in Germany, 21; Great Depression, 32; health care, 32; in Hong Kong, 36, 37, 38; immigrant workers, 5, 28, 29–31; income grants, 38–39; in India, 25; inequality, 35; International Labour Organization (ILO), 28; ISI (import-substitution industrialization), 35, 37; in Italy, 21, 22; in Japan, 23; in Kenya, 34; labor market regimes, 20–21; land reform, 5, 26; in Latin America, 19, 23, 24, 25, 27, 30–31, 36, 38; liberal regimes, 21, 22; market role, 22; in Mauritius, 32, 34; means-tested welfare, 5, 21, 26, 38; minimum income, 32; in Netherlands, 21; in New Zealand, 23, 32; noncontributory schemes, 29, 31, 36; open economies, 28; path dependence, 20; pauperist regimes, 5, 26–27, 28, 29; in Philippines, 25; the poor, 28, 35–38; in Portugal, 22; privatization of pension systems, 19; reform from above, 33; reform of, 38–39; rights-based welfare, 26; in Singapore, 25, 26; social assistance schemes, 19, 38; social democratic regimes, 21, 22; social insurance, 38; in the South, 19, 23–39; in South Africa, 24–25, 27, 28, 31, 32–33, 34, 37, 38; in South Korea, 37, 38; in southern Europe, 22; in Spain, 22; stages of welfare-regime making, 29; state role, 22; in Sweden, 21; in Taiwan, 38; three-part typology of, Esping-Andersen's, 4, 19–24; three-part typology of, Seekings', 5, 26–27; "trajectories" *vs.*, 23; in Trinidad and Tobago,

32; unemployment, 20–21; in United States, 21; wage-arbitration systems, 23; workerist regimes, 5, 26–27, 28, 29, 34
welfare spending, religiosity and, 149–150
welfare states: development of, 273; employment, 51; in Germany, 251; mature welfare states (*see* OECD); religiosity, 153; taxation, 72–73, 75, 78, 91–92; unemployment, 57; unions, 5–6
Wellstone, Paul, 324
Western Europe, unemployment in, 5
the "what's the matter with Kansas" problem, 9, 188
White, Gordon, 25
Wilensky, Harold, 93n6
Wilhelm I, Emperor of Germany, 251
Willoch, Kaare, 73
Wilson, Rick K., 122
Winfrey, Oprah, 312
Wissel, Rudolf, 260–261, 261
women's rights, 238n19
Wong, C., 204
workerist welfare regimes, 5, 26–27, 28, 29, 34
workers' compensation, religiosity and spending on, 152, 163, 166, 168, 170, 179n21
World Bank: *Averting the Old-Age Crisis*, 19; "Political Economy of Poverty, Equity and Growth," 24; social insurance, 38; tax data, 94n14; welfare for the elderly, 25
World Health Organization, 7, 107
World Values Survey, 152, 153, 238n21

Yakovlev, Ekaterina, 142n4

Zaller, John, 311–312
Zambia, 112
Zanakis, S., 101
Zentrum (Center Party), 259, 260–261
Zhuravskaya, Evgeny, 142n4
Zimbabwe, 112
Zogby polls, 312, 317, 336n11

.

www.ingramcontent.com/pod-product-compliance
Lightning Source LLC
Chambersburg PA
CBHW022134020426
42334CB00015B/885